Library of
Davidson College

THE LAMB AND THE ELEPHANT

But because our understanding cannot in this body found itself but on sensible things, nor arrive so clearly to the knowledge of God and things invisible, as by orderly conning over the visible and inferior creature, the same method is necessarily to be followed in all discreet teaching.
JOHN MILTON, *Of Education*

The order of God's creatures in themselves is not only admirable and glorious, but eloquent; then he that could apprehend the consequences of things, in their truth, and utter his apprehensions as truly were a right orator.
JOHN HOSKINS, *Directions for Speech and Style*

Manie times also under the selfesame words they comprehend some true understanding of Naturall Philosophie or sometimes of politike governement and now and then of divinitie, and these same sences that comprehend so excellent knowledge we call the Allegorie which Plutarch defineth to be when one thing is told and by that another is understood.
SIR JOHN HARINGTON, *Preface to* Orlando Furioso

Hence poetry is something more philosophic and of graver import than history, since its statements are of the nature rather of universals, whereas those of history are singulars. By a universal statement I mean one as to what such or such a kind of man will probably or necessarily say or do—which is the aim of poetry, though it affixes proper names to the characters. . . .
ARISTOTLE, *Poetics*

The Lamb and the Elephant

IDEAL IMITATION AND THE CONTEXT OF RENAISSANCE ALLEGORY

*Poetry ... is like a river ...
wherein the little lamb may wade,
and the great elephant freely swim.*

By John M. Steadman

THE HUNTINGTON LIBRARY
SAN MARINO • CALIFORNIA
1974

Published with the assistance of the
UNION PACIFIC RAILROAD FOUNDATION FUND

COPYRIGHT © 1974
HENRY E. HUNTINGTON LIBRARY AND ART GALLERY
SAN MARINO, CALIFORNIA
LIBRARY OF CONGRESS CATALOG CARD NUMBER 73-93874
STANDARD BOOK NUMBER 0-87328-062-8
DESIGNED BY WARD RITCHIE
PRINTED IN THE UNITED STATES OF AMERICA
BY ANDERSON, RITCHIE & SIMON

CONTENTS

Foreword		vii
Preface		xv
I.	Innovation and Tradition: The Problem of the Renaissance	3
II.	The Recovery of Antiquity	25
III.	Classical Tradition and Renaissance Epic	53
IV.	The Garment of Doctrine: Imitation and Allegory	71
V.	Image and Idea: Imitation and Allegory	106
VI.	Invention and Design: Idea and Form	146
VII.	Invention and Disposition: Theme and Structure	180
VIII.	The End of the Renaissance: The Problem of Periodization	213
	Epilogue	232
	Index	245

FOREWORD

Addressed primarily to the student of English literature, this book endeavors to view the poetry of the British Renaissance in the larger European context. Stressing the continuity of the Renaissance poetic tradition with medieval and post-Renaissance theory and practice, it reconsiders the problem of periodization, the validity of art-historical and political categories in literary scholarship, and the limited contexts in which our standard definitions of the Renaissance and its phases can be significant.

The focal point of this study is the principle of "ideal" presentation—the illustration of abstract universals or class concepts through concrete sensuous particulars—as seen against the background of changing poetic and rhetorical ideals, varying relationships to classical models and authorities, and altering conceptions of the literary genres and of the rules of poetic imitation. By tracing the vicissitudes of this principle through medieval, High Renaissance, "mannerist," and neoclassical modes and styles, this essay attempts to elucidate the shifting relationships between image and idea in the literature of the period, its variables as well as its constants, and the changing frame of reference that conditioned the Renaissance allegory and exemplum.

Of the major sections in this book, the first chapters summarize the problem of defining the Renaissance and survey the relationship between medieval tradition and the study and imitation of the ancients. Though most of this material is familiar to the specialist, this section may serve as a general introduction to the period for the nonspecialist. Chapters four and five, devoted to aspects of Renaissance poetic theory, analyze the tension between two modes of ideal representation: the traditional allegorical method and neo-Aristotelian conceptions of mimesis as the probable and verisimilar imitation of an action. Chapters six and seven reexamine the meaning of invention and disposition in Renaissance theory: their rhetorical background and their significance for the principles of literary and pictorial composition. The final chapter is concerned with the later stages of Renaissance style and the problem of periodization.

In revaluing the frame of reference and the critical terminology

Foreword

that the modern literary historian brings to the study of Renaissance literature, I have attempted to indicate the weakness as well as the strength of the Renaissance frame (or frames) of reference. Throughout the period there was, on the whole, a notable discrepancy between theory and practice. The traditional categories of style and the conventional distinctions in genre often seem virtually irrelevant to works that claim conformity to the "rules," and they are frequently too rigid and too stereotyped to serve as reliable guides in comparing the styles and craftsmanship of different authors. In theory, men of letters usually tended to think in terms of absolute norms of structure and genre and style; in practice, they frequently followed contemporary taste. Few of them came squarely to grips with the problem of cultural and historical relativity in literary and artistic standards. Though some were bold enough to assert the independence of the moderns from ancient precept and example, the majority of theorists considered the arts of poetry and rhetoric as a discipline almost as universally applicable as the art of logic itself, and the rules of the genres as scarcely less binding than those of the syllogism. In actual practice, on the other hand, poets often treated the precepts of the *ars poetica* as cavalierly as the principles of *ars logica*. The ideal framework that the Renaissance critic imposed on the flux of literary history is no less untrustworthy than the categories that the twentieth-century cultural historian projects on the continuity of *Geistesgeschichte*, the history of man's thought. It cannot be accepted uncritically, for it was based on a false conception of literary history and of the nature of the poetic genres. Yet it cannot be ignored, for it is the frame of reference in terms of which men of the Renaissance usually judged the literature of the classical and medieval past and the productions of their own contemporaries and in terms of which, in varying degrees, they composed and defended their own work.

Despite their frequent interaction, literary history and literary theory are, perhaps, ultimately irreconcilable—as incompatible as Heraclitus and Parmenides. The theorists may impose ideal patterns on the historical process—discriminating periods and styles and genres—but these rarely fit all the particulars to which they allegedly apply. As abstractions they sometimes offer a distorted and incom-

Foreword

plete picture of the particulars to which they *do* apply, and they inevitably disrupt the continuity of the historical process itself. The patterns that are valid in a restricted sense, for literary historian and theorist alike, are structures of thought systematized by particular individuals in particular works at particular points in time—the pattern of a specific poem or painting, the organized erudition of a Renaissance commonplace book or theological manual, a treatise on natural or moral philosophy, or (for that matter) an *ars poetica*. These we may study with a modest hope of accuracy and precision, for they are, even when they deal with abstractions, concrete facts. Other patterns—the secondary abstractions that we impose on the uncertain currents of social and intellectual history and the multiplicity of literary and artistic works—are less verifiable; and towards these we should preserve at best a healthy skepticism.

In examining Renaissance conceptions of "ideal imitation," I have placed primary emphasis on the technical problems involved in communicating an abstract universal through concrete particulars by means of allegory and simile or metaphor or by personification and example. Since writers of the period shared their concern for "noumenal mimesis" with medieval and post-Renaissance authors, it seems advisable to summarize some of the persistent problems involved in defining and delimiting the Renaissance and in evaluating its continuity with medieval and post-Renaissance traditions. Similarly, since "imitation of the idea" is often associated with "imitation of the ancients" and with "imitation of nature" in Renaissance artistic and literary theory (often with allusions to Zeuxis' eclectic approach to the problem of rendering an ideal beauty), one cannot overlook the equally controversial question of the ambiguous and often contradictory relationships of Renaissance poets and artists to classical models.[1]

On the whole, all of these problems defy generalization, and any "solution" must necessarily be tentative—and, in a sense, metaphoric. Not only do our own critical and historical categories differ significantly from those that men of the Renaissance employed, but the same terms did not always possess the same meaning for men of the period. It is no less dangerous to impose intellectual abstractions on the shifting forms of literature and art than on the flux of history;

Foreword

and the vocabularies that observers (the Renaissance observers no less than moderns!) employ to describe general movements are apt to distort the concrete data of literature or history in the very process of attempting to interpret them and to render them intelligible. The concepts and formulae that we must necessarily employ in recognizing historical or literary trends and in communicating our formulations are inevitably subjective or intersubjective. They are instruments of cognition, but they modify and transform the actual objects of our study in making them accessible to cognition. The principle of indeterminism is as applicable to artistic and literary history and to cultural history as it is to modern physics.

The raw material of intellectual and social history alike is indigestible; we can assimilate it only after it has been thoroughly pounded, seasoned, mixed, and baked or broiled into a palatable compound—a confection acceptable to the limitations of our own intellectual constitutions. The categories of literary history must inevitably be no more than abstractions from particulars—the artifacts of a philological gastronomy, the broths and extracts, conserves and distillations of some scholastic Brillat-Savarin.

To friends and colleagues at the Henry E. Huntington Library and the University of California, Riverside, I am grateful for valuable criticism and editorial assistance. Professors Hallett Smith, Robert Wark, and Daniel Donno generously read much of the manuscript. The aquiline vision of Mrs. Lillian Bean, Dr. Edwin Carpenter, Mrs. Jane Evans, Mrs. Winifred Freese, Mrs. Noelle Jackson, and Mrs. Betty Leigh Merrell has been an indispensable aid in the preparation of this book. For helpful suggestions for the lecture which formed the nucleus of this book, I am indebted to Professor William Elton, Dr. Allan Nevins, Dr. A. L. Rowse, Professor Paul Zall, and Professor D. D. Hale. In planning and writing this book I am deeply indebted for advice and encouragement to my Riverside colleagues Professors Stanley Stewart and Kathleen Williams, to my Huntington colleagues Miss Mary Isabel Fry, and Dr. Ray Allen Billington, and to Dr. James Thorpe, Director, and Dr. John Edwin Pomfret, former Director of the Henry E. Huntington Library.

John M. Steadman
The Henry E. Huntington Library

Foreword

NOTES

[1] The interconnection between the principles of imitating abstract ideas, imitating nature, and imitating the works of the ancients rests on the conception that nature is an imperfect *artifex*, that she is rarely able to embody the ideas or forms of natural species in particular individuals and retain a perfect resemblance to the ideal in its pristine and transcendental perfection, that the artist must therefore delineate an ideal form or universal in his own mind rather than copy meticulously any single particular object in nature, that the ancient masters portrayed an idealized nature and consequently provide a better guide than the actual productions of nature herself. For the history of this principle in Renaissance artistic theory, see Erwin Panofsky, *Idea, A Concept in Art Theory*, trans. Joseph J. S. Peake (Columbia, S. C., 1968).

In antiquity Horace had advised the poet to study the Greek masterpieces with meticulous care, and Cicero had recommended to the orator the examples of Greek eloquence as well as the teachings of Hellenic philosophy. Quintilian, in turn, writing in a later (and, in his own opinion, a decadent) age, had proposed Latin authors of an earlier generation—including Cicero himself—as models of style. From Cicero and Quintilian, Renaissance humanists inherited an emphasis on art (precept), study and imitation of "classical" writers, and exercise or *praxis*, in the education of an orator and humane writer. The same threefold or fourfold schema had also been extended to the poet. Education in eloquence (in prose and poetry alike) thus involved close critical analysis of classical texts with an eye to imitating them and learning thereby to perfect one's own style. This educational program and "aesthetic" ideal confers a certain degree of unity on the period extending from the late fourteenth century in Italy to the mid-seventeenth century in England. The rhetorically oriented curriculum at St. Paul's, the London school that John Milton attended, is far closer to the ideals of Petrarch and to the curricula of his fifteenth-century successors than to those of our own day. Nevertheless there remains a considerable degree of continuity between Renaissance rhetoric and poetics and those of the Middle Ages, the so-called "baroque" era, and indeed the period of the Enlightenment. One would be reluctant, therefore, to accept this ideal as the principal *differentia* of the Renaissance. In this period, as in the ages that immediately preceded and followed it, there was frequent tension between the demands of eloquence and those of "solid" learning, between rhetorical and apodeictic methods, between techniques of persuasion and those of logical demonstration. In the Renaissance the "quarrel of the arts" was scarcely less pronounced than in the Middle Ages, in the late seventeenth century, or in our own day.

As readers familiar with Panofsky's *Idea* and the complementary studies by Lee and Mahon will recognize, throughout this book I have given the phrase "ideal imitation" a broader meaning than the more technical use traditional in art criticism. Students of Lomazzo, Zuccaro, and Bellori have been understandably concerned primarily with conceptions of an ideal beauty rather than with moral absolutes—i. e. with the formal design of composition (and the formal proportions of the individual figures within a composition) rather than with dogmatic content. Though I have attempted to avoid confusing these different senses of the term, its ethical and aesthetic implications, it would be unwise (as well as unhistorical) to insist on a rigid distinction. The Renaissance was no less sensitive to the virtue of beauty than to the beauty of virtue; and in theory and practice the two concepts sometimes converged. By synthesizing the doctrines of the *Phaedrus* and the *Symposium*—the beauty of *phronesis* (moral wisdom or virtue) and the ladder of love—apologists for art and literature alike could profess to be janitors of the realm of ideas, utilizing sensuous beauty as a means of ascent not merely to the Idea of the Beautiful but to the Idea of the Good.

As many of them were well aware, the Platonic Ideas of Truth and Beauty were

Foreword

ultimately one with the Idea of the Good; the word *kalos* could denote moral as well as physical beauty, just as *kakos* could refer to ugliness of character or person. Moreover, in Renaissance literary and art theory, notions of beauty in formal structure and in style were closely linked with other kinds of universals and class-concepts through the principle of decorum. The ideal of perfection in proportion or in character (in harmony of body or of soul) naturally varied according to species—with recognized categories or types for psychological temperaments and social functions as well as for age or sex or biological kinds. In discussing the Idea of a heroic poem, a critic might logically examine the Idea of a perfect hero (the ideal warrior or captain or councillor or orator or king) and the Idea of heroic virtue itself. This would entail moral as well as aesthetic considerations, leading him beyond problems of formal disposition or plot structure and style to problems of decorum in personal attributes *(attributa personarum)* and the doctrines of moral philosophy.

Similarly, to depict a beautiful body is an aesthetic problem (though the term "aesthetic" may be anachronistic in a Renaissance context); but to suggest thereby a "beautiful soul," of which the body is merely the vehicle, involves moral concepts. Insofar as sensuous design conduces to spiritual harmony, it involves ethical as well as purely aesthetic values. "His harmonica'l and ingeniose Sould did lodge in a beautifull and well proportioned body," John Aubrey wrote of John Milton. The Renaissance never forgot this Platonic commonplace. Reflected in the pedagogical slogan, *mens sana in corpore sano*, it underlies the critical thought of the age, making it difficult for critics of a later period to disentangle ethical from aesthetic arguments, or to evaluate adequately the very different intents of poet and painter in employing the same arguments and commonplaces.

In one form or another, both poets and painters might apply the correlation between sensuous vehicle and higher intellectual or spiritual value (inherent in the Platonic correlation between beautiful body and beautiful soul) to the ideal of an ethically oriented verbal or pictorial rhetoric. In defending their respective arts both might appeal to the same commonplaces. The fact remains, however, that the majority of these arguments had been invented in defense of verbal eloquence, on behalf of rhetoric or of poetry; and these rarely made allowance for the differences between visual and verbal media. (Indeed the wide-spread doctrine *ut pictura poesis* and the notion of rhetorical "colors" tended to blur the distinction still further.) This sometimes lends an unreal character to the art theory of the Renaissance, significantly heightening the divorce between theory and practice even more than in the verbal arts. For, though the issues have originated in practice—in the rivalry of contemporary schools—they are often formulated and debated in terms of classical rhetorical or poetic or philosophical disputes. Poets might profess to emulate painters through elaborate passages of ecphrasis or description (topographias, chronographias, prosopographias, and the like), but any visual appeal (other than typographical) must inevitably be indirect; the only direct sensuous immediacy must necessarily be aural rather than visual, through the ear rather than the eye. On the other hand, the poet might depict character or passion or thought, moral or affective states and the "wily subtleties and refluxes" of the soul more immediately than the painter, who must rely for the greater part on the expressive potentialities of expression and gesture—fixing incident in a sort of paralyzed motion, character in applied physiognomy, and emotion in an arrested ballet. It is hardly surprising, therefore, that Renaissance theorists should frequently blur the ethical and aesthetic senses of "Idea," that art historians should stress the Idea of Beauty or formal design, and that literary theorists should emphasize the imitation of moral absolutes.

The concept of ideal representation underlying Renaissance theories of both visual and verbal arts is not radically different from medieval views, and in the light of recent studies of medieval rhetoric, poetic, and aesthetics, some of the traditional

Foreword

differentiae between medieval and Renaissance would seem to demand qualification. Neither the theory of ideal nor literal imitation is new. The concept of beauty as harmony or proportion, and an interest in mathematical structures in art and literature alike, occur in both periods. The difference between medieval and Renaissance is essentially one of emphasis. The humanistic emphasis on the pleasure-principle in education and the exploitation of its aesthetic and moral implications involve rhetorical and poetic commonplaces current in antiquity and accessible to the Middle Ages. The quarrel of the arts—between logic and rhetoric, philosophy and eloquence—and the attempt to reconcile them through a learned poetry and oratory—likewise belongs to both eras. What is new and different is the stress on the classics as the model for imitation of both nature and ideas—and of an ideal beauty of form and design.

Further ambiguities are inherent in the art-historical and literary use of the terms "classic" and "ideal." Wölfflin applies the former term specifically to the art of the High Renaissance, but extends it (along with the complementary term "baroque") to what he regards as analogous phases of development in the art of other periods and cultures. Curtius similarly sees "classical" and "mannerist" as complementary or antithetical qualities recurring in the literature of various epochs and societies. Again, though extensive discussions of the doctrine of ideal imitation occur in the writings of so-called mannerist or baroque theorists (cf. Lee, Mahon, Blunt, and Panofsky on Lomazzo, Federico Zuccari, and Bellori), art historians have sometimes emphasized the contrast between the "ideal art" of the High Renaissance, with its "idealized and normative objectivization," and the "sharply opposed" attitude of "the anticlassical style, normally called Mannerism"; Walter Friedlaender, *Mannerism and Anti-Mannerism in Italian Painting*, ed. Donald Posner (New York, 1965), p. 5. For a comprehensive study of the problem of human proportions in painting and sculpture, see Erwin Panofsky, *Meaning in the Visual Arts* (Garden City, N.Y., 1955), pp. 55-107.

The concept of art as the sensible vehicle of the intelligible universal belongs to the Middle Ages as well as the Renaissance. Federico Zuccari can quote Saint Thomas Aquinas on the idea and on art as the imitation of nature—though significantly omitting, as Panofsky observes *(Idea*, pp. 230-31), a crucial sentence in Aquinas' *Physicà*. The Platonic commonplace of sensuous beauty and earthly love as a means of ascent to intellectual beauty and heavenly love underlies much of the erotic poetry of the late Middle Ages and the Renaissance. On the other hand, despite the inevitable indebtedness of medieval to classical authors and the imitation of the classics in medieval literature, the emphasis on the ancients as models both for an idealized nature and for the harmonious design appropriate for the several poetic species belongs primarily to the Renaissance. Though many Renaissance poets might, like their medieval counterparts, be content simply to incorporate classical allusions and echoes or isolated imitations of particular passages, it is the emphasis on classical structure and formal design that sets many of their contemporaries apart from medieval tradition and realigns them with classical tradition.

There remained, of course, a tension in Renaissance poetics not only between diverse conceptions of imitation (literal and ideal, formal and stylistic and moral) but also between Christian and pagan conventions. In that idealizing age, the classical mode did not invariably meet the exorbitant claims of the ideal schema. The notion of ideal imitation could undercut the classics themselves on both moral and aesthetic grounds. (These were, indeed, closely interrelated through the principle of decorum.) Preoccupation with the ideal of heroic virtue might result in discrediting the heroes of classical epic as deficient in true (i.e. Christian) heroism, while preoccupation with formal design might lead to the censure of Homer in comparison with Virgil. Testing the rules of poetic theory against the classical models themselves and

Foreword

vice versa, the Renaissance critic was frequently compelled to revise and reassess both.

It is significant, however, that both Lomazzo and Zuccari chose to entitle their treatises on art, different though they were in orientation, by the fashionable term *Idea*. For Lomazzo's neo-Platonic aesthetics and his indebtedness to Ficino and for Federico Zuccari's Aristotelian-scholastic viewpoint, see Panofsky, *Idea*, pp. 85-99, 129-53, 230-33. Zuccari's neo-Aristotelian views on matter and form (p. 230) parallel Tasso's observations on matter and form in the heroic poem. For Zuccari's distaste for mathematical theory, see p. 80. For the "art-theoretical doctrine of Ideas, insofar as it is concerned with the problem of beauty" in the High Renaissance and for cinquecento interpretations of the term *idea*, see Panofsky, pp. 63-68.

In a study of this sort one is painfully aware of the limitations of one's own terminology—and the dangers as well as the necessity of large-scale generalizations. Such phrases as "Renaissance humanism," "Renaissance classicism," "ideal imitation," or "imitation of the ancients" unfortunately suggest a uniformity of approach that did not, and could not, exist in fact. The values that men of the Renaissance sought and found in the art and literature of antiquity (and the works of the ancients themselves) were too diverse to be reduced to a single formula. Moreover, in concentrating on Renaissance theories of mimesis one may easily underestimate their affinities with medieval tradition. For the concepts of "ideal imitation" (Panofsky, Lee) and "redeemed eloquence" and the Ciceronian "correlation between eloquence, wisdom and virtue" (Colish) are common to both the Middle Ages and the Renaissance— a legacy from classical rhetoric and poetics. So are the conception of poetry as fiction (a "made" or "constructed" artifice) and the complementary emphases on allegorical and literal meaning, fabulous marvels and realistic representation (verisimilitude). Resisting the temptation to reduce their art to a single mode or formula, medieval and Renaissance poets normally recognized diverse poetic species, in some of which truth to nature, in others apparent violation of nature in the interest of the idea, might prevail. Platonic and Aristotelian doctrines concerning the nature and origin of ideas were current in both periods. The conception of an art which might be simultaneously true to nature and to the idea—probable and verisimilar on the literal level but enriched by a deeper allegorical meaning—was accessible to both medieval and Renaissance poets.

It is not the professed attempt to represent either the natural or the ideal realm (or both) that principally differentiates medieval from Renaissance poetics or art theory. Nor is it the significantly greater range of classical authorities available to the man of the Renaissance. The major difference resides largely in the Renaissance acceptance of classical masterpieces as models for an ideal *structure*, (as well as for an idealized but lifelike representation of natural objects and for eloquent expression)—in the endeavor to imitate the *formal* design as well as the verbal style of classical works. In the opinion of many Renaissance readers, the ancients had not only achieved a union of wisdom and eloquence and an apparent fidelity to the truth of ideas and the truth of nature; they had also succeeded in realizing the ideal patterns of the several poetic genres—the perfect "form" or Idea of an heroic poem, or of a lyric or comedy or tragedy.

For the Renaissance poet and artist were frequently preoccupied not only with moral universals (the idea of a perfect councillor or warrior or governor) but also with the idea of beauty (often defined as harmony or symmetry or proportion) and with the ideal patterns or paradigms appropriate for various genres and subjects. These they sought (or frequently professed to seek) in the works of antiquity. To imitate the ancients was simultaneously to imitate nature, to imitate ethical or political universals, and to imitate an idea of formal beauty or proportion.

PREFACE

He perceived that poetical creations are not vain and simple fables or marvels, . . . but that beneath them are hid the sweetest fruits of historical and philosophical truths, so that the conceptions of the poets cannot be fully understood without history and moral and natural philosophy.

[What Gregory said of Scripture] may also be said of poetry, namely, that in the same account it discloses the text and its underlying mystery. Thus at the same moment by the one it disciplines the wise, and by the other it strengthens the foolish. It possesses openly that by virtue of which it may nourish little children, and preserves in secret that whereby it holds rapt in admiration the minds of sublime thinkers. Thus it is like a river . . . wherein the little lamb may wade, and the great elephant freely swim.

GIOVANNI BOCCACCIO, *The Life of Dante*

Though these words were written shortly after the middle of the fourteenth century, they were, on the whole, valid throughout the Renaissance. Sixteenth-century mythographers drew heavily on Boccaccio's *Genealogy of the Gods*, which applies the same theory of historical and philosophical allegory to the elucidation of pagan myth. Milton possessed a copy of Boccaccio's *Vita di Dante* and possibly utilized it for his remarks in *Comus* on ancient poets taught by the heavenly muse. Francis Bacon detected hidden philosophical mysteries in the myths of the Gentiles, though he regarded the myth as possibly anterior to the philosophical content. In Renaissance eyes, Boccaccio's conception of the allegorical method of poetry was strengthened by classical and late-classical interpretations of Homer and Virgil, by medieval and Renaissance exegesis of Ovid, by the example of Dante and Spenser, by allegorical commentaries on the epics of Ariosto and Tasso, Graziani and Marino, and by the tradition of classical and Renaissance mythography and iconography. The literary world of the Renaissance was, like the world itself, a *mundus symbolicus*. It is symptomatic of the continuity of medieval and Renaissance tradition—and of the strength of the classical tradi-

Preface

tion in both periods—that twentieth-century medievalists should regard Boccaccio's views as representative of medieval theories of allegory, while modern Renaissance specialists quote them with equal approbation as indicative of Renaissance opinion.

There is, moreover, a certain poetic justice in Boccaccio's reference to Saint Gregory in this context. For the allegorical method of Scriptural interpretation, exemplified in the Biblical exegesis of Origen and Saint Augustine and in Gregory's commentary on the Book of Job, had been indirectly influenced by the allegorical methods of classical mythographers and Homeric commentators.

1.

This essay reexamines two interrelated problems in Renaissance poetry: the imitation of universals and the imitation of ancient or modern exemplars in literature or art—the illustration of "archetypes" and the evocation of "prototypes" or "ectypes."[1] Within the last fifty years numerous iconological and literary studies have explored the interrelationship between image and idea in the visual and verbal arts of the Middle Ages and the Renaissance against the background of a continuous though variable mythographical and rhetorical tradition and a persistent though varying dependence on classical and Biblical imagery.[2] These have emphasized the interconnections not only between poetry and painting, but also between both of these arts and the methods of rhetoric and the doctrines of moral philosophy. The principle of "ideal" representation frequently involves the assumption that poetry and painting should serve ethical or doctrinal ends. As the handmaidens of philosophy or theology, public servants of church or state, they aim to portray abstract universals through concrete particulars. Embodying the ideas of virtues and vice—intelligible but invisible essences—in sensuous images capable of striking the imagination and impressing the memory, they may simultaneously delight the sense, instruct the understanding, and move the will.

Though the last of these functions originally applied to rhetoric and was subsequently extended to poetry and painting by Renaissance theorists, the essential basis of what we may call "noumenal mimesis" had already been formulated in classical antiquity. En-

Preface

riched and sometimes obscured by theories of Scriptural allegory, it remained a commonplace of medieval and Renaissance poetics, surviving well into the nineteenth century. In medieval literature and art it frequently underlies the exploitation of the dream-vision as a method for impressing the forms of virtues and vices and other separated essences on the fantasy through sensuous images, and the use of illustrative exempla as instruments of instruction and persuasion.[3] In the Renaissance it conditions the theory of allegory, the conception of the "pattern-hero" or exemplary protagonist in epic poetry, the logical and rhetorical functions of similes and other figures of comparison, and the vogue of emblems and enigmas and mysteries. In both periods it is often associated with the *topos* of art as a mirror of nature, an image of the visible or invisible world—or with the Renaissance analogy between the theater of the world and its epitome, the stage.

In the Renaissance the conception of ideal representation was further complicated by the interrelationship between rhetoric and poetic.[4] Both Plato and Cicero had insisted that the orator ought to know the true forms of wisdom and virtue in order to exercise his office with justice and responsibility.[5] Medieval poetics had often been closely associated with rhetoric, and poetry itself had been regarded as an instrument of moral persuasion as well as instruction and delight. In Renaissance theory, the triple functions of rhetoric —to teach, delight, and move—were extended to poetry and art. The poet or painter persuaded his audience or spectators to righteousness through concrete sensory images of abstract intelligible essences, illustrating the intrinsic beauty of virtue or the deformity of vice through external forms and depicting the contrary rewards of good and evil. Portraying spiritual states through the rhetoric of the flesh, he employed the language of sense to move his public to the contemplation of universal ideas or of spiritual truths above reason. Like his medieval predecessors, he dehorted the beholder from earthly to celestial values and from temporal to eternal goods through the methods of analogy and comparison or contrast.

Though this summary is substantially valid for both medieval and Renaissance aesthetics, it nevertheless oversimplifies a complex and various body of poetic doctrine.[6] In theory there were sometimes

Preface

significant variations; and in practice poets often refused to be bound by theory, either disregarding theory altogether or selecting precisely whatever rules or principles they might find helpful in composing a particular kind of poem for a specific audience and neglecting the rest. We should not assume that the majority of medieval or Renaissance poets followed any single literary theory consistently or scrupulously or that they consciously subordinated poetics to the ends of theology or moral philosophy. Moreover, many of the more idealistic conceptions of the ethical and religious functions of poetry were rhetorically conditioned. They occur frequently in the context of apologies for poetry or rhetoric, or for humane letters and pagan myth, against the claims of rival disciplines and the accusations of the detractors of poetry. In emphasizing the superior ontological status of poetry as an imitation of universal ideas and in stressing the moral and political benefits of catharsis, Aristotle is rebutting Plato. In arguing that Homer is a better teacher than Crantor and Chrysippus, Horace is affirming the superiority of the poetic exemplum as an instrument of moral instruction to the jejune methods of professional philosophers. Milton and Valvasone[7] made analogous claims for the superiority of poetry to scholastic theology, and Petrarch for Aristotle's inferiority to Cicero as a moralist: "Ille docet attentius, quid est virtus, urget iste potentius, ut colatur virtus."[8]

Cicero's most eloquent plea for the humanities occurs in a judicial defense for the poet Archias. The fourteenth and much of the fifteenth book of Boccaccio's *Genealogy of the Gods* are apologies for poetry and for pagan myth; it is significant that, by stressing the affinities of poetic allegory with mystical theology, the apologist endeavors to counter the attacks of "demonstrative" or scholastic theologians. Sidney's exaltation of the poet's office occurs in an "apology" or "defense" against Gosson's invective against poetry. Mazzoni's vindication of the allegorical method appears in a defense of Dante's *Commedia*. Neither Tasso nor Davenant could be regarded as a disinterested theorist in his speculations on the nature of heroic poetry; and the former's "Allegoria" to his epic would appear to be, in large part, an afterthought, an ex post facto rationalization. Spenser's letter to Raleigh endeavors to prevent possible misinterpretation of his "dark conceit." Milton's more extended discus-

Preface

sions of the lofty office of the poet occur in passages of "ethical proof" in his polemical treatises. His discussion of the moral function of tragedy in the preface to *Samson Agonistes* defends his own practice in modeling his drama according to the "rule" of the ancients instead of contemporary dramatic practice. The humanists' emphasis on the moral function of poetic and rhetorical eloquence and on the ethical utility of classical history and poetry and oratory were, in part at least, a justification for their own academic discipline and pedagogical methods.

Though we should not doubt the sincerity of such claims (for Milton and Spenser seem to have practised what they preached), we should not overlook their apologetic or polemical context. Utility and nobility *(honestas)* were traditionally two of the principal topics for rhetorical persuasion. Apologists for various arts and sciences —astronomy and mathematics, painting and sculpture, architecture and music, metaphysics and theology, alchemy and Bacon's "experimental philosophy"—naturally appealed to these commonplaces in extolling or defending their own disciplines against the claims of rivals. The defenders of poetry did likewise, emphasizing the profitable and honorable character of their art. Its utility depended ultimately on its moral and religious functions and its service to state and church. Its nobility resided traditionally in the altitude of its subject matter or in the antiquity and dignity of its origin.

Men of the period still believed in a hierarchy of the arts and sciences; the point at issue was not the principle of hierarchy, but the order of the arts, their proper orientation, and their use or abuse. The objects of astronomy were nobler than those of geography, inasmuch as the starry heavens were superior to the earth—a *topos* that Milton skilfully inverts in *Paradise Lost*. Painters, sculptors, and architects vied with one another in tracing the antiquity of their respective arts back to the creation of the world. Poets, in turn, extolled their own art not only by arguing its utility as an instrument of instruction and persuasion, but also by stressing its nobility: the visionary and vatic character of the bard, his ability to contemplate the invisible mysteries of the spiritual realm and express them symbolically in verse, the divine objects and celestial origin of poesis. By associating the methods of poetry with the symbolic methods of

Preface

Scripture and mystical theology, with the veiled symbols of a mythical *prisca theologia*, or with the signatures and hieroglyphics that the Creator himself had impressed on nature, the apologist was in effect elevating the poet himself into a mystagogue and hierophant—a mediator between *visibilia* and *invisibilia*—and emphasizing the celestial themes and the divine nature of poetry.[9]

The epithet "divine science," already transferred from metaphysics to theology, was applied to poesis. The poet, like the hero, became a *divinus vir;* and his works "divine." Poetry and its sister, music, were arts as ancient as the creation of the world, when the morning stars had sung together and the sons of heaven shouted for joy—or perhaps older still. In Milton's insistence on the celestial origin and antiquity of his "heavenly muse," we should recognize not only a contrast between sacred and profane, divine and secular poetry, but also an attempt to stress the *honestas* of his muse, an art divine in its source and antedating the visible creation. For other poets of the late Renaissance who, apparently unlike Milton, identified the heavenly muse with the Third Person of the Trinity, coeternal and coequal with Father and Son, the *ars poetica* would literally be a "divine science,"[10] associated from eternity with the supreme Deity himself. The Spirit who inspired the *poema sacro*, the divine poem, was the same Spirit who had moved upon the face of the aboriginal waters at creation and who had spoken through the prophets.

The complicated symbolic traditions—pictorial and literary, pagan and Biblical, classical and medieval—accessible to the Renaissance *poeta doctus* were both an aid and an obstacle to poetic invention. Horace's injunction to follow tradition *("aut famam sequere")* or to observe *convenientia* (consistency or decorum), the imitation of classical models as a humanistic pedagogical technique, and the conscious effort of many poets to emphasize the continuity of tradition by borrowing from vernacular authors as well as from the ancients themselves could restrict the scope of the poet's invention as well as the "disposition" and "elocution" of his work. At the same time, the complexity and variety of these traditions might afford ample opportunities for innovations within the tradition, for combining elements derived from diverse sources or even from various traditions in a new and fresh way. By following tradition, the poet invested his

Preface

image with probability and authority; through his innovations on tradition he could achieve *maraviglia* or surprise. Milton combines pagan and Biblical traditions in this way, just as Boiardo and Ariosto had combined motifs derived from classical epic and myth with romantic, and, less notably than Tasso and Spenser, with Christian, traditions.

The symbolic value of both classical and Biblical traditions had been enriched, moreover, not only by the use that other writers had made of them (for, in a sense, most poetic exploitation of classical myth or Biblical typology tends either to reinforce or to alter its original significance), but also by an extensive body of allegorical and moral commentary. As a result many of the conventional symbols had become polysemous. Invested with a variety of traditional meanings, they constituted a vocabulary that the author might share in common with at least the more erudite members of his audience, a vocabulary conventional enough to be intelligible, but sufficiently ambiguous to permit the author to choose and select which meanings or combination of meanings he preferred to emphasize. Actaeon might have one significance in a neo-Platonic and neo-Hermetic treatise, other implications in invectives against curiosity or lust or the cost of hunting, and still a fifth sense in a comedy on cuckoldry.

One of the principal advantages of many of these motifs, for Renaissance artists and poets alike, consisted precisely in the fact that they had long since entered the public domain. Even the enigmas and mysteries and hieroglyphs that delighted the amateur mystagogues of the period were in large part conventional. Though the traditional symbols might occasionally, as in the case of neo-Hermetic writers, serve as the vehicle for abstruse alchemical and metaphysical doctrines, they were usually associated with commonplaces of moral or natural philosophy, with conventional topics of invention. Like their medieval predecessors, Renaissance painters and poets frequently regarded (or professed to regard) their art as the handmaiden of moral philosophy or of theology and politics. Theoretically, verbal and visual arts alike aimed at secular or spiritual felicity as their final cause. Both imitated the same objects—actions and characters and passions, nature and the art or poetry of the past, and the ideas or "forms" of virtues and vices. Both utilized the de-

Preface

vices of synecdoche and metonymy, etymology and paronomasia, as writers on emblematic wit sometimes observed. Both made use of the resources of allegory and exemplum, the principles of decorum and verisimilitude and probability, the notions of original genius and divine inspiration, the concept of the marvelous, the distinctions between the subject matter and styles of various genres. Both resorted, in part at least, to the familiar topics of invention. Treatises on painting and sculpture often employ the concepts and vocabulary of Horatian and Aristotelian poetics, while treatises on poetry frequently draw parallels from the visual arts. Both, in turn, reveal the influence of rhetorical theory in their vocabulary ("argument" or "theme," "disposition" and "invention"), in their development of the distinction between unadorned matter or theme and extrinsic ornament or "colors," and in their insistence on the superior force of the sensuous image or example in impressing the imagination, instructing the intellect, delighting the senses, and moving the passions, the appetites, and the will. This emphasis on sensuous beauty as a means of arousing love for the abstract idea—the ideal forms of the virtues—derives partly from Platonic and Ciceronian theories of the interrelationship between rhetoric and moral philosophy and partly from Biblical conceptions of the visible forms of nature as images of the invisible qualities of their creator, the rhetoric of Deity.

The interdependence of artistic and poetic theory with rhetoric is scarcely less marked in the Renaissance than the topical organization of so many of the florilegia and manuals of the period—the commonplace books, the compendia of divinity and theological *loci communes*, the topical indices to emblem books and iconologies, mythographies and collections of proverbs. Art theory had not yet emancipated itself from poetics, nor had poetics freed itself successfully from rhetoric. Iconographers drew much of their material from ancient poetry, while poets and painters alike turned to the same mythographical and iconological manuals for inventions. Medieval theory had interpreted Horace's poetics against the background of rhetorical theory, and sixteenth-century commentators often read Aristotle's *Poetics* in the light of their understanding of Horace or of Aristotle's *Rhetoric* and *Politics*. Theoretically, poetry, painting, and rhetoric alike were regarded, on the whole, as instru-

Preface

ments of moral persuasion and accordingly subject to the ends of church or state as well as to the tastes of an individual artist or his patron. Organization by topics assisted the painter, as well as the poet and the orator, in "inventing" his arguments, in finding the myth or history that might best exemplify his theme, or the proverb that might strengthen his argument through the persuasive force of "common opinion" and tradition, or the prototypes in ancient art or literature that could lend to his treatment the authority of antiquity. In the case of a Scriptural image or theme, this could represent the authority of divine testimony. For the men who regarded the pagan myths and mysteries and the Egyptian hieroglyphics as the veiled statements of a *prisca theologia* these too could possess a superhuman authority, either as the mysteries of a secret tradition or merely as fabulous corruptions of Biblical truths.

In examining these adaptations of older traditional symbols, classical or Biblical, medieval or early Renaissance, this book will limit its horizon specifically to Renaissance contexts. To broaden it to include twentieth-century theories of symbolic forms and mythopoeic thought, and the insights of anthropologists and psychologists, would not only raise additional questions—problems better suited to the methods of the behavioral sciences than to those of literary scholarship—but also introduce embarrassing anachronisms.[11] Though these may provide interesting analogies and contrasts with Renaissance mythography—just as they have sometimes illuminated or obscured the treatment of mythical themes in classical art and literature—they are apt to distort one's understanding of particular works. The critic cannot assume that the symbolic vocabularies of different cultures, or even of different historical epochs, are essentially interchangeable, that they possess the same ontological status or semantic value, or that they stand in the same relationship either to abstract ideas or to subliminal "archetypes." Perhaps comparative studies of the Alcheringa ("dreamtime") of Australian aborigines, the trances of Kalmuck and Kara-Kirghiz shamans, the iconology of peyote visions, and the reconstructed rituals of cavemen of Auvergne will someday produce fresh and hitherto unexpected insights into Renaissance mythography, but this task must remain a challenge for future scholars.

Preface

Renaissance conceptions of myth and symbol were significantly narrower than our own. For the most part, the writers and artists of the period regarded them as sensuous expressions of universal ideas rather than as strictly "symbolic forms" according to Cassirer's definition. In a truly symbolic mode, as our own contemporaries define it, the thing signified cannot be expressed or conceived apart from its sign or symbol. For most Renaissance writers, however, these were separable, belonging to two distinct levels of sense and planes of reality, visible and intelligible. Though there are significant exceptions—especially in symbolic statements of negative theology, inasmuch as the supreme Deity remains incomprehensible either through abstract ideas or concrete symbols—in the majority of cases the meaning of a myth or an allegory or an exemplum was a general concept, an idea that could be abstracted from particulars like a kernel from a nutshell. Though invisible or only dimly visible to the senses, it could be clearly contemplated by the intellect.

The emblematic story or picture thus served a dual purpose in accordance with the dual nature of man, that "great Amphibium," and the divided and distinguished worlds in which he lived. The distinction between literal and allegorical senses corresponded to the dichotomy of flesh and spirit, to the distinction between sense perception and cognition of ideas, and to the Platonic division between the phenomenal and transcendental worlds, the aesthetic and noumenal realms, probability and certitude, opinion and truth. Whether allegorical or hieroglyphic, both the verbal and the visual icon served as the vehicle of a universal idea, capable of stirring the imagination and arousing the will. As a mediator between the realm of phenomena and the realm of ideas, it was a means of ascent, emotional as well as intellectual, to the plane of universals. Though it was necessarily a "dark" conceit, like the shadows in Plato's cave or the forms in St. Paul's enigmatic mirror, its obscurity was the inevitable result of clothing an intellectual abstraction in the ornaments of rhetoric or art. Though the universal is comprehensible only to the intellect, its essential beauty or foulness can be impressed on the imagination through the language of sense.

There are, of course, variations on this pattern. The hidden sense may refer to particulars—a specific individual or a certain event, as

Preface

in historical allegory, in prophetic dream visions, or in certain Biblical types—rather than to a general idea. In Christian allegory the principal opposition may lie between the realms of reason and faith, or human and divine knowledge, rather than between sense and idea. If the concealed meaning is anagogical, it refers to spiritual entities or conditions that cannot be cognized by the intellect and can be conceived only by analogy or comparison. A similar elusiveness characterizes the symbolic expressions of mystical experience and frequently of neo-Platonic and Hermetic doctrines. These are, however, exceptions to the dominant tradition in Renaissance allegory. Here the symbolic referent is normally a universal idea; though dimly shadowed through its external vehicle (variously described as husk or integument, glass or veil or garment), it can be abstracted and contemplated by the intellect. The poet or painter expects his audience (or the "fit" and "few" among them) to "unhusk" the kernel, extracting the general concept from the particulars that both conceal and reveal it— in short, to apply to art the methods of learning they normally applied to nature. Epistemologically, this view of allegory could fit both Platonic and Aristotelian theories of knowledge—the recollection of half-forgotten ideas through contemplating their sensuous images and their progressive clarification and definition through Socratic dialectic, the abstraction of universals from particulars through inductive reasoning and their systematic organization through deductive inference.

The visual or verbal exemplum involved an analogous ascent from particular to universal. Unlike allegory and metaphor, however, the example did not necessarily entail the substitution of one object for another or a transference of meaning from the proper species to a different species or genus. Except for the allegorical exemplum, the example is normally a particular that can be regularly subsumed under the general category to which it properly belongs, the universal idea which, as exemplum, it illustrates and signifies. Unlike allegory and personification, which may denote concrete particulars as well as general concepts, the exemplum usually illustrates a general idea, even though it usually and characteristically approaches the universal by inductive inference from concrete particulars.

Like allegory, personification may represent either a universal idea or a particular; but unlike allegory it does not involve the substitution of one sense or one species for another. The name itself identifies the general concept or the particular object represented, and the figurative element consists almost entirely in investing a fleshless abstraction or a force of nature with a human form and voice and symbolic attributes. Nevertheless, the actions and apparel of such a figure may be allegorical, and her attendants often include allegorical and exemplar personages as well as other personifications. The range of traditional personifications was sufficiently comprehensive to include mythical deities like Eros and Hades, the divinities Fortuna and Virtus and Victory, natural forces and topographical features (Nature, Boreas and Zephyr, Tiber and Nile), cities and countries and continents (Roma, Egypt, Asia), the arts and sciences, moral and theological abstractions, and miscellaneous concepts like Time and Fame, Pleasure and Incontinence, True and False Education. Classical and medieval tradition had left a rich symbolic vocabulary on which Renaissance poets and artists could draw at will, or which they could amplify through their own inventions.

Though these and other symbolic modes—Biblical types, parables and enigmas, emblems and hieroglyphs, heraldic devices and natural signatures—could be differentiated in theory, they tended to overlap in practice; and one should not overstress the distinctions between them. Their essential function was to illustrate or mask a general idea or another particular, and in practice both artists and poets tended to combine them or employ them interchangeably. In classical myth and poetry, personifications sometimes intermingle with gods and heroes—Power and Force in *Prometheus Bound*, Death in *Alcestis*, and a variety of abstractions in Virgil's underworld. One encounters a similar congregation of mythical deities and personified abstractions in the medieval dream-visions of Guillaume de Lorris, Jean de Meung, and Chaucer. In Spenser's epic, personifications mingle freely with allegorical figures drawn from myth or chivalric legend or hagiography or from the poet's own imagination. Milton's Hell (peopled by Biblical devils, pagan divinities, and classical monsters) is guarded by the personifications Sin and Death. Dante, on the other hand, makes comparatively little use of personifications, preferring to illustrate the nature of virtues and vices through the

Preface

"transumptive" method of allegory and the method of the exemplum. Lesser poets might well have crowded heaven and hell and purgatory with personified virtues and vices. Dante veils these abstractions under historical or mythical figures: Virgil and Statius, Matelda and Beatrice, Cerberus and Pluto and Geryon, Centaurs and giants, or illustrates them through literary or historical exempla.

2.

The classical myths could function both as allegories and as exempla. Through the continuity of mythographical and iconographical tradition, and through long exploitation in plastic and verbal art, many of them had acquired conventional and comparatively stable meanings. Insofar as the allegorical significance of the pagan divinities had become traditional, they could now function virtually as personifications. After long usage the "veil of allegory" had become threadbare. With very little eyestrain the reader could make out the figure of chastity or the orb of the moon under the mask of Diana, the power of sensual love and beauty under the fable of Venus, or the nature of wisdom and eloquence in the myth of Mercury. In such instances there would be little disguising or masking of meaning; and the technical distinction between personification and allegory would be largely academic and pedantic. In effect, all three divinities could serve as *personae* for the abstract ideas or natural powers with which they had traditionally been associated by allegorists and mythographers. The gods of wind and wine and warfare served practically as *personae* for these ideas; there would be little difference either in meaning or in perspicuity whether the poet referred explicitly to Bacchus or wine, to Ceres or grain, Mars or war, and to Aeolus or the wind. Just as myth and symbol tend to become rationalized as allegory and exemplum, conventional allegory may easily become virtually indistinguishable from personification.

In the case of more obscure readings of ancient myth—esoteric interpretations, new interpretations invented by the poet or his contemporaries, accommodations of mythological conventions to different intellectual and historical contexts—a genuinely allegorical mode would still be possible; and the pagan deities might indeed be enig-

Preface

matic and hieroglyphical figures. Though the common interpretations of Diana and Venus and Bacchus and Mercury had reduced them to little more than personifications, the less familiar interpretations advanced by neo-Platonists, Hermeticists, and other partisans of occult traditions or mystical and negative theologies managed to invest these symbols with an element of obscurity, the veil of darkness usually associated with the integuments of allegory.

Thus the Renaissance taste for mysteries and hieroglyphs and covert allegories was, in fact, self-defeating. As these symbolic vocabularies became more widely known, they lost the charm of secrecy and the beauty of strangeness. A secret divulged is no longer a secret, and a mystery made manifest ceases to be mysterious. A code that has been deciphered is no longer effective for cryptograms. As the taste for esotericism became more fashionable, the esoteric inevitably became exoteric. Once the veil had been drawn, the husk removed, the hieroglyph interpreted, the types and shadows understood, the traditional symbolic vocabulary offered comparatively few opportunities for "dark" conceits; and to achieve novelty one must alter either the symbol itself or its referent. The poet or artist must either invest his vocabulary of symbols with new and more difficult senses or else substitute fresh symbols for hackneyed conventions. He could also endeavor to achieve innovation and surprise by combining the old symbols and conventional symbols in a new and different way. Finally, a skillful poet or artist might employ the conventional symbol in its traditional sense, yet invest it with apparent novelty and *maraviglia* through sheer technical brilliance, the virtuosity of his *maniera*. Even though the enigma or emblem and its meaning might be thoroughly familiar to his audience, he could consciously surround it with an atmosphere of mystery through his description of setting. In epic and romance, the locale of such tableaux—underground caverns, enchanted castles and gardens, the temples of pagan divinities, distant islands and forests and mountaintops—can recreate an atmosphere of the strange and marvelous, even though the poet's symbols are thoroughly conventional and have long since lost their obscurity and their enigmatic quality.

In historical allegories, where one particular substitutes for another, both particulars, literal and allegorical, may potentially serve as moral exempla, illustrating an abstract universal through two parallel stories represented on two different levels. Both the persons and action symbolized, and the persons and action that obliquely shadow or embody them, may serve as inductive proofs for the same ethical, political or religious doctrine. Similarly, Biblical types, and the antitypes they foreshadow, may function as examples of the same abstract virtues or vices. Just as the historical events of the Old Testament may refer allegorically to events in the New Testament, according to the fourfold pattern of scriptural exegesis, but also signify moral (tropological) concepts and spiritual (anagogical) states, their New Testament referents may exemplify the same ethical abstractions or foreshadow the same spiritual and eschatological patterns. In Michael's prophetic survey of world history in the concluding books of *Paradise Lost*, the Old Testament examples of the "one just man" bearing witness to the true faith against the contumely or violence of corrupt or apostate worldlings function as "shadowy Types" of Christ; nevertheless, like the exemplum of Abdiel in Raphael's earlier account of the angelic war, type and antitype alike function as examples of constancy and the better fortitude of patience and heroic martyrdom, inductive proofs for the superior heroism of the martyr or "witness" in the cause of truth. Adam is taught chiefly by the "example" of Christ that suffering for truth's sake is "fortitude [heroic valor or *virtus*] to highest victory." In *Lycidas*, the thinly veiled pastoral allegory expresses particulars through particulars, substituting two fictional shepherds for two historical persons, scholars at Cambridge; but the significance of these feigned personae and the actual characters they signify extends beyond the particular to the universal, to the general offices and rewards of poet or priest.

Spenser's Letter to Raleigh moves easily from the general to the particular referents of his allegory and from ethical abstractions to concrete historical situations. In his "generall intention" the poet means to signify "glory" through his Faery Queene, but in his "particular" intention he signifies the "person" of Queen Elizabeth—conceived in her public "person" as "a most royall Queene or Empresse"—and her kingdom in Faery land. In Belphoebe he portrays her private "person" as "a most vertuous and beautifull Lady." In

Preface

the "person" of Arthur he has portrayed "the image of a brave knight, perfected in the twelve private morall vertues" and especially in magnificence (magnanimity). Twelve "other knights" function as "patrones," perhaps in the dual sense of patterns as well as protectors of the twelve "other vertues." Moreover, Spenser makes little distinction between the instructive force of example and allegory. In the "Persons" of Agamemnon and Ulysses, Homer had "ensampled" a "good governour and a vertuous man," and Spenser proposes to do likewise, following the example of "antique Poets historicall" like Homer and Virgil and their successors, Ariosto and Tasso. The methods of allegory and example are grouped together and contrasted with the method of precept: some "had rather have good discipline delivered plainly in way or precepts, or sermoned at large . . . then thus clowdily enwrapped in Allegoricall devises. But . . . So much more profitable and gratious is doctrine by ensample, then by rule."

Spenser is writing within the tradition of Horatian poetic theory with its emphasis on profit and delight *(prodesse* or *delectare, utile* and *dulce)*. Though other poets would advance additional reasons for the pedagogical merits of exemplum and allegory, including the paradoxical stress on perspicuity and obscurity, he bases his argument on the principle of pleasure, including the traditional seicento argument in favor of the multiple heroes and interlacing plots of the romance—the increased pleasure afforded by variety of subject matter—and also on the Horatian and Aristotelian criterion of probability. In order to render his moral discipline "most plausible and pleasing," he has colored it with "an historicall fiction, the which the most part of men delight to read, rather for variety of matter, then for profite of the ensample. . . ." In these days all things are "accounted by their showes, and nothing is esteemed that is not delightfull and pleasing to commune sence." In embodying the twelve moral virtues in twelve "patrones," in addition to Prince Arthur, the principal hero, he has attempted to give "more variety" to the history. Like many of his contemporaries, who endeavored simultaneously to imitate an action, an ideal of heroic virtue, and the models bequeathed by the ancients and their Renaissance successors, he at-

Preface

tempts not only to provide examples of abstract virtues, but also to follow the "ensample" of earlier poets. His dedicatory sonnets refer alternately to the "shady vele" of allegory as a vehicle for "th'antique glory of thine ancestry" and to the "brave ensample of long passed daies,/In which trew honor yee may fashioned see. . . ." Moreover, both Spenser and Harvey utilize the term "type" for historical allegory: "that true glorious type of thine,/The Argument of mine afflicted stile"; "that faire Ilands right:/Which thou doest vaile in Type of Faery land/Elyzas blessed field that *Albion* hight."

Such exempla and allegories may serve the ends of demonstrative as well as deliberative rhetoric, providing arguments for praise or blame as well as for exhortation or dehortation. In addition to employing concrete particulars as images for general concepts, the writer may evoke the latter primarily in order to extol or deride specific individuals among his own contemporaries. Although personifications of Heroic Virtue or Magnanimity or Beauty or Clemency and exemplary or allegorical representations of these qualities through specific historical or mythical characters may maintain the pretense of "ideal imitation," in many cases the artist's chief end is the praise of a patron or the excoriation of enemies. To extol a man or woman as Virtue itself—as absolute Fortitude or Prudence, ideal Beauty or Chastity, the norm and essence of the moral and theological virtues rather than merely one out of many representative examples—is a form of encomiastic hyperbole that heightens the merits of the person praised. In many Renaissance works the author's actual end in portraying universals may not be the imitation of an idea so much as the idealization of an individual. Fortunately, he could accomplish both aims simultaneously. In a representation of Hercules and his exploits a poet or artist might allegorically shadow Heroic Virtue in general and his own patron in particular, and these two different referents of his symbol would effectively reinforce each other. Through the same image he would, in effect, be praising his patron on two levels, comparing him specifically with Hercules and also identifying him with the ideal pattern or archetype embodied in the Hercules image. Thus Donne's hyperbolic praise can be simultaneously directed to the dead Elizabeth Drury and to the Idea of

Preface

Woman; his delineation of the universal serves to magnify the particular (the deceased daughter of his patron), while the particular, in turn, serves to illustrate and exemplify the abstract virtues appropriate to perfect womanhood.

One should not underestimate the degree of divergence between theory and practice in Renaissance poetry or plastic art. Not only did theorists themselves vary widely on many essential points, but poets and artists often treated the aesthetic doctrines of their contemporaries with considerable freedom. In interpreting and evaluating their works by the aesthetic categories of their period, we may, indeed, be applying criteria almost as arbitrary—concepts almost as extrinsic to the works themselves—as the critical values of the nineteenth or twentieth century. One may easily exaggerate a writer's dependence on contemporary theory, and accordingly judge him by principles of composition or interpretation that may have exerted little or no direct influence on his own creation. Similarly, there is a significant difference between allegoresis as a method of composition and as a method of interpretation. A poet or painter may desire to arouse curiosity and suspense through a judicious use of obscurity and mystery, but he will rarely want to baffle his public altogether. On the other hand, an exegete desiring to adapt Homeric or Virgilian narratives to the ethos of philosophers and theologians, or to find answers to problems of medieval and Renaissance society in the Old or New Testaments, may be compelled to exercise considerable ingenuity in extracting the message he is looking for. The more abstruse allegories, and the more difficult and far-fetched interpretations, are often ex post facto, superimposed on a work by commentators or possibly by the author himself. We should not assume rashly that medieval or Renaissance poets wrote, or contemporary artists carved or painted, according to the same allegorical methods that they and their predecessors had attributed to the ancients. If they had actually invested their works with the polysemous complexity that mythographers had imposed on pagan myth and Christian exegetes on the text of Scripture, they could hardly have expected to be intelligible to even the most erudite of audiences. On the whole, the Renaissance allegorical "system," and perhaps the medieval symbolic system likewise, existed more in the minds of commentators and exe-

Preface

getes on the works of others than in the minds and hands of practicing artists and poets.

3.

Though the visual arts are tangential to this study, it has been impossible to ignore them. Poets and artists inherited the same mythological traditions and consulted the same mythographical manuals, borrowed the same motifs from the same classical authors and exhibited the same eclecticism in adapting and combining them in new syntheses. Treating the same historical or mythical subjects, depicting the same virtues or vices, glorifying the same patrons, they frequently encroached on one another's domain: painters by endeavoring to realize dramatically isolated moments of crisis in a continuous narrative action; poets through descriptive detail and visual imagery. Both utilized proverbs and *sententiae*—standard rhetorical devices scarcely less conventional in emblem literature and drama than in oratory—and both exploited etymology (the argument "from the name") as a source of verbal or visual wit. Both on occasion recognized the same distinction between icastic and fantastic imitation. Both employed feigned images (eidola) as sources of instruction, persuasion, and delight.

Poetry and painting shared the same topics as well as the same ends; and just as the latter frequently based its inventions on literature, the former could draw on iconographical tradition for its own conceits. Though Milton's hybrid figure of Sin possesses numerous analogues in classical and Renaissance literature, she acquires additional propriety in his epic on the Fall through the iconographical tradition that had endowed the serpent of Genesis with similar form. Similarly, Una's lamb—an embarrassing encumbrance on a dangerous quest—derives primarily from pictorial representations of St. George's combat with the dragon. As the sheep intended as a companion-sacrifice to the dragon, it had long been an attribute of the virgin rescued by St. George. It remains an identifying attribute in Spenser's verbal picture, though the virgin is no longer Cleodolinda, but Una—the one Catholic and Apostolic church.[12]

In examining the adaptation of traditional mythological and iconographical motifs by various poets, I have necessarily restricted this

Preface

study to specific passages in particular works instead of comparing entire poems as organic wholes, subordinating problems of disposition and style to topics of invention, emphasizing the representation of abstract ideas and passing over other, equally important objects of imitation: action and character, passion and thought.

4.

In limiting this study to the representation of *intelligibilia* (universals) through *sensibilia*—to the images of abstract ideas portrayed in allegories or exempla by poets or painters—one must neglect other, potentially richer aspects of the relationship between *visibilia* and *invisibilia:* the approach to the *arcana Dei* through mystical theology, through the signatures and correspondences impressed on the visible creation by the unseen Creator, or through the manifested attributes of the unmanifested Deity in Christ the Logos; the representation of separated substances through accommodating them to the limitations of human sense, imagination, and reason; Biblical typology and the symbolism of the liturgy. The complex issue of Renaissance number symbolism has been excluded primarily because it requires fuller discussion than can be afforded here. Its importance for the structure of Dante's *Commedia* and for medieval and Renaissance church architecture has long been recognized by scholars. More recently, Fowler has stressed its significance for Spenser, and Martz for the poetry of Donne; but its relevance to Milton's verse still remains controversial. Though Renaissance treatises on art sometimes refer to the symbolic significance of geometrical forms, much of their discussion of mathematical proportions is conditioned by other factors: the need for accuracy, compositional requirements such as foreshortening and perspective, and "correct" proportions for the human form, the desire to demonstrate the nobility of painting by linking it with mathematics and emphasizing its certitude, and, above all else, the conception of beauty in terms of symmetry, proportion, and harmony.[13] The psychological power of harmony, whether in music or verse or the visual arts, to arouse and allay the passions and to shape character had interested both Plato and Aristotle; and it had subsequently been rationalized in terms of hidden sympathies or cor-

Preface

respondences in the human soul. As *musica humana*, the harmony of the human soul and body, was the analogue of artificial or instrumental music and of the *musica mundana* of the cosmos; the artificial harmony of numbers possessed the power to set the soul itself in harmony with the universe. Music itself was, of course, a mathematical art; perhaps indeed "all arts aspire to the condition of music." The "harmonious numbers" of verse or the proportions of a mathematically composed painting or sculpture or building ("frozen music") might possess powers comparable to those of Timotheus and Amphion. An adequate study of Renaissance number symbolism and of "the hidden soul of harmony" must consider music theory—which lies, unfortunately, beyond the scope of this study.

Recent criticism has, however, sometimes exaggerated the element of "cosmic symbolism" in Renaissance literature and over-stressed the concept of the poem as "heterocosm." Though painters might recognize the macrocosm-microcosm ratio and numerical and astrological correspondences between the parts of the human body and those of the world, they were not, as a rule, painting an *imago mundi* when they sat down to compose a portrait. Though dramatists might exploit the proverbial analogy between the theater and the world, they invested their comedies and tragedies with localized settings, selected characters, and particularized actions. Though they might draw general inference about the way of the world, their plays were not, as a rule, world symbols. The majority of allegorical representations of the world, in fact, are not concerned with its proportions, but with its moral significance: the topos of *mundus mare* in emblem books and illustrations of Fortune (and perhaps in the Anglo-Saxon elegies, "The Wanderer" and "The Seafarer"), the world as labyrinth or *selva oscura* in Milton's *Comus* and Dante's *Inferno*, or the world as Vanity Fair or a Fair Field Full of Folk in Bunyan and Langland. Even the great "cosmic epics" of the late Middle Ages and the late Renaissance, Dante's *Commedia* and Milton's *Paradise Lost*, are designed less as images of the cosmos than as moralized and spiritualized cosmology. In both instances the cosmos has been, so to speak, restructured tropologically and anagogically to express moral and spiritual contraries in spatial terms. Though Milton's setting is universal in scope, embracing "Heav'n, Hell, Earth, Chaos,

Preface

All," and though his narrative comprehends the creation and corruption of the world and its ultimate destruction and renovation, the plot centers on a single action in a localized setting within a few instants of time. The universe of the *Commedia* is topically structured, its geography and uranography systematically arranged according to the principal commonplaces of medieval ethical theory. The scale of nature and the structure of the cosmos function as images for the hierarchy of virtues and vices.

The imagery of the "occult" sciences in Renaissance literature and art likewise presents special problems, which would require more detailed examination than is possible here. There is a partial truth in the observation that "classical antiquity . . . lay hidden behind demonic antiquity" and that "for a long time logic and magic coexisted peacefully side by side. . . ."[14] Nevertheless, despite the valuable researches of recent scholars, the application of this material to the interpretation of particular works of art and creative literature often remains ambiguous. Some of Thomas Vaughan's alchemical poems might easily be regarded as little more than conventional love lyrics; fortunately, in several instances, the author himself has supplied the key to their deeper allegorical significance. Again, though the prose treatises of Thomas Vaughan and Jakob Boehme are often saturated with alchemical terminology, they frequently employ this vocabulary metaphorically and allegorically as a vehicle for Christian theological doctrines—symbolic equivalents for mystical experience and for regeneration and sanctification, resurrection and glorification. Vaughan frequently combines Biblical and alchemical imagery, and in this way can transform the philosopher's stone into Christ the Rock, the cornerstone despised by the builders.

Though recent scholarship has emphasized the possibility of a magical intent in Renaissance poetry and art, the critic may encounter difficulties in demonstrating such an intent in a particular painting or poem, over and above the more conventional aesthetic concern with mimesis and proportion. Though certain poets or artists may have attempted to follow the principles of natural magic in their pictorial or dramatic representations of astrological divinities, or their use of mathematical ratios in pictures and buildings, or in musical and poetic forms and meters, it is easier to argue the theoreti-

Preface

cal and general possibility of this view than to find definitive evidence in particular and concrete works of art. The use of astrological or alchemical or mathematical symbolism as imagery in art does not necessarily indicate that such images were intended to *operate* as astrological forces; nor does the exploitation of imagery based on universal analogies prove that such correspondences were intended to be magically efficacious as well as mimetically and rhetorically convincing. The same symbolic relationships between *sensibilia* and *intelligibilia*, or between earthly and celestial forms and powers, might operate rhetorically or "magically," as a mode of conceptualization and communication or as a form of sympathetic magic. The former is the normal modus operandi of Renaissance symbol and allegory, and even though the possibility of an intended magical efficacy cannot be altogether excluded, it is usually hard to prove. The rhetorical and poetic adaptation of correspondences as arguments from analogy and ingenious conceits does not necessarily involve a positive belief in universal analogies as physical and metaphysical realities and it should not be mistaken for "magical" or quasi-magical exploitation of correspondences as cosmic principles, operative throughout the universe and linking the various grades and ranks in the scale of being from matter up to spirit.

Perhaps the most significant aspects of the search for "correspondences" in Renaissance literature are not the parallels between verbal and visual arts, or the analogies between microcosm and macrocosm, but the conscious parallels or contrasts between Christian and classical art and thought, and the attempt to utilize analogies between the civilizations of the ancients and the moderns for the instruction and admonition of the latter. Men of the period were conscious of similarities as well as dissimilarities between ancients and moderns or between sacred and ethnic culture; these analogies recur in the historical and ethicopolitical as well as the literary and artistic thought of the period. "The central intellectual problem of the Renaissance," a modern historian observes, "was to find what Aby Warburg once called a compromise formula, an *Ausgleichsformel*, that would enable men to live comfortably with classical forms and Christian convictions, trust in man and trust in God, vigorous secular energies and a tenacious ascetic ideal" (Gay, p. 270).

Preface

The psychology of poetic representation is no less important than the "psychology of pictorial representation" recently explored by E. H. Gombrich in his excellent *Art and Illusion*, 2nd ed., rev., (Princeton, 1961); but it demands a kind of investigation—exhaustive, detailed, comprehending several highly specialized disciplines—that lies beyond the scope of this book. Underlying medieval and Renaissance theories of stylistic and generic distinctions and concepts of the functions of rhetoric and poetics are presuppositions concerning the relationship of visual and verbal media to faculty psychology.[15] These not only concern the relation of *sensibilia* to *intelligibilia*, and of sensuous and affective images to abstract ideas. They also involve the analogy between poetic vision and the visionary experience of the dreamer (whether this is the delusion of the lover or the revelation of the prophet) and the relationship between sense and reason in poetry or rhetoric and in inductive or deductive logic. During this period, poetic theory and practice are comparatively flexible, capable of embracing a wide and various range of aesthetic alternatives. They move, with relative freedom, between the extremes of dream experience and waking experience, between conceptions of poetry as phantasm and as probable imitation. The poet's emphasis (or that of the critic) may range fairly readily between the ideals of marvel and verisimilitude—between the fabulous or enigmatic image and the probable or convincing image. Both poles can be found in Chaucer as in Milton.

Despite the greater range of classical authors accessible to Renaissance scholars, there was substantial continuity between medieval and Renaissance rhetorical or poetic theory. This is apparent not only in a common indebtedness to Horace and Donatus, to the *Rhetorica ad Herennium* and Cicero's *De Inventione*, but also in assertions of the poet's freedom to mix truth with fiction in the interests of art—a liberty asserted by Alain de Lille in the twelfth century as well as by Tasso in the sixteenth and Edward Phillips in the late seventeenth. According to *The Complaint of Nature*, poets sometimes "combine historical events and imaginative fancies, . . . to the end that from the harmonious joining of diversities a finer picture of the story may result."[16]

Preface

Notes

[1] Cf. Merritt Y. Hughes, *Ten Perspectives on Milton* (New Haven and London, 1965), pp. 165-95.

[2] Cf. Erwin Panofsky, *Idea: A Concept in Art Theory*, trans. Joseph J. S. Peake (Columbia, S.C., 1968); Erich Auerbach, *Mimesis: The Representation of Reality in Western Literature*, trans. Willard Trask (Garden City, N.Y., 1957); E. H. Gombrich, *Norm and Form: Studies in the Art of the Renaissance* (London, 1966); Douglas Fraser, Howard Hibbard, and Milton J. Lewine, eds., *Essays in the History of Art Presented to Rudolf Wittkower* (London, 1967); Denis Mahon, *Studies in Seicento Art and Theory* (London, 1947; Charles S. Singleton, ed., *Art, Science, and History in the Renaissance* (Baltimore, 1967).

Among recent studies of Milton's imagery, see C. A. Patrides, "*Paradise Lost* and the Theory of Accommodation," *TSLL*, 5 (1963), 58-63; Roland Mushat Frye, *God, Man and Satan* (Princeton, 1960); William G. Madsen, "Earth the Shadow of Heaven: Typological Symbolism in *Paradise Lost*," *PMLA* 75 (1960), 519-26; James Whaler, "The Compounding and Distribution of Similes in *Paradise Lost*," *MP* 28 (1931), 313-27; Jackson I. Cope, *The Metaphoric Structure of "Paradise Lost"* (Baltimore, 1962); Joseph H. Summers, *The Muse's Method* (Cambridge, Mass., 1962); Christopher Waldo Grose, "Some Uses of Sensuous Immediacy in *Paradise Lost*," *HLQ* 31 (1968), 211-22.

[3] In considering the complementary and sometimes antithetical relationship of the exemplum to the allegory ("concretion *versus* abstraction") and the relationship of both to either universal or particular referents, I have employed the term *exemplum* (or example) in a fairly broad sense. I apply it not only to exemplary actions and narratives (a sense familiar to students of Renaissance poetics and of medieval sermon literature), but also to individual persons (historical, legendary, or fictional) whose character and actions have become so well known that the poet can allude to them merely by name as examples of particular virtues and vices, or of good and evil fortune or fame, without elaborating their past history. He can cite Lucretia, for instance, as an example of chastity, Troilus as an unfortunate and Theseus as an unfaithful lover, Hercules and Samson as exemplars of strength, without necessarily repeating the stories of their lives as complete narrative exempla. I have usually avoided the term *exemplar* since it could lead to confusion between the concrete instance or example and the ideal archetype. In neo-Platonic writings the term "exemplary virtues" frequently refers specifically to the divine persons themselves, or sometimes to the paradigms or archetypal ideas in the divine mind. As both the idea and its image can be termed exemplars, the latter could be described as "an exemplar of an exemplar"; to avoid this confusion of senses, I shall restrict the term *exemplum* to the illustrative concrete particular (whether person or narrative) and designate exemplary virtues as paradigms or archetypal ideas.

[4] In the following pages I shall generally employ the terms "ideal imitation" and "ideal representation" more or less interchangeably, despite the ambiguities and occasional anachronisms of this terminology. Though there is no inherent contradiction between the concepts of poetry as fable or fabulous allegory, as moral exemplum, and as imitation (or between the ideals of the poet as imitator and as maker), the emphasis on the mimetic functions of poetry derives largely from Platonic and Aristotelian poetics, while the emphasis on imitation of classical models as a means of mastering the techniques of eloquence (in poetry and prose alike) derives largely from the influence of Cicero, Quintilian, and the pseudo-Ciceronian *Rhetoric to Herennius*.

Preface

Though the definition of poetry as an imitation of an action is widespread during the late Renaissance, earlier theorists tend to stress the fabulous and allegorical character of poetry rather than its essentially mimetic nature. Writers on poetics do not normally refer to allegory as the "imitation" of ideas; and it is difficult to find an accurate common term for the delineation of universals through the veil of allegory and through the imitation of an exemplary action. For want of a better term, I shall refer to both as diverse modes of "ideal representation." In addition, there are embarrassing ambiguities in the use of terms like *idea* and *imitation*. Renaissance critics may apply the former term to categories of style and the paradigms of the several poetic genres, to the plot or structure of a poem or the formal design of a painting, to the norms of virtues and vices or to the definitions or class-terms for various species and subspecies of men or beasts or plants and minerals, to the plan or schema in the artist's mind, and to the sense impression or mental image of a particular object. *Imitation* may refer to the representation of abstract universals or concrete particulars, to the delineation of action or character or passion or thought, to the representation of external nature or internal ideas, or to the close study and emulation of classical and modern writers.

The student must also take into account the shifting boundaries between poetics and rhetoric and logic, and the different modes of handling abstract concepts in these several arts. A tendency to confuse the provinces of these organic or "instrumental" arts was apparent not only in the Middle Ages but also in the Renaissance, and theorists were constantly compelled to redefine their relationship and their areas of jurisdiction. Varchi maintained that whereas rhetoric achieved its end by persuasion, poetry attained its end "by imitation or representation." While the former utilized the enthymeme as its principal instrument, the latter relied chiefly on the example; J. E. Spingarn, *A History of Literary Criticism in the Renaissance*, 2d ed., (New York, 1954), pp. 34, 50-51; Ronald David Emma and John T. Shawcross, eds., *Language and Style in Milton*, (New York, 1967), p. 197; see also Roland Mushat Frye, "Rhetoric and Poetry in *Julius Caesar*," *Quarterly Journal of Speech*, 37 (1951), 41-48; Wilbur Samuel Howell, "Rhetoric and Poetics: A Plea for the Recognition of the Two Literatures," *The Classical Tradition: Literary and Historical Studies in Honor of Harry Caplan*, ed. Luitpold Wallach (Ithaca, 1966), pp. 374-90. Jacopo Mazzoni argued that "the credible as credible [and persuasive] is the subject of rhetoric and the credible as marvelous is the subject of poetry . . ."; Allan H. Gilbert, ed., *Literary Criticism, Plato to Dryden* (Detroit, 1962), pp. 370-71, 388. In Tasso's opinion, "rhetoric treats the false not in so far as it is false but in so far as it is probable; but the probable in so far as it has verisimilitude pertains to the poet"; Gilbert, p. 473; cf. ibid., pp. 412, 460 for Sidney's views. For wonder *(maraviglia, meraviglia)* as an affective aim of poetry, see James V. Mirollo, *The Poet of the Marvellous: Giambattista Marino* (New York and London, 1963).

Finally, in emphasizing the cognitive functions of poetic imitation and style, we must not neglect their affective functions nor the analogy with the function of pathetic proofs in rhetoric. In stressing the theory of ideal representation, we must not underestimate the frequency with which poets and artists tacitly or vocally demonstrated their independence from theory, pursuing the *dulce* with little or no concern for the *utile* and seeking no other end than pleasure. In considering the principle of *mimesis* we should not underplay the principle of "making." A likeness to reality could only be achieved by laborious and calculated art. The poetic icon or eidolon was a *constructed* image; and the principle of "ideal imitation" applied not only to moral universals but also to the form and design of the work and to the "idealized nature" so conveniently accessible in the masterpieces of the ancients. Illusionism is not inconsistent with the principle of ideal imitation. Though certain sixteenth and seventeenth-century theorists sometimes emphasize their opposition, it could be argued

Preface

that (on the contrary) the more vivid and lifelike the sensuous imitation, the greater its effectiveness as the vehicle of abstract ideas or spiritual values. By setting past or future events, the forms of virtues and vices, and celestial or infernal states immediately before the eyes, by seeking the qualities of *enargia* or *evidentia* (vividness), the poet or artist could persuade and move his audience more effectively. His verbal or visual image served as a kind of "evidence" or testimony, making the spectator temporarily an eyewitness of the remote events and invisible concepts described. This conception of the role of the sensuous image in embodying the invisible idea recurs in both the rhetorical and the poetic theory of the Renaissance and it provides a link with the literary theory of the medieval and baroque periods. Essentially, there is little radically new or different in the alleged "mannerist" or "baroque" tension between sensuality and spirituality, phenomenal and transcendental orders of reality—in spite of recent critical opinion to the contrary. These antitheses are inherent in traditional theories concerning the relationship of rhetoric and poetic to philosophy or theology. Ideally, these "organic arts" serve the latter most effectively through appealing to the senses and the passions in order to awaken knowledge and love of abstract ideas, through exploiting the phenomenal realm of opinion in the interest of the transcendental realm of apodeictic and certain knowledge. This concept of the function of eloquence recurs in classical and medieval, Renaissance and "baroque" periods (though it is not always the dominant theory), and one cannot regard it as a *differentia* of "the baroque" (as certain critics have done).

[5]Cf. Joseph Anthony Mazzeo, "St. Augustine's Rhetoric of Silence: Truth vs. Eloquence and Things vs. Signs," in *Renaissance and Seventeenth-Century Studies* (New York and London, 1964), pp. 1-28. Mazzeo observes that Saint Augustine "brought rhetoric back to where Plato had left it in the *Phaedrus*, where eloquence and rhetoric are based on truth in contrast to mere show. . . ." See also Marcia Lillian Colish, *The Mirror of Language: A Study in the Medieval Theory of Knowledge* (New Haven and London, 1968). See also the notes by Merritt Y. Hughes on *Comus*, line 218, and *Paradise Regained*, Book III, line 11, in John Milton, *Complete Poems and Major Prose* (New York, 1957), pp 95n, 505n; and my note "Herbert's Platonic Lapidary: A Note on 'The Foil' " in *Seventeenth-Century News*, 30 (1972), 59-62. See also Erwin Panofsky, *Idea, A Concept in Art Theory*, trans. Joseph J. S. Peake (Columbia, S.C., 1968), pp. 3-4, 11-18, on Plato's remarks concerning the "poietic" or "heuretic" painters, who attempt to "do justice to Idea in their works," and on Cicero's adaptation of Plato's theory of ideas to "the image of perfect eloquence in the mind."

[6]The term "aesthetics" is, of course, anachronistic when applied to the Middle Ages and Renaissance. See Joseph H. Summers, "Herbert's Conception of Form," in *The Metaphysical Poets*, ed. Frank Kermode (Greenwich, Conn., 1969), p. 233n, on "Baumgarten's invention of 1750" and Kristeller's "admonition concerning the historical impropriety of the word *aesthetic*" in the context of Saint Augustine's thought.

[7]In the preface to his *Angeleida*, Erasmo da Valvasone quotes Horace's praise of Homer (Epistle 2, Book I) for expressing better and more fully than Chrysippus and Crantor "quid sit pulchrum, quid turpe, quid utile," adding that persons incapable of understanding Scotus or Saint Thomas Aquinas could learn much about theology from pious poets: "Non altramente anchora molte cose apprenderebbono di quelle, che dalla sacra Theologia derivano coloro, che ne Scoto intendono, nè San Tomaso, se da pietosi Poeti cantate fossero. . . ." In *Areopagitica* Milton similarly praises Spenser as "a better teacher than *Scotus* or *Aquinas*." See my "Milton, Valvasone, and the Schoolmen," *PQ* 37 (1958), 502-04.

Preface

[8] D. W. Robertson, Jr., *A Preface to Chaucer* (Princeton, 1962), p. 79.

[9] Ibid., pp. 15, 25-26, 56, 65.

[10] See Leah Jonas, *The Divine Science: The Aesthetic of Some Representative Seventeenth-Century English Poets* (New York, 1940); Lily Bess Campbell, *Divine Poetry and Drama in Sixteenth-Century England* (Cambridge, 1959).

[11] Though the current interest in Renaissance visual and verbal imagery has frequently been stimulated by psychological and anthropological researches into the nature of myth and symbol and by the methods of phenomenology, these highly technical disciplines demand specialized skills usually beyond the competence of most literary or art historians. Among recent psychological-anthropological approaches to art and literature, see E. H. Gombrich, *Art and Illusion* (Princeton, 1960); Herbert Read, *Icon and Idea* (New York, 1965); Wayne Shumaker, *Literature and the Irrational* (New York, 1966); Erich Fromm, *The Forgotten Language* (New York, 1957); Benjamin Lee Whorf, *Language, Thought, and Reality* (Cambridge, Mass., 1964); Anton Ehrenzweig, *The Hidden Order of Art* (Berkeley and Los Angeles, 1971); Philip Wheelwright, *The Burning Fountain* (Bloomington and London, 1968); J. S. Kasinin, ed., *Language and Thought in Schizophrenia* (New York, 1964); C. G. Jung, *Psyche and Symbol*, ed. Violet S. de Laszlo (Garden City, N.Y., 1958); John Middleton, ed., *Myth and Cosmos* (Garden City, N.Y., 1967); C. G. Jung and C. Kerényi, *Essays on a Science of Mythology* (New York and Evanston, 1963); Claude Lévi-Strauss, *Structural Anthropology* (Garden City, N.Y., 1967); Wolfgang Köhler, *Gestalt Psychology* (New York, 1947); Joseph Campbell, *The Hero with a Thousand Faces* (New York, 1956); Mircea Eliade, *Myth and Reality*, trans. Willard R. Trask (New York and Evanston, 1968).

For Elizabethan imagery, see Rosemond Tuve, *Elizabethan and Metaphysical Imagery* (Chicago, 1947); Hallett Smith, *Elizabethan Poetry: A Study in Conventions, Meaning, and Expression* (Cambridge, Mass., 1952). For classical imagery, see Marsh H. McCall, Jr., *Ancient Rhetorical Theories of Simile and Comparison* (Cambridge, Mass., 1969).

Among useful studies of medieval and Renaissance poetics and rhetoric, see Bernard Weinberg, *A History of Literary Criticism in the Italian Renaissance*, 2 vols. (Chicago, 1961); J. E. Spingarn, *A History of Literary Criticsim in the Renaissance*, 2d ed. (New York, 1954); Charles Sears Baldwin, *Medieval Rhetoric and Poetic* (New York, 1928); idem, *Renaissance Literary Theory and Practice* (New York, 1939); Ida Langdon, *Milton's Theory of Poetry and Fine Art* (New Haven and London, 1924); J. W. H. Atkins, *English Literary Criticism: the Medieval Phase* (New York and Cambridge, 1943); idem, *English Literary Criticism: the Renaissance* (London, 1947); idem, *English Literary Criticism: Seventeenth and Eighteenth Centuries* (London, 1951); idem, *Literary Criticism in Antiquity* (Cambridge, 1934); Wilbur Samuel Howell, *Logic and Rhetoric in England, 1500-1700* (Princeton, 1956); Walter J. Ong, S. J. *Ramus: Method, and the Decay of Dialogue, From the Art of Discourse to the Art of Reason* (Cambridge, Mass., 1958); idem, *Ramus and Talon Inventory* (Cambridge, Mass., 1958); Lily Bess Campbell, *Divine Poetry and Drama in Sixteenth-Century England* (Cambridge and Berkeley, 1959); William G. Crane, *Wit and Rhetoric in the Renaissance* (New York, 1937); Jerrold E. Seigel, *Rhetoric and Philosophy in Renaissance Humanism; The Union of Eloquence and Wisdom, Petrarch to Valla* (Princeton, 1968); Frances A. Yates, *The Art of Memory* (Chicago, 1966); Ruth Wallerstein, *Studies in Seventeenth-Century Poetic* (Madison, Wis., 1950); Bernard Weinberg, ed., *Trattati di poetica e retorica del Cinquecento*, 3 vols. (Bari, 1970-72); Edmond Faral, ed., *Les arts poétiques du XIIe et du XIIIe siècle* (Paris, 1958); Kathryn A. McEuen, *Classical Influence upon the Tribe of Ben* (Cedar Rapids, Iowa, 1939); Louis L. Martz, *The*

Preface

Poetry of Meditation, rev. ed. (New Haven and London, 1962; G. Gregory Smith, ed., *Elizabethan Critical Essays,* 2 vols. (Oxford, 1904); J. E. Spingarn, ed., *Critical Essays of the Seventeenth Century,* 3 vols. (Oxford, 1908-09); Vincent M. Bevilacqua, "*Ut Rhetorica Pictura:* Sir Joshua Reynolds' Rhetorical Conception of Art," *HLQ* 34 (1970), 59-78; John R. Spencer, "*Ut Rhetorica Pictura:* A Study in Quattrocento Theory of Painting," *Journal of the Warburg and Courtauld Institutes,* 20 (1957), 26-44; Erwin Panofsky, *Idea;* E. H. Gombrich, *Norm and Form, Studies in the Art of the Renaissance* (London, 1966); Rensselaer W. Lee, *Ut Pictura Poesis: The Humanistic Theory of Painting* (New York, 1967).

In "Una fonte 'retorica' per il Barocco a Torino," Andreina Griseri interprets Tesauro's views on "symbolic art" (such as emblems and *imprese*) as a pictorial rhetoric and stresses the influence of his iconographic and rhetorical concepts on the decorations in the Palazzo Reale in Torino; see Douglas Fraser et al., eds., *Essays in the History of Art Presented to Rudolf Wittkower* (London, 1967).

Among recent studies of Renaissance emblem literature and iconography, see Arthur Henkel and Albrecht Schöne, eds., *Emblemata, Handbuch zur Sinnbildkunst des XVI. and XVII. Jahrhunderts* (Stuttgart, 1967) and the reviews by Henri Stegemeier, *JEGP* 67 (1968), 656-72, and by William S. Heckscher and Cameron F. Bunker, *RQ* 23 (1970), 59-80; Albrecht Schöne, *Emblematik und Drama im Zeitalter des Barock* (Munich, 1964); Rosemary Freeman, *English Emblem Books* (London, 1948); Mario Praz, *Studies in Seventeenth-Century Imagery,* 2d. ed. (Rome, 1964); Henry Green, *Shakespeare and the Emblem Writers* (London, 1970); Gertrud Schiller, *Iconography of Christian Art,* trans. Janet Seligman, vol. I (Greenwich, Conn., 1971); Erik Iverson, *The Myth of Egypt and its Hieroglyphs in European Tradition* (Copenhagen, 1961); Ernest Friedrich von Monroy, *Emblem und Emblembücher in den Niederlanden, 1560-1630,* ed. Hans Martin von Erffa (Utrecht, 1964); Liselotte Dieckmann, *Hieroglyphics: The History of a Literary Symbol* (St. Louis, Mo., 1971); André Grabar, *Christian Iconography: A Study of its Origins* (Princeton, 1968); the papers collected in *Research Opportunities in Renaissance Drama,* ed. Samuel Schoenbaum, vols. 13-14 (Evanston, 1972), and the works cited in my "Bibliographical Note" in the same volume.

In discussing the three parts of the emblem (motto or *inscriptio, pictura,* and epigram or *subscriptio*), Holger Homann emphasizes the "ideal priority of the picture." The *res picta* is simultaneously *res significans;* the picture is not self-explanatory, but its higher sense is concealed and is first discovered in the *subscriptio.* "Das eigentlich Emblematische ist also, dass das in der *pictura* Dargestellte nicht nur als Seiendes, sondern auch als Bedeutendes vorgestellt wird: die *pictura* ist also nicht Verbildlichung des Textes, sondern der Text nimmt seinen Ausgang von dem in der *pictura* Abgebildeten und zeigt dessen verborgene, das Dargestellte übersteigende Bedeutung auf" (Holder Homann, *Studien zur Emblematik des. 16. Jahrhunderts* [Utrecht, 1971], pp. 14-15).

On emblematic scenes in Shakespeare's romances and on the relationship between literal and figurative, representational and emblematic, mimetic and poetic modes, see Douglas L. Peterson, *Time, Tide and Tempest: A Study of Shakespeare's Romances* (San Marino, Calif. 1973), pp. 60, 112, 125, 219-220, 243.

On the philosophy of symbolic forms, see Susanne K. Langer, *Philosophy in a New Key* (New York, 1948); idem, *Feeling and Form* (New York, 1952); Ernst Cassirer, *Language and Myth,* trans. Susanne K. Langer (New York, 1953); idem, *The Philosophy of Symbolic Forms,* trans. Ralph Manheim, 2 vols. (New Haven and London, 1953, 1955); Alfred North Whitehead, *Symbolism, Its Meaning and Effect* (New York, 1959); Martin Foss, *Symbol and Metaphor in Human Experience* (Princeton, 1949); Erwin Panofsky, "Die Perspektive also 'Symbolische Form,'" *Vorträge der Bibliothek Warburg* (1924-25); W. K. Wimsatt, Jr., *The Verbal*

xliii

Preface

Icon: Studies in the Meaning of Poetry (Lexington, 1954). On problems of literary symbolism, see Robert M. Browne, "The Typology of Literary Signs," *College English* 33 (1971), 1-17.

On Renaissance mythography, see Douglas Bush, *Mythology and the Renaissance Tradition*, new rev. ed. (New York, 1963); idem, *Pagan Myth and Christian Tradition in English Poetry* (Philadelphia, 1968); Patricia Merivale, *Pan, the Goat-God, His Myth in Modern Times* (Cambridge, Mass., 1969); DeWitt T. Starnes and E. W. Talbert, *Classical Myth and Legend in Renaissance Dictionaries* (Chapel Hill, 1955).

On the mythopoeic imagination, see S. H. Hooke, *Middle Eastern Mythology* (Baltimore, 1963); Theodor H. Gaster, *Thespis* (New York, 1961); Henri Frankfort, et al., *Before Philosophy* (Baltimore, 1949); Harry Slochower, *Mythopoesis: Mythic Patterns in the Literary Classics* (Detroit, 1970); for concepts of myth in twentieth-century fiction and criticism, see John B. Vickery, ed., *Myth and Literature: Contemporary Theory and Practice* (Lincoln, Neb., 1969).

On symbolic landscape, see David M. Bergeron, "Symbolic Landscape in English Civic Pageantry," *RQ* 22 (1969), 32-37; John R. Knott, Jr., "Symbolic Landscape in *Paradise Lost*," *Milton Studies*, vol. 2 (1970), pp. 37-58.

See also John D. Boyd, *The Function of Mimesis and Its Decline* (Cambridge, Mass., 1968); George Converse Fiske, *Lucilius and Horace: A Study in the Classical Theory of Imitation* (Westport, Conn., 1971); Hermann Koller, *Die Mimesis in der Antike: Nachahmung, Darstellung, Ausdruck* (Berne, 1954); Ferruccio Ulivi, *L'imitazione nella poetica del Rinascimento* (Milan, 1959); Harold O. White, *Plagiarism and Imitation During the English Renaissance* (New York, 1965); Willem Jacob Verdenius, *Mimesis: Plato's Doctrine of Artistic Imitation and Its Meaning to Us* (Leiden, 1962).

For *sapientia et eloquentia* as a medieval educational *topos* and for its relation to Augustinian views on rhetoric and doctrine, see John Block Friedman, *Orpheus in the Middle Ages* (Cambridge, Mass., 1970), pp. 101-02.

For humanist and neoclassical attitudes toward the music of the ancients and for seventeenth-century identifications of music with rhetoric, see John Hollander, *The Untuning of the Sky: Ideas of Music in English Poetry, 1500-1700* (New York, 1970), pp. 3, 17, 162, 174-220.

[12]Cf. Francis Bond, *Dedications of Patron Saints of English Churches* (London, New York, etc., 1914), p. 153; on Cleodolinda, Karl Künstle, *Iconographie der christlichen Kunst*, vol. 2 (Freiburg im Breisgau, 1926), p. 269, observes that the king's daughter is frequently called Aja or Margaretha, as well as Cleodelinde. In Alexander Barclay's *The Life of St. George*, ed. William Nelson (EETS #230, London, 1955), the virgin is called Alcyone (p. 40).

[13]Cf. Panofsky's essay "The History of the Theory of Human Proportions as a Reflection of the History of Styles," in *Meaning in the Visual Arts* (Garden City, N.Y., 1955), pp. 55-107. Renaissance theorists regarded the "proportions of the human body" as "visual realization of musical harmony," reduced them to mathematical principles, endowed them with mythological and astrological significance, or identified them with the proportions of buildings and parts of buildings (pp. 91-92). Affricano Colombo "appended to his small book on the planets . . . a theory of proportions for painters and sculptors. . . ." In this "fusing of astrological doctrines with the theory of proportions," Panofsky perceives (p. 97n) a "characteristic attempt at reinterpreting Leonardo's scientific naturalism in the spirit of cosmological mysticism." Francesco Giorgi's *Harmonia mundi totius* (Panofsky, pp. 100n, 102n) finds "correspondences between the human body and Noah's ark." In contrast to these Renaissance treatises, the canon of human proportions written by the Arabian

Preface

"Brethren of Purity," who flourished in the ninth and tenth centuries (pp. 76-77), "was not supposed to furnish a method for the pictorial rendering of the human figure, but was intended to give insight into a vast harmony that unifies all parts of the cosmos by numerical and musical correspondences."

Noah's ark was also a type of the church, and mathematical symbolism frequently conditioned ecclesiastical architecture. As Anthony Blunt observes (*Artistic Theory in Italy, 1450-1600* [London, Oxford, New York, 1962], pp. 127-30), Palladio recommended a circular design for churches as "the most perfect form" and a symbol of "the unity of God, His infinite essence, His uniformity, and His justice." St. Charles Borromeo ("the only author to apply the Tridentine decree to the problem of architecture"), on the other hand, rejected the circular form as pagan and required a cruciform church. Cataneo preferred the form of the cross as "the symbol of redemption" but argued that its proportions should be "those of a perfect human body...."

[14] Peter Gay, *The Enlightenment* (New York, 1966), p. 259, citing Aby Warburg. Among recent studies of Renaissance occultism, see D. P. Walker, *Spiritual and Demonic Magic from Ficino to Campanella* (London, 1958); Wayne Shumaker, *The Occult Sciences in the Renaissance: A Study in Intellectual Patterns* (Berkeley and Los Angeles, 1922); Frances A. Yates, *Giordano Bruno and the Hermetic Tradition* (New York, 1969); Edgar Wind, *Pagan Mysteries in the Renaissance* (New Haven, 1958); Jean Seznec, *The Survival of the Pagan Gods*, trans. Barbara F. Sessions (New York, 1953); Don Cameron Allen, *Mysteriously Meant: The Rediscovery of Pagan Symbolism and Allegorical Interpretation in the Renaissance* (Baltimore and London, 1970); Allen G. Debus and Robert P. Multhauf, *Alchemy and Chemistry in the Seventeenth Century* (Los Angeles, 1966). Renaissance Pythagoreanism has been investigated by S. K. Heninger, Jr. in *Touches of Sweet Harmony: Pythagorean Cosmology and Renaissance Poetics* (San Marino, 1974). Miss Yates (*Bruno*, p. 81) notes the continuity of Renaissance magic with "medieval magic and also the transformation of that tradition into something new." Just as "the images of the gods were preserved through the Middle Ages in astrological manuscripts, reached the Renaissance in that barbarized form, and were then reinvested with classical form through the rediscovery and imitation of classical works of art," in "the same way, astral magic comes down in the mediaeval tradition and is reinvested with classical form in the Renaissance through the rediscovery of Neoplatonic theurgy." Though Ficino's magic is "closer in outlook, practice, and classical form to the Emperor Julian than it is to *Picatrix*," nevertheless "the substance of it reached him through *Picatrix*, or some such similar text-books, and was transformed by him back into classical form through his Greek studies."

See also Fritz Saxl and Hans Meier, *Verzeichnis astrologischer und mythologischer illustrierter Handschriften des lateinischen Mittelalters* (Heidelberg, 1915, 1927; London, 1953); Aby Warburg, *Gesammelte Schriften* (Hamburg, 1932-).

[15] For discussion of medieval and Renaissance theories of the fantasy in relation to poetry and rhetoric, see *inter alia* Osgood's introduction and notes to his translation of sections from Boccaccio's *Genealogy of the Gods*, Charles Dahlberg's studies of the *Romance of the Rose*, McKeon's work on the Augustinian tradition in rhetoric, Karl Wallace on Bacon's theory of the imagination, Murray Bundy's studies on the imagination, Stahl's translation of Macrobius, D. W. Robertson, Jr., and Bernard Huppé on the poetry of Chaucer and Langland, Edgar de Bruyne's *Etudes d'esthétique médiévale*, and Erwin Panofsky's *Idea*. For an analysis of the rhetorical and logical basis of Renaissance imagery, the principle of "sensuous immediacy" or "sensuous vividness," the "garment of style" and the concept *ut pictura poesis*, imitation in literature as "making an artful construct" or "artifact," and Platonic and

Preface

neo-Platonic and Aristotelian conceptions of the representation of the "essence" or "ideal form" or "universal," see Rosemond Tuve, *Elizabethan and Metaphysical Imagery* (Chicago, 1961), pp. 3-9, 25, 41-44, 50-116, and passim. See also Christopher Waldo Grose, "Some Uses of Sensuous Immediacy in *Paradise Lost*," HLQ 31 (1968), 211-22.

[16]Alain de Lille, *The Complaint of Nature*, trans. Douglas M. Moffat, Yale Studies in English, vol. 36 (1908), p. 40. For evidence of the "availability of Latin classics very early in the 12th century," see Alain de Lille, *The Anticlaudian*, trans. William Hafner Cornog (Univ. of Penn. diss., 1935), pp. 40-42.

THE LAMB AND THE ELEPHANT

Chapter I

INNOVATION AND TRADITION: THE PROBLEM OF THE RENAISSANCE

WE OF THE twentieth century,[1] though we boast of being legitimate heirs of the Renaissance, have radically altered our patrimony.[2] Our ancestors talked about voyaging to the moon, but never seriously attempted to go there. Theirs was a flight of fancy only, or of prophetic imagination—like Astolfo's "two-staged" ascent by Hippogriff and by chariot of fire. What was fantasy to them has become an achieved reality for us, a document of oral and visual history competing for space on our television channels. Their poetry has become our technology; and the gulf that separates us from them is partly our own creation—a price we have paid for our scientific progress. Nevertheless, this too is part of our Renaissance legacy as well as a bequest from the sagacious serpent of Eden. Our aircraft and submarines and armored tanks implement the conjectures of Renaissance engineers. Dr. Strangelove is the lineal descendant of Dr. Faustus. What a twelfth-century humanist once said about the value of the ancients for his own age may apply equally well to our own century and its debt, for good or for evil, to the sixteenth:

> We are like dwarfs set on the shoulders of giants, from which we can see more and further things than they, not so much from the keenness of our own sight or the magnitude of our own stature, but because we are sustained and raised up by their gigantic proportions.[3]

To us, who look back on the Renaissance as Renaissance men themselves looked back to classical antiquity—through a romantic haze that makes distant objects appear larger than life—its monuments and the men who made them seem indeed to be of "gigantic proportions." Their creations impress us today like Cyclopean stonework—a massive and incredible achievement. We find ourselves repeating, as others have exclaimed at Tiryns and Mycenae,

The Lamb and the Elephant

"surely a race of giants *did* build here!" Nevertheless, the most ecstatic tourists are fully aware that there were no giants in the Argolid, and the more skeptical among us may doubt the reality of the Renaissance. Perhaps, like the Cyclopes and the Titans, this too is a myth. Yet, before we discard the legend altogether (which would be throwing out the baby with the bath) or attempt to euhemerize it, extracting a kernel of historical truth from the layers of enveloping legend, we should ask ourselves what we actually understand by this term. What does the Renaissance really mean?

Unfortunately it has meant altogether too many things. A movement—or a complex of movements. A style—or a syndrome of styles. A period—but precisely when this period began and ended we are not yet sure. In fact, we frequently misunderstand one another, easily deceived by the fallacy of equivocation. When A is talking about a movement, B misinterprets his remarks as a reference to period or style. C uses several very different senses interchangeably without realizing it, and thus confounds confusion. D loses himself in the vicious circle of his own definition, defining the period in the terms of the movement, the movement in terms of the style, the style in terms of the period, and hence "finds no end in wand'ring mazes lost." If we are still debating the significance of the Renaissance, part of the responsibility lies with the term itself—its ambiguity, its multiplicity of meanings. As Hobbes sensibly observed, "ambiguous words are like *ignes fatui;* and reasoning upon them is wandring among innumerable absurdities. . . ."[4]

Words are "wise men's counters," the same author reminds us; "they do but reckon by them. . . ."[5] "Renaissance" may look golden and ring like gold; and even the lexicographer, counting his word-hoard, may overlook the possibility of alloy. Nevertheless, this term cannot always pass as solid currency; its meaning and value often vary widely in different contexts. Before accepting it as valid coinage, we should not lose sight of the fact that it is actually a counter to reckon by—a convenient term that may or may not correspond to reality, that may or may not have concrete historical significance.

Many a Renaissance scholar, in fact, suffers from the disease of "semantic Humpty-Dumptyism." You recall the passage in Lewis Carroll's *Through the Looking-Glass:*

Problem of the Renaissance

"But 'glory' doesn't mean 'a nice knock-down argument,'" Alice objected.

"When *I* use a word," Humpty Dumpty said, in rather a scornful tone, "it means just what I choose it to mean—neither more nor less."

"The question is," said Alice, "whether you *can* make words mean so many different things."

"The question is," said Humpty Dumpty, "which is to be master—that's all."

"That's a great deal to make one word mean," Alice said in a thoughtful tone.

"When I make a word do a lot of work like that," said Humpty Dumpty, "I always pay it extra."[6]

Perhaps the fate of this character should be a warning to us, an object lesson in verbal hubris. If there is indeed a "tyranny of words," then the Renaissance, that age of despots, has apparently been the most tyrannical of all, the most arbitrary and the most difficult to dethrone. Among words that are shadow, not substance—idols of the forum, as Bacon calls them—this is one of the most elusive. A specter that haunts the marketplace, evading the grasp of the scholar and the light of critical analysis, it may yield perhaps to exorcism.

For the Renaissance, alas, is not merely a word, but an incantation. Like "Sesame," it can set doors ajar, but all too often it unlocks the wrong one. We expect the same magic syllables to open very different portals: humanism and science, Reformation and counter-Reformation, empiricism and rationalism, scepticism and fideism, mathematics and poetry. We apply the same formula to northern and southern Europe, to Italy and the Low Countries, to England and Spain—to Petrarch in the fourteenth century and to Milton in the seventeenth.

A password that admits us everywhere, a skeleton key that opens every door, can be a distinct embarrassment. Locks and bolts, cabinets and compartments become meaningless. As one scholar warns us, the term Renaissance is so vague that it "should never be used without qualification, such as the Medical Renaissance in France, or the Mathematical Renaissance in Northern Italy."[7]

Worse still, this Idol of the Marketplace is a rhetorical figure, a

The Lamb and the Elephant

metaphor of rebirth. We are, in fact, disputing about the significance of a trope.

1.

Now what—precisely—does this metaphor mean? What basis does it have in reality? To raise these questions is to invite easy generalizations that seem to clarify central issues but may actually distort them by making them appear simpler and more sharply defined than they really were. Clear and distinct ideas may be indispensable to a Cartesian rationalist, but for the literary and cultural historian they may do violence to the complexities of the society he is endeavoring to understand. To subject half-lights and shadows to rational analysis is to destroy them. Besides the ambiguity of the "Renaissance," the tacit assumptions underlying its various senses are often highly questionable; in attempting to clarify these senses the critic may, in fact, be anatomizing a chimaera. The tools of literary and historical scholarship are his own fabrications. Such concepts as historical epochs, intellectual trends, and artistic styles represent his own abstractions from concrete particulars. Though these idealized types and formulas are too convenient to discard, they can compromise as well as facilitate his understanding of historical events and particular works of art. While they enable him to discourse rationally about a vast number of particulars that he could not possibly consider individually—to manipulate literary genres and entire cultures like building blocks and to shuffle centuries and continents together as easily as an astronomer juggles with stars—they are essentially his own creation, and they may prejudice his further interpretation of particulars. The patterns he perceives in history are of his own making; he not only abstracts them from historical data, he also imposes them on the raw material of history. The nominalist may justly be skeptical both of the periodization of history and of attempts to isolate cultural trends and to define literary and artistic styles.

Generalizations about literary genres and styles or about historical movements and periods are usually valid only within comparatively narrow limits. They are approximate and tentative statements belonging to a different level of meaning (and perhaps a different order of reality) from that of the concrete phenomena they profess to interpret and classify. They are an ideal order abstracted from literary and historical data like a tailor's measurements for a suit, and subsequently reimposed on literary history like the finished clothes. Whether they fit or not depends ultimately on the accuracy of the craftsman's abstractions, the validity of his paradigm.

The patterns constructed by the historian and the literary theorist are no less ideal and almost as artificial as those of the painter, and on occasion they may be just as subjective. Conceptions of an epoch or a poetic genre may vary as widely as pictures of the same scene by different artists. They are oversimplifications of literature and history, just as a line drawing is an oversimplification of a landscape. To vary the image, they are distillations from experience and bear roughly the same relation to concrete events that a highball bears to a cornfield.

When applied to the literary and cultural history of the Renaissance, such generalizations can be especially treacherous. Modern interpretations frequently clash with one another and with Renaissance opinions. Men of the fifteenth and sixteenth centuries themselves often tended to hypostatize historical epochs, oversimplifying the characteristics of classical and medieval society as well as the attributes of their own culture. In many instances, moreover, their observations on all three periods were conditioned by rhetorical demands, consciously or unconsciously modified by their polemical intent. In considering their use of the metaphor of rebirth, we should bear in mind Huizinga's warning against a monolithic conception of the Renaissance:

The picture displayed by the Renaissance is one of transformation and hesitation, one of transition and intermixture of cultural elements. Anyone seeking in it a total unity of spirit capable of being stated in a simple formula will never be able to understand it in all its expressions. Above all, one must be prepared to accept it in its complexity, its heterogeneity, and its contradictions, and to apply a pluralistic approach to the questions it poses. Whoever casts out a single schema as a net to capture this Proteus will only catch himself in the meshes.[8]

Huizinga's admonition is applicable not only to the concept of the Renaissance as a period but also to the study of its intellectual movements and literary and artistic styles. In searching for a simple formula one is apt to select one facet of the Renaissance as a norm and to misconstrue the numerous variations from this norm either as reactions to and against the Renaissance or as a combination of Renaissance and counter-Renaissance elements. Just as art historians have distinguished an "anti-Renaissance" style, literary historians have posited a "counter-Renaissance" movement. Some distinguish specifically anti-Renaissance phases in the art and thought of the period. Some exaggerate the differences between Renaissance culture and that of the late Middle Ages and the seventeenth and eighteenth centuries. Others recognize the importance of these links with medieval and modern tradition, but nevertheless underplay their specifically Renaissance aspects. Interpreting these examples of continuity retrospectively as medieval survivals or proleptically as foreshadowings of the age of the Royal Society and the Enlightenment, the historian tends at times to neglect or underestimate the degree to which they are also Renaissance phenomena, an integral part in the total culture of the period. (The implication that they are *essentially* medieval or modern unfortunately suggests that they are merely alien and anachronistic intrusions in the Renaissance, or indeed that they are really aspects not of the Renaissance, but of a counter-Renaissance. In considering the problem of the Renaissance as a period, one should be extremely careful as to what aspects (if any) of its culture one excludes from the "Renaissance movement" or "Renaissance style.")

Any definition, moreover, must take account of its variety and complexity and should avoid positing a sharp break with the cultures of the preceding and following centuries. To look too assiduously for the *differentiae* of a culture may result in overemphasizing features of minor importance in its actual value structure. Some of the most important aspects of Renaissance civilization in the eyes of men of the period may be precisely those features that the twentieth-century historian tends to label medieval or modern.

Finally, one should observe equal caution in the labels one assigns to the diverse intellectual movements and artistic styles of the period. Attempts to impose the categories of art history on intellectual and

Problem of the Renaissance

literary history have been greeted with applause and skepticism. Art historians still encounter difficulty in defining "mannerism" and "baroque" and in applying these terms to particular works, and it is still questionable whether literary criticism has gained or lost in precision by importing them. Conventional designations for varieties of prose style—Attic and Asiatic, Ciceronian and libertine, Senecan and Tacitean—can be just as indefinite as the conventional labels for poetic styles—Petrarchan and metaphysical, *concettismo* and *culteranismo*—and just as difficult to apply to specific authors. Terms like "anti-Ciceronianism" and "anti-Petrarchism" tend to become catchalls. Critics sometimes apply them indiscriminately to major and minor variations on the Ciceronian and Petrarchan traditions, to moderate objections against these writers and to more radical protests. A critic may analyze the style of a single author—Donne or Herbert or Browne—without losing himself or his readers in verbal quicksands. Nevertheless, when he attempts to define larger categories, such as metaphysical style, baroque style, or mannerism, and to impose these definitions on particular passages of verse or prose he is on less substantial ground.

2.

Whatever doubts we and our contemporaries may entertain about the metaphor of renascence, many of the humanists and artists of the period were largely free from such uncertainty. From Petrarch and Boccaccio in the fourteenth century to Milton in the seventeenth we find men of letters alternately condemning their age for barbarism and extolling it for the revival of learning.[9] For these the Renaissance was primarily a movement, though they also associated it with ideas of period and style. Inevitably conditioning the character of the age and reshaping literary and artistic modes, the "rebirth" was, in their opinion, not only a consciously conceived rhetorical and pedagogical program but also an integral part of the universal cycle of generation and corruption, growth and decay. It was simultaneously historical process and literary platform.

Moreover, for many writers of the period the metaphor of regeneration—the rebirth of the arts and sciences after centuries of torpor—seemed to refer primarily to Latin learning, to the diffusion of humanistic methods in the study and imitation of Roman authors. But not exclusively. The image of rebirth also extended to Greek and Hebrew, and even to Arabic and Aramaic—all of them "native languages to the ancients."[10] In defending *Tetrachordon*, Milton significantly based his apology on the humanistic study of the Greek language, invoking the shade of the early English humanist who had taught "*Cambridge* and *King Edward* Greek." The metaphor of rebirth was successively transferred from the recovery of classical eloquence to the development of vernacular literature and, by extension, to recent achievements in other disciplines—to the arts of design, to iconology and the recovery of the images of the ancient gods, to mythography and the rediscovery of the hidden sense of classical myths, to theology and the recovery of the *philosophia Christi* and evangelical *veritas*, to geography and the discovery of new continents, to technology and the exploitation of new inventions.[11] The same trope could apply to the methods of humanistic education and to the reorientation of literary taste and rhetorical style, to the rediscovery of lost or neglected writings and the correction of familiar but corrupted texts, to the actual imitation of classical art and to experiments with proportion and symmetry theoretically (if not historically) grounded on the alleged mathematical premises of classical aesthetics.

The metaphor of rebirth was also extended to movements and trends that sometimes appeared to run counter to other aspects of the Renaissance. Coupled with the Biblical concept of regeneration, it recurred in the idea of the "reformation" of church and state. Dissociated from the imitation of the ancients and directed against the adoration of classical authority, it reappeared (in different, but related, images) in Bacon's ideal of an "instauration" of learning and in Browne's hope for an "exantlation" of truth. The *topos* of a revival of learning and the associated metaphors of rebirth and renovation could apply to divine and human learning, to arts and sciences, to veneration and contempt of classical authority. In the controversies of that polemical age they could provide rhetorical ammunition for the apologists of the moderns as well as for the champions of the ancients.

Though the metaphor of rebirth was international in scope, it

Problem of the Renaissance

sometimes possessed a different significance for Italy and the transalpine states. For the Italian, it frequently held the additional connotation of a national regeneration, the recovery of his native heritage and, in part at least, the revival of the glories of Roman antiquity. Though it proved impossible to restore the political structure of ancient Rome, as a few patriots had vainly endeavored to do, the Italian could attempt to restore its language, to revive its poets and historians, to convert its arts into instruments for celebrating regional governments or for eulogizing the Roman see.[12] Though arms could not restore the greatness of the past, as Machiavelli had hoped they might, perhaps letters might succeed—expelling barbarisms if not barbarians and reconquering the language and eloquence if not the empire of Rome. For other peoples the metaphor of rebirth presented a rather different challenge. For them it was a matter of national pride to digest the Italian achievement, to vie with the Italian humanists in their mastery of classical learning, to resettle the awakened and now peripatetic Muses on their own stony soil.

As humanistic learning crossed the Alps and the seas to civilize the outlanders, the myth of the Renaissance became in due course a "progress of the arts," a triumphal procession of the Muses (thoroughly grounded in the principles of humanist Latin or the elegances of the Italian tongue) through the courts and schools of the barbarian north and west.[13]

3.

Though it would be perverse to discount contemporary views of the age, it would be naïve to accept them without qualification. We cannot take the Renaissance entirely at its own valuation or on its own terms. As many of our own contemporaries have recognized, the metaphor of rebirth needs qualification; so does an equally familiar commonplace, the imitation of the ancients. The spokesmen of the new learning greatly exaggerated both its breach with the Middle Ages and its fidelity to antiquity.

Thus far we have approached the metaphor of rebirth in terms of contemporary attitudes towards the Renaissance as a movement rather than in terms of Renaissance style and the characteristics of the Renaissance as a historical period. The social and political char-

The Lamb and the Elephant

acteristics of the age lie beyond the scope of this study; they belong primarily to the social historian rather than to the student of literature. The analysis of Renaissance styles is equally complicated and pertains as much to art history as to literary criticism. We shall consider both of these problems only insofar as they are directly relevant to the myth of the Renaissance and the image of rebirth. Though the Renaissance does not have the same meaning when considered as a movement, as a style, or as a historical period—nor even the same significance when applied to different arts and sciences—these various senses are intimately interrelated. To examine the idea of "imitating" the ancients necessarily involves the reexamination of Renaissance styles. To reconsider cinquecento attitudes toward the Middle Ages naturally raises the question of the Renaissance as a historical period.

Though Sarton has defined the Renaissance as a reaction against medieval scholasticism or Arabic influences, this explanation apparently confuses cause and effect.[14] What appears on the surface to be a struggle between medieval and Renaissance modes of thought is in large part a rivalry between different learned disciplines and different pedagogical emphases. It is comparable to the rivalry between theological, medical, and legal faculties in medieval and Renaissance universities, to the twelfth-century antagonism between the rhetoricians of Orleans and the logicians of Paris, and to Boccaccio's polemics against jurists and philosophers as enemies of poetry. Attacks on scholastic methodology continue throughout the period and well into the seventeenth century, attracting humanists and scientists alike and enlisting such singular companions-at-arms as Bacon and Erasmus, Milton and Hobbes. Scholasticism was almost as solidly entrenched in many European universities during the Renaissance as in the Middle Ages, and Renaissance attacks on its methods are essentially a continuation of a late medieval struggle.

During the course of the Renaissance, moreover, scholastic and humanistic learning frequently tended to combine. School divines lectured from texts edited by humanist scholars. Conversely, philosophers like Pico della Mirandola and poets like Donne and Cleveland made extensive (though sometimes facetious) use of the terminology of the schools. Attacks on Aristotelian doctrine were often

Problem of the Renaissance

couched in Aristotelian terms. Reformation theologians might simultaneously inveigh against the scholastic doctors as sophists and against the humanists as neopagans, but many of them had been trained both in classical literature and in scholastic theology. Though humanists continued to attack scholasticism as a relic of monastic ignorance and to condemn its technical vocabulary as barbarous, the majority of schoolmen in the sixteenth and seventeenth centuries had tasted the fruit of humanistic learning. Though some had found it too sweet for their palates and others thought it indigestible without a heavy dose of orthodox doctrine, many of them, who achieved ecclesiastical preferment, had been generous patrons of the arts. Moreover, in the context of fifteenth- and sixteenth-century learning, scholastic methodology was not as obscurantist as its humanistic critics liked to believe. In certain disciplines it was a more effective instrument of communication than humanistic rhetoric. It is significant that the scientists of the seventeenth century often felt it imperative to reject not only the language and methods of scholasticism but also the stylistic embellishments of humanist eloquence. Though the technical jargon of scholastic physics might not enjoy the sanction of Ciceronian usage, it provided a more exact scientific language than the classical vocabulary and rhetorical ornaments of contemporary humanists. Scholastic science would eventually be overthrown not by humanist polemics but by the scientific methods of the "new philosophy." Humanist attacks were directed less against its doctrines than against its methodology and its language, against its neglect of poetry and rhetoric, and against its deficiencies as a pedagogical instrument.

Indirectly, humanistic philology may have hastened the decline of scholastic philosophy by providing critical texts of the major classical philosophers and setting up rivals to the authority of Aristotle: publishing the works of Plato and the early neo-Platonists, reviving Stoic and Epicurean doctrines, resurrecting classical atomists and empiricists and skeptics, editing the mathematical and mechanical treatises that would stimulate the scientific speculation of the seventeenth century. On the whole, however, the humanist polemic against scholasticism was motivated less by dislike for its physical and metaphysical doctrines than by distaste for its methodology and by envy of a powerful and hostile rival. Humanism was not so much a revolt or reaction against scholastic learning as a rival discipline—a course of study centered upon rhetoric and poetry and history rather than logic, and stressing the arts of persuasion rather than syllogistic demonstration. Though their apologies for poetry and other *studia humaniora* were sometimes directed against scholastic adversaries, the principal arguments on which the humanists constructed their defense were conventional in both classical and medieval traditions—the divine origin of poetry and its nobility as a "divine science" like metaphysics and theology; its utility as a vehicle of moral and natural philosophy and as an instrument for ethical persuasion; the wholesome truth concealed under a pleasing fiction; the instructive force of example; and the pedagogical efficacy of instruction combined with delight. When Milton extols Spenser as a more effective teacher than Scotus and Aquinas, his statement may look like a reaction against the schoolmen, but it is actually an echo of Horace's preference for Homer over Crantor and Chrysippus.

4.

America has been defined as the air space between New York and Los Angeles, and perhaps this analogy will hold for Renaissance ideas of the period between the fall of Rome and the age of Dante and Petrarch. Even though the terms "Middle Ages" and "Renaissance" are modern inventions, both concepts are implicit in Renaissance images of the death and rebirth of learning and the exile and recall of the Muses. The myths of a dark age and a golden age were complementary and interdependent. Initially at least, both were conceived in terms of the fate of the arts and, somewhat provincially, in terms of the destiny of Italy; by purifying the Latin tongue from barbarian accretions and purging the arts of design from "Gothic" and Byzantine elements, Italians were in effect restoring their native heritage, the civilization of Rome. Since the model for reformation belonged to Latin antiquity, the imitation of the ancients became, in a sense, a patriotic duty. Philology could serve as the instrument of cultural and national rebirth.

Accomplished rhetoricians, skilled in the techniques of praise and blame, most humanists were aware of the argumentative force of contraries. In extolling their own mission and the merits of their classical models they were frequently compelled, consciously or unconsciously, to undervalue the achievements of medieval civilization. The myth of a "Gothic" style survives in our own architectural vocabulary. The learning of the Middle Ages they condemned as monkish ignorance and the sophistry of friars. Its arts they despised as barbarous. Even in the mid-seventeenth century Milton could still appeal to the *topos* of medieval barbarism to discredit the use of rhyme, "the Invention of a barbarous Age. . . ."

The Renaissance humanist's view of his own age and his attitude toward medieval civilization were inevitably conditioned by his idealized and often oversimplified view of antiquity. If his own era held the promise of a golden age, it was because his contemporaries had learned how to interpret and imitate the classics. If medieval art and literature differed from those of antiquity, then they must, *a fortiori*, be degenerate and corrupt. We are far more aware than he of the complexities and contradictions inherent in classical culture, of the differences between the classical models and his own imitations, and of the persistence of medieval elements in his art and thought. To a far greater extent than he was willing to admit, he built, as we can perceive, on medieval foundations.

In most branches of learning—philosophy, literature, art, and even architecture—there was substantial continuity with the preceding era. It is preferable, therefore, to speak of a "reformation" of the arts and sciences, rather than a rebirth. The late Middle Ages were not, as we know, a "dark age." Modern scholars speak with justification of earlier "renascences"—the Carolingian renaissance and the twelfth-century reawakening—as well as the Renaissance of the fourteenth century. When Vasari tells us that "Gothic . . . edifices, to us moderns, are rather to the discredit than the glory of the builders," it is he who seems laughable—not the architects of Chartres cathedral.

The truth is that the Renaissance is not an isolated summit, but a peak on a plateau. It does not soar abruptly out of an intellectual abyss, but from the *altiplano* of the late Middle Ages. What one finds, in effect, is not a sudden transition from aesthetic nadir to

The Lamb and the Elephant

zenith, from cultural darkness to light, but a new development inspired by antiquity yet still deeply indebted to medieval achievements. Under the classical façade one finds the foundations and pillars not of some pagan temple, but of some medieval church or guildhall or feudal castle. The underlying structure of Renaissance civilization still remains medieval in many respects, even though the surface has been remodeled in a more fashionable style. Medieval civilization has undergone a radical reorganization of taste, or (in Sarton's words) a "transmutation of values."

We cannot explore in detail the complex social and intellectual factors that produced this reorientation and fostered the illusion of rebirth. So far as poetry and rhetoric are concerned, the primary cause of the revolution in literary taste appears to have been the labors of the Italian humanists in recovering, editing and translating classical texts; in restoring the classical genres; in choosing what they believed to be the best classical exemplars as models for imitation and as the basis for instruction in the schools; and, finally, in adapting to the vernacular the principles of classical composition and style.[15]

Their labors bore fruit not only in literature, but indeed in practically the whole cycle of arts and sciences. With the invention of printing, they were able to provide Western Europe with standard texts—not merely belles lettres, but also classical works in other fields: architecture, medicine, philosophy, and allied disciplines. As one scholar observes, "the [scientific] scholarship of the Renaissance was dominated by philologists."[16] Another stresses the role of Renaissance scholarship in disseminating the work of Vitruvius and thus turning "Renaissance architecture to an academic art."[17] Sixteenth-century editions of Aristotle's *Poetics* helped to reshape critical theory. Erasmus's edition of the New Testament provided additional ammunition for the Reformers. Ficino's translations contributed to the fusion of Renaissance Platonism and Hermeticism. Editions of Stoic, Epicurean, and skeptical philosophers strengthened the reaction against Aristotle. It is hardly surprising, therefore, that the Renaissance humanist grossly underestimated the preceding age and often misunderstood his own. Medieval scholasticism had placed what seemed an exorbitant emphasis on logic; the humanist emphasis, on the other hand, was predominantly rhetorical or grammatical.

Problem of the Renaissance

Scholasticism's principal achievements were confined, on the whole, to areas excluded from the humanists' jurisdiction. Scholastic pedagogy had tended to emphasize precept; humanistic education stressed the value of the example. Scholastic Latin seemed barbarous and inelegant; the humanist sought to restore the Latin tongue at its purest and best by imitating the style of classical authors. The texts on which the medieval schoolmen had relied were often corrupt or incomplete; the humanist attempted, by a study of the manuscript tradition, to reestablish the original versions.

Within relatively narrow limits, then, there is truth in the humanists' view of the Middle Ages and of their own age. So far as classical philology and the transmission of classical texts were concerned, these dedicated Latinists were, in large part, justified in speaking of medieval barbarism and corruption and in regarding their own endeavors as a return to classical purity. In the limited context of the Latin language and its literature, the myth of the Renaissance is real.

It becomes less real, less valid, however, when placed in a broader context. Partly by analogy, other disciplines—architecture, sculpture, painting, theology—echo the terminology of the humanists. As Vives' treatise on the subject indicates, men of the period were acutely sensitive to the "corruption of the arts"—and zealously dedicated to their restoration. Like the Latinists, these artists and scientists indicted the preceding age for "corrupting" their several disciplines and lauded their own period for "reviving" the arts, for "restoring" them to their pristine principles and antique excellence. But, unlike the Latinists, they were not altogether justified in making such claims. In these fields, the metaphor of the Renaissance sometimes seems more an ideal than a reality, less an achievement than a boast.

The Renaissance was an age of mythographers, and not the least of its achievements was that it created its own myth—a legend so attractive, so powerful that we have not yet succeeded in "euhemerizing" it—in isolating the core of truth behind it. There is some justification in its principal claims—the revival of learning, the imitation of antiquity—but these are only half-truths. In the myth, classicism and the rebirth of the arts are usually inseparable; but in fact they are two very different things.

The Lamb and the Elephant

NOTES

[1] Portions of this chapter and of Chapters II, III, and IV were first presented in a lecture on "The Renaissance in Literature: Innovation and Tradition" at the University of California, Riverside, in November 1965. The original address was one of a series of talks delivered by various speakers on the general theme "The Renaissance and Twentieth-Century Man," at the kind invitation of Professor William Elton.

[2] For more detailed discussion of topics covered in this chapter, see Wallace K. Ferguson, *The Renaissance in Historical Thought* (Cambridge, Mass., 1948); idem et al., *The Renaissance: Six Essays* (New York, 1962); idem et al., *Facets of the Renaissance* (New York, 1963); George Clarke Sellery, *The Renaissance: Its Nature and Origins* (Madison, Wis., 1950); Tinsley Hilton, ed., *The Renaissance* (Madison, Wis., 1964); Hiram Haydn, *The Counter-Renaissance* (New York, 1950); Douglas Bush, *Mythology and the Renaissance Tradition in English Poetry*, rev. ed. (New York, 1963); Jean Seznec, *The Survival of the Pagan Gods*, trans. Barbara F. Sessions (New York, 1961); John Addington Symonds, *The Renaissance in Italy* (New York, 1960); Jacob Burckhardt, *The Civilization of the Renaissance in Italy* (New York, 1950); R. R. Bolgar, *The Classical Heritage and Its Beneficiaries* (New York, 1964); Myron P. Gilmore, *The World of Humanism* (New York, 1962); Federico Chabod, *Machiavelli and the Renaissance*, trans. David Moore (New York, 1965); J. Huizinga, *Erasmus of Rotterdam*, trans. F. Hopman (London, 1953); J. E. Spingarn, *A History of Literary Criticism in the Renaissance*, 2d ed. (New York, 1954); Charles Homer Haskins, *The Renaissance of the Twelfth Century* (New York, 1964); J. Huizinga, *The Waning of the Middle Ages*, trans. F. Hopman (Garden City, N.Y., 1954); Bernard S. Levy, ed., *Developments in the Early Renaissance* (Albany, 1972); Werner L. Gundersheimer, ed., *The Italian Renaissance* (Englewood Cliffs, N.J., 1965); Paul O. Kristeller and Philip P. Wiener, eds., *Renaissance Essays* (New York and Evanston, 1968); Paul O. Kristeller, *Eight Philosophers of the Italian Renaissance* (Stanford, Calif., 1964); Arturo B. Fallico and Herman Shapiro, eds. and trans., *Renaissance Philosophy*, 2 vols. (New York 1967, 1969); Hans Baron, *The Crisis of the Early Italian Renaissance* (Princeton, 1966); idem, *From Petrarch to Leonardo Bruni* (Chicago and London, 1968); Marie Boas, *The Scientific Renaissance, 1450-1630* (New York, 1962); A. Rupert Hall, *The Scientific Revolution, 1500-1800*, 2d ed. (Boston, 1962); Ernst Cassirer, *The Individual and the Cosmos in Renaissance Philosophy*, trans. Mario Domandi (New York and Evanston, 1963); Edgar Wind, *Pagan Mysteries in the Renaissance*, rev. and enl. ed. (New York, 1968); Erwin Panofsky, *Studies in Iconology* (New York, 1962); idem, *Meaning in the Visual Arts* (Garden City, New York, 1955); Rensselaer W. Lee, *Ut Pictura Poesis: The Humanistic Theory of Painting* (New York, 1967); Heinrich Wölfflin, *Principles of Art History*, trans. M. D. Hottinger (New York, 1950); Charles Sears Baldwin, *Renaissance Literary Theory and Practice* (New York, 1939); J. W. H. Atkins, *English Literary Criticism: The Renascence* (London, 1947); Marvin T. Herrick, *The Fusion of Horatian and Aristotelian Literary Criticism* (Urbana, 1946); Bernard Weinberg, *A History of Literary Criticism in the Italian Renaissance*, 2 vols. (New York, 1961); Lily B. Campbell, *Divine Poetry and Drama in Sixteenth-Century England* (Cambridge, Berkeley and Los Angeles, 1959); Horst Meller and Hans-Joachim Zimmermann, eds., *Lebende Antike, Symposion für Rudolf Sühnel* (Berlin, 1967); R. W. Southern, *Medieval Humanism and Other Studies* (New York and Evanston, 1970); J. H. Plumb, *The Italian Renaissance* (New York and Evanston, 1965); Eric Cochrane, ed., *The Late Italian Renaissance, 1525-1630* (New York and Evanston, 1970); Johan Huizinga, *Men and Ideas*, trans. James S. Holmes and Hans van Marle

Problem of the Renaissance

(New York, Evanston, and London, 1970); Peter Burke, *The Renaissance Sense of the Past* (London, 1969); C. D. O'Malley, "Tudor Medicine and Biology," *HLQ* 32 (1968), 1-27; S. K. Heninger, Jr., "Tudor Literature of the Physical Sciences," *HLQ* 32 (1969), 101-33, 249-70; W. R. Elton, "Shakespeare and the Thought of his Age," in *A New Companion to Shakespeare Studies*, ed. Kenneth Muir and S. Schoenbaum (Cambridge, 1971), pp. 180-98; Eugenio Battisti, *L'antirinascimento* (Milan, 1962); Giuseppe Saitta, *Il Pensiero italiano nell'Umanesimo e nel Rinascimento*, 2d ed. (Florence, 1961); Eugenio Garin, *La cultura filosofica del Rinascimento italiano* (Florence, 1961); Johan Huizinga, *Dutch Civilization in the Seventeenth Century and Other Essays*, trans. Arnold J. Pomerans (New York and Evanston, 1969); Anthony Molho and John Tedeschi, eds., *Renaissance Studies in Honor of Hans Baron* (Dekalb, Ill., 1971); Heinz Otto Burger, *Renaissance Humanismus, Reformation. Deutsche Literatur im europäischen Kontext* (Berlin and Zürich, 1969); Annabel M. Patterson, *Hermogenes and the Renaissance: Seven Ideas of Style* (Princeton, 1970); Nancy S. Struever, *The Language of History in the Renaissance: Rhetoric and Historical Consciousness in Florentine Humanism* (Princeton, 1970); Jerrold E. Seigel, *Rhetoric and Philosophy in Renaissance Humanism: The Union of Eloquence and Wisdom, Petrarch to Valla* (Princeton, 1968); Brian Vickers, *Classical Rhetoric in English Poetry* (London and New York, 1970); Ernst Cassirer, *The Platonic Renaissance in England*, trans. James P. Pettegrove (Austin, Texas, 1953); Peter Dronke, *Poetic Individuality in the Middle Ages; New Departures in Poetry, 1000-1150* (Oxford, 1970); O. B. Hardison, Jr., ed., *Medieval and Renaissance Studies* (Chapel Hill, 1971); D. S. Chambers, *Patrons and Artists in the Italian Renaissance* (Columbia, S.C., 1971); Peter Burke, *Culture and Society in Renaissance Italy, 1420-1540* (New York, 1971); John Larner, *Culture and Society in Renaissance Italy, 1290-1420* (New York, 1971). G. W. Trompf, "The Carolingian Renaissance," *Journal of the History of Ideas*, vol. 34 (1973), pp. 3-26, distinguishes the general and specific senses of the term *renaissance* and suggests that the Carolingian renaissance could be "brought into sharper focus if . . . treated comparatively with cultural developments in the fifteenth and sixteenth centuries." On Renaissance humanism and historiography and the problem of the Renaissance, see Peter Burke, *The Renaissance Sense of the Past* (London, 1969) and idem, "The Sense of Historical Perspective in Renaissance Italy," *JWH* 11 (1969), 615-32; *El transito de la Edad Media al Renacimento* (Madrid, 1967); Hugh Trevor-Roper, ed., *The Age of Expansion: Europe and the World, 1559-1660* (New York, 1968); Donald J. Wilcox, *The Development of Florentine Humanist Historiography of the Fifteenth Century* (Cambridge, Mass., 1969); Maurizio Bonicatti, *Studi sull' Umanesimo, Secoli XIV-XVI* (Florence, 1969); August Buck, *Die Humanistische Tradition in der Romania* (Bad Homburg, 1968); Werner L. Gundersheimer, ed., *French Humanism, 1470-1600* (New York, 1969); Paul O. Kristeller, *Der italienische Humanismus und seine Bedeutung* (Basel, 1969); Pierre Mesnard, *Erasme ou le Christianisme critique* (Paris, 1969); L. D. Reynolds and N. G. Wilson, *Scribes and Scholars; A Guide to the Transmission of Greek and Latin Literature* (London, 1968); Giovanni Santinello, *Studi sull' umanesimo europeo* (Padua, 1969); Franco Simone, *Umanesimo, Rinascimento, Barocco in Francia* (Milan, 1968); Roberto Weiss, *The Renaissance Discovery of Classical Antiquity* (Oxford, 1969); Carroll W. Westfall, "Painting and the Liberal Arts: Alberti's View," *JHI* 30 (1969), 487-506; Andre Chastel, *The Myth of the Renaissance, 1420-1529* (Geneva, 1969); Anne Denieul-Cormier, *The Renaissance in France, 1488-1559* (New York, 1968); Antonia McLean, *Humanism and the Rise of Science in Tudor England* (New York, 1972); Georges Duby, *Fondements d'un nouvel humanisme, 1280-1440* (Geneva, 1966). On Renaissance humanism and rhetoric, see Theodore K. Rabb and Jerrold E. Seigel, eds., *Action and Convention in Early Modern Europe* (Princeton, 1969); Hanna H. Gray, "Valla's *Encomium* of St. Thomas Aquinas and

The Lamb and the Elephant

the Humanist Conception of Christian Antiquity," in *Essays in History and Literature Presented by Fellows of The Newberry Library to Stanley Pargellis* (Chicago, 1965), pp. 37-51.

For the Elizabethan Renaissance, its social and cultural patterns, and its artistic and intellectual achievements, see John Buxton, *Sir Philip Sidney and the English Renaissance* (London, 1954); Hardin Craig, *The Enchanted Glass: The Elizabethan Mind in Literature* (New York, 1936); Arthur B. Ferguson, *The Articulate Citizen and the English Renaissance* (Durham, N.C., 1965); Albert Feuillerat, *John Lyly: Contribution à l'histoire de la Renaissance en Angleterre* (Cambridge, 1910); Sidney Lee, *The French Renaissance in England* (Oxford, 1910); A. L. Rowse, *The England of Elizabeth: The Structure of Society* (London, 1951); idem, *The Expansion of Elizabethan England* (London and New York, 1955); idem, *The Elizabethan Renaissance*: vol. 1, *The Life of the Society* (London, 1971), and vol. 2, *The Cultural Achievement* (London, 1972); Hallett Smith, *Elizabethan Poetry: A Study in Convention, Meaning, and Expression* (Cambridge, Mass., 1952); E. M. W. Tillyard, *The English Renaissance, Fact or Fiction?* (Baltimore, 1952); Louis Booker Wright, *Middle-Class Culture in Elizabethan England* (Chapel Hill, 1935).

For relationships between English and Italian Renaissance culture, see Lewis Einstein, *The Italian Renaissance in England* (New York, 1913); John Rigby Hale, *England and the Italian Renaissance* (London, 1954); John L. Lievsay, *Stefano Guazzo and the English Renaissance, 1575-1675* (Chapel Hill, 1961); Napoleone Orsini, *Studi sul rinascimento italiano in Inghilterra* (Florence, 1937); George B. Parks, *The English Traveler to Italy* (Rome, 1954); idem, "The Decline and Fall of the English Renaissance Admiration of Italy," *HLQ* 31 (1968), 341-57; Mario Praz, *The Flaming Heart* (Garden City, N.Y., 1958); F. T. Prince, *The Italian Element in Milton* (Oxford, 1954); Roberto Weiss, *Humanism in England During the Fifteenth Century* (Oxford, 1941).

[3]Cf. Bernard of Chartres in Friedrich Heer, *The Medieval World*, trans. Janet Sondheimer (New York, 1963), p. 122.

[4]Thomas Hobbes, *Leviathan, Parts One and Two*, ed. Herbert W. Schneider (Indianapolis and New York, 1958), p. 50.

[5]Ibid., p. 42.

[6]Lewis Carroll, *Alice's Adventures in Wonderland* and *Through the Looking-Glass* (London, 1971), pp. 190-191.

[7]George Sarton, *Appreciation of Ancient and Medieval Science During the Renaissance* (New York, 1961), p. ix.

[8]Huizinga, *Men and Ideas*, pp. 286-87.

[9]For these and other representative quotations from Renaissance authors on the revival of learning, see James Bruce Ross and Mary Martin McLaughlin, eds., *The Portable Renaissance Reader* (New York, 1958), pp. 79, 81-83, 123 ff., 138, 140 ff., and passim. Boccaccio boasted that "In our age ... more illustrious men have come from heaven, generous spirits who wish to raise up again ... the oppressed art of poetry, and to recall it from exile into its former abode." Leonardo Bruni declared that his own century, "like a golden age," had "restored to life the liberal arts, which were almost extinct: grammar, poetry, rhetoric, painting, sculpture, architecture, music, the ancient singing of songs to the Orphic lyre, and all this in Florence." Boccaccio extolled Petrarch for restoring "Apollo to his ancient temple" and the Muses "to their pristine beauty," while Bruni praised the same author for "recognizing and restoring to life the ancient elegance of style" after the barbarians had "almost completely extinguished all knowledge of letters." Valla expressed confidence

Problem of the Renaissance

that Latin eloquence, "the language of Rome, will shortly grow stronger than the city itself, and with it all disciplines will be restored." In Italy, Vasari recognized a "restoration" or "second birth" of the arts of design—painting, sculpture, architecture—comparable to the revival of literature. Joachim von Watt extolled Rudolph Agricola for summoning "the noble Muses to cross the Alps themselves into those German lands which had earlier shown no power of acquiring a knowledge of letters." Hailing the revival of "polite letters, which were almost extinct," and their cultivation by Scots, Danes, and Irishmen, Erasmus voiced the "confident hope that not only morality and Christian piety, but also a genuine and purer literature, may come to renewed life or greater splendor...." In his *Antibarbarorum liber* he defended humane letters and classical literature against hostile attack, and he compared the labors of the humanists in restoring ancient texts to the labors of Hercules. Cf. William Heckscher, "Reflections on Seeing Holbein's Portrait of Erasmus as Longford Castle," in *Essays in the History of Art Presented to Rudolf Wittkower*, ed. Douglas Fraser et al (London, 1967), pp. 128-48; and Craig R. Thompson in *RQ* 25 (Summer, 1972), 192: "Si ullis hominum laboribus hoc cognominis debetur ut *Herculani* dicantur, eorum certe vel maxime deberi videtur, qui in restituendis antiquae veraeque litteraturae monimentis elaborant."

The *topoi* of the revival of learning and the exantlation of truth were also applied to Hermetic philosophy (Yates, *Bruno*, p. 236). For Bruno, Copernicus' achievements were the "dawn which was to precede the full sunrise of the ancient and true philosophy after its agelong burial in the dark caverns of blind and envious ignorance...." Bruno compares himself to the inventor of the first ship, to the Argonauts, and to Columbus: "what then shall be said of him who has found a way to mount up to the sky...?" In *Giordano Bruno and the Hermetic Tradition*, (pp. 159-63), Frances Yates emphasizes the distinction between the Renaissance "humanist tradition"—"the recovery of the Latin texts, of the literature of Roman civilization..., and the attitude to life and letters which arose out of that recovery" in the fourteenth and fifteenth centuries—and a second Renaissance "experience," the "recovery of the Greek texts and their ensuing new philosophical revelation in the fifteenth century." In her opinion, "these two Renaissance experiences are of an entirely different order, using different sources in a different way, and ... making their appeal to different sides of the human mind," and differing in their attitude to chronology and textual scholarship, to the Middle Ages, and to religion. These contrasting emphases—on "literature and history," "rhetoric and good literary style," and on "philosophy, theology, and also science (at the stage of magic)"—reflect the "contrast between the Roman and the Greek mind." As she observes (p. 252), Bruno, "looking in quite a different direction from Erasmus, sees humanism, not as the new learning which has superseded mediaeval barbarism, but as the destroyer of the philosophical tradition."

See also Hallett Smith, "Tamburlaine and the Renaissance," in *Elizabethan Studies and Other Essays in Honor of George F. Reynolds*, University of Colorado Studies Series B. Studies in the Humanities, vol. 2 (1945), pp. 126-31 on Loys Le Roy's *La Vicissitude ou Variété des Choses en l'Univers* (1575). Stressing the "concurrence of arms and learning," Le Roy regarded Tamburlaine as representative of the modern age, observing that the "restitution" of tongues and all disciplines had begun during that monarch's reign and that Petrarch and Boccaccio were his contemporaries. In Le Roy's opinion, the principal characteristics of his own age were the "restoration of tongues and knowledge"; the invention of printing, the mariner's compass, and artillery; geographical exploration and discovery; and new diseases and divers sects in religion.

On the *topoi* of the medieval decay of learning and the Renaissance revival and migration of the arts, cf. Milton's academic exercises. In the Seventh Prolusion he attributes the decay of piety and religion to the medieval decay of learning. In the

The Lamb and the Elephant

whole continent of Europe "several centuries ago all liberal arts had perished, and the Muses who preside over them now, had abandoned the universities of that time. A blind inertia possessed and pervaded everything. In the schools nothing except the absurd dogmas of the doddering monks was heard. . . ." In the oration preceding his Sixth Prolusion he declares that "when the laws of our Republic of Letters were first laid down, letters had only recently been brought to these shores from distant lands" and "skill in Greek and Latin was very rare and unusual. . . ." See John Milton, *Complete Poems and Major Prose*, ed. Merritt Y. Hughes (New York, 1957), pp. 616, 624. Milton's prolusion "Against Scholastic Philosophy," delivered in the Public Schools at the University of Cambridge, echoes traditional humanistic complaints against scholasticism. He condemns its poverty of matter and its inelegance of style: "No flowers of rhetoric relieve this lifeless, flaccid, crawling stuff, but the jejune, juiceless style matches its thin substance. . . ." He finds it lacking in both profit and delight, and then contrasts the impotence of "these wretched, squalid studies" with the affective and persuasive powers of the *studia humaniora*—poetry, rhetoric, and history. The "futile and barren controversies and wordy disputes" of scholastic philosophy "are impotent to move the affections of the heart; they simply stupefy and benumb the mind." They "have filled men's breasts with thorns and briars and have brought endless discord into the schools, which has marvellously impeded the scholars' happy progress." Moreover, they accomplish nothing "for the good of society or for the honor or profit of our fatherland"; they are impotent "either to teach eloquence or to develop wisdom or to stir men to brave actions" (Hughes, 605-06).

On the ideal of the learned orator, instructed in the cycle of arts and sciences and capable of speaking effectively on almost any given subject, cf. Cicero's *Orator* and *De Oratore* and Quintilian's *Institutio Oratoria;* on the ideal of the learned poet, cf. Horace's *Ars Poetica;* and on their interrelationship, cf. J. E. Spingarn, *A History of Literary Criticism in the Renaissance* (New York, 1925). Both ideals involve a fusion of wisdom and eloquence and a concern for matter *(res)* as well as style *(verba)*. For medieval and Renaissance views on the interrelationship between wisdom and eloquence, see the recent studies by Colish, Mazzeo, McKeon, Seigel and Karl Wallace. In his Seventh Prolusion Milton asserts that "nothing mean or mediocre is tolerable in an orator any more than it is in a poet, and that it behooves an aspirant to true, and not merely specious eloquence, to be instructed and perfected in an all-around foundation in all the arts and in every science" (Hughes, p. 622). Cf. Joseph Anthony Wittreich, Jr., " 'The Crown of Eloquence': The Figure of the Orator in Milton's Prose Works," and John F. Huntley, "The Images of Poet and Poetry in Milton's *The Reason of Church-Government*," in *Achievements of the Left Hand: Essays on the Prose of John Milton*, ed. Michael Lieb and John T. Shawcross (Amherst, 1974), pp. 3-54; 83-120.

[10]Cf. Loys Le Roy, quoted in Ross and McLaughlin, p. 105.

[11]Cf. Seznec on medieval and Renaissance traditions in the representation of the pagan gods. Despite differences in "outward appearance," images of pagan deities in Renaissance art are "in spirit very close" to medieval images (p. 109); it is misleading to speak of the "death of the gods" with the "decline of the ancient world" and their "resurrection" in the Italian Renaissance. Nevertheless, it was "merely the content of the images of the gods which survived. The garment of classical form had disappeared, having gradually been shed in favor of barbaric disguises which made it impossible to identify the wearers" (p. 149). Rightly seen, the Renaissance is "in no sense a sudden crisis" but "the end of a long divorce. It is not a resurrection, but a synthesis" (p. 213). "The triumph of the ancient gods in Renaissance Italy and then in Europe as a whole, and the immense place which they occupy in the art and literature of the sixteenth century," reflect the influence of contemporary manuals and

Problem of the Renaissance

dictionaries, and it was not "until the middle of the sixteenth century that Italy saw a renewal of the authentic mythographical tradition" (pp. 219, 224).

For the debt of Renaissance artists to medieval treatises on perspective, see Herbert Read, *Icon and Idea* (New York, 1965), pp. 149-50. Ghiberti's "Commentaries" reveal indebtedness to "Arabic sources, particularly . . . the Optics of . . . Alhazen" (c. 965-1039). "The whole of this tradition is deductive: it assumes the presence of certain ideal laws in nature, and art becomes an illustration of these laws rather than a direct experience of reality. Beauty is conceived solely in terms of harmonic proportion." John of Peckham's work on perspective "was very popular in the thirteenth century and was probably known to the brothers Van Eyck."

For mythography, see Don Cameron Allen, *Mysteriously Meant: The Rediscovery of Pagan Symbolism and Allegorical Interpretation in the Renaissance* (Baltimore and London, 1970). On *philosophia Christi*, cf. Raymond Himelick, trans., *The Enchiridion of Erasmus* (Bloomington, Ind., 1963), p. 30.

Pride in original achievement and in conformity to antique example are frequently closely associated in Renaissance encomium. Writers praised their contemporaries for being first in the field, or else first since the ancients; for free invention or for fidelity to antique precedent. The *topos* of novelty and originality in deed or in subject matter had long been a conventional argument for praise. It can be traced from Horace through Boiardo, Ariosto, and Milton. Curtius has examined its continuity in classical, medieval, and Renaissance literature. See Ernst Robert Curtius, *European Literature and the Latin Middle Ages*, trans. Willard R. Trask (New York and Evanston, 1953), p. 86. The revival of classical genres and styles or the adaptation of classical forms to Biblical subject matter could be represented by contemporary eulogists either as a new development or as a restoration of ancient tradition. Renaissance writers are conscious of an impressive list of "firsts." Petrarch and Mussato are crowned with laurel, like the poets of antiquity. In his oration on the dignity of man, Pico della Mirandola argues that it is "ignoble, as Seneca says, to know only by way of commentary, and, as if the discoveries of the ancients had closed the road for our industry. . . ." He proposes "the concord of Plato and Aristotle, believed by many before now, but adequately proved by no one." He has "put down the seventy-two new physical and metaphysical doctrines" that he has "thought out in Aristotelian and Platonic philosophy," bringing forward "a new philosophy" at "a tender age." He has also "brought forward something else new, the ancient system of philosophizing through numbers." See Pico della Mirandola, *On the Dignity of Man*, trans. Charles Glenn Wallis (Indianapolis and New York, 1965), pp. 24-25.

[12] See Hans Baron, *The Crisis of the Early Italian Renaissance* (Princeton, 1966) and Myron P. Gilmore, *The World of Humanism* (New York, 1962).

[13] Cf. Seznec, p. 219, on this facet of the Renaissance myth.

[14] See Sarton in *The Renaissance: Six Essays*, p. 56.

[15] See Paul Oskar Kristeller, *Renaissance Thought*, vols. 1 and 2 (New York, 1961, 1965). For the search for manuscripts of Greek and Latin antiquity by Italian humanists, see John Addington Symonds, *Renaissance in Italy*, vol. II, The Revival of Learning (New York, 1960), pp. 92-117; Leo Deuel, *Testaments of Time: The Search for Lost Manuscripts and Records* (New York, 1965), pp. 3-51.

[16] Sarton, *Appreciation*, pp. 168-69.

[17] Geoffrey Scott, *The Architecture of Humanism*, 2d ed. (New York, n.d.), pp. 146 ff. For the "role of humanists at the papal court during the first years of the fifteenth century," Bruni's distinction between the truth of history and the exaggerations of eulogy, and the humanist *topos* of "restoring studies long interrupted," see

The Lamb and the Elephant

Gordon Griffiths, "Leonardo Bruni and the Restoration of the University of Rome (1406)," *RQ* 26 (1973), 1-10. See also R. R. Bolgar, ed., *Classical Influences on European Culture A.D. 500-1500* (Cambridge, Eng., 1971); R. R. Bolgar, "Humanist Education and Its Contribution to the Renaissance" in *The Changing Curriculum*, ed. Malcolm Seaborne (London and New York, 1971) and rev. by Edward P. Mahoney in *RQ* 25 (1972), 473-74; Charles Trinkhaus, *In Our Image and Likeness: Humanity and Divinity in Italian Humanist Thought*, 2 vols. (Chicago & London, 1970); A. H. T. Levi, ed., *Humanism in France at the End of the Middle Ages and in the Early Renaissance* (Manchester, 1970).

Chapter II
THE RECOVERY OF ANTIQUITY

THE CLASSICAL TRADITION had proved unusually hardy. The Mediterranean stock had persisted in medieval art and learning, even though it had undergone striking mutations. Surviving its transplantation to the western islands and the forests of northern Europe, it had remained green during the subarctic twilight of the barbarian Völkerwanderungen. It had burgeoned in the glacial chill of monastic scriptoria. In cathedral schools and universities it had bloomed periodically like the Glastonbury thorn; from the same buried root sprang the prickly subtleties of scholastic logic and the variegated and sometimes overscented flowers of rhetoric. Like Darwin's biological species, the classical genres had mastered the technique of survival by adapting themselves to changing cultural environments and climates of opinion. These mutations and variants had become part of the literary ecology of the Middle Ages; and in the Renaissance they would be subjected to selective breeding, cross-fertilized with chosen exemplars of the original ancestral species.

The arts had already experienced a series of "rebirths." (The term is an exaggeration, however, since the arts had never actually died out, and perhaps it would be more accurate to speak of their transformations.) In at least one instance this had resulted in the evolution of a style that appeared to run counter to the classical "representational tradition." As Panofsky has observed, "classical images were faithfully though often clumsily copied in Carolingian manuscripts and lingered on in their derivatives"; at a later date, however, they were replaced by "representations of an entirely non-classical character as soon as the Middle Ages had achieved a style entirely their own."[1] Flourishing vernacular literatures had developed, especially in western Europe, frequently combining French and Provençal, Germanic and Celtic elements with classical themes. Instead of reviving a dead or moribund art or literature, the artists and writers of the Renaissance grafted their classical or pseudoclassical aesthetic ideals upon the stock of a living medieval tradition. They achieved a reformation of style, but this was essentially a reformation of arts and letters that were already thriving. They imposed classical forms—or what they believed to be classical forms—on existing literary and artistic modes.

1.

In a variety of fields—the history of science as well as that of art and literature—modern scholars have discredited the Renaissance myth of a decisive "break" with classical tradition during the Middle Ages followed by an equally decisive revival and restoration of classical art and learning. Though they acknowledge a different kind of historical awareness in medieval and Renaissance authors, they have qualified Renaissance ideas of a rebirth of the arts and sciences and a return to the literary and artistic principles of antiquity. Iconographers have noted the survival of medieval and Oriental elements in Renaissance treatments of classical mythological themes. Poets and artists derived their notions of pagan iconography not only from classical sources but indirectly from manuals and dictionaries that often showed little direct knowledge of classical art. In their illustrations of pagan mythology Renaissance artists frequently copied one another; the imitation of classical models was frequently indirect, based on secondary sources. Though Panofsky regards the "reintegration of classical themes with classical motifs" as a distinguishing characteristic of the Italian Renaissance—a phenomenon that differentiates this movement from the "numerous sporadic revivals of classical tendencies during the Middle Ages"—he also reminds us that "this reintegration could not be a simple reversion to the classical past." Renaissance artists "could not simply renew the art of the Greeks and Romans"; instead, they had to "strive for a new form of expression, stylistically and iconographically different from the classical, as well as from the medieval, yet related and indebted to both."[2]

When Renaissance authors set out, like antiquarian knights-errant, in quest of the classical past, they were not always inspired by the same motives. Some were seeking broader, more detailed, and more reliable information about pagan antiquity. Others were looking

The Recovery of Antiquity

for a more effective key to understanding the classical authors and, in particular, for interpreting the allegorical meanings hidden beneath the ancient myths. Others were searching for models to improve their own mastery of Latin poetry and prose.

For Boccaccio, the principles of classical poetry were the most reliable guide for the modern poet. Though he praised Dante for rediscovering the fountain of the Muses, "lost many centuries ago," he was aware that Dante had reached it, "not by the path that the ancients had followed, but by certain byways entirely unknown to our ancestors. . . ." Petrarch, on the other hand, "rejecting the principles of writers who . . . had hardly touched on the threshold of poetry, began to follow the ancient path," opening the "way for himself and for those who wished to ascend after him" and cleansing "the fount of Helicon. . . ."[3] The poetry of antiquity provided the surest and safest guide for the modern poet.

Boccaccio himself regarded poetry not only as a form of theology but also as a political instrument, an "agency of regeneration in the State."[4] His *Genealogy of the Gods* is notable, however, not only for its exaltation of poetry as a form of natural and moral philosophy and a *prisca theologia*, but for its sense of distance from antiquity. Boccaccio was painfully conscious of the fragmentary character of classical mythology, and he repeatedly employed the imagery of *sparagmos* (dismemberment) to emphasize the magnitude of his task. Later humanists would employ similar imagery, and Milton would adapt the same image to Reformation theology.[5] "The names and tribes of gods and their progenitors," Boccaccio declared, "are scattered hither and yon all over the world. Here a book and there another has something to say on the subject." "Everywhere . . . I will find and gather, like fragments of a mighty wreck strewn on some vast shore, the relics of the Gentile gods." "I can quite realize this labor to which I am committed—this vast system of Gentile gods and their progeny, torn limb from limb and scattered among the rough and desert places of antiquity and the thorns of hate, wasted away, sunk almost to ashes; and here am I setting forth to collect these fragments, hither and yon, and fit them together, like another Aesculapius restoring Hippolytus."[6]

In attempting to uncover the allegorical meaning concealed beneath absurd fables, "to tear the hidden significations from their tough sheathing," Boccaccio recognized the impossibility of fully recovering "the authors' original intentions"; his confession may serve as an index of his consciousness of the gulf between classical antiquity and his own age:

> Who in our day can penetrate the hearts of the Ancients? Who can bring to light and life again minds long since removed in death? Who can elicit their meaning? ... The Ancients departed in the way of all flesh, leaving behind them their literature and their famous names for posterity to interpret according to their own judgment. But as many minds, so many opinions.[7]

2.

The reverence for antiquity and the close study of classical authors had not been uncommon in the Middle Ages. Classical themes had occurred frequently in both Latin and vernacular literature, and the ideal of imitating the styles of the ancients was by no means unknown. As Bolgar points out, "The twelfth-century scholars adopted classical instances, classical arguments to illustrate the conclusions of their own experience just as they used classical metres and figures in their essentially medieval poems." Walter of Châtillon, for example, was "no pedestrian imitator." He displayed a "genuine appreciation of the overall form and characteristics of his genre," reproducing "not only the detail, but also the generalities of the classical epic."[8] Panofsky similarly calls attention to "a proto-humanistic movement, viz., an active interest in classical themes regardless of classical motifs, centered in the northern regions of Europe, as opposed to the proto-Renaissance movement, viz., an active interest in classical motifs regardless of classical themes, centered in Provence and Italy."[9] Chaucer's medieval dream-visions frequently took as their point of departure the work of some classical author. Few medieval or Renaissance humanists would have quarreled with his assertion that

> ... out of olde bokes, in good feyth,
> Cometh al this newe science that men lere.

The ancient Latin poets were "classics" for the Middle Ages as for the Renaissance.

The Recovery of Antiquity

In philosophy and science meanwhile, late medieval scholars had attempted to restore the texts of standard Greek authors either by direct translation from their original tongue or indirectly through Arabic. For medieval and Renaissance scholars alike, the chief authorities in the majority of learned disciplines belonged on the whole to classical or early Christian antiquity. Poets attributed their fables to classical authors; encyclopedists cited classical authorities; scholastic theologians based their *summas* on selections from patristic writers and Biblical texts. The attempt to restore and reform learning by going back, as far as possible, to the ancient authorities themselves was scarcely less characteristic of the medieval schoolmen in their thorny scientific disciplines than of the Renaissance humanists in their own wide and airy fields, the *loci amoeni* of humane literature.

As a rule, neither medieval nor Renaissance scholars approached the classics with negative capability. Both were accustomed to reading the text with the aid of later commentaries and secondary authorities. In early printed editions of classical authors medieval and Renaissance commentators frequently appear cheek by jowl, the philological and rhetorical scholia of the Renaissance scholar complementing the logical analysis, rhetorical notes, and paraphrases of his medieval predecessor.

Finally, there was substantial continuity between the rhetoric and poetics of the Middle Ages and those of the Renaissance. The doctrine of literary genres, the ideal of decorum, the distinction between three principal levels of style, the ornaments of rhetoric were common to both periods. Medieval authors could draw on Horace's *Ars Poetica*, Cicero's *De Inventione*, and the pseudo-Ciceronian *Rhetorica ad Herennium*. A few possessed some knowledge of Aristotle's *Poetics* through a Latin translation from Averroes' paraphrase. Though the Renaissance possessed a much wider range of classical works on rhetoric, these tended to complement rather than undermine the classical rhetoricians known to the Middle Ages. The principal reorientations of rhetorical theory occurred comparatively late in the Renaissance; Ramus' revision of the conventional division between logic and rhetoric belongs to the late sixteenth century.[10] Similarly, it was not until the mid-sixteenth century that Aristotle's

Poetics exerted a decisive influence on critical theory, and even this work was usually read in the light of Horatian doctrines.[11] By that time, the Renaissance in Italy was nearing its close.

For medieval and Renaissance authors alike, the fundamental principles of rhetoric and poetics were based on classical authority. However different the results of their labors, writers of both periods were convinced that they were observing the principles of "art poetical" as set forth by the ancients and interpreted by the moderns —the very principles that underlay the masterpieces of the classical poets and orators. How far their success had been due to nature or to art, to intuitive or deliberate exploitation of the rules, was a different matter.

Despite the greater diversity and complexity of Renaissance rhetoric and poetics, they exhibited significant continuity with medieval theory. Though there were also major differences, some of these seem to have originated primarily in a more exact and comprehensive knowledge of the texts of classical poets and orators, and only secondarily in the rediscovery of theoretical treatises. Though writers in both periods might disregard the rules altogether or treat them with considerable license, Renaissance authors frequently turned to the practice as well as the theory of the ancients for guidance. Their medieval predecessors, on the other hand, were sometimes content to apply theoretical principles without systematically investigating precisely how and why the classical writers themselves had utilized them. In the preface to *Samson Agonistes* Milton significantly preferred classical models to classical theory as an authoritative guide; the three Greek tragic poets were "the best rule to all who endeavor to write Tragedy."

In conceptions of the classical genres, medieval and Renaissance poetic theory often diverged widely. In their discussions of comedy and tragedy medieval theorists had sometimes blurred the distinction between dramatic and narrative poetry. Some of the classical forms had been virtually abandoned, supplanted by newer and more popular species. Others had become accommodated to medieval genres and had lost much of their original form. The revival of the ancient literary genres, the elimination of certain medieval misconceptions, and the partial correction of others marked a significant turn in the evolution of Renaissance poetic theory. This development, however, was due not only to the recovery of "lost" critical treatises on poetics but to the intensive study of classical poems.

Although both of these developments in Renaissance critical theory exerted a profound influence on the literature of the period, the major divergences between medieval and Renaissance poets in their exploitation of the classical tradition cannot be primarily attributed to different attitudes towards the authority of the ancients or towards the principles (as medieval and Renaissance writers understood them) of classical rhetoric and poetics. Other contributing factors—differences in the literary tastes of the audience, in the selection of classical models, and in the degree of individuality permitted the author—were likewise of secondary importance. The tastes of courtly circles in both periods were sometimes remarkably similar, and medieval and Renaissance poets had read and admired many of the same authors. The most significant reasons for their differences were apparently the quality and degree of their imitation of classical writers and the methods by which they learned and mastered the technique of imitation. At this point one encounters, inevitably, the concept of the Renaissance not merely as a movement or as an age, but as the self-conscious and systematic pursuit of stylistic perfection. Like many of the artists of the cinquecento, the poets sought to reconquer the style and manner of the ancients, the *stilo antico*.

3.

Twelfth-century humanism, as Bolgar points out, tended to focus attention "on the detail rather than on the broad general characteristics of the ancient authors," picking and choosing "on the basis of an unsystematic knowledge" of antiquity. That the later humanists succeeded in achieving a more systematic imitation of "classical language and style" and a more "detailed understanding of ancient ways of thought" was due in large part to their exploitation of the "note-book and heading method" as a pedagogical technique. Encouraging the student to organize the fruits of his classical studies rhetorically as a "mnemonotechnical aid" by systematically listing words and phrases, rhetorical ornaments, and epithets and by compiling proverbs, exempla, and other potential arguments under topical headings, this technique demanded a close study of classical texts. This in turn facilitated the mastery of classical style and the exploitation of classical ideas. "The effect of reading the Greek and Roman authors with a view to imitation was precisely to fix in the mind the details of ancient history and ancient life."[12]

The "key to the whole complex development of Humanism during the fifteenth century" and to some of the differences between medieval and fifteenth-century literature is to be found, Bolgar suggests, in the diffusion of this educational technique. "At the end of the fourteenth century, the cultural tradition of the West bore the recognisable imprint of the Middle Ages. By the end of the sixteenth, the mediaeval elements had been replaced by others drawn from the Graeco-Roman heritage; and in between these two limits of time, we find that the method of study in general use is based on the analysis of the classical texts and the memorization of linguistic and illustrative detail."[13]

The program of classical studies in Renaissance grammar schools aimed simultaneously at the perfection of linguistic skill and moral character. By intensive study of classical authors of the "best" periods the student was expected to learn correct Latinity, to acquire the linguistic mastery indispensable for broadening his knowledge of antiquity and the neo-Latin learning of his own time. By rhetorical exercises based on these authors he would not only perfect his own Latin style, but would master techniques of persuasion that could be effectively deployed in the vernacular. By observing patterns of heroic excellence he would be persuaded to shun ignoble ease for the more strenuous ways of virtue. Offering patterns for moral as well as literary imitation, the poetry and history of antiquity could form character as well as style.

The grammar-school curricula of the period throw significant light on the classical knowledge that poets shared with educated contemporaries and on the rhetorical orientation of humanistic education. The imitation of classical authors (and we cannot afford to overlook the fact) was essentially a technique for acquiring eloquence, a method for learning to speak and write well. The topical headings of the notebooks assisted the orator to invent or "find" appropriate arguments for his own thesis and to anticipate those of his opponent. They were a heritage of classical and medieval rhetoric, and their influence is apparent not only in the widespread use of the commonplace-book, but in numerous additional aids to rhetorical invention—florilegia, compendia of proverbs, emblem-books, and even mythographical and iconographical manuals. The method of Bacon's *Essays* owes much to this topical organization of arguments pro and con. The same commonplaces of rhetorical invention served the painter and the sculptor as well as the poet and the orator. As Bevilacqua points out in a recent study, the emphasis on "invention" persists in art theory as late as Sir Joshua Reynolds.[14] The word lists of the humanist educator, in turn, lead to the selective lexicons and dictionaries of the late fifteenth and sixteenth centuries and the manuals of phrases and epithets.

In addition to the notebook-and-heading method, other pedagogical techniques tended to encourage close imitation of classical authors in the formation of style.[15] The student composed elegies and verse epistles, epigrams and odes in imitation of classical genres. He was required to translate passages from Latin into the vernacular and back again, and to compare his own Latin version carefully with the original. He composed orations and *suasoriae* in the classical manner on set themes. He delivered "showpieces" at academic exercises, and acted in classical or neo-Latin comedies on festal occasions. The imitation of the ancients, the mastery of the Latin tongue, and the cultivation of rhetorical technique went hand in hand.

Though some of the humanists may have regarded the imitation of classical models as an end in itself, for the majority it was rather a means to an end, limited by the rhetorical objectives it was designed to serve. It is in this context that we must assess the criticism that Erasmus and Harvey and other humanists directed against the excessive zeal of certain imitators of Cicero. It is against the same background of rhetorical theory, moreover, that we must consider the limitations of humanist methodology. As recent scholars justly complain, Renaissance annotators tended at times to violate the unity and integrity of the work they professed to explain.[16] Instead of considering the development of the author's argument, they frequently broke up the text into convenient fragments, providing each passage with an *explication de texte* and annotating phrases, allusions, and ideas with parallel passages drawn from other works by the same writer or from altogether different authors. In this respect the techniques of analysis they brought to the study of the classics could prove a major obstacle to full appreciation and understanding. Concentration on the parts tended to obscure the whole; it became difficult to see the forest for the trees.

Critics have also protested against the eclectic nature of many Renaissance compositions, against the tendency to cite a wide variety of authors without making sufficient allowance for the different contexts in which these allusions originally appeared.[17] This tendency also seems to have resulted, in part, from the rhetorical emphasis of classical studies in Renaissance grammar schools. By encouraging the student to mine the classics for *res* as well as *verba*, for convincing arguments as well as elegancies of style, humanist pedagogy had indirectly fostered an eclectic exploitation of classical materials. The same tendency had been further aggravated by the eclectic nature of Renaissance manuals and other rhetorical aids. It would be a mistake, however, to regard this approach as indiscriminate or unsystematic. Its weakness was that it was too systematic and that the discrimination was made primarily on rhetorical grounds. Here again the rhetorical orientation of classical studies could prejudice the understanding of antiquity and distort the imitation of the ancients.

4.

The relationship to antiquity was a chronic obsession of the Renaissance, and it is still fundamental to an understanding of the period. Nevertheless, it was too complex, too diverse, and sometimes too contradictory for clear definition. "Antiquity" is not less equivocal than "Renaissance," and like the latter it cannot be reduced to a simple formula. The relationship between the two eras is doubly ambiguous, for it is a relationship between equivoques. Not only is there a potential difference between our own conception of this relationship and the way the Renaissance conceived it, but the relationship itself is rather a complex of relationships—a confused tangle

The Recovery of Antiquity

of knots and lines of affinity—than a simple bond. In certain contexts it is a relationship between particular works, concrete events, or historic individuals. In others it is a relationship between ethical and political abstractions or between idealized concepts of genre and style. Sometimes it is a relationship between broader and more elusive categories—between classical and contemporary society, or ancients and moderns.

The terms of comparison and the nature of the comparison have varied widely. The ancients whose works served as poetic or rhetorical models or as doctrinal authorities often belonged to different periods, various intellectual disciplines, and diverse national cultures. The Renaissance scholars and artists who turned to them for inspiration and instruction frequently belonged to different professions or to rival schools within the same profession. In different fields the "revival of learning" proceeded at different rates and at different times; the scientific renaissance and the literary renaissance might overlap, but they did not coincide. The accessibility of classical models and the degree of conscious imitation varied widely in literature and the visual arts. Though poets and orators might possess an embarrassing wealth of antique exemplars, painters were compelled to rely on relics of classical sculpture, literary descriptions, and their own experience of anatomy, mathematics, and optics. Whereas the writer might choose at will among the "best authors" of the "best periods," the sculptor had to rely largely on copies of major works or on originals by lesser masters. The painter, in turn, had access to very few examples of ancient painting; nothing at all had been preserved from the work of the artists most highly praised in antiquity. Though men of the period could study Virgil and Homer, Cicero and Demosthenes, or Seneca and Terence at first hand, they could never consult the actual works of Zeuxis and Apelles and Polygnotus. The painter could not directly imitate a classical exemplar as could the poet or orator. In practice the ideal of imitating the ancients could never mean the same thing to Bembo and to Raphael.

In painting, the return to antiquity could mean the perpetuation of allegorical monstrosities based on poems in the Greek anthology or Hellenized versions of Egyptian hieroglyphs, the imitation of gestures and costumes on late Roman sarcophagi, the mathematical or anatomical construction of human figures, or historical decorum in the representation of classical subjects. In architecture, it could denote the revival of the Vitruvian orders and theatrical settings, the reproduction of rosettes from the vaults of an imperial bath or basilica, or the reintroduction of cosmatesque mosaics in a Christian church. In epigraphy it could signify the conjunction of Roman capital letters with Carolingian minuscule and the italic script of Renaissance humanists.

In most fields the ideal of a reversion to antiquity meant a recovery of the actual knowledge formerly possessed by the ancients and subsequently corrupted, scattered, and obscured. This entailed more than the rediscovery and publication of neglected texts, the close comparison of classical authors, and antiquarian scrutiny of archeological materials. It meant returning to primary sources, going behind and beyond medieval tradition and secondary sources to the principal authorities themselves, to the actual texts of Galen and Hippocrates, Plato and Aristotle, Archimedes and Hero and Ptolemy, Dioscorides and Oppian, Plutarch and Tacitus and Livy, Pliny and Vitruvius. Renaissance distrust of medieval Latin and Arabic tradition was not entirely founded on prejudice; it was partly motivated by a legitimate preference for primary rather than derivative authorities, a desire to drink at the clear and uncontaminated fountainhead of classical tradition rather than from the muddy and unpalatable waters of its medieval outlets.

Occasionally, this ideal narrowed to antiquarian curiosity. The attempt to remaster the knowledge held by antiquity became at times little more than a search for knowledge *about* antiquity. Though the pedantries of the antiquarians might earn the ridicule of their contemporaries, they nevertheless left their imprint on the arts. Poets and painters alike sometimes consulted the scholars for mythological and iconographical details. Hostile critics readily seized upon apparent violations of historical accuracy. Increasing familiarity with the details of classical history and the life and thought of the ancients on the part of the poet or artist and his contemporaries inevitably affected his treatment of classical subjects. The demands of verisimilitude, probability, and decorum could no longer be satisfied (as

The Recovery of Antiquity

was so often the case in the late Middle Ages) by portraying Greek and Roman warriors as contemporary knights, and Thebes and Troy as medieval towns. The "reintegration" of classical themes and classical motifs, which Panofsky regarded as characteristic of Renaissance art in contrast to the art of the late Middle Ages, probably resulted in part at least from the impact of a wider and more detailed acquaintance with antiquity (a knowledge facilitated both by the methods of the humanistic educators and the detailed investigations of the antiquarians) on the ideals of decorum and verisimilitude in artistic imitation.

These aesthetic principles were accessible to medieval as well as Renaissance writers and artists through a fusion of rhetorical theory and Horatian poetics. That the two periods often differ markedly in their application of these principles is partially due to the greater awareness of historical distance and the more intimate knowledge of antiquity that the Renaissance poet and his audience brought to his classical subject or theme. The medieval writer or artist could achieve verisimilitude and probability by "medievalizing" his subject, investing his characters with contemporary manners and apparel, enlivening his actions with medieval jousts and tourneys, feasts and hunting scenes, preserving the social decorum of a feudal culture, introducing realistic details reminiscent of contemporary life or idealized conventions reminiscent of medieval romances. He arrayed classical philosophers in the robes of medieval doctors, ancient warriors in the armor of medieval knights. He portrayed the matter of Greece and Rome just as he depicted that of Britain and France—in the context of late medieval ideals of courtesy and chivalry. Though many of these ideals persisted well into the Renaissance and beyond, the Renaissance artist or poet could not as a rule avail himself of the same license that his medieval predecessor had found so convenient. He was more frequently compelled to dress his classical worthies in antique armor and to endow them with at least the semblance of classical *ethos*.

Here again we encounter a substantial continuity between the poetic and rhetorical theory of the late Middle Ages and the Renaissance, but a significant difference in their application of theories and in the quality and degree of their imitation of antiquity.

The Lamb and the Elephant

5.

The archaizing and antiquarian tendencies of the Renaissance are a complex phenomenon, and their roots in the regional and national cultures of contemporary Europe are too deeply buried and too widely extended for the literary critic to uncover. They require the spade of the social historian and perhaps the drill of the depth psychologist. But they are not, of course, unique to the Renaissance. They bear more than a superficial resemblance to archaizing trends in other periods and in other societies—in the sculpture of the late Roman empire, the decor of Napoleonic France, the Gothic revival in Britain. Like these, they involve a sense of historical distance, a simultaneous awareness of the continuity and discontinuity of tradition, a nostalgia for a vanished splendor, and an attempt to reestablish contact with a heroic age by reviving at the very least its external forms and styles. At their most grandiloquent, they belong to the rhetoric of empire and the rodomontade of national glorification. In their less pretentious forms, they may exhibit more than a trace of cultural uncertainty, a tremulous groping after social identity and the reassurance of a historic tradition. In the Tudor steakhouses of the prairie states, the classical praenomina of the Deep South, the Biblical names of New England we may detect a latent element of self-doubt under the overt self-assertion. Perhaps the analogy will hold true for the Herculeses and Hippolytuses, the Caesars and Alexanders, and even the Endymions and Narcissuses of the Renaissance.

Such archaizing tendencies occur fairly frequently in different societies, different periods, and different art forms; and their social and aesthetic significance may vary with each of these factors. Even within the same period and the same society, they may not possess precisely the same significance in different arts or sciences. Archaizing trends in poetry and painting and music, in rhetoric and philosophy, or in religious liturgy and doctrine may sometimes run parallel, but they may also conflict with one another. In the broader area of comparative literature or comparative sociology, the significance of such trends may vary even more widely; and the critic should be wary of the easy assumption that similar factors underlie archaizing styles in late classical and Carolingian and Renaissance art or in the

The Recovery of Antiquity

art of the T'ang or Sung, Ming or Ch'ing dynasties. In many instances these archaizing movements give expression to contradictory values within the same culture; and though they may reflect certain tensions within a particular society and a particular stage of development, they may also run counter to other contemporary trends. They are rarely representative of the society as a whole. On occasion they can prove deceptive. The apparent orientation toward the past may really be a program for the future; the retrospective glance toward the glories of antiquity may actually be a prospectus for future progress. Major innovations may be consciously or unconsciously disguised under traditional forms.

In the Renaissance, as in many other "archaizing" periods, the imitation of the ancients held political and ethical implications beyond its significance for the arts and sciences. For many men of the period, as for a number of medieval writers, classical antiquity was a heroic age, providing patterns of martial valor and civic virtues as well as standards of learning and eloquence. The arms and arts had flourished together, and the imitation of antiquity comprised the virtuous exploits of the ancients as well as their poetry and oratory. Just as late medieval authors sometimes extolled the combination of "chivalry" and "clergy" in ancient Greece and Rome and in their own societies,[18] Renaissance writers frequently coupled martial and intellectual excellence in their eulogies of classical civilization and the achievements of their contemporaries. The civil virtues and political greatness of the ancients served as topics of exhortation and praise in a wide variety of political contexts. Writers could apply them to popes or to emperors, to monarchies or republics, to the states of the Italian peninsula or to the "barbarian" nationalities of northern and western Europe.

With a little ingenuity the veneration of classical civilization could be accommodated to the civic pride of the Italian states or to the national vanity of the barbarian realms. Many of the latter claimed descent from Greek or Trojan worthies and could therefore boast genealogical links with the classical world. The interest in classical antiquity could stimulate additional interest in their own national past. Admiration for the epics of Greece and Rome could inspire French and English, Spanish and Portuguese poets to glorify

The Lamb and the Elephant

their own peoples in heroic verse, accomplishing for their own countrymen what Virgil and Homer had done for theirs.

In some of the vernacular epics of the period one encounters a deliberate medievalism in style and content along with an equally conscious imitation of the classics. In attempting to evoke the heroic atmosphere of Arthurian Britain in an allegory of Elizabethan England, Spenser combined elements derived from classical and Renaissance epic and from medieval romance, modeling his style and language partly on Virgil, partly on Ariosto, and partly on Geoffrey Chaucer. In the unreal continuum of epic romance, where localized space tends to become lost in a geographically indefinite and essentially moralized locality, and where historical time contracts or expands into a mythical time, he can introduce near and distant scenes, remote and contemporary events without apparent inconsistency. St. George and Prince Arthur can meet in Faeryland. The same indefinite locale and indeterminate duration can place Hesiod's monsters and an emblem of Isis in the center of the Reformation struggle and bring Elizabeth's policies in Ireland and on the Continent into the cycle of Arthur's adventures.

Spenser's allegorical vision operates as a solvent, fusing Biblical and classical, medieval and Renaissance, Italian and French and British allusions into a moral pageant that is simultaneously within and beyond time, like the realm of ideas itself. Under the pretext of celebrating the legendary past of his country—the Britain of Prince Arthur in the heroic age of chivalry—he is portraying the virtues and vices of his own society, eulogizing Elizabeth and many of her courtiers, yet reproaching many of his contemporaries for degenerating from the example set by their ancestors, proposing the past both as a model for imitation and as an argument for contemporary praise or blame.

Spenser is primarily depicting through concrete and sensuous images an abstract world of moral universals—a transcendental order that is nevertheless immanent in his own society and in the societies of the past, manifested no less in poetic fable than in ancient and modern history—and perhaps (as both Aristotle and Sidney had maintained) more clearly. He is imitating the ideal forms of the virtues and vices; and, though in portraying them he has his eye fixed

The Recovery of Antiquity

on actual historical examples as well as on his own mythical fictions and the inventions of other poets, there is no inherent inconsistency in this union of the mythical, the historical, and the ideal. The concrete particulars—historical and mythical exempla alike—participate in, and are subsumed under, the general idea. Precisely because it *is* a universal, it can comprehend individuals belonging to widely different ages and traditions—Biblical and classical, medieval and Renaissance—and the poet may without inconsistency turn to all of these sources for materials to flesh out the abstract idea. He is depicting an archetypal realm, though in a Platonic rather than a Jungian sense; a mythical world, though as Renaissance mythographers, rather than twentieth-century anthropologists, conceive this term. Like the dream time of Australian aborigines, Spenser's chivalric age lies in a mythical past that exists outside of time and can only be recapitulated symbolically and through ritual participation in the present. Yet its timelessness is of a different order, deriving directly from Platonic (and to some extent Aristotelian) theories of universals; and its ritual participation is solidly based on the "participation" (in the technical idiom of Platonic doctrine) of the sensuous and concrete particulars of his fable in the general idea. The sensuously realized *historia* functions as a point of comparison for interpreting and validating (or invalidating) contemporary society, but also as a means of entry into the transcendental realm of exemplary virtues and paradigms.

6.

The classicism of the Renaissance has usually been overstressed. It represents, after all, only one facet—albeit a highly important one—of a complex and sometimes contradictory culture. Aside from numerous evidences of the actual continuity of medieval and Renaissance tradition, there are significant examples of conscious "medievalism" on the part of Renaissance writers and artists. In early "mannerist" painters, recent critics have detected a deliberate retrospection, an attempt to circumvent the High Renaissance achievement and return to an earlier and less classical style, seeking inspiration from earlier Renaissance painters or from northern artists who had not entirely outgrown the older tradition. The macaronic element in writers like Rabelais and Burton and the scholastic wit of some of the "Metaphysical" poets may be consciously ironic, undercutting the very traditions they are echoing; nevertheless, such tongue-in-cheek pedantry for comic or satiric ends is itself a medieval tradition. The romance tradition, in turn, not only derives much of its material and its stylistic conventions from medieval sources, but sometimes affects a deliberate medievalism, partly to foster the illusion of antiquity and a sense of the continuity of the genre, but partly through genuine delight in the manner and matter of the old tales. The antiquarian interests of the Renaissance are not restricted to classical antiquity.

Imitating ancient models meant, on the whole, following their example rather than literally copying them. Though a writer or artist might occasionally demonstrate his virtuosity by composing a play or carving a statue so meticulously classical in style as to deceive his contemporaries, these were *tours de force;* in the greater part of his work the same poet or sculptor would be more interested in displaying his originality and impressing on his style and subject the stamp of his own *ingenio* than in mimicking the style of another artist, however ancient.[19] The ancients themselves had encouraged the formation of a personal style through studying a variety of authors, and poets and painters alike were advised to follow the example of the painter who had selected the best features of several different models to form the image of a perfect beauty. For many Renaissance writers, classical literature provided "models" and even "rules" for imitation, but these were essentially guides to composition, not stereotypes. The ancients were constitutional monarchs, not tyrants, and their rules and models left ample scope for originality in invention and freedom in disposition and style.

Unlike an earlier generation of critics, we must not overestimate either the fidelity or the extent of Renaissance classicism. Later ages achieved a clearer understanding, a closer imitation, of antiquity; yet we value them less—and rightly so. The Madeleine in Paris is surely more classical than San Lorenzo or Saint Peter's, and it is patently inferior to both. The same Pisan sculptors who consciously imitate classical drapery (and hence appear to foreshadow the "Renaissance") are also responsible for introducing French Gothic sculp-

The Recovery of Antiquity

ture into Italy (and thus seem to perpetuate a "medieval" style). The emphasis on perspective—so characteristic of Renaissance painting—is primarily a legacy from medieval optics, with very little influence from classical art. For all its classicism, the Temple of St. Francis, which Alberti designed for Sigismundo Malatesta, is structurally very unlike the temples of antiquity. The façade is, in effect, a Roman triumphal arch superimposed on a Christian chapel. In art and literature alike, Renaissance classicism is sometimes functional; more often it is little more than ornament.

When we compare Renaissance classicism with that of earlier renascences, we note several striking differences. Unlike its predecessors it is predominantly secular rather than clerical. It is broader, for it embraces virtually the whole cycle of arts and sciences. It is more thorough both in its understanding of antiquity and its recovery of classical texts. It approximates more nearly the spirit and outlook of the ancients. It makes a far greater—and more enduring—impact on the vernacular languages and literatures.

Nevertheless, however profound its influence on all the arts, classicism is not the only key to the period. It does not provide a satisfactory formula for the early Renaissance painters in France and the Low Countries, the sculptors of Germany, or indeed for the Italian and Spanish primitives. Nor, for that matter, does it comprehend several of the most important facets of the Italian Renaissance. In its progress through northern and western Europe the Renaissance carried with it not only the humanists' enthusiasm for classical literature, but also many elements that were specifically Italian. In France, in Italy, in Spain a predilection for Italian culture often went hand in hand with the veneration of antiquity. If Athens was the "school of Hellas" and the university of Rome, Florence was the academy of Italy—and ultimately of all western Europe.[20]

The Renaissance was, in fact, primarily an Italian achievement. Though northern and western Europe made their own distinctive contributions, they derived much of their literary inspiration and scholarship from the south. The period was essentially an interlude of Italian cultural dominance, preceded and followed by the cultural hegemony of France.

One result was a time lag in the diffusion of Renaissance civilization. When it finally flowered in England, it was overripe in Italy; it had already begun to go to seed on its native soil. This, in turn, led to a singular anachronism in the English Renaissance. Chaucer at the end of the fourteenth century and the Tudor poets in the sixteenth were linked by a common debt to Petrarch and Boccaccio as well as to French tradition; one of his lyrics reappears in Tottel's *Miscellany*, apparently mistaken for a contemporary work. Influences from the early and late Renaissance often reached Britain simultaneously, sometimes directly from Italy, sometimes indirectly through France and Spain. Quattrocento, cinquecento, seicento authors contended for place, side by side with the Pléiade. In their zeal for Continental modes, English poets frequently donned old and new fashions together—Italian doublet, Spanish "slops," Dutch cuffs, with perhaps a French ruff thrown in for good measure. But the costume fitted, and the poets themselves were usually indifferent to the inconsistency.

For, in fact, the cultural lag operated to their advantage. It allowed them to draw on virtually the whole Renaissance tradition, combining elements from the best Continental authors regardless of period and country. It enabled them—even in the sixteenth century—to retain the freshness of the early Renaissance.

Another result was the popularity of styles that were essentially Italian rather than classical—in art and music, in behavior and dress, in calligraphy and poetry. Italian *novelle* achieved wide popularity, and—either in their original form or in English or French translation—furnished plots for English drama. Italian comedies found translators or imitators. The Senecan tradition in Italian tragedy produced echoes in France and England. Italian lyrical genres—the sonnet, the madrigal, and even the anti-Petrarchan burlesque—resounded in English halls. English poets often took their themes and imagery directly from Italian sonneteers or indirectly through French imitators. The ghost of Machiavelli stalked the English stage, or sat—an embarrassing presence—at councils of state. English courtiers and writers read and deplored Aretino. Spenser imitated Ariosto and Tasso. Harington and Fairfax translated them. Italian merchants and princes became stock figures of English comedy and tragedy. Italian dramatic innovations—such as pastoral drama and tragicom-

The Recovery of Antiquity

edy—became fashionable on the English stage. Italian verse forms—the canzone, the hendecasyllabic madrigal, *terza rima, ottava rima*, blank verse—penetrated English poetry. The triumph of Italy seemed complete even at the very moment when Englishmen were most vigorously denouncing the *inglese italianato* as an incarnate devil.

Yet, like classicism, the Italian influence is only one of many strands that make up the complex fabric of the English Renaissance. The thrill of discovery that made the classical world—the "realms of gold"—as exciting as the new El Dorados beyond the seas also affects the Englishman's attitude toward his near neighbors and towards his own national past. If the Italian achievement seems new and exciting to him, so does that of Spain and Portugal, Germany and the Low Countries, France and Switzerland. He is alive to the contemporary movements in these countries—artistic, literary, or spiritual. He reflects this interest in the scope and breadth of his translations. In England, as on the Continent, the Renaissance is truly international.

Yet all the same, our Renaissance Englishman is intensely self-conscious about his own past, both historical and legendary. He reads and assimilates Arthurian romance and the satire of Langland, writes histories and chronicles, adapts them to the stage and to narrative verse. He reveres Chaucer ("well of English undefyled," and "pure well-head of Poesie"; *FQ* 4.2.32.8 and 7.7.9.3-4) and through diction and metrics alike he relates his own poetry to the Chaucerian tradition. The Prologist in Shakespeare's *Pericles* is a medieval Englishman, John Gower.

The classics remain the most significant factor in the Renaissance, but scarcely less important is the interplay between the various vernacular traditions. The Renaissance in northern and western Europe is a volatile and sometimes explosive compound—an unstable fusion of classical, Italian, and indigenous traditions.

7.

The Renaissance goal of imitating the ancients was in many ways a foredoomed failure. How could one reproduce the *essentials* of antique art without reviving antiquity itself? How could one accurately imitate the classics without restoring the society, the civilization, the political and religious milieu that had produced them? How could men of the period reconcile the conflicts between Graeco-Roman values and their own? Not only must they reckon with profound social and spiritual differences, they must also attack such problems as a different subject matter, the requirements of the vernacular, the tastes of patron and audience—all formidable obstacles to the reimposition of classical form. And how should they resolve the differences among the ancients themselves, the internal contradictions of a classical tradition that had extended well over ten centuries and embraced the whole Mediterranean world? Like the Renaissance itself, classical antiquity had been an age marked by controversy and contradiction. Like the Renaissance, it had derived its dynamism largely from inherent and even irreconcilable tensions. Could it ever be reduced to the stasis of an archetype, the inflexible rigor of an abstract norm?

More than a few Renaissance classicists thought that it could, and acted on this assumption. As a result they were constantly compelled to shift, to compromise, to mediate between authors long dead, to reopen controversies abandoned centuries ago. In this sense the Renaissance was a glorious anachronism.

Antiquity resisted the attempt to force it into so rigid a mold. Classical civilization was far too complex for that, and classical authorities far too divided. Nonetheless, with indefatigable energy, the Renaissance set about the formidable task of bringing unity out of diversity, of finding a common frame of reference for Plato and Aristotle, Virgil and Homer, Seneca and Euripides. Iconographers synthesized the emblematic traditions of Greece and Egypt, Judea and Rome. Neo-Platonists extracted a perennial philosophy out of a theosophical salmagundi—an *olla podrida* of doctrines Hermetic, Platonic, Pythagorean, Orphic, cabalistic, Brahmanic, and Gymnosophical. Historians strove to reconcile classical chronology with Biblical, Chaldean historiography with Egyptian. Poets and critics wrestled with the discrepancies between classical practice and theory.

By idealizing antiquity, these men of the Renaissance usually over-

The Recovery of Antiquity

simplified it. By treating it as a norm, they frequently reduced the complexity of a dead civilization to the radical unity of an abstract idea, transforming the historical realities of the classical world into a Platonic archetype. The principles that underlay the classical achievement seemed to many of them permanently valid, significant not for an age but for all time, and as binding for the fifteenth century as for antiquity itself.

This tendency, though hardly universal in the Renaissance, was nevertheless widespread enough to distort the vision of the past. Blinded by the universal, the classicist sometimes stumbled over particulars. Elevating antiquity to an ideal, he could never quite come to grips with its diversity.

Moreover, besides the inherent contradictions of antiquity, Renaissance syncretism faced a more fundamental challenge. It must adapt classical ideals to the conventions of a very different age and altogether different countries. If it could not transplant the classical tradition, root and branch, on alien soil, it must at least attempt to graft it on the native stock.

"Captive Greece," declaimed Horace, "took her fierce victor captive and brought the arts into rustic Latium."[21] Renaissance Europe experienced a similar conquest. Nymphs abandoned their ancestral streams to colonize the Tagus and the Seine, the Thames and the Severn, the Cam and the Mulla. The Muses, like Cato, learned alien tongues in their old age. The dethroned gods of Hellas sought sanctuary in court, cathedral, and classroom. Yet they were seldom at ease there. Perhaps (as Milton put it) the age was too late, the climate too dank. Perhaps they were reluctant to sing the songs of Parnassus in a strange land. Or perhaps they found their new roles uncongenial. Could Jove himself restore justice to the court of the Renaissance despot? Should Mars willingly discard the javelin to load a musket or prime a cannon? Would chaste Diana relish her own part in the masquerade—as the aging Virgin Queen of England or the mistress of the King of France?

Yet even though the Renaissance poet or artist was seldom consistently faithful to antiquity, rarely exact in imitating classical models, his failure was a happy one. Antiquity gave him standards of excellence as well as of form and style—and in his own way he met them. At times he even surpassed his models. The happy interaction of two worlds—"one dead," the other not altogether "powerless to be born"—the fruitful dialogue between classical ideals and contemporary tastes, resulted in a new creation neither antique nor medieval. Indebted to both, the Renaissance was essentially of neither. It was *sui generis*.

Paradoxically, its success was partially rooted in its failure. We value the age for its own achievements, not for its approximation to antiquity. However zealously many of its literary theorists cherished the ideal of imitation, it was essentially a creative rather than an imitative age.

The Renaissance movement, in a sense, restored the classical tradition. But it was also compelled at every turn to innovate, to alter tradition. Its dynamism sprang in part from a crisis in authority. By accepting the classics as standards, it undertook a double burden—first, the onus of resolving the conflicts in the classical tradition itself; secondly, the problem of accommodating the classical legacy to other traditions and other authorities, both spiritual and secular. This task of reconciliation severely taxed the Renaissance capacity for synthesis.

In this context it is much easier to understand the complex interaction of classicism with Reformation and Counter-Reformation; Reuchlin's attempt to reconcile Pythagoras and the Cabala with the New Testament; and Ficino's search for a common ground for Platonism and Christian theology. Some thinkers deftly evaded the crisis through the doctrine of the "double truth." Others, like Agrippa, sought to cut the Gordian knot by banishing the secular arts and sciences as vanities and leaving room only for faith. The same crisis of authority underlay the problems that confronted poets and critics. These faced the task of adapting classical form to national or Biblical subject matter and reconciling the ethics of modern Europe with the poetics of ancient Greece.

The Renaissance crisis of authority and its intrinsic contradictions were never effectively resolved. If they have ceased to exist today, it is because history has bypassed them or because they have taken a radically different form. To enter the humanist's world, one had to accept his law and creed, the permanent validity of classical au-

The Recovery of Antiquity

thority. But one could not help doubting it. One could not remain long in the humanist's culture without questioning its basic postulates, without challenging both the jurisdiction and the accuracy of the ancients.

For, in fact, the very veneration of antiquity eventually brought its authority under question. A close examination of classical texts revealed not only the inconsistencies of their authors, but also their inaccuracies in the light of observed fact. If the Renaissance begins on a note of enthusiasm for the revival of classical learning, it draws to an end with a more critical estimate of the ancients. "Away with antiquities," exclaims Bacon, "and citations or testimonies of authors[!]"[22] The "outstanding characteristic of [Leonardo's] genius," declares one critic, "lies in his categorical rejection of all 'principles of authority,' and in his assertion of the exclusive value of experiment."[23] For Milton, the doctrines of Greek philosophy are "false, or little else but dreams, / Conjectures, fancies, built on nothing firm." The Greek poets fare scarcely better: "Remove their swelling Epithetes thick laid / As varnish on a Harlots cheek, the rest, / Thin sown with aught of profit or delight, / Will far be found unworthy to compare / With *Sion's* songs...."[24]

Idols should be left on pedestals and preferably in dim light. When they are dismounted and subjected to scrutiny, one discovers the feet of clay.

On the whole, the Renaissance was neither slavish in its imitation of classical models nor consistent in its reliance on classical authorities. For the most part, it revered the ancients without subservience and, indeed, with a certain independence. It obeyed them at times—strictly or loosely—and when it chose it disregarded them. This is true not merely of literature, but also of other disciplines. Sarton divides the Renaissance scientists into two groups—"the imitative and the non-imitative or creative," scholars who revived and expounded the scientific doctrines of antiquity and men of less erudition but greater originality.[25] Despite the dominance of philology, there was an increasing tendency to supplement classical texts on anatomy and botany with fresh information. There were notable advances in mathematics and astronomy, and classical geography was revolutionized by the new discoveries of the voyagers.

The Lamb and the Elephant

A similar tension between innovation and tradition characterized the architecture of the period. As Geoffrey Scott observes, this "is more imitative than any style of building that preceded it." It is, in a sense, a "transcript of classical style." Yet imitation did not preclude originality. However "eagerly" Renaissance architects "welcomed..., quoted, illustrated, [and] praised" the "Rules" of Vitruvius, "they felt themselves at total liberty to disregard [them]."[26]

8.

In painting and sculpture, the Renaissance achieved the same compound of tradition and innovation, imitation and originality. As Wölfflin points out, the fifteenth and sixteenth centuries both desired to be "antique," but "each understood the antique in a different way.... With unerring feeling artists picked from [their] admired models [the "antique figures"] only those things which they themselves understood, that is, those things which they had already mastered for themselves; and we may even say that the repertory of antique sculpture... not only had no effect on the course of the stylistic development of modern art, but that it did not even lead to any premature developments."[27]

The same pattern held true in literature. Writers venerated the poetic doctrines and models left by Greece and Rome, but they usually showed considerable freedom and variety in following them. And it was just this interplay of convention and innovation, this tension between imitation and originality, that gave Renaissance literature its distinctive character and value. Most authors paid lip service to classical ideals, but each understood them and adapted them in his own way. Each worked out his own compromise between the classical archetype and the demands of his audience, his subject matter, his language, and his own personal taste. The result was an art frequently stamped with intense individuality.

The Recovery of Antiquity

NOTES

[1] Erwin Panofsky, *Meaning in the Visual Arts* (Garden City, N.Y., 1955), pp. 48-49.
[2] Ibid., p. 54.
[3] James Bruce Ross and Mary Martin McLaughlin, eds., *The Portable Renaissance Reader* (New York, 1958), p. 124.
[4] Charles G. Osgood, *Boccaccio on Poetry* (Indianapolis and New York, 1956), p. xliii.
[5] Cf. *Areopagitica*, in John Milton, *Complete Poems and Major Prose*, ed. Merritt Y. Hughes (New York, 1957), pp. 741-842.
[6] Osgood, pp. 9-13.
[7] Ibid., p. 11.
[8] R. R. Bolgar, *The Classical Heritage and Its Beneficiaries* (New York, 1964), pp. 220-21.
[9] Panofsky, p. 47.
[10] Cf. Catherine Dunn, ed. *The Logike of Peter Ramus* (Northridge, Calif., 1969); and Wilbur Samuel Howell, *Logic and Rhetoric in England, 1500-1700* (Princeton, 1956), on Rudolph Agricola's conception of the relationship between logic and rhetoric and the influence of his *De Inventione* at Cambridge. Dunn, p. xvii, also notes the influence of Ramon Lull's thirteenth-century treatise, the *Ars Magna*, on the Continent during the early sixteenth century.
[11] Cf. Bernard Weinberg, "From Aristotle to Pseudo-Aristotle," in *Aristotle's Poetics and English Literature*, ed. Elder Olson (Chicago and London, 1965), pp. 192-200.
[12] Bolgar, pp. 220, 265, 269, 272, 297.
[13] Ibid., 265, 296, 301.
[14] See Vincent M. Bevilacqua, "*Ut Rhetoric Pictura:* Sir Joshua Reynolds' Rhetorical Conception of Art," *HLQ* 34 (1970), 59-78. For the influence of Italian humanism on Renaissance conceptions of the visual arts, and for the relationships between rhetoric and painting, see Michael Baxandall, *Giotto and the Orators: Humanist Observers of the Painting in Italy and the Discovery of Pictorial Composition, 1350-1450* (Oxford and New York, 1971) and the review by Charles Trinkaus in *Speculum* 48 (1973), 548-50.
[15] See Donald Leman Clark, *John Milton at St. Paul's School: A Study of Ancient Rhetoric in English Renaissance Education* (New York, 1948).
The humanists' defense of their program in education echoed the traditional arguments employed by apologists for poetry and oratory—the value of pleasure as a pedagogical stimulus; the efficacy of sense experience in acquiring a knowledge of abstract ideas, and concrete examples in illustrating universal concepts; the ethical, political, and religious utility of the *studia humaniora;* the peculiar persuasive and instructive force of a judicious combination of matter and style, *res et verba*. Milton's tractate *Of Education* (Hughes, pp. 630-39) remains faithful to the essentials of humanist educational theory, though he presents his plan as a new and still unimplemented reform and though he incorporates elements derived from seventeenth-century theorists. Although he shares the ideal of "the reforming of education" with Hartlib, Comenius, and Dury, the pattern he outlines is one that he professes to find in antiquity. His course of study is "likest to those ancient and famous schools of Pythagoras, Plato, Isocrates, Aristotle and such others, out of which were bred up such a number of renowned philosophers, orators, historians, poets, and princes."

The Lamb and the Elephant

..." Nevertheless, in at least one respect his school will surpass those of the ancients; instead of training youth for either the military or the academic life, Milton's "institution of breeding" will be "equally good for peace and war." The authors he prescribes are almost exclusively classical writers, with a sprinkling of modern commentators on the classics. Like many of the humanists, he stresses matter as well as eloquence, "solid things" as well as words, and he condemns his rivals on the grounds of both *res* and *verba* (In the schools and universities our youth waste time "either in learning mere words or such things chiefly as were better unlearned.") Milton proposes to begin with "arts most easy" and proceed gradually to more difficult studies; to progress from *sensibilia* to *intelligibilia* and from *visibilia* to *invisibilia;* to employ "proper eloquence" to lead his students "in willing obedience, inflamed with the study of learning and the admiration of virtue ..."; and to make the acquisition of linguistic skills both easy and delightful. He stresses the moral, patriotic, and religious ends of education; and (like many other humanist educators) he reiterates the topic of *honestas* (nobility). This is "the best and noblest way of education"; "a complete and generous education," "a virtuous and noble education"; and it is designed to produce "brave men and worthy patriots, dear to God and famous to all ages," men capable of performing "justly, skilfully, and magnanimously all the offices, both private and public, of peace and war."

[16] Cf. Weinberg in Olson, pp. 192-200.

[17] Ibid.; Ettore Mazzali in Cochrane, pp. 134-48, et al.

[18] Cf. Chrétien de Troyes, Cligès, in Jean Seznec, *The Survival of the Pagan Gods*, trans. Barbara F. Sessions (New York, 1961), pp. 18-19. Cf. also Loys le Roy on arms and arts; Hallett Smith, "Tamburlaine and the Renaissance," in *Elizabethan Studies and Other Essays in Honor of George F. Reynolds*, University of Colorado Studies Series B. Studies in the Humanities, vol. 2 (1945), 126-31.

[19] On Michelangelo's "forgery of a Sleeping Cupid, which was exhibited in Rome as a genuine antique" and on his "pseudo-antique statue" of Bacchus, see Edgar Wind, *Pagan Mysteries of the Renaissance*, rev. and enl. ed. (New York, 1968), pp. 177-82. Wind regards Michelangelo's "pseudo-antique sculpture" as "the exact parallel to certain literary performances which ... aimed at a similar deception," such as Bembo's Latin epigrams, and Alberti's comedy *Philodoxus* and "false Lucians."

[20] For Milton's praise of Italy as "the lodging-place of *humanitas* and of all the arts of civilization" and his admiration of Florence above all other cities "because of the elegance, not just of its tongue, but also of its wit," see *The Complete Prose Works of John Milton*, ed. Don M. Wolfe, vol. 4 (New Haven and London, 1966), pp. 609, 615; cf. George B. Parks, "The Decline and Fall of the English Renaissance Admiration of Italy," HLQ 31 (1968), 341.

[21] Horace, *Epistles*, II, l., ll 156-57, "Graecia capta ferum victorem cepit et artis intulit agresti Latio."

[22] See *Parasceve ad Historiam Naturalem et Experimentalem*, quoted in Virgil K. Whitaker, *Francis Bacon's Intellectual Milieu* (Los Angeles, 1962), p. 2.

[23] G. C. Argan in René Huyghe, *Larousse Encyclopedia of Renaissance and Baroque Art* (New York, 1964), pp. 118 ff.

[24] *Paradise Regained*, IV, 291-350.

[25] See George Sarton, *Appreciation of Ancient and Medieval Science During the Renaissance* (New York, 1961), pp. 168-69; and Sarton's essay in Wallace K. Ferguson et al., *The Renaissance: Six Essays* (New York, 1962), pp. 55 ff.

[26] Geoffrey Scott, *The Architecture of Humanism*, 2d ed. (New York, n.d.), pp. 141 ff.

[27] Heinrich Wölfflin, *Classic Art* (Greenwich, 1961), pp. 246-47.

Chapter III
CLASSICAL TRADITION
AND RENAISSANCE EPIC

>>>>>>:<<<<<<

IN LITERATURE, as in painting and architecture, the imitation of classical models was merely one of several interrelated factors in the transformation of the arts. In antiquity itself, close study and imitation of the masters of earlier periods had been a standard pedagogical device—a means of supplementing precept by example, and doctrine by practice—and they retained this office more or less intact in Renaissance literary and artistic education. The problem of reviving and reforming the arts in conformity with classical precedent and example usually presented a dual aspect, both cognitive and practical. Though the study of antiquity might be an end in itself, it was usually conceived rather as a means to the end of practice. Knowledge about antiquity stimulated and facilitated the emulation of antiquity. The reclamation of the wisdom of the ancients—the recovery of lost texts, the emendation of corrupt texts, the reinterpretation of ambiguous texts—was designed to further the progress of contemporary arts and sciences by basing them more firmly on the principles discovered by the ancients and the examples left by the ancients.

Insofar as the precepts and examples of classical writers could serve as guides to correct speech, and the imitation of classical works as guides to the correct imitation of nature and ideas, they were means to the end of effective eloquence. Their end was practice; and in practice Renaissance writers often treated them with considerable license. Even when the modern consciously set out to imitate a classical model, he was apt to encounter technical difficulties imposed by linguistic and prosodic conventions, the tastes and expectations of his audience, the character of national literary traditions, and the requirements of structural organization, ethical decorum, and subject matter. Some of these difficulties are apparent in the Neo-Latin literature of the period (that international fashion which came nearest to reclothing the Muses in archaic dress) and in the burgeoning vernacular traditions of Western Europe.

1.

The Neo-Latin poet was spared many of the problems that vexed the modern tongues. Writing in a language that had long ago reached its perfection, a language fixed forever in the literature of the Augustan age, he was under no compulsion to fashion his own idiom. He inherited a standard; he did not need to create one. He could borrow images and entire phrases from ancient models with comparative ease, imitating the vocabulary and syntax of classical poets and following the classical rules for quantitative verse. There was a distinct advantage in imitating the ancients in their own tongue, in the hard and polished idiom of marble.[1]

But there were also undeniable disadvantages. Though the Latin tongue might enable a poet to reach an international audience of learned men, it would make his work largely unintelligible to many of his countrymen. Neo-Latin dramas could reach only a specialized audience; Neo-Latin lyrics would be unintelligible to many of the gentlewomen to whom they were addressed; and Neo-Latin epics celebrating the greatness of the national past would be accessible to only a fraction of the nation.

More significantly, the Neo-Latin poet could rarely hope to rival his ancient models in excellence. Despite his exceptional proficiency in Latin metrics, Milton was keenly aware of this limitation, and it undoubtedly influenced his choice of the English language as the medium of his major narrative and dramatic poetry. On the whole, in spite of the high prestige and indubitable merit of Neo-Latin verse, it was frequently overshadowed, both in quality and in quantity, by the vernacular literature. This, in its own right, might amply justify the metaphor of rebirth.

Nevertheless, for many a Renaissance poet, the choice of the vernacular entailed peculiar difficulties. As a living language, it was subject to further development or decay. Already some of his predecessors had become unintelligible; further changes could render his own work archaic and perhaps obsolete. The limited resources of the native vocabulary, variations in regional dialects, and different levels of speech and style also challenged him. He must, perforce, create his own language and poetic diction. In Italy, Dante's *De Vulgari Eloquentia* had attempted to refine the written language and to establish an "illustrious vernacular" (as he terms it)—"vulgare illustre, cardinale, aulicum, et curiale"—as a standard. His successors debated the rival claims of Tuscan and other dialects as the proper medium for verse or prose. In France, Du Bellay's *Défense et illustration de la langue française* proposed that the French language imitate more perfect tongues, such as Greek, Latin, and Italian; in their extensive borrowings from these languages the Pléiade followed this principle.[2] On the other hand, Malherbe displayed equal zeal for the vernacular, but maintained a diametrically opposite attitude toward the problem of improving it; reacting against the Pléiade, he endeavored to purge the French tongue of foreign accretions. British authors self-consciously plundered alien tongues to "enrich" their own, while the purists among their fellow-countrymen strove to rid the language of foreign, pedantic, and "inkhorn" terms. Spenser cultivated a deliberate archaism by drawing much of his vocabulary from Chaucer's "well of English undefyled." Milton embellished his verses with idioms taken from Greek and Hebrew, Latin and Italian, as well as from earlier English poets—Chaucer, Spenser, Shakespeare, Sylvester, Jonson, Fairfax, and others. In thus refashioning their native languages as a poetic medium, authors achieved a variety in diction and style and a marked individuality that few Neo-Latin poets could attain. Regarding their own languages as imperfect instruments that still required enrichment and purification, they produced a literary language that might vary significantly among different writers and in different genres—a linguistic vehicle that was sometimes a highly personal and individualized creation.

Differences between classical and vernacular syntax further heightened the difficulties that confronted the poet who desired to approximate the *stilo antico* in the vernacular tongues. Though these problems might seem negligible in the case of modest genres like the eclogue, they became more formidable in ambitious forms like the epic, where the poet deliberately sought a more complicated style, more dignified and formalized and more remote from common speech. Theoretically the heroic poet should maintain an elevated and magnificent style appropriate to the dignity of his subject matter and capable of arousing marvel and admiration; and in the opinion of several Renaissance critics, one means of achieving such a style was to distort the normal word order of conversational prose, departing as far as possible from familiar usage in syntax as well as in vocabulary. The success of this technique in classical literature, however, had depended largely on the nature of Greek and Latin grammar. In these tongues the variety of inflectional forms had permitted extensive variation in word order without obscuring the sense. In the vernacular tongues, where the older inflectional endings were breaking down, an inverted word order meant a sacrifice of clarity. Nevertheless, both Tasso and Milton exploited this device in their epics on the hexaemeral tradition, *Il Mondo Creato* and *Paradise Lost*.

Similarly, the nature of the vernacular tongues severely hampered the attempt to revive classical prosody. Quantitative meter was a near impossibility. Though various poets or theorists favored it—Tolomei in Italy, Baïf and Taille in France, Drant and Webbe, Campion and the "Areopagus" in England—their efforts were, for the most part, egregious failures.[3] Instead of grafting classical metrics on the modern languages, vernacular poets were forced to look for substitutes—syllabic verse in Italy and France, accented verse in England. Milton's versification represents a more complex achievement; his epics reflect the influence of the syllabic pattern common in Italy as well as the stressed meters of the native English tradition.

2.

The choice of the vernacular raised a further problem largely extrinsic to Latin poetry. Should the modern poet imitate the unrhymed verse of the ancients or the rhyming stanzas of his native tradition? Though hotly debated in Italy and subsequently in England and France, this issue was never resolved. The Italian defenders of blank verse praised its flexibility. It was admirably suited (they argued) to "the continuation of the thoughts from one verse into another" and to the "concatenation of senses and constructions." They defended it positively by appealing to the example set by clas-

Tradition and Renaissance Epic

sical poets, negatively by condemning rhyme as a barbaric legacy from the "dark ages." Milton's stated views often echo the opinions of his Italian predecessors. Dismissing rhyme as "the Invention of a barbarous Age, to set off wretched matter and lame Metre," arguing that "the learned Ancients" had avoided the "jingling sound of like endings" as "a fault . . . both in Poetry and all good Oratory," he emphasizes the same quality that earlier critics had perceived in blank verse—"the sense variously drawn out from one Verse into another."[4]

In Italy and England, blank verse soon established itself in drama, but never managed to dominate the other genres. Poets like Alamanni and Rucellai employed it for short didactic poems modeled partly on Virgil's *Georgics* or on Horace's *Ars Poetica*. Several English and Italian poets—Surrey, Liburnio, Caro, Hippolito de Medici—utilized it as the most appropriate medium for translations of the *Aeneid*. Nevertheless, with a few notable exceptions—Trissino's *Italia Liberata*, Tasso's *Il Mondo Creato*, Milton's *Paradise Lost* and *Paradise Regained*—blank verse made little headway in the epic. The principal vehicle for the heroic poem remained the hendecasyllabic *ottava rima* stanzas (rhyming *ababab cc*) popularized by Boccaccio and by numerous other writers of romantic epic—Boiardo and Berni, Ariosto and Pulci, and both Bernardo and Torquato Tasso. In England, narrative poets likewise tended to neglect blank verse in favor of forms analogous in length and structure to the *ottava rima*. Even though Chaucer's rhyme royal (a seven-line stanza rhyming *ababbcc*) and the eight-line stanza of The Monk's Tale and "An ABC" *(ababbcbc)* may have been derived from French *ballade* stanzas rather than from the Italian *ottava rima*—and subsequently have served as models for the development of the Spenserian stanza[5]—the use that Chaucer and Spenser and their successors made of these stanzaic forms in their narrative poetry bears a closer resemblance to the function of the *ottava rima* stanza in Italian romance-epic than to the French *ballade*. The length of these stanzaic units facilitated the use of various devices of amplification and encouraged a leisurely and easy development of the narrative. Since the level of style was traditionally associated with the length of its periods and their components—cola, semicola, commas, etc.—the use of long and well-rounded forms like these stanzaic blocks of seven, eight, or nine stanzas could be regarded as appropriate to the elevated style of heroic poetry. At the same time, their close resemblance to lyrical stanzaic forms made them appropriate vehicles for amorous complaints and occasional songs, the arguments of courtship, and descriptions of the changing moods and sentiments of lovers and the varieties of romantic landscape.

Vernacular heroic poets faced the further necessity of finding adequate substitutes for the classical hexameter. In Italy, Trissino had favored the hendecasyllabic line as the best modern equivalent for the heroic verse of antiquity. The hendecasyllable had been Dante's medium in the *terza rima* verses of the *Commedia*, and the *ottava rima* stanzas of Boccaccio and his successors had established the eleven-syllable line as the standard in heroic poetry. In England the nearest equivalent was the five-foot line (generally decasyllabic or hendecasyllabic, but with varying stresses and frequent departures from an iambic pentameter pattern), utilized by Chaucer and by most epic and dramatic poets. French poetry, on the other hand, often retained the hexameter, but altered its metrical pattern, utilizing a dodecasyllabic line; and, unlike many Italian and English dramatists, French dramatic and epic poets usually preferred the rhyming couplet as a medium instead of blank verse or *ottava rima*. Even though Du Bellay favored the use of blank verse in imitation of the ancients, it never became as prominent in France as in Italy and England.

Thus in diction, syntax, and versification alike, the vernacular poet was forced to modify classical practice. Unable to imitate the ancients in every respect, he must adapt their precedent and their precepts to the demands of his own language and seek a viable modern equivalent. Paradoxically, his very loyalty to the classical models and the classical tradition compelled him to innovate.

3.

Turning from problems of language and verse to those of form and structure, one finds a similar interplay between classical and native traditions. The most persistent of the genres—lyric and satire,

Tradition and Renaissance Epic

epic and romance—were hardy perennials that had continued to flourish during the medieval winter. The late Middle Ages had developed a new theatrical tradition, which had restored the drama to the stage after a long period of dissociation, in which the real nature of dramatic imitation had become obscured. The task that faced Renaissance poets and critics was not to create a native poetic tradition *ex nihilo*, but to reshape the existing genres in a classical mold, to reform them after the rule and pattern of antiquity.

Thus in theory, and often in practice, the Renaissance revived the laws of the classical genres and reimposed them on contemporary poetry. Aristotle's *Poetics* and Horace's *Ars Poetica* acquired a quasi-legislative authority, and the attempt to explain and reconcile them produced a formidable body of commentaries—chiefly in Italy, but also in France, the Low Countries, and England. Poetics, like logic, was an authoritive discipline, with definitive rules and principles. It was (in Milton's words) "that sublime art which in Aristotle's *Poetics*, in Horace, and the Italian commentaries of Castelvetro, Tasso, Mazzoni, and others, teaches what the laws are of a true epic poem, what of a dramatic, what of a lyric, what decorum is (which is the grand master-piece to observe)."[6]

This exaggerated stress on theory is symptomatic of the intellectualism that characterized other arts of the period—painting, architecture, sculpture. The rationalism of the age is reflected not only in countless treatises on poetics, but also in conscious efforts to conform to classical precept and precedent. In attempting to restore the ancient genres, poets imitated the odes of Horace, the lyrics of the elegiac poets, the tragedies of Seneca and the Greeks, the comedies of Plautus and Terence, the epics of Homer and Virgil. But they often wrote with one eye on their models, the other on the theorists. At times they strove to be more "correct" than their exemplars, more classical than the classics themselves. The same despotism of theory appeared in the literary controversies that racked the age. Almost every major poem provoked critical assaults and apologies. Pellegrino and Tasso condemned Boiardo and Ariosto for disregarding unity of action. The Accademia della Crusca subjected Tasso's *Gerusalemme Liberata* to attack. Guarini's pastoral tragicomedy *Il Pastor Fido* was condemned by Denores and his fellows as a spurious genre.

The Lamb and the Elephant

Critics accused Dante of violating Aristotle's rules and confusing the literary species—or defended him on the same grounds. Speroni's tragedy *Canace* aroused the hostility of Giraldi and his followers. The classics themselves were not immune to attack, and even Homer came under fire for violating the principles of decorum.

The chief targets of the theorists were violation of the unities and indecorum in character and style. The multiple plots and loose structure of romantic epic and popular drama contradicted the laws of composition. The mixture of comic and tragic elements in the same poem confused the genres. Baseness or vice in heroic characters flouted decorum. When Sidney condemned the contemporary drama for bringing the same person from youth to old age in a single hour, he was basing his argument on the unity of time. When Tasso and other critics attacked the romances for portraying many exploits of many heroes, they were upholding the unity of action. When Milton censured the Greek poets for celebrating "the vices of thir Deities and thir own," he founded his charge on literary as well as moral grounds; their poems were "ill-imitated" and thus violated the essentials of poetic art.[7] When he condemned "ignorant and libidinous poetasters" who have "scarce ever heard of that which is the main consistence of a true poem, the choice of such persons as they ought to introduce, and what is moral and decent to each one," he appealed to the principle of decorum.[8]

Nevertheless, there was a marked discrepancy between theory and practice. The currents of the Renaissance were too powerful to be hemmed within the narrow channels of classical precept. Though poets rarely challenged the authority of the ancients, they ignored it when convenient and rationalized their innovations when necessary. Giraldi Cinzio and Pigna defended the romance as a new genre to which Aristotle's rules did not apply. Guarini justified his tragicomedy by appealing to Plautus and the Greek tragedians. Iberian critics defended the irregularities of the national stage on the grounds of popular taste or "new conditions." If "the Spanish drama adjusted itself to the rules and laws of the ancients," declares one apologist, "it would proceed against the requirements of nature.... The great Lope [de Vega] has done things over and above the laws of the ancients, but never against these laws."[9] With the virtually unique exception of Ben Jonson, the English theater produced its greatest works in partial indifference to the "rules." Some of the most influential Renaissance epics were irregular by classical standards, and even the heroic poems of Milton and Camoëns and Tasso failed to satisfy the criteria of many neoclassical readers. Bembo might urge Ariosto to write a true epic instead of a romance,[10] and Harvey might similarly warn Spenser against imitating Ariosto. Nevertheless, both of these poems achieved a popularity—and a high literary excellence—that the epics of Trissino and Alamanni, for all their painstaking fidelity to the model of the *Iliad*, never achieved. Despite its bias toward rigidity and formalism, Renaissance theory was too divided, too complex, too diverse to command unqualified allegiance, and Renaissance practice was even less consistent. Both were ambiguous enough to leave ample scope for originality. Even an archclassicist like Milton could be undecided on the essential principles of structure—"whether the rules of Aristotle [for the epic] are strictly to be kept, or nature to be followed, which in them that know art, and use judgment, is no transgression, but an enriching of art...."[11]

4.

However complicated the issues of language and form might become, the problem of subject matter was equally perplexed. Should the heroic or tragic poet seek his material among the fancies of his own imagination, from the fables and legends of other writers, or from history? If he chose a historical subject, in turn, should he treat secular or sacred themes, ancient or recent events? These issues were hotly debated by Renaissance critics, and in practice as well as in theory poets themselves varied significantly on these points.

Most critics agreed on the purpose of the epic. Its function was to imitate heroic virtue and praise heroic deeds. But what sort of heroic virtue, what kind of deeds? Should the poet portray pagan or Christian heroism, physical or spiritual victories? What type of person should he choose as his hero, his ideal "pattern"? What kind of character should he glorify?

The striking diversity that the Renaissance displayed in answering such questions reflects the conflicting pressures of the age. The

The Lamb and the Elephant

example of the ancients—classical or Biblical—seemed to dictate either a national or a religious theme. Homer had celebrated the triumphs of Greece, Virgil those of the founder of Rome. Hence, by analogy, the modern poet ought to glorify the achievements of his own countrymen. Spenser celebrated the legendary hero of Britain —Prince Arthur—and England's patron saint, St. George. Camoëns described the exploits of Vasco da Gama and his companions—Portuguese heroes who surpassed the achievements of the Argonauts. Milton planned a heroic poem on Arthur or some other "king or knight" before the Norman conquest. Trissino narrated the liberation of Italy from the Goths. Ronsard began a *Franciade* to glorify his country's past.

Nevertheless, an influential minority preferred Biblical themes. Vida's *Christiad* and Sannazaro's epic on the virgin birth were not only widely read, but encouraged the development of a tradition of the divine epic on the Continent and in England. Du Bartas' *Divine Weeks and Works* was one of the most popular poems of its day, and his brief epic on Judith was frequently translated. Moreover, the Scriptures not only contained potential subjects for heroic poetry, but provided a model epic that had been inspired by the Holy Ghost. The Book of Job was a heroic poem that emphasized spiritual rather than physical warfare and celebrated the "better fortitude of patience" rather than force. This "divine poem" profoundly influenced Milton's conceptions of heroic virtue and of moral temptation as heroic ordeal.

Popular or aristocratic fashions in romance sometimes governed choice of subject. The Este family at Ferrara enjoyed romances of chivalry, and their court poets catered to this taste. The epics of this circle usually dealt with conventional romantic themes and heroes. Boiardo and Ariosto described the feats of Roland (Orlando). The elder Tasso related the exploits of Amadis of Gaul, while his son devoted a short epic to the Carolingian hero, Rinaldo. In his *Gerusalemme Liberata* Torquato Tasso sought to combine the formal unity of classical epic with the charm and variety of the romance, and he introduced the Carolingian romantic hero, Rinaldo, anachronistically into the historical setting of the First Crusade. Alamanni attempted a similar fusion of romantic content and classical form,

Tradition and Renaissance Epic

basing his *Giron il Cortese* on a French romance, and choosing an Arthurian theme for his *Avarchide*. In the latter work, so meticulously modeled on the *Iliad*, Lancelot usurped the place of Achilles, Arthur assumed the role of Agamemnon, and Vivian played a double role—as the Lady of the Lake, but also as a stand-in for Thetis.

The subject matter of Renaissance epic mirrored the tensions and contradictions of the age. To the classic argument of wars ("tristia bella"), poets added the conventional themes of the romance—love, enchantment, and the chivalric quest. Epics on Biblical heroes and heroines—Judith and Esther, David and Joseph—rivaled the traditional poems on secular worthies. In several instances Renaissance historical figures—Fernandez Gonzalo, Henry IV of France, Prince Maurice of Nassau—replaced legendary champions and rulers of antiquity and the Middle Ages as epic persons, just as canonized saints—Ignatius, Francis of Assisi, Louis of France—substituted occasionally for ancient pagans and Carolingian knights. Even within the same poem mythology and Christian angelology might coexist in uneasy tension, just as the same hero or heroine might combine classical and Renaissance, pagan and Christian ideals of virtue or valor in a new but highly unstable compound.

Ancient legend and myth furnished the argument for many Italian epics.[12] G. B. Giraldi Cinzio celebrated the exploits of Hercules, Basinio Basini the adventures of the Argonauts and of Meleager, and Giambattista Marino the love of Venus and Adonis. Maffeo Vegio not only composed a thirteenth book to Virgil's *Aeneid*, completing the story with the marriage of Aeneas and Lavinia, but also wrote epics on Astyanax and on the Golden Fleece. Francesco Bolognetti emulated Virgil by writing a second *Aeneide* himself. In addition to a poem on Ulysses, Lodovico Dolce produced two narrative works in *ottava rima*—*L'Achille* and *L'Enea*—by interweaving ("tessendo") the stories of Homer's *Iliad* and Virgil's *Aeneid*. Scipione Herrico also turned to the story of Troy for inspiration, developing Achilles as a romantic hero like Orlando in an epic entitled *Iliade ovvero l' Achille innamorato*.

Other heroic poems were devoted to classical history rather than myth. Girolamo Graziani wrote on Cleopatra. Francesco Bolognetti composed an epic *(Il Constante)* on the attempt of a Roman patri-

The Lamb and the Elephant

cian to free the emperor Valerian from captivity. Several heroic poets celebrated the exploits of the elder or the younger Scipio. Petrarch's Latin epic, the *Africa*, and Bernardino Berti's *Scipione Africano* were devoted to the conflict between Rome and Carthage; and, according to Antonio Belloni, other poems on this subject were composed by Francesco Baitello (the author of a *Scipiade*) and Luigi Joele (the poet of *Cartagine soggiogata*).

Other epic poets derived their subjects from late classical, medieval, or modern history. Ercilla based his *Araucana* on a military campaign in which he himself had participated. Other writers attempted to bridge the gap between the purely religious argument and the secular themes of love and war by describing battles between the faithful and the infidel, or between the orthodox believer and the heretic. Constantine, Clovis, and other Christian rulers became epic heroes. Francesco Bracciolini's *Croce racquistata* and Gabriele Zinani's *Eracleide* dealt with the struggles of the Byzantine emperor Heraclius against Persia. In Giangiorgio Trissino's *Italia Liberata da i Goti* and Gabriello Chiabrera's *Italia Liberata overo delle Guerre de' Goti*, the Gothic enemy were partisans of the Arian heresy. Another epic by Bracciolini, *La Bulgheria convertita*, celebrated the conversion of the Bulgars. Nevertheless, in the majority of heroic poems of this type the principal antagonist was Islam. In the romance-epics of Boiardo and Tasso the immediate context was Charlemagne's struggles with the Moors and their allies. A later work, Graziani's *Conquest of Granada*, (1650), celebrated the final defeat of the Moors in Spain. Other poems—Tasso's *Jerusalem Delivered*, Pietro Angelio da Barga's *Sirias* ("expeditio . . . Christianorum principum, qua Hierosolyma ductu Goffredi Bulionis . . . à Turcarum tyrannide liberata est"), and Giovanni Leone Semproni's *Boemondo overo Antiochia Difesa* concerned the Crusades. Margharita Sarrocchi's *La Scanderbeide* described the Albanian hero's warfare with the Turks. The decisive naval victory by Don John of Austria over the Turks inspired a flood of heroic verses on the Battle of Lepanto: Francesco Bolognetti's *Christiana vittoria*, Caraffa's *Austria*, and two poems entitled *Vittoria navale* by Benamati and Tronsarelli. Anton Francesco Oliviero's *Alamanna* concerned Charles V's warfare against Lutheranism and the Schmalkaldic League of Protestant princes. Religious warfare was likewise a dominant motif in Lope de Vega's *La Dragontea*—a poem directed against Sir Francis Drake —and in Spenser's *Faerie Queene*. The same *odium theologicum* reappeared in Milton's miniature epic on the Gunpowder Plot.

Yet, in that age of poetic zealotry and literary bigotry, it is refreshing to encounter one heroic poem specifically devoted to the exploits of the Grand Turk, Mahomet II. Giovan Mario Filelfo's *Amiride* demonstrates that the Renaissance was capable, in a few rare instances at least, of transcending its national and sectarian loyalties and honoring valor and *virtù* even in an enemy.

Giulio Malmignati's *L'Enrico, ovvero Francia conquistata* celebrates the wars of Henry IV. Cantalicio's *Gonsalvia* describes the Neapolitan victories of Fernandez Gonzalo and the expulsion of the Aragonese dynasty from that city. A spate of heroic poems on the new world followed the voyages of Columbus and his successors: Giovanni Giorgini's *Il Mondo nuovo*, Tommaso Stigliani's poem of the same name, and Lorenzo Gambara's *De navigatione Christophori Columbi*.

The expediency of flattering a patron also conditioned the choice of epic subject. More heroic in fiction than in fact, Renaissance princes took their places as epic heroes, alongside Theseus and Hercules, Ulysses and Godfrey. Francesco Sforza of Milan inspired the *Sforziades* of Francesco Filelfo and Antonio Cornazzano. Porcellio's *Feltria* extolled the deeds of Federico da Montefeltro, duke of Urbino. The same poet also reaped the rewards of flattery from Alfonso I of Aragon for a poem on the latter's victorious entry into Naples. The wars of Sigismundo Malatesta of Rimini provide the argument for Basinio Basini's *Hesperis*. In this work the poet exploited the resources of mythology to eulogize the condottiere's mistress; etherealized into the daughter of Zephyr, she becomes the virtuous nymph Psyche. Giovan Mario Filelfo's *Cosmiade* and *Lorenziade* extol the Medici family. Mantuan's *Trophaeum Gonzagae* celebrates Francesco Gonzaga's victory over the French. At Ferrara, more famous poets—Boiardo, Ariosto, Tasso—describe imaginary exploits by alleged or legendary ancestors of their patron. Alamanni praises the equally legendary progenitors of the dukes of Berry. Spenser's allegory shamelessly flatters a whole gallery of

The Lamb and the Elephant

Elizabethan notables—the Queen herself, the earl of Leicester, Lord Grey, Sir Walter Raleigh, and many others.

5.

In literature as in other arts, the Renaissance transformed aesthetic tastes and revolutionized structure and style. By returning to classical principles it reshaped—recreated—European literature.

Yet the result, paradoxically, was not uniformity but variety. Each poet had to work out his own compromise between classical and native traditions. Each had to make his own innovations. Taken as a whole, Renaissance literature—in subject, style, and form—exhibits a richness and variety unsurpassed by its classical models or its mediaeval precursors.

Only in a very limited sense did the Renaissance approximate antiquity. But the attempt to do so stimulated a rivalry between ancients and moderns that eventually dethroned antiquity. His very allegiance to Parnassus and Helicon paradoxically inspired the Christian poet to "soar above th' *Aonian* Mount." Similarly, the veneration of classical authority eventually led the scientist and philosopher to seek knowledge beyond the classical texts, to establish the quest for truth on firmer grounds than authority or tradition.

From the vantage point of the twentieth century, we have, perhaps, a clearer view of the Renaissance achievement than the age itself could attain. No longer constrained by the "rules" of Aristotle, no longer confined by the example of Virgil or Horace, Cicero or Seneca, we can evaluate Renaissance civilization on very different grounds—by standards that the age itself might not have accepted. We can respect it for qualities that many of its own critics usually overlooked. We can esteem it primarily not for its fidelity to classical tradition, but for its innovations, its variations, its originality.

In the very failure of these poets and artists lies their outstanding success. If they often fell short of the classical principles and models they revered, they nevertheless left their own mark. In fact, they have become our own classics.

In one sense, the Renaissance is with us still. Its movements have never completely lost their momentum. Its styles have outlived the period that evolved them. They still survive in our own age, yet sometimes in a very different form. Like Proteus, they are adept at transforming themselves.

Nevertheless, this influence is, for the most part, indirect. Despite our debt to the Renaissance, we have in many respects outgrown it. What can a modern chemist learn from Paracelsus or Dr. John Dee? Renaissance science retains its value only for the historian. And what of the arts? In our approach to the classics we are infinitely farther removed from the world of the cinquecento humanists than were our parents; in educational techniques, still farther. "The advantages of a classical education are twofold—," declared an eighteenth-century scholar; "it enables us to look down with contempt on those who have not shared its advantages, and also fits us for places of emolument not only in this world, but in that which is to come."[13] Such a boast might still have been valid two generations ago, but it is no longer pertinent today. Even though the humanist tradition still survives in classical scholarship, it hardly survives elsewhere; and the classical disciplines themselves are fighting for life.

In the sciences we no longer look to the ancients for guidance. In the arts we have evolved new styles of our own, styles that seem better adapted to our current needs and interests. The Renaissance modes that satisfied our grandparents have grown obsolescent with the old Beaux Arts tradition in Europe and the "Genteel Tradition" in this country. A half-accomplished revolution in taste has displaced them.

It would be shortsighted to lament this change and futile to contend against historical drift. We live in the age of Saarinen, not Bramante; of Picasso, not Leonardo. Contemporary civilization has struggled to emancipate itself from the Renaissance, just as Renaissance society strove to free itself from the Middle Ages. Neither has altogether succeeded, but in both cases the attempt has produced a fresh outlook, a reformation of styles, a "transmutation of values." But mutability entails penalties as well as rewards. In both instances an older synthesis, another system of values, has been lost.

The chief value of the Renaissance for our century is, perhaps, neither its style nor its doctrine, but its humanity. In a culture that has become so specialized that our arts and sciences no longer speak the same language, we need the wider outlook of the Renaissance *uomo universale*, the unitive vision of Renaissance art, the Renaissance legacy of proportion and perspective. In a pragmatic society dizzied by its pursuit of progress, we need, perhaps, a glimpse of more permanent values—that stable, unchanging realm of ideas which so haunted the Renaissance Platonist. In a civilization depersonalized by its own technology, we need the humanistic orientation of Renaissance literature with its cardinal emphasis on man.

Our age has, indeed, gone far towards realizing the ideal of Bacon and his near-contemporaries—the "exantlation of truth," that Thomas Browne hailed so eagerly, the mastery of nature that also excited Descartes. Yet the New Atlantis has proved very unlike the Utopia its prophet predicted. Twentieth-century man has made formidable strides toward mastering external nature. But he has not yet succeeded (to echo a very characteristic Renaissance cliché) in mastering himself. Yet for the Renaissance, as for antiquity, this was the golden maxim. "*Gnothi seauton. Nosce teipsum.*"

Every generation borrows from the past what it needs, what it finds most significant for its own sensibility. Ours is no exception. We no longer need precisely what Shelley and Byron, Goethe and Schiller took from the Renaissance, what David and Delacroix found there, or what it once meant to Winckelmann and Pater, to Browning and Symonds, or to Reynolds and Blake and Wren. Neither Renaissance civilization nor the classical culture it sought to imitate can serve as standard and model for us today. Neither retains the authority to impose laws of thought or style. These belong to the past; they are obsolete. But the achievement itself is not obsolete, has not lost its relevance or validity. In scope, in power, in magnitude, in variety, it seems unsurpassed by anything before or since. It still possesses the magnetic power to draw us—if only vicariously and at a great distance—into the Renaissance experience.

The age of the giants is over, but their work remains. If we see farther than they, it is because we have built on their foundations, because we stand on their shoulders.

Tradition and Renaissance Epic

NOTES

[1] See Douglas Bush, ed., *A Variorum Commentary on the Poems of John Milton* (New York, 1970), I, 8-9 on the attempts of the neo-Latin poets "not only to imitate the ancients in subject matter, attitude, and manner, but to adapt ancient idiom to modern subjects, to write about their own world as an ancient—or a Christianized ancient—might have written."

[2] For the influence of Sperone Speroni's *Dialogo delle lingue* on du Bellay's (and Ronsard's) *Deffense et Illustration de la langue francoyse*, see A. J. Krailsheimer, *The Continental Renaissance, 1500-1600* (Harmondsworth, 1971), pp. 23, 45, 41. For Bembo's attempt to transpose "the principle of imitation from the Classical languages to Italian," his choice of Petrarch as "the unique model for verse composition" in his own vernacular poetry, and his attack in *De Imitatione* on "the eclecticism practised by earlier humanists," see Krailsheimer, pp. 31, 141-49. For Speroni's (and Bembo's) "solution of a vernacular humanism capable of raising modern literature to the level of Greek and Latin perfection by the careful imitation of antiquity based on the recognition of the peculiar needs of each language and age," Scaliger's views on imitation of the "second nature" of art, Herrera's praise of Garcilaso's verse as a stylistic norm for Spanish as a literary language and his conception of poetic composition as a "matter of artifice and contriving," see Krailsheimer, pp. 35-37, 43. For the "vernacular humanism" of sixteenth-century Italy, Spain, and France, which "replaced the predominantly Classical interests of Italian humanism in the preceding age," see Krailsheimer, p. 107.

[3] For discussion of the quantitative verse of the English Renaissance, see Hallett Smith, *Elizabethan Poetry: A Study in Conventions, Means, and Expression* (Ann Arbor, 1968), pp. 270-72; William Nelson, *The Poetry of Edmund Spenser: A Study* (New York and London, 1965), p. 19. For the role of Daniel Rogers as a mediator between the Pléiade and the "Areopagus"—"that much-disputed literary group which was active in London in the late 1570s and which involved such names as Edmund Spenser, Sir Philip Sidney, Gabriel Harvey, Edward Dyer, Fulke Greville, and . . . any number of literary lights in various combinations"—see James E. Phillips, "Daniel Rogers: A Neo-Latin Link Between the Pléiade and Sidney's 'Areopagus' " in *Neo-Latin Poetry of the Sixteenth and Seventeenth Centuries* (Los Angeles, 1965), pp. 5-28. Apropos of the "Areopagus," Tucker Brooke, in *A Literary History of England*, ed. Albert C. Baugh (New York, 1948), pp. 436-37, maintains that "groups of young scholars, including Spenser, Sidney, and Dyer in London and the Harvey brothers at Cambridge, were seriously concerned to follow up a hint of Ascham's and work out a new English prosody on classical quantitative lines." For the distinction between "prosody" and "versification" and for a critique of recent scholarship on Milton's English verse, see Edward R. Weismiller, "Studies in Verse Form in the Minor English Poems," in *A Variorum Commentary on the Poems of John Milton*, vol. II, ed. A. S. P. Woodhouse and Douglas Bush (New York, 1972), pp. 1007-87; and idem, "The 'Dry' and 'Rugged' Verse," in *The Lyric and Dramatic Milton, Selected Papers from the English Institute*, ed. Joseph H. Summers (New York and London, 1965), pp. 115-52.

[4] See my "Verse Without Rime: Sixteenth-Century Italian Defences of *Versi Sciolti*," *Italica* 41 (1964), 384-402.

[5] Cf. Tauno F. Mustanoja, "Chaucer's Prosody," in *Companion to Chaucer Studies*, ed. Beryl Rowland (Toronto, New York, and London, 1968), pp. 74-75.

The Lamb and the Elephant

[6] Cf. Ida Langdon, *Milton's Theory of Poetry and Fine Art* (New Haven, 1924), p. 225.

[7] *Paradise Regained*, IV, 340.

[8] James Holly Hanford, *A Milton Handbook*, 4th ed. (New York, 1947), p. 375.

[9] J. E. Spingarn, *A History of Literary Criticism in the Renaissance*, 2nd ed. (New York, 1954), pp. 232 ff., quoting Alfonso Sanchez.

[10] Ibid., p. 117.

[11] Hanford, *Milton Handbook*, p. 373.

[12] This discussion of Renaissance epic themes is based largely on Antonio Belloni, *Storia dei generi letterari italiani: il poema epico e mitologico* (Milan, n.d.). See also R. A. Sayce, *The French Biblical Epic in the Seventeenth Century* (Oxford, 1955); Watson Kirkconnell, *The Celestial Cycle* (Toronto, 1952); Barbara Kiefer Lewalski, *Milton's Brief Epic: The Genre, Meaning, and Art of* Paradise Regained (Providence and London, 1966); Leicester Bradner, *Musae Anglicanae: A History of Anglo-Latin Poetry, 1500-1925* (New York and London, 1940); Burton O. Kurth, *Milton and Christian Heroism: Biblical Epic Themes and Forms in Seventeenth-Century England*, Univ. of California Publications, English Studies, vol. 2 (Berkeley and Los Angeles, 1959); C. M. Bowra, *From Virgil to Milton* (London, 1948); Davis P. Harding, *The Club of Hercules: Studies in the Classical Background of* Paradise Lost, Illinois Studies in Language and Literature, vol. 50 (Urbana, 1962).

[13] M. L. Clarke, *Greek Studies in England* (Cambridge, 1945), pp. 13-14.

Chapter IV
THE GARMENT OF DOCTRINE: IMITATION AND ALLEGORY

GENERALIZATIONS ABOUT medieval or Renaissance poetics are at best only partially true, and general statements about imitation and allegory are no exception. All the same, one is justified in recognizing a partial shift in emphasis in late Renaissance theory from allegoresis to mimesis as the essential method of poetry and its principal *differentia* from rhetoric.[1] This shift in emphasis reflects the influence of Aristotle's *Poetics* during the latter part of the sixteenth and during the seventeenth centuries. Nevertheless, this development represented, on the whole, an alteration rather than a radical breach in the continuity of medieval and Renaissance tradition. Medieval poetics had inherited a theory of verisimilitude and probability through Horace's *Ars Poetica* and a theory of imaginative "presentation" through classical and medieval doctrines of the role of the imagination in sense perception and in dream-visions.[2] Conversely, the older traditions concerning the allegorical method of poetry and the pristine philosophy concealed beneath the poetic fictions of the ancients persisted well into the seventeenth century, along with a taste for the symbolic modes of enigmas and emblems and hieroglyphs, the occult correspondences of Hermetic philosophy, the allegorical trappings of romance and masque, and the typological and prophetic symbolism of the Scriptures. Cesare Ripa's *Iconologia*, which appeared in the last decade of the sixteenth century and was frequently reprinted thereafter, remained an influential manual for artists and poets throughout the eighteenth century. The ideals of imitation and allegory coexisted, without apparent conflict, in Tasso's "Allegoria" to his *Jerusalem Delivered*. A later generation of neoclassical critics sometimes objected to an extensive use of allegory as incompatible with "realistic" imitation, but these were men of the Enlightenment, not of the Renaissance.

The Lamb and the Elephant

1.

Theoretically and historically, for medieval and Renaissance writers alike, allegory could both conceal and reveal.[3] Disguising historical persons and events under convenient fictions, masking the principles of natural and moral philosophy or the doctrines of metaphysics and theology under the veil of fabulous inventions, it could also serve (like its counterpart, mystical theology) as an instrument of revelation. By investing abstract concepts and separated substances with sensuous form, it made them more readily accessible to the human imagination, simultaneously instructing the understanding and moving the will. For Boccaccio, the essential difference between poetry and rhetoric resided in the poet's allegorical method. Horace's dictum that poets ought either to instruct or to delight had, moreover, become fused with allegorical theories derived both from classical antiquity and from Biblical hermeneutics. The notion that poetry should delight through its fictions and instruct through its allegorical meaning was a commonplace, if not an axiom, of both medieval and Renaissance criticism. This conception of the allegorical nature of poetry and its value as an instrument of instruction served as a principal argument for the defense of the *ars poetica* against attacks by champions of rival disciplines and (more specifically) against ethical and theological censure.

It also conditioned the exegetical techniques applied to the interpretation of classical and medieval or Renaissance authors. In the study of these later writers—as in the interpretation of the poetry of Homer and Virgil and Ovid, the understanding of gentile mythology and iconography, and the exegesis of scripture—allegorical techniques of interpretation served a variety of ends: to enrich the doctrinal content of the text, to moralize apparent improprieties, to emphasize the interconnection between image and idea, cortex and kernel, or (in modern terminology) "vehicle" and "tenor." These techniques inevitably affected the actual practice of poets themselves, though precisely how far or in what degree remains uncertain. Though the majority of medieval and Renaissance poets may have possessed at least a superficial awareness of allegorical methods of interpretation, they did not all write allegories, nor did they in-

Imitation and Allegory

variably maintain the allegorical element consistently even within the same poem. They could on occasion introduce extended historical or discursive or fictional passages into the midst of a formal allegory, or conversely insert allegorical episodes into the midst of a non-allegorical poem on a historical subject. As Rosemond Tuve has wisely warned us, we should not expect a continuous allegory even in an allegorical poem, or look for a hidden significance in every episode of its narrative or every detail of its descriptions.

In some instances, the poet's own allegorical interpretation appears to have been, in large part, superimposed on his poem *ex post facto*, as in the allegories of Tasso and Graziani. In the "Argument" to his *Heroic Frenzies* Bruno goes out of his way to disclaim this kind of Parthian shot. He insists that his erotic imagery is a divine allegory, like that of the *Song of Songs*—even though his readers might believe that he had added the allegory afterwards:

Thus anyone could be easily persuaded that my primary and fundamental intention may have been to express an ordinary love, which may have dictated certain conceits to me, and afterwards, because it had been rejected, may have borrowed wings for itself and become heroic; for it is possible to convert any fable, romance, dream and prophetic enigma, and to employ it by virtue of metaphor and allegorical disguise in such a way as to signify all that pleases him who is skillful at tugging at the sense, and is thus adept at making everything of everything, to follow the word of the profound Anaxagoras.[4]

Instances of such retrospective allegorizing have been noted in Petrarch's writings.[5] Indeed, Petrarch himself, and Francis Bacon after him, were fully aware that the covert meanings that they had perceived in the fables of earlier writers might not have been originally intended by the poets themselves. In several cases (as in the poetry of Chapman or in Dante and other poets of the *dolce stil nuovo*) the allegorical element, though intrinsic and essential, reflected the language of a literary cult or coterie, intelligible to the few but largely inaccessible to the vulgar. In other works the veil of symbol was as thin as the "subtyl coverchef of Valence" worn by Chaucer's Venus. A sophisticated audience should have encountered little difficulty in following the allegory of the *Romance of*

73

the Rose or the occasional allegorical passages in Boiardo and Ariosto. Despite the complex meanings that exegetes like Fornari discovered in the *Orlando Furioso*, its subtlety derives largely from a different trope—*ironia* rather than *allegoria*.[6]

On the whole, the court poets of the late Middle Ages and the early Renaissance were compelled to accommodate their allegorical techniques to the capacities and skills of their audience, covering their intent but not very deeply—concealing their meanings like a child's Easter eggs in places where they might easily be discovered. The pleasure resided not merely in the fiction itself, but also in the treasure hunt for hidden significances.

2.

In attempting to read any medieval or Renaissance allegory whose meaning is not immediately apparent (perspicuous at first glance like the hero's encounter with variants of Fortuna and Circe in epic or romance, and like Milton's allegory of Sin and Death), or intelligible in the light of emblem books and mythographies and lexicons, the modern scholar may find the allegorical tradition as embarrassing as an albatross about his neck. He cannot discard it altogether, but it distinctly interferes with the performance of his routine duties. Its very range and variety sometimes make it an unreliable guide for the interpretation of a particular work. Usually a specific poem can best be understood in terms of its relationship to particular facets of the allegorical tradition rather than to the tradition as a whole. Similarly, though the scholar cannot afford to ignore medieval and Renaissance theories of allegory, these too may distort his interpretation.

For the majority of these authors, moreover, allegory was not a literary genre, but a mode of discourse. Essentially it was a rhetorical figure—a trope, like metaphor and metonymy and irony—expressing the poet's real intention through words or symbols that appeared on the surface to have a different significance. Its mode, like that of Dante's *Commedia*, was "transumptive" (i.e. metaphorical) and thus involved a deliberate substitution or transference of meaning. The allegorical mode could be applied to a wide variety of literary species—pastoral, epic, lyric, comedy, tragedy, epithalamion, satire—and its characteristics might vary widely in these different genres and even in poems belonging to the same literary kind. Personifications, like Reason and Dame Philosophy, were numerous in allegory; but strictly speaking, these were examples not of *allegoria*, but of another rhetorical figure, *prosopopoeia*.[7] The poet might also derive his images from puns, like Milton's play on the name of his fellow student Rivers in *Vacation Exercise*, or on the etymology of words, as reflected in the punishment of schismatics and hypocrites in Dante's *Commedia*. In practice the allegorical mode had outgrown the rhetorical figure *allegoria*, absorbing other rhetorical figures in the process. Although these retained their original identity, they had in fact become allegorical conventions. Similarly, allegorical fashions tended at times to transform the traditional literary kinds, producing pastorals that were primarily satires or complaints on the state of the clergy, romances that were predominantly psychomachias, and lyrics that were thinly disguised astronomical observations or alchemical hymns.

The allegorical tradition was further complicated by the interplay between classical and Biblical conventions. Poets frequently attempted to justify their art by comparing the allegories of the ancient Gentiles with the symbolic visions of Scripture and by emphasizing the analogy between poetry and mystical theology. The classical myths had been allegorized by the ancients themselves as well as by medieval and Renaissance expositors. These interpretations sometimes differed profoundly. Classical mythographers had distinguished several different Joves and Hercules. Etymologies of mythical names differed substantially. Even when following the conventional modes of interpretation—euhemeristic or historical, physical or scientific, and moral—there were numerous differences among classical authorities. Aside from these discrepancies in ancient mythography, allegorical interpretations of the pagan gods were further complicated by the infiltration of Oriental images and interpretations of the planetary deities during the late Middle Ages.[8]

The tradition of Scriptural allegoresis was equally complicated. The symbols themselves were ambiguous and polysemous; in different Scriptural contexts the same symbol might possess a variety of

The Lamb and the Elephant

diverse and even contradictory meanings. There were different opinions as to the number of senses in the Scriptures; though the fourfold classification (historical, allegorical, tropological, anagogical) was traditional, some commentators preferred a threefold or sevenfold division.[9] In the *Convivio* Dante felt compelled to distinguish between the allegorical sense according to poets and according to theologians; and scholars are still debating which kind of allegory he was actually following in his *Commedia*.[10]

3.

In the Renaissance the problems of the allegorist were in some respects complicated—in other respects simplified—by neoclassical literary ideals, by a more extensive and intensive knowledge of classical texts (including fresh mythographical and iconological materials) and by Reformation principles of Biblical exegesis.

Though medieval theologians generally recognized the importance of the literal or historical sense of Scripture as the foundation of the allegorical interpretations, they did not as a rule question the validity of these higher levels of meaning. Although certain Rabbinical scholars (such as Rashi, Rashbam, and Joseph Bekhor Shor) and Catholic commentators (like Andrew of St. Victor, Herbert of Bosham, and Nicholas of Lyra) emphasized the literal interpretation of the Biblical text,[11] the principal attacks on the allegorical senses came from the Reformers. Whereas Erasmus extolled the spiritual over the literal reading, Luther and the majority of his followers insisted on the literal sense alone, with due allowances for Scriptural metaphors, Old Testament typology, and the veiled imagery of the prophetic and apocalyptic books. This hermeneutical revolution tended to deprive the Protestant allegorist of the elaborate superstructure of allegorical senses elaborated by patristic commentators and disseminated through the *Glossa Ordinaria*. Nevertheless, it did not cut him off entirely from the medieval tradition. In varying degrees he could still derive his imagery from Biblical metaphors, from Old Testament types, and from the visions and prophecies of both testaments. Moreover, since vernacular translations of the Bible were now in the hands of the laity, he could apply Scriptural im-

Imitation and Allegory

agery to contemporary events (as medieval poets had also done) with reasonable expectations of being understood.

Like the allegorical senses of Scripture, liturgical symbolism had been radically curtailed by the Reformation. Outward and visible signs of inward, spiritual, and invisible graces had diminished with the sacraments. Evangelical plainness replaced the subtle language of ceremony and gesture and color. In the Church of England, the liturgy—the garment of devotion—remained, on the whole, as controversial an issue as ecclesiastical vestments. The uses that Anglican poets could make of liturgical imagery were conditioned, in part at least, by their High or Low Church sympathies. Like rhetoricians, ecclesiastics debated the question of appropriate style, the merits of naked simplicity or sensuous ornament. Critics of the liturgy combined Biblical images of the *meretrix* with traditional literary denunciations of the cosmetics of rhetoric and meretricious allurements of verbal adornment.[12]

With more intensive and extensive knowledge of classical literature and sculpture, the mythographical and iconographical traditions of the Middle Ages seemed increasingly obsolete. Though Boccaccio's *Genealogy of the Gods* remained influential, and Renaissance scholars continued to cite Fulgentius, Lactantius, St. Augustine, and other late classical writers known to the Middle Ages, the mythographical and iconographical traditions of the Renaissance were based, in large part, on materials unknown to their medieval predecessors—Greek literature and Roman statues and coins, the iconologies of Philostratus and Callistratus, the Homeric allegories of Stoics and neo-Platonists, mythological allusions in Apollonius' *Library* and the histories of Herodotus and Diodorus of Sicily, the Byzantine commentaries of Tzetzes and Eustathius, the lexicons of Suidas and Photius and Hesychius. The rich accretions of Greek materials, their conflicting testimony on the classical myths and their meaning, and the disagreement among Renaissance scholars themselves compounded the difficulties that the Renaissance poet must face in exploiting classical myth in his own allegories and communicating his covert meaning to his audience.

The Oriental elements that had appeared in the iconography of the gods during the late Middle Ages were, on the whole, replaced by classical conventions. Nevertheless, these too survived well into the Renaissance, apparently through the continuity of astrological and magical tradition. The decans reappear in the frescoes of the Palazzo Schifanoia in Ferrara, and Ficino's descriptions of the planetary gods bear a demonstrable resemblance to the talismans described in *Picatrix*.[13]

The mythological tradition that the Renaissance poet had inherited was already equivocal and polysemous. Its inherent ambiguity was increased by the conjectures of the mythographers themselves and by the attempts of different philosophers—Ficino, Pico della Mirandola, Bruno, Francis Bacon, and others—to reinterpret the classical gods and myths in the light of their own personal and (in some instances highly idiosyncratic) doctrines. The poets themselves were responsible for further inventions and interpretations, converting local rivers into divinities, composing fables or adapting legends to enhance their importance. Spenser described the wedding of the streams of Ireland. Milton adapted Geoffrey of Monmouth's legend to the purposes of the masque, introducing the river-goddess Sabrina (the Severn) as a means of resolving the complications of his masque-plot. Camões and Garcilaso praised the nymphs of the Tagus, French poets the nymphs of the Seine. The poet could also draw on local legends, false etymologies, or etiological myths connecting his fable with classical or Biblical antiquity. Behind Camöens' epic, *The Lusiads*, lies the tradition that Portugal had received its name Lusitania from Bacchus' companion Lusus, just as Lisbon (Ulyssipona) had been named for Odysseus. In Ronsard's incomplete epic, the Trojan Francus (Astyanax) is the founder of France.[14] Milton once hoped to celebrate the arrival of another Trojan, Brutus, on British shores. The legend of Gathelus and his wife Scota, eponymous ancestors of the Goidelic Celts and the Scots (and contemporaries of Moses as well), found its way into the Scottish histories of Hector Boece and Bellenden and into Holinshed's *Chronicles*. Spenser did not hesitate to invent or adapt the names of Queen Elizabeth's remote ancestors.

The Renaissance poet was also free to compose his own myths. Fracastoro's shepherd Syphilus bestowed his name on the disease.[15] Milton invented a liaison between Bacchus and Circe to provide an appropriate genealogy for Comus; and in *L'Allegro*, after giving the traditional parentage for Euphrosyne, he added an alternative genealogy of his own invention.

The Renaissance mythological tradition was neither fixed nor static; it was fluid, shifting, and changing. The variety of mythical and allegorical possibilities that confronted the poet permitted him to select precisely the details and significances that suited him best. The act of utilizing the mythological tradition was itself a mode of invention and an act of creation.

4.

Humanistic pedagogical methods and their aesthetic consequence —the growing importance of neoclassical literary ideals—also conditioned the techniques of the Renaissance allegorist. In attempting to teach a correct and eloquent Latinity, modeled on that of classical authors of the "best periods," humanistic educators had emphasized close study of the texts of the principal orators, historians, and poets, and close imitation of their styles. It was not enough for the student merely to master the vocabulary and grammar and rhetoric of the ancients; he must also learn to apply them in the ancient manner, after the fashion of the classical authors themselves. In treating classical themes, moreover, he must endeavor to preserve historical as well as literary decorum, portraying the ancients in terms of the mores and conventions of antiquity rather than those of the Middle Ages or the Renaissance. This literary emphasis on the *maniera antica* is analogous to the reintegration of classical style and classical subject that Panofsky has noted in the visual and plastic art of the Renaissance. It resulted, in large part, from greater historical and archaeological knowledge of antiquity, from humanistic imitation of classical style, and from neoclassical emphasis on probability and verisimilitude in poetic representation and on fidelity to the principles of the classical genres.

Nevertheless, it would be a mistake to exaggerate this influence, or to posit a sharp cleavage with medieval tradition. Medieval poets had on occasion imitated the classical genres: the epics of Virgil, Lucan, and Statius; Senecan tragedy; Terentian comedy; Virgilian pastoral. Various medieval "humanists," such as John of Salisbury, Richard de Bury, and Joseph of Exeter, had achieved a Latin style, in prose or poetry, that the Renaissance could regard as exceptional in a "barbaric" age.[16] Medieval treatises on poetics acknowledged the importance of verisimilitude and probability. Ovid continued to be widely imitated and frequently allegorized during the Renaissance. Two of the most popular Renaissance genres, the sonnet and the romance, were medieval forms, though later writers attempted to accommodate them to classical genres: the sonnet to the Horatian ode and the epigram; the romance to the epic or to the Alexandrian and Byzantine romances.

Sixteenth-century authors continued to imitate vernacular writers of the late Middle Ages or early Renaissance—Chaucer, Boccaccio, Petrarch, Dante; and the heroes of medieval epic and romance (Roland and Oliver and Charlemagne, Arthur and Lancelot and Gawain, Amadis of Gaul, the Cid) retained their popularity well into the sixteenth and seventeenth centuries. They owed their survival partly to courtly and popular taste, but sometimes to the conscious effort to emulate the example of classical poets. By drawing on national legends for his epic or romantic argument and enriching his style with archaisms derived from earlier vernacular poets, more than one Renaissance poet attempted to accomplish for his own nation what Homer and Virgil had achieved for Greece and Rome: celebrating the heroic and half-legendary past of his own nation or of medieval Christendom in a heroic poem; creating an artificial epic language through the conscious use of archaic words and formulas; observing decorum by relating chivalric legend or national history in an old-fashioned style reminiscent of chronicles and romances—an idiom deliberately intended to evoke the national past. Such conscious archaization could on occasion serve as a device for undercutting and ridiculing medieval and romance conventions, but it could also heighten decorum. If classical themes should be depicted according to the *maniera antica*, then *a fortiori* medieval themes might appropriately require a "Gothic" or romantic style and manner. Poets and artists were by no means consistent on this point, of course; and on the question of the appropriate decorum for treating Biblical or pagan, classical or medieval themes, Renaissance writers

Imitation and Allegory

varied widely in practice. Few achieved the harmony of Hebraic and Hellenic decorum apparent in Milton's *Samson Agonistes*.

The conventions of the medieval romance in Boiardo and Ariosto and the numerous Chaucerian echoes in Spenser heightened the sense of the past and reinforced the author's exaltation of medieval chivalry in comparison with modern times. Such medieval archaism in Renaissance poetry sometimes reflected a genuine awareness of the distance between classical antiquity and medieval antiquity, in addition to the gulf between both of these ages and modern times. Moreover, this conscious use of medieval conventions by Renaissance writers in order to evoke the sense of the past differed in function from the medieval transformation of classical gods and heroes and Biblical worthies into medieval knights and ladies: Joshua and Alexander into contemporary warriors, Venus and the Virgin into medieval queens. Both kinds of "medievalization" entailed the observance of decorum and verisimilitude, but their treatment of these principles was conditioned by different attitudes toward historical distance and discontinuity. In the former instance, the poet was emphasizing the sense of historical distance; his "medievalized" style was accommodated to his medieval subject, just as the "antique" style of his contemporaries had been adapted to their classical subject matter. In the other instance, however, the poet blurred the sense of historical distance, partly because he was insufficiently acquainted with classical antiquity or because he realized that his audience was largely unfamiliar with the ancient past. The ideal of historical decorum in poetry and painting alike had not yet been fully developed. Probability and verisimilitude consisted in making his representations plausible and convincing to his own contemporaries usually in contemporary terms, exploiting conventional notions of the attributes appropriate to different categories of rank and character without scrupulous regard for differences in historical and geographical milieu. The same general type might serve for Theseus and Arthur and Charlemagne. Verisimilitude would require fidelity rather to the general type than to historical differentiation; the image would seem convincing if it conformed to the conventional, albeit idealized, schema for a medieval prince or knight. Such schemas were, however, often strongly influenced by antiquity—through descriptions in Virgil and Ovid and Boethius and other classical or late classical writers, or through discussions of decorum, verisimilitude, and personal attributes inherited from ancient rhetoric and poetics.

The medieval poet might be conscious of the distances that separated him from pagan and Biblical antiquity, or from postclassical times and what we should term the earlier Middle Ages, but he did not as a rule differentiate their historical settings with clarity, precision, or consistency. He might allude to the past in order to enhance the authority of his own poetic argument, to justify the presence of the supernatural, or to censure the present age. (References to the past in Chaucer's Franklin's Tale, the Wife of Bath's Tale, and "The Former Age" serve such purposes.) Gothic and classical and Biblical antiquity tended at times to merge, like mountains in distant landscapes; and fantasy and historical reality to become as indistinguishable from one another as clouds and crags. As in the case of landscape paintings, such vagueness—in the decorum of time as in that of space—increased the sense of remote distances.

Nevertheless, we should not overstress the differences between medieval and Renaissance poets in their attitudes toward historical decorum. The latter tended, not infrequently, to convert classical and medieval worthies into Renaissance princes and courtiers, or to invest Biblical saints with the attributes of classical heroes and heroines. On the Renaissance stage, where conventions of costuming might involve overt historical inconsistencies, all of the *dramatis personae* in a Greek or Roman setting might appear in modern dress. In other instances, a few characters might assume clothing deliberately reminiscent of antiquity, while their fellow-actors continued to wear Renaissance garb. In the representation of ancient or medieval personages, literary decorum and verisimilitude might, in different circumstances, involve ignoring or emphasizing historical distance, alternatively stressing their points of resemblance or dissimilarity with the moderns. To make a Greek or Roman personage or a Biblical character seem "like the reality" might entail accommodating him to recognizable Renaissance moral and social categories; but it might alternatively entail emphasizing his differences from men of the sixteenth century. Although the moderns could hardly avoid

Imitation and Allegory

seeing the ancients as moderns writ large, projecting classical schemata on the present and Renaissance schemata on the remote past, their tendency to accommodate their images of antiquity to the expectations of their own contemporaries was usually just as much the product of conscious rhetorical or poetic artifice as the result of a limited historical perspective. Analogies between ancient and modern, like Plutarch's parallels between Greek and Roman worthies, might serve as deliberative or demonstrative arguments.

Like medieval romances, medieval allegorical conventions persisted well into the Renaissance, along with allegorical materials derived directly from classical sources. The humanists themselves defended poetry on allegorical grounds. Allegorized mythographies and iconographies; collections of hieroglyphics and emblems, often designed expressly for the use of poets and painters, sculptors and masque-designers, allegorical commentaries on Homer and Virgil, Ovid and Dante; allegorical exegeses of Ariosto and Tasso—these aids to symbolic interpretation and composition circulated widely. Mazzoni justified the apparent improbabilities and impossibilities of Dante's *Commedia* on the basis of its allegorical content; these apparent absurdities were credible as symbols of hidden truths.

Allegory remained, on the whole, as fashionable in the Renaissance as during the Middle Ages; and its appeal for the learned was enhanced by admiration for Plato's fables and smooth conceits, for the *prisca theologia* of Orpheus and Hermes Trismegistus, for the occult sapience concealed in Egyptian hieroglyphs, and for the book of nature as an emblem-book writ large, manifesting the invisible secrets of the spiritual world through visible but cryptic signs.

5.

Thus, despite the persistence of allegorical conventions and the substantial continuity of medieval and Renaissance literary traditions, humanistic pedagogy and neoclassical theory tended to alter and restrict the scope of the allegorist. The major classical authorities on the art of poetry had defended its ethical and social utility on non-allegorical grounds, and it was no longer necessary to justify poetry (as Boccaccio had done) by stressing its allegorical content.

The Lamb and the Elephant

Horace had emphasized the value of the poetic exemplar as a source of moral instruction. In Odysseus, Homer had provided a pattern of wisdom, thereby teaching the principles of moral philosophy more effectively than professional philosophers like Chrysippus and Crantor. For Aristotle, the ethical value of poetry consisted largely in its ability to purge the passions and to portray universal ideas. It could serve, therefore, as an instrument both of moral purification and of philosophical instruction. For both theorists, the moral utility of the poem depended, in large part, on its effectiveness as poetry—its fidelity to the principles of correct imitation and construction. Although medieval poetics and rhetoric had elaborated and systematized the principles of decorum inherited from classical antiquity—propriety and *convenientia* in genre and subject matter, character and style—the application of these principles during the Renaissance tended to become more rigid after closer examination and imitation of classical models and after the diffusion of Aristotle's *Poetics*. In epic and drama especially, decorum seemed to demand a reformation of late medieval or early Renaissance conventions of mixing light and serious matters, comic and tragic characters and incidents, and low and elevated imagery and diction. For many Renaissance critics, it became, as it did for Milton, "the grand masterpiece to observe."

Verisimilitude and probability in the incidents of the plot, in character, and in the thought or sentiments of the *dramatis personae* were scarcely less important, and in many instances they severely circumscribed the writer's opportunity for introducing the marvelous. The formal arrangement of the incidents of the plot—for Aristotle, the "soul" of the poem—became a major issue in theories of dramatic and epic construction. The poetic imitation must be convincing on the literal level, even though it might contain a deeper allegorical meaning. The supernatural element must be rationalized (as Tasso suggested) through the use of the "Christian marvelous" (the agency of angels and demons) or through the spells of sorcerers. In this way the fabulous metamorphoses of classical myth and the enchanted gardens of medieval romance could appear probable and plausible. In such *mirabilia*, moreover, the poet might find ample scope for introducing covert allegories, as in the enchanted gardens and palaces of Ariosto and Tasso and Spenser.[17]

Imitation and Allegory

Neoclassical theory not only rationalized poetic method, but tended to bypass allegorical problems by emphasizing alternative arguments for the moral utility of poetry, and to undercut the traditional allegorical methods by stressing probability and verisimilitude.[18] The eventual though incomplete triumph of neoclassical principles during the seventeenth century over the older medieval and Renaissance allegorical traditions probably resulted, however, not only from the authority and logic of the neo-Aristotelian critics themselves, but also from a combination of other factors: admiration of classical models, Cartesian rationalism on the Continent, and the linguistic reforms associated with the new science in England.

Nevertheless, the restrictive influence of neoclassical theory on poetic allegory was limited. Dante's allegory and Ariosto's romance, written before the development of Italian neo-Aristotelian theory, were alternately attacked and defended by late cinquecento critics; but the controversies that surrounded them were more significant for the development of theories of epic and romance than for the popularity and influence of either poet. Tasso's practice was not always consistent with his own theories; thus he introduced an allegory of Fortune into the *Jerusalem Delivered* without rational justification. Spenser may have profited from critical controversy over the plotting of epic and romance in attempting to link the separate books and actions of his romance-epic through the person of Prince Arthur and the final unwritten scene at Gloriana's court—thereby reconciling the romance's variety of heroes and actions with the structural and narrative unity that neo-Aristotelian criticism demanded of the epic plot. This did not appreciably affect his allegorical method, however; the rationale of his scenes and episodes and characters results primarily from their allegorical significance (whether moral or historical or physical) rather than from probability and verisimilitude in the neoclassical sense.

The allegory retained its popularity among Spenser's seventeenth-century imitators—Fletcher's physiological allegory of the human microcosm and the neo-Platonic allegory of Henry More. In *Il Penseroso* and in his early prose, Milton acknowledged his delight in allegorical romance:

The Lamb and the Elephant

> Of Tourneys and of Trophies hung,
> Of Forests, and inchantments drear,
> Where more is meant than meets the ear.

Masques and pageants also afforded the poet ample scope to exploit the allegorical resources of classical mythology. In *A Masque* Milton not only introduced a neo-Platonic *daimon* and the classical god of nocturnal revelry and feasting, but explicitly emphasized the allegorical truth concealed in the mythological fables of the ancient "Poets taught by th' heav'nly Muse...." The neoclassical epic usually offered fewer opportunities for allegory. In *Paradise Lost* Milton invested hell with mythical beasts, assigned Sin and Death to Hell-gate, peopled Chaos with the divinities of the Abyss, invented a Limbo of Vanities on the outer shell of the cosmos, and linked the world with Hell and Heaven by a stupendous causeway and a golden chain. Though he confined his allegories primarily to isolated episodes in his poem, he felt free to introduce them without any rational justification other than their symbolic meaning.

This apparent breach of verisimilitude seemed, in the eyes of a later generation of critics, to violate the principles of imitation; and some of them accorded it grudging admiration as a brilliant flaw or censured it as an absurdity. In his life of the poet, Dr. Johnson,[19] who had already objected to the "confusion of spirit and matter which pervades the whole narration of the war of heaven," found the allegory of Sin and Death "undoubtedly faulty." Allegorical persons have no "real existence," and "to give them any real employment, or ascribe to them any material agency, is to make them allegorical no longer, but to shock the mind by ascribing effects to nonentity." Even though Euripides had brought Death upon the stage, and Aeschylus introduced Violence and Struggle as active *dramatis personae*, no precedents could justify the absurdity of this allegory.

6.

Though neoclassical theory and taste restricted the role of the allegorist, they did not banish him altogether from Parnassus. There was still room for him on the lower slopes, in satires like *Absalom*

Imitation and Allegory

and *Achitophel,* in polemical works like *The Hind and the Panther,* or in mock-heroic poems like *The Dunciad.* Pope's burlesque method enabled him to exploit allegorical machinery (along with other epic conventions) simultaneously as an object and an instrument of ridicule, organizing his fable around the impressive figure of the goddess Dulness and the metaphor of the "uncreating Word"—a personification-allegory he would probably have ridiculed in a regular epic. Johnson accorded the allegorist the license of introducing personifications—though *allegory* had meant far more than *prosopopoeia* for the majority of medieval and Renaissance writers. Allegorical conventions persisted in neoclassical painting and sculpture; and if they were somewhat less prominent in literature, the reason is to be sought not only in literary theory but also in such ambiguous and indefinable factors as "taste" and "climate of opinion."

Though the direct influence of the new rationalism and empiricism—the fashionable "mechanical" and "experimental" philosophies and their linguistic reforms—may have been exaggerated, their indirect influence in shaping sophisticated taste may have been more lethal to the ideals of the allegorists. Despite the sidereal mysticism of Kepler and the apocalyptic mysticism of Newton, the alchemical or Hermetic occultism of Sir Kenelm Digby and Sir Thomas Browne, the new science was, on the whole, hostile to alchemical and astrological speculations and to the system of natural magic and cosmic correspondences on which they were based. The antiquity and authority of the Hermetic writings had been discredited. The Cartesian emphasis on clear and distinct ideas as an epistemological criterion left little scope for dark conceits as a source of truth. Psychological theory emphasized the unreliability of the imagination; and divines, the dangers of enthusiasm. Rational theology was safer than mystical theology, and less hazardous to the peace of church or state. Biblical scholars usually stressed the literal sense of Scripture rather than its allegorical content. Christian physicotheologians and apologists were, on the whole, more concerned with demonstrating the rational foundations of their creed than with elucidating its hidden mysteries. Christianity is "not mysterious," Toland argued, and John Smith stressed its "reasonableness." For many of their contemporaries it seemed far more important to reconcile the findings of modern science with the revealed truths of religion than to extract the doctrines of both from pagan allegories. The classical poets were at last so firmly established, on the basis of literary merit alone, that there was no longer any necessity for justifying their study on the grounds of allegorical content. Despite the prolonged controversy over the relative superiority of ancients and moderns, recent scientific discoveries and new advances in philosophy had clearly challenged the authority of the ancients; if the classical scientists and philosophers were no longer undisputed masters, there would be little point in turning to the classical poets for instruction in physics and metaphysics. Similarly, the spokesmen for a natural theology could find a firmer foundation for their doctrines in logical demonstration and mathematical physics than in the *prisca theologia* concealed in ancient myths.

With the decay of the allegorical approach to Scripture and of the symbolic interpretation of the book of nature, two of the traditional supports for poetic allegory were undermined. Poetry must be judged primarily in terms of its overt conformity to the laws of poetics and the principles of ethics rather than on the basis of its allegorical significance. When Pope "stoop'd to Truth, and moraliz'd his song" *(Epistle to Dr. Arbuthnot)*, he felt compelled to forsake the mazes of Fancy. For Boccaccio and for perhaps the greater part of Renaissance poets, on the other hand, the labyrinth of fable had been a direct path to truth—provided the poet and his reader held fast to the clue. The very essence of poetry was the sensuous representation of moral absolutes. Just as the task of the poet (the "maker" or *fictor*) was to veil morality in pleasing fictions, the task of the interpreter and the exegete was to moralize the inventions of the imagination.

7.

Though there is no inherent contradiction between critical insistence on verisimilitude and probability in imitation and an emphasis on hidden allegorical content—and though both of these principles occur in classical, medieval, and Renaissance theory—they frequently coexist in uneasy tension; and in the late Renaissance and during the eighteenth century this sometimes verges on

Imitation and Allegory

open conflict. Though later critics continue to emphasize the function of poetry and rhetoric in providing sensuous representations of moral universals, they often prefer the probable or "realistic" *exemplum* as a vehicle for this "ideal" representation rather than the marvelous but apparently incredible allegory. In contrast to the poetics of the late Middle Ages and early Renaissance, critical discussions of the essence and function of poetry shift from the allegorical to the mimetic—from the principle of *hiding* an ideal meaning in a symbolic and metaphorical vehicle that is overtly incredible, improbable, and unreasonable to the principle of *revealing* or illustrating the ideal meaning through an exemplary narrative or figure that is consistently credible, probable, rational, and "like the reality."

To a certain extent both of these principles coexist in the poetry of John Milton, and the shift in critical emphasis during the late Renaissance and the period of the Englightenment may be best illustrated by Samuel Johnson's strictures against the "allegory" of Sin and Death in *Paradise Lost*.

Johnson granted the poet a limited use of allegorical personifications, acknowledging their license to "exalt causes into agents, to invest abstract ideas with form, and animate them with activity." Nevertheless, "such airy beings are, for the most part, suffered only to do their natural office, and retire. Thus Fame tells a tale, and Victory hovers over a general, or perches on a standard; but Fame and Victory can do no more." Johnson could allow Milton (like Fletcher) to portray Sin as the portress of Hell, and he could permit her and her son to direct Satan back to the infernal regions on a subsequent occasion. Nevertheless he could not sanction their physical intervention in the "real" actions of the poem. When these personified abstractions temporarily stop Satan's journey and when Death offers him battle, "the allegory is broken." Similarly, in constructing the bridge over Chaos to assist Satan on his return, they again violate the principles of allegory, "because the difficulty of Satan's passage is described as real and sensible, and the bridge ought to be only figurative."[19]

The bridge between Hell and the fallen world is, of course, symbolic, like the golden chain connecting the newly created cosmos with Heaven. The infernal causeway and the celestial stairs are alike "mysteriously meant." The causeway is no less a metaphor than the Biblical allusions to the "way of death" (Jeremiah xxi.8) and the "broad way" leading to destruction (Matt. vii.13), which underlie Milton's allegorical fiction—the Scriptural foundations, so to speak, of his pontifical arch, the piers of his extended metaphor. The primary utility of this detail is not its role in the plot—facilitating Satan's return to Hell—but its allegorical significance.

The encounter at Hell-gate is similarly significant primarily on the allegorical plane. The dungeon where sin is punished by eternal death is appropriately guarded by personifications of Death and Sin. Not only is Satan's enterprise an act of sin, that will be punished by more stringent penalties and an intensification of the pains of spiritual death, but its ends and results are the sin and death of mankind. The alliance at Hell-gate prepares directly for the symbolic entrance of Sin and Death into the world after the fall of man and for their establishment as Satan's universal vicegerents (an echo of Pauline imagery) until their final destruction by Christ. Though Sin and Death intervene actively in Milton's narrative, as Johnson correctly perceived, neither figure is essential to the plot; and Milton's principal reason for elaborating these personifications and investing them with active roles is their thematic and ethical function rather than their narrative value or the ornamental "beauty" (Johnson's phrase) of the allegory.

By personifying sin and death, Milton gives concrete expression to the major concepts inherent in his poetic argument: man's transgression of the law and its fatal consequences. His theme is the act of sin that brought death and misery into the world, both by narrative imitation and through allegorical symbols, portraying Adam's trespass and the spiritual and physical corruption that follows its consummation through direct narration but giving them additional emphasis and focus through endowing these abstract concepts with shapes and personalities. Prosopopoeia complements, but does not conflict with, mimesis, and the tragedy of Adam's fall affects us more powerfully after our earlier vision of the foulness of evil. These personifications bring into focus the more general and dispersed descriptions of sin and spiritual death that Milton has already developed in the first two books of the epic and that he will develop fur-

Imitation and Allegory

ther through his narratives of the angelic war, the transgression of Adam, and the future history of the world.

The recognition scenes at Hell-gate and beside the newly erected bridge over Chaos are complementary episodes. Structurally, they occur at the beginning and end of Satan's enterprise immediately before his outward voyage and immediately before his return journey, just after his departure from Pandaemonium and just before his return to his Capitol to announce his success. Framing his enterprise, and framed by Hell scenes that represent the reenactment and/or punishment of his own crime, these encounters between Milton's counterhero and his progeny at crucial moments in the fable emphasize the moral pattern—sin and death, crime and punishment—underlying Satan's pseudo-heroic assault on mankind as well as the moral structure underlying Adam's transgression. Adam and Eve and their posterity, Satan and the serpent and his peers (his instrument or his accessories in crime) are implicated in the same act of transgression; and as personified abstractions, Sin and Death represent the common guilt and punishment of them all. Milton's allegory is far more than the mere decorative incident that critics have sometimes supposed it to be; it highlights two of the principal concepts inherent in the argument and primary action of his poem. His representation of Eden and original innocence is framed by these symbolic descriptions of the original evils that destroy the happy garden and the felicity of its original inhabitants. Contraries are more sharply defined through their opposition; and after the loathsome figures at Hell-gate, the image of a world still uncontaminated by corruption and a humanity still free of sin and death strikes the reader with greater force and pathetic irony.

The scavenger imagery with which Milton invests this pair, comparing them to dogs and vultures, reinforces the parallel that scholars have noted already between *Paradise Lost* and the *Iliad*. In the proposition of his epic, Milton's reference to the death and miseries that man's first sin has brought into the world parallels Homer's reference to the death and miseries that Achilles' wrath has brought upon his companions—despatching the souls of heroes to Hades and leaving their bodies as prey to beasts and birds. The latter allusion to the scavengers is conventional heroic imagery (common in Ger-

The Lamb and the Elephant

manic and Celtic and Slavic as well as in classical epic). In developing it allegorically in terms of sin and death, Milton is maintaining epic decorum and heightening the analogy between the dire results of Adam's disobedience and those of Achilles' disastrous anger.

Finally, these personifications serve both to magnify the heroism of the Son and to extol the providence of the Father. The heroes of classical myths—Hercules and Theseus, Perseus and Bellerophon—proved their valor and served the public good by slaying monsters; and their exploits had frequently been moralized specifically as the triumph of rational virtue over irrational vice. Similar combats with monsters—orcs and dragons, giants and ogres and harpies—were traditional in medieval and Renaissance epic; and these too had sometimes been allegorized as psychomachias. The victories of Ariosto's heroes over strange beasts had been moralized in this way, and in the *Faerie Queene* Spenser had usually made the ethical or religious significance of such conflicts clear without the aid of commentaries. The heroism of the Son, who will someday defeat Sin and Death through the merits of his Passion and ultimately destroy Satan and the perverted world, is enhanced by his conformity to the traditional heroic pattern of monster-slaying. Finally, their very greed—their hunger for carrion and appetite for decay—serves the ends of purification. As scavengers—destined first to lick up the draff and filth left by man's polluting sin, and finally to be destroyed by divine wrath—they exhibit the power of divine providence to bring good out of evil and convert the instruments of corruption into means of purification.

In developing his epic argument—the fall of man—and emphasizing its moral significance, Milton has employed two different, though related, modes of narrative presentation: first and primarily, the imitation of an action in the sense that neo-Aristotelian critics usually understood this term; secondly, the allegorical mode. Both methods involve fictional inventions, and the deliberate addition of sensuous details to render the remote events immediate and the abstract ideas concrete. Both entail the conscious creation of poetic images as means of instructing the intellect, affecting the passions, and moving the will by striking the imagination more forcefully. Both are representations of abstract ideas or historical actions, though

Imitation and Allegory

they differ in the degree to which, on the surface at least, they observe the principles of probability and verisimilitude.

Milton's plot—the imaginative and fictional elaboration of what he believed to be an historical event—is, on the whole, both probable and verisimilar on the literal level. Raphael's narrative of the angelic war—also a fictional and imaginative imitation of Biblical history—requires an understanding of the language of accommodation. The angel is compelled to adapt the divine mysteries—"The secrets of another World"—to the limitations of the human mind, delineating "what surmounts the reach / Of human sense" in sensuous imagery and "lik'ning spiritual to corporal forms, / As may express them best...." Raphael's history is the world's first epic poem, and (like later poets) he expresses *invisibilia* in terms of *visibilia*. In combining Scriptural imagery with details reminiscent of Gentile mythology, moreover, Milton is following the commonplace (expressed later in *Paradise Regained*) that the pagan myths were corruptions of divine truths revealed to the patriarchs. In the later epic he exploits this *topos* to oppose *Hebraica veritas* and Hellenic falsehood, like the personified Alithia *(Alethia)* and Pseustis of the medieval *Ecloga Theoduli*. In the mythical conventions of Raphael's story, however, he is also stressing (as possibly in his earlier allusion to the heavenly Muse in *Comus*) the common origin of Biblical tradition and poetic fable in divine revelation. Here again there is a parallel with the arguments of Boccaccio in the *Vita di Dante* and the *Genealogy of the Gods of the Gentiles*.

Both of these narratives—Milton's story of Adam's fall and Raphael's account of the fall of the angels—imitate the abstract idea. They not only possess the authority of history, therefore, but they are (by neo-Aristotelian standards) more "philosophical" than history. Poetically and didactically, they function as historical and ethical *exempla*, as inductive proofs of the nature and rewards of disobedience. Poetic justice, as so often in literary theory and practice, is the vehicle for expressing moral justice; and the poem itself becomes an instrument of moral philosophy. Though the reader could be expected to draw the appropriate inference for himself, abstracting the general idea or *moralitas* from the particular example, Milton, like other poets, leaves no room for misunderstanding. Raphael himself

The Lamb and the Elephant

points the moral of his story—eminently relevant to his audience on the brink of a similar fall:

> ... let it profit thee to have heard
> By terrible Example the reward
> Of disobedience; firm they might have stood,
> Yet fell; remember, and fear to transgress.

Raphael is a "divine Historian," Michael a divine "Seer" or prophet. Nevertheless his predictions consist almost entirely of episodes that were already past events for Milton and his contemporaries. Like the argument of his epic and the content of Raphael's story, they possessed the authority of Biblical history, and like these they functioned as historical and ethical examples. Even the prophecies of the Second Advent, which conclude this prophetic sequence, had formerly seemed imminent rather than distant to the poet and many of his compatriots, immediately and personally relevant to contemporary history, to the political and ecclesiastical conflict in which they themselves were actively engaged, and to national crises that few of them could escape. Even though Milton may have abandoned his earlier views on the imminence of the Last Judgment, the predictions that concluded Michael's survey of future history (now largely past history) were intimately involved with the tragic history of his own time; and they possessed an historical immediacy that the twentieth-century reader can recapture only in imagination.

Though Milton amplifies a few of these *exempla*, such as the story of Noah, more than others, he subjects none of them to the extensive elaboration that he had accorded Raphael's narratives of the fall of the angels and the creation of the world. The tradition of epic prophecy did not, as a rule, relate future events in minute detail. Normally it included an extensive survey of the future (now the past), celebrating the destiny of a nation or an institution or a family by extolling its principal leaders and their exploits and devoting greater space to contemporary worthies, frequently the poet's actual or potential patrons and their close relatives. Milton adapts this tradition to his theme of man's disobedience and punishment. Michael's prophecy replaces the masque of worldly miseries and the final promise of the Messiah that conclude his drafts for a drama on the fall. In the context of the epic, they redound, on the whole, to the shame rather than the glory of the protagonist's race—to the praise of the "one just man" or the elect few in various ages and to the condemnation of the vast majority. Milton amplifies the examples of Noah and Christ to stress the opposition between divine grace and human sin, but he develops neither of these episodes on the scale of Raphael's account of the angelic war and the six days' works.

Milton's allegory is not essential to the plot. As in other poetic accounts of Adam's fall, Satan could have escaped from hell without the intervention of an infernal portress, and returned without the assistance of a causeway. The primary value of these episodes is to underline the moral significance of the action, emphasizing the interconnection of crime and punishment by personifying them and stressing their significance for the fate of fallen man and fallen angel alike by making them active participants in the plot. Moreover, by treating these allegorical figures as *dramatis personae* (like the symbolic figures of Wisdom, Justice, Mercy, Conscience, Death, etc. in his early drafts for a tragedy on the fall) and bringing them into direct personal relationships with a "real" historical character like Satan, Milton attempts to heighten the illusion of reality, endowing abstract concepts with sensuous form and depicting moral relationships in terms of physical actions. He is combining the epic marvelous with verisimilitude, even though this is verisimilitude in a highly specialized sense.

Nevertheless Johnson's criticism is essentially sound. Though he overlooks the ethical and thematic relevance of these episodes and though we may not share his low opinion of their artistry, he has identified one of the aesthetic principles underlying the method of both scenes, the confrontation of real and allegorical personages and their mutual participation in actions that are neither entirely "real" nor altogether symbolic. The poet has mixed his modes, and accordingly his narrative cannot be consistently interpreted on either the literal or the allegorical level alone.

Though such admixture is conventional in Renaissance romance—the fays and sorceresses Dragontina, Falsirena, and Morgana in Boiardo, for instance, or the mansions of Ariosto's Alcina and her sister Logistilla—it is not uncommon in heroic poetry consciously

The Lamb and the Elephant

modeled on classical epics. Trissino introduces a personification of incontinence—Acratia—into his epic on Belisarius' liberation of Italy from the Goths. Camoëns personifies the Cape of Good Hope as a menacing giant.

In Tasso's epic on the First Crusade, Armida's enchanted palace could be rationalized on the literal level as the result of witchcraft, but the personification of Occasio or Fortuna who steers the boat to the enchanted island is explicable only on the allegorical plane. Milton's mixture of literal and allegorical modes is a Renaissance epic convention.

NOTES

[1] Boccaccio countered ethical objections to poetry chiefly by appealing to its allegorical method and its moral sense. Sidney defended the poetic art against similar charges partly on allegorical grounds but primarily by arguing that it imitated moral ideas. Milton, in turn, based his argument for the ethical function of tragic poetry on the concept of catharsis, arguing that poetry could purge the passions of its audience by arousing their delight in beholding passions well imitated. Cf. Charles G. Osgood, trans., *Boccaccio on Poetry* (Indianapolis and New York, 1956), pp. 39-54, 62-69, 78-87, 121-23. For the influence of Boccaccio's *Genealogy of the Gods* and its relation to medieval and Renaissance conceptions of allegory, see D. W. Robertson, Jr., *A Preface to Chaucer* (Princeton, 1962); Jean Seznec, *The Survival of the Pagan Gods*, trans. Barbara F. Sessions (New York, 1961); Michael Murrin, *The Veil of Allegory: Some Notes Toward a Theory of Allegorical Rhetoric in the English Renaissance* (Chicago and London, 1969). For Sidney's views, see O. B. Hardison, Jr., ed., *English Literary Criticism: The Renaissance* (New York, 1963), pp. 107-19, 123-25. Though Sidney primarily emphasizes the power of the poet's feigned images of virtues and vices (which couple the "generall notion" with the "particular example") to move and persuade to virtue and truth, he also repeats the commonplace of the universal knowledge concealed "under the vayle of fables" and the "many misteries contained in Poetrie, which of purpose were written darkely, least by prophane wits it should bee abused" (p. 145). For Milton's opinion see the Preface to *Samson Agonistes*, "Of that sort of Dramatic Poem which is call'd Tragedy."

In defending poetry against accusations of lying and violating the truth, both medieval and Renaissance authors (Boccaccio, Sidney, Mazzoni, Tasso, and others) frequently appealed to the argument from verisimilitude as well as to the argument from allegory. They stressed the fictive nature of poetry and its concern with probable and convincing resemblances (apparent truths and, on occasion, idealized likenesses) rather than with exact copies of existing objects or literal fidelity to historical events. For Ronsard's endeavor to justify his *Franciade*'s flagrant departures from history—urging his audience to read his epic "as the work of a poet and not as the treatise of an historiographer" and maintaining that the arguments of his classical models were "also built upon verisimilitude rather than truth"—see Bodo

Imitation and Allegory

L. O. Richter, "Ronsard and Belleforest on the Origins of France," in *Essays in History and Literature Presented by Fellows of The Newberry Library to Stanley Pargellis*, ed. Heinz Bluhm (Chicago, 1965), p. 69.

See Morris Bishop, *Petrarch and His World* (Bloomington, Ind., 1963), pp. 178-79, for the discussion of poetics by Ennius in Petrarch's *Africa;* "All that has to do with history, the practice of virtue, the lessons of life, the study of nature, is the realm of poetry, only on condition that things otherwise bald and bare be hidden under a shroud, and that they deceive the sight by a thin veil, now hiding, now revealing." In hiding himself under "a varied, agreeable cloud," the poet imposes a long but pleasant labor on the reader, in order that "the sense may be the more difficult in the search, the more delightful in the discovery." See also the translation of Petrarch's Coronation Oration in Ernest Hatch Wilkins, *Studies in the Life and Works of Petrarch* (Cambridge, Mass., 1955), pp. 300-13. In this work Petrarch quotes Lactantius' statement that the poet's office consists in taking "things that have really come to pass" and transforming them "by means of subtle figures into things of a different sort," along with Macrobius' assertion that Homer "was setting truth before the wise under the cloud of a poetic fiction when he spoke of Jove as going to the ocean with the other gods, that is, with the stars. . . ." Under "the veil of fictions," Petrarch continues, poets "have set forth truths physical, moral, and historical . . ." and the "difference between a poet on the one hand and a historian or a moral or physical philosopher on the other is the same as the difference between a clouded sky and a clear sky, since in each case the same light exists in the object of vision, but is perceived in different degrees according to the capacity of the observers." Moreover, poetry is "all the sweeter since a truth that must be sought out with some care gives all the more delight when it is discovered" (Wilkins, pp. 306-07). See also the discussion of Petrarch's Coronation Oration in Ricardo J. Quinones, *The Renaissance Discovery of Time* (Cambridge, Mass., 1972), pp. 120-21.

[2]On verisimilitude, probability, and propriety of persons and things, see Cicero, *De Inventione*, trans. H. M. Hubbell (London and Cambridge, Mass., 1949), p. 18, "Inventio est excogitatio rerum verarum aut veri similium quae causam probabilem reddant . . ."; p. 70, "Ac personis has res attributas putamus: nomen, naturam, victum, fortunam, habitum, affectionem, studia, consilia, facta, casus, orationes"; pp. 84-86, "That is probable which for the most part usually comes to pass, or which is a part of the ordinary beliefs of mankind, or which contains in itself some resemblance to these qualities, whether such resemblance be true or false." Cf. Harry Caplan, ed. and trans., *Rhetorica ad Herennium* (Cambridge, Mass., and London, 1954), p. 3, "Inventio est cogitatio rerum verarum aut veri similium quae causam probabilem reddant." See also, Edmond Faral, ed., *Les arts poétiques du XIIe et du XIIIe siècle* (Paris, 1958), pp. 119-51, 310-11, 380. According to Matthieu de Vendôme's *Ars Versificatoria* (Faral, p. 135), ". . . si quaelibet res describatur, in expressione descriptionis maximum fidei praetendatur nutrimentum, ut vera dicantur vel veri similia, juxta illud Oratii: [*Poet*. 119]

Aut famam sequere aut sibi convenientia finge."

For the views of John of Garland, see Giovanni Mari, ed., *Poetria magistri Johannis anglici de arte prosayca metrica et rithmica*, Romanische Forschungen, vol. 13 (1902). John quotes "Tullius in secunda rhetorica: Inventio est rerum verarum et verisimilium excogitatio, que causam probabilem reddat" (p. 887); in the section "De decem [*sic*] actributis personi ex quibus loci rethorici eliciuntur," John lists "undecim actributa persone": "nomen, natura, convictus, fortuna, habitus, consilium, affectus, studium, casus, factura, oracio" (p. 939). According to Francesco Sansovino's *La Retorica* (1543), "L'invenzione secondo Tullio non è altro ch'una imaginazione di cose vere o almeno che abbian sembianza di vero, la quale imaginazione sia di maniera ch'ella possa render la causa probabi!e inanzi a color a' quai si favella"; Weinberg, *Poetrica e Retorica del Cinquecento*, I, 454. Cf. Bernardino Daniello, *La Poetica* (1536) on verisimilitude; Weinberg, I, 254. See Aristotle's discussion of imagination in *De Anima* (Book III, Chapter 3), in *The Works of Aristotle*, J. A. Smith, trans., W. D. Ross, ed., vol. 3 (Oxford, 1931). The name *phantasia* has been derived from *phaos* (light), inasmuch as "sight is the most highly developed sense" and it is "not possible to see without light." Imagination is different, however, from "either perceiving or discursive thinking, though it is not found without sensation, or judgment without it." Imagining "lies within our own power whenever we wish (e.g. we can call up a picture, as in the practice of mnemonics by the use of mental images), but in forming opinions we are not free: we cannot escape the alternative of falsehood or truth." Accordingly, imaginative activity is not the "same kind of thinking as judgment." Imagination is not sense, for "sensations are always true," but "imaginations are for the most part false"; and imaginative visions may appear in dreams, when one's eyes are shut and one is exercising neither the faculty nor the activity of sight. Imagination is "that in virtue of which an image arises for us"; and because imaginations remain in the organs of sense and resemble sensations, men are sometimes guided by them "because of the temporary eclipse in them of mind by feeling or disease or sleep."

For sensible criticism of the "severely moralistic approach" to Elizabethan and Restoration drama, see Harriett Hawkins, *Likenesses of Truth in Elizabethan and Restoration Drama* (Oxford, 1972).

[3]For recent studies of medieval and Renaissance allegory, see Murrin, op. cit.; Edwin Honig, *Dark Conceit: The Making of Allegory* (New York, 1966); Rosemond Tuve, *Allegorical Imagery: Some Mediaeval Books and Their Posterity* (Princeton, 1966); Paul Piehler, *The Visionary Landscape: A Study in Medieval Allegory* (London and Montreal, 1971); Boyce Allen Judson, *The Friar as Critic* (Nashville, Tenn., 1971); Edward A. Bloom, "The Allegorical Principle," *ELH* 18 (1951), 163-90; W. Roy Mackenzie, *The English Moralities from the Point of View of Allegory*, Harvard Studies in English, vol. 2 (1914); R. E. Kaske, "Chaucer and Medieval Allegory," *ELH* 30 (1963), 175-92; Robert Worth Frank, Jr., "The Art of Reading Medieval Personification Allegory," *ELH* 20 (1953), 237-50; Dolora Cunningham, "The Jonsonian Masque as a Literary Form," *ELH* 22 (1955), 108-24; Dale Herron, "The Focus of Allegory in the Renaissance Epic," *Genre* 3 (1970), 176 ff.; C. A. Merrick, "Neoplatonic Allegory in Calderón's *Las Fortunas de Andrómeda y Perseo*," *MLR* 68 (1972), 319-27; Raimund Rütten, "Symbol und Mythus im altfranzözischen Rolandslied," *Archiv*, vol. 4 (Braunschweig, 1970); Gérard Cames, *Allégories et symboles dans l'hortus deliciarum* (Leyden, 1971); Danilo L. Aguzzi, "Allegory in the Heroic Poetry of the Renaissance" (diss. Columbia Univ., 1959); A. A. Parker, *The Allegorical Drama of Calderon* (Oxford, 1968); Pietro Cali, *Allegory and Vision in Dante and Langland: A Comparative Study* (Cork, 1971); Dietrich Walter Jöns, *Das 'Sinnen-Bild': Studien zur allegorischen Bildlichkeit bei Andreas Gryphius* (Stuttgart, 1966); A. M. Cinquemani, "Henry Reynolds' Mythomystes and the Continuity of Ancient Modes of Allegoresis in Seventeenth-Century England," *PMLA* 85 (1970), 1041-48; Angus Fletcher, *Allegory: The Theory of a Symbolic Mode* (Ithaca, N.Y., 1964); Don Cameron Allen, *Mysteriously Meant: The Rediscovery of Pagan Symbolism and Allegorical Interpretation in the Renaissance* (Baltimore and London, 1970); C. S. Lewis, *The Allegory of Love* (Oxford, 1936); Archimede Marni, *Allegory in the French Heroic Poem of the Seventeenth Century* (Princeton, 1936); A. D. Nuttall, *Two Concepts of Allegory* (London, 1967); Desirée Hirst, *Hidden Riches: Traditional Symbolism*

Imitation and Allegory

from the Renaissance to Blake (London, 1964); Ellen Douglass Leyburn, *Satiric Allegory: Mirror of Man* (New Haven, 1956); James I. Wimsatt, *Allegory and Mirror: Tradition and Structure in Middle English Literature* (New York, 1970); Bernard F. Huppé and D. W. Robertson, Jr., *Fruyt and Chaf: Studies in Chaucer's Allegories* (Princeton, 1963); F. P. Pickering, *Literature and Art in the Middle Ages* (London, 1970); Roberta D. Cornelius, *The Figurative Castle* (Bryn Mawr, Pa., 1930); Guy de Tervarent, *Attributs et symboles dans l'art profane, 1450-1600* (Geneva, 1958); John V. Fleming, *The Roman de la Rose: A Study in Allegory and Iconography* (Princeton, 1969), John MacQueen, *Allegory* (London, 1970).

On allegory in antiquity, see Herbert Anthony Musurillo, *Symbol and Myth in Ancient Poetry* (New York, 1961); Reinhart Hahn, *Die Allegorie in der antiken Rhetorik* (Tübingen, 1967).

On Dante's allegory of poets, Charles S. Singleton, *Dante Studies I* (Cambridge, Mass., 1954); Richard Hamilton Green, "Dante's 'Allegory of Poets' and the Medieval Theory of Poetic Fiction," *CL* 9 (1957), 118-28; Phillip Damon, "The Two Modes of Allegory in Dante's *Convivio*," *PQ* 40 (1961), 144-49.

Among recent studies of Spenser's allegory, see Angus Fletcher, *The Prophetic Moment: An Essay on Spenser* (Chicago and London, 1971); Harry Berger, *The Allegorical Temper* (New Haven, 1957); Hsin-chang Chang, *Allegory and Courtesy in Spenser* (Edinburgh, 1955); Kathleen Williams, *Spenser's World of Glass* (Berkeley, 1966); Edwin Greenlaw, *Studies in Spenser's Historical Allegory* (Baltimore and London, 1932); A. C. Hamilton, *The Structure of Allegory in the Faerie Queene* (Oxford, 1961); Graham Hough, *A Preface to the Faerie Queene* (New York, 1963); William Nelson, *The Poetry of Edmund Spenser: A Study* (New York and London, 1963); Thomas P. Roche, Jr., *The Kindly Flame* (Princeton, 1964); Paul J. Alpers, *The Poetry of The Faerie Queene* (Princeton, 1967); idem, *Elizabethan Poetry: Modern Essays in Criticism* (New York, 1967); Roger Sale, *Reading Spenser: An Introduction to the Faerie Queene* (New York, 1968); Thomas K. Dunseath, *Spenser's Allegory of Justice* (Princeton, 1968); Frank Kermode, *Shakespeare, Spenser, Donne: Renaissance Essays* (London, 1971); Jane Aptekar, *Icons of Justice: Iconography and Thematic Imagery in Book V of the Faerie Queene* (New York, 1969); R. F. Hill, "Spenser's Allegorical 'Houses,'" *MLR* 65 (1970), 721-33; D. Douglas Waters, "Errour's Den and Archimago's Hermitage: Symbolic Lust and Symbolic Witchcraft," *ELH* 33 (1966), 279-98; A. C. Hamilton, "Spenser's Treatment of Myth," *ELH* 26 (1959), 335-54; John B. Bender, *Spenser and Literary Pictorialism* (Princeton, 1972); Michael Murrin, "The Varieties of Criticism," *Modern Philology* 70 (1973), 342-56; Kathleen Williams, "Vision and Rhetoric: The Poet's Voice in *The Faerie Queene*," *ELH* 36 (1969), 131-44.

Among recent studies of number symbolism, see Christopher Butler, *Number Symbolism* (London, 1970); Alastair Fowler, *Spenser and the Numbers of Time* (New York, 1964); idem, *Triumphal Forms: Structural Patterns in Elizabethan Poetry* (Cambridge, 1970); Alastair Fowler, ed., *Silent Poetry: Essays in Numerological Analysis* (London, 1970); Gunnar Qvarnström, *Poetry and Numbers* (Lund, 1966); Vincent Foster Hopper, *Medieval Number Symbolism* (New York, 1938); Maren-Sofie Røstvig et al., *The Hidden Sense and Other Essays*, Norwegian Studies in English, no. 9 (Oslo, 1963).

On the medieval exemplum, see Frederic C. Tubach, *Index Exemplorum: A Handbook of Medieval Religious Tales* (Helsinki, 1969). See also Edwin Habel, ed., "Die Exempla honesta vitae des Johannes de Garlandia, eine lateinische Poetik des 13. Jahrhunderts," *Romanische Forschungen* 29 (1911), 131-54; G. R. Owst, *Literature and Pulpit in Medieval England*, 2d ed., rev. (Oxford, 1961). For the medieval exemplum and its relation to parable, see Osgood, p. 60; for myth and fable as exemplum, see Juan de Mena, *El Laberinto de Fortuna o las Trescientas,* ed. José Manuel Blecua (Madrid, 1968), p. xxxi.

[4] Giordano Bruno, *The Heroic Frenzies,* trans. Paul Eugene Memmo, Jr. (Chapel Hill, 1966), p. 63.

[5] I am indebted to Professor Daniel Donno for this point.

[6] For Sir John Harington, the poet's license to feign is rooted in the practice of the ancients (who "wrapped as it were in their writings divers and sundry meanings which they call the sences or mysteries thereof") as well as in Aristotle's definition of poetry as an art of imitation. Poetry is an "honest fraud in which (as *Plutarch* saith) he that is deceived is wiser then he that is not deceived and he that doth deceive is honester then he that doth not deceive." Since the art of poetry is "but an imitation (as *Aristotle* calleth it)," poets are "allowed to faine what they list. . . ." In the literal sense (which is "the utmost barke or ryne") they "set downe, in manner of an historie, the acts and notable exploits of some persons worthy memorie; then in the same fiction, as a second rine and somewhat more fine as it were nearer to the pith and marrow, they place the Morall sence, profitable for the active life of man, approving vertuous actions and condemning the contrarie." Beneath these senses lies the allegorical sense, "which *Plutarch* defineth to be when one thing is told and by that another is understood." See "A Preface or . . . Briefe Apologie of Poetrie" in *Ludovico Ariosto's Orlando Furioso Translated . . . by Sir John Harington,* ed. Robert McNulty (Oxford, 1972), pp. 4-5. In his "Advertisement to the Reader," Harington argues that "the matter of the booke" tends to virtue. His marginal notes quote "apt similitudes and pithie sentences or adages with the best descriptions and the excellent imitations and the places and authors from whence they are taken." At the end of each book he comments on the history, the moral, the allegory ("some things that are meerely fabulous, yet have an allegorical sence which every bodie at the first shew cannot perceive"), and the allusion ("fictions to be applied to some things done or written of in times past, as also where it may be applied without offence to the time present"); McNulty, pp. 16-17. At the end of the volume he provides "A Briefe and Summarie Allegorie," noting the virtuous and vicious "examples" proposed by Ariosto, the opposition of good and bad love and of virtue and pleasure, the "patternes" of honorable love and lewdness, the "patterne" of gratitude, and the "verie Idea and perfect example of a true knight." The allegorical sense is "the verie kyrnell and principall part or as the marrow and the rest but the bone or unprofitable shell, or according (. . . using *Tassoes* comparison) like to the pill that is lapped in suger and given a child for a medicin . . ."; McNulty, pp. 558-68.

Ariosto has applied his whole work and all its parts to "two principall heads and common places, namely, *Armes* and *Love,* in both which men commit great oversights and from both which proceed manie great enormous disorders both in publique and privat. . . . And this is the cause that mine author hath propounded many examples, but especially two"—i.e. Orlando's madness and Rogero's sojourn at Alcina's court of pleasure—"in the which men may see their frailtie in the . . . passion of love"; McNulty, p. 559. The "other common place is of armes which indeed is more pertinent to matters of state (as tother is to privat life and manners), and in this mine author hath carried his invention verie daintily and well worth the marking. For he propoundeth to us the example of two mightie Emperours, one of which directed all his counsells by wisedome, learning, and Religion. But the other being rash and unexperienced ruined himself and his countrie . . ."; McNulty, p. 566. For Harington's unacknowledged debt to Gioseffo Bononome's remarks on "l'armi & gli amori" as the "due capi, over luoghi comuni" and as "la divisione: & la materia over soggetto di tutta l'opera," see McNulty, pp. xxx-xxxi. For the analogy with Spenser, who likewise sings of wars and loves and of knights and dames, and dif-

Imitation and Allegory

ferentiates between public and private virtues, see William Nelson, *The Poetry of Edmund Spenser: A Study* (New York and London, 1965), pp. 120, 204-05.

In stressing Harington's debt to the allegorical commentaries of Bononome and Fornari, McNulty nevertheless notes significant differences in their theories of allegory. Whereas Harington "seems to understand allegory . . . as a series of unrelated arbitrary levels which may be applied virtually from outside in writing or interpreting a story," Fornari bases his conception of the allegorical sense on the correspondences existing between the intellectual (or supercelestial) world, the celestial world, the sublunary world, and the human microcosm. According to Anaxagoras, there is "somma convenenza" among these four worlds, and all that exists in one has likenesses in the other three. Hence St. John informs Ariosto (35.18.3-4) that

> Ogni effetto convien che corrisponda
> In Terra, e in ciel, ma con diversa faccia.

Hence the names of earthly things are often given to heavenly things, and from this principle proceeds "la disciplina d'ogni senso allegorico." Hence the writer or expositor of allegorical verses must know the nature of these worlds "& che cosa dell'un mondo corrisponda, & si raffronti à quella dell'altro . . ."; McNulty, pp. xxxvii-xxxviii. Cf. Graham Hough, *A Preface to the Faerie Queene* (New York, 1963), p. 119; and *Paradise Lost* V, 574-76: ". . . though what if Earth/Be but the shadow of Heav'n, and things therein / Each to other like, more than on Earth is thought?"

Mindful of the fable of Hercules' Choice, Harington construes Alcina's country as "the court of pleasure" and Logistilla's residence as "vertue" and "wisedome" (McNulty, pp. 79, 122, 559-62). Ariosto's tale of the two sisters—the legitimate daughter all but totally dispossessed and her power usurped by her illegitimate sister—represents the rebellion of the "nature of man" (i.e. "our appetite or affection") against reason: "And now every part of the body engenders such seeds of concupiscence that nature is become a bastard sister to reason and usurpes that governement that is due onely to her and leaveth her onely one castell . . . , so that reason is retirde as it were to her principall fortresse, to the head, the rest of this kingdome being possessed (by *Alcyna*) by pleasure and fond delights. Now then, what marvell is it if this new *Hercules* . . . (i.e. Ruggiero) do with so great difficulty and through so many impediments clammer up to this stately seat of *Logistilla* . . ." (p. 563). Ruggiero's "Griffeth horse" signifies "the passion of the mind contrarie to reason that carries men in the aire, that is, in the height of their imaginations, out of Europ, that is, out of the compasse of the rules of Christian religion and feare of God, unto the Ile of *Alcyna*, which signifieth pleasure and vanities of this world." In addition to reason, virtue, and wisdom, Logistilla also represents "the true Christian religion," impugned by rival faiths and by their cousin heresy and their grandsire Atheism" (pp. 79-80). The eccesiastical meaning with which Harington invests Ariosto's Logistilla thus roughly parallels the significance of Spenser's Una.

For Harington, Erifilla represents covetousness (McNulty, pp. 80-89). The magician Atlanta "may signifie Cupid or that fond fancie that we call love"; his enchanted palace symbolizes the labyrinth of love (pp. 57, 79-80, 565-66). The benevolent sorceress Melissa figures "both preachers and philosophers that shew us by the ring (which hath bene expounded before to be reason) our foule errors and our wandring courses and so makes us see our owne deformities and the deformitie of that we esteeme so dearely. . ." (p. 89; cf. p. 100). The four ladies sent to rescue Ruggiero represent the four cardinal virtues (p. 122).

Like Fornari, who did not hesitate to drag in an allegorical interpretation by the hair (*per li capelli;* McNulty, pp. xxvii, xxxv), Harington is aware that allegorical readings may be the invention of the expositor rather than the author. On occasion he leaves their discovery to the private taste and judgment of his readers. On other occasions he tentatively proposes an allegorical reading while retaining a healthy skepticism as to whether Ariosto had intended it. On the other hand, certain allegories strike him as obvious and inevitable. "For the Allegorie in this Canto I find not much to be said except one should be so curious to search for an allegorie where none is intended by the Author him selfe; yet an allegorie may not unfitly be gathered of the description of Bayardos following *Angelica* . . ."; McNulty, p. 28. "For the Allegorie of this booke much might be said of *Atlant*, of his horse and his shield, but I will only touch what I thinke will be thought most worth the noting and let passe the rest for each mans private conceipt"; p. 56. "Finally, the fortification of the castle, the fuming pots of stone, the situation and height, and every thing that is said of the man, the horse, the house, the shield, are so easie to understand in allegoricall sence as I thinke it needlesse to proceede anie furder in this matter"; p. 57. "Allegorie there is none in this booke at all"; p. 69. "The rest of this whole booke is an Allegorie so plaine to those that will indeed looke heedfully into it as needs no exposition, and it is continued in the next booke and in a manner there expounded to the understanding of any reasonable capacitie; yet for plainnes sake I will touche some things with my accustomed breefenes and leave the rest to the discreet reader to scan and to applie to his owne profite"; p. 79. "Infinite matter more might be applied in allegoricall sence out of this booke if I would covet to stand upon everie small matter, for . . . these two bookes be in a manner a meere allegorie from the beginning to the ending"; p. 89. "In the description of Discord and Fraud and finding Silence in the house of sleepe, being long since banished from philosophers and divines, the allegorie is so plaine as it were time lost to expound it because it expounds it selfe so plainly . . ."; p. 163. "Historie nor Allegorie nor scant any thing that is good can be picked out of this bad booke . . ."; p. 324. "Of the Allegorie I have not much to say because myne authour him selfe expounds it so plainly . . ."; p. 409.

William Nelson observes that Orazio Toscanella "describes Ariosto's method in just the way that Spenser describes his own," placing "several virtues in several individuals, one virtue in one character and another in another character, in order to fashion out of all the characters a well-rounded and perfect man"; Nelson, *The Poetry of Edmund Spenser: A Study* (New York and London, 1965), p. 121; cf. p. 323 for the views of Pigna on the multiple heroes of romance, depicted in "all those honorable actions which are sought in a perfect knight."

[7]See R. W. Frank, Jr., "The Art of Reading Medieval Personification-Allegory," *ELH* 20 (1953), 237-50; cf. D. W. Robertson, Jr., *A Preface to Chaucer* (Princeton, 1962), pp. 248-49, on the iconographically described "character" and the personified abstraction in Chaucer's poetry.

[8]See Seznec, op. cit., passim.

[9]See Beryl Smalley, *The Study of the Bible in the Middle Ages* (Notre Dame, 1964), pp. 41-42; cf. pp. 9, 20-23, 28, 90-94, 100-09.

[10]See Charles S. Singleton, *Dante Studies*, vols. I and II (Cambridge, Mass., 1954, 1958); Aleramo P. Lanapoppi, "La *Divina Commedia*: allegoria 'dei poeti' o allegoria 'dei teologi'?", *Dante Studies* (Dante Society of America), vol. 86 (1968), 17-39; *Convito* II, Chapter 1; Edward Moore, ed., *Tutte le opere di Dante Alighieri* (Oxford, 1894), pp. 251-52; Robert Hollander, *Allegory in Dante's Commedia* (Princeton, 1969).

[11]See Smalley, pp. 150-95.

[12]For the application of the fourfold exegetical schema to the liturgy, see Gulielmus Durandus' *Rationale divinorum officiorum*.

Imitation and Allegory

[13]Cf. Frances A. Yates, *Giordano Bruno and the Hermetic Tradition* (New York, 1969), pp. 52-57, 70-72; Seznec, pp. 62n, 74.

[14]Cf. Seznec, pp. 19-20, 24-36, on medieval and Renaissance legends of the Trojan origin of the Franks, the descent of the Burgundians and the house of Navarre from Hercules, and the role of Brutus and Hesperus, Italus and Tuscus and Brabo, as the eponymous ancestors of other European nations. For the Trojan myth in the Renaissance, see Bodo L. O. Richter, "Ronsard and Belleforest on the Origins of France," in *Essays in History and Literature Presented by the Fellows of The Newberry Library to Stanley Pargellis*, ed. Heinz Bluhm (Chicago, 1965), pp. 65-80; R. E. Asher, "Myth, Legend and History in Renaissance France," *SF* 13 (1969), 409-19. For the relationships between German and Italian humanism and their influence on Renaissance reinterpretations of the Teutonic past, see Frank L. Borchardt, *German Antiquity in Renaissance Myth* (Baltimore and London, 1971) and the review by Lewis W. Spitz in *Speculum* 48 (1973), 733-36. Spitz notes the cultural rivalry between Germanic and Italian humanists and the need felt by the former "to create a worthy national past for their people."

[15]According to Fracastoro's poem Syphilus, shepherd of King Alcithöus, was punished by the disease "as a punishment for neglecting the worship of Apollo, and was cured by a decoction of the sacred tree Guaiacum after he had confessed his impiety and promised repentance"; see the Introduction by James Johnston Abraham in Heneage Wynne-Finch, trans., Fracastoro's *Syphilis sive Morbus Gallicus* (London, 1935), p. 18.

[16]In *The History of Britain*, Milton hails Joseph of Exeter as "the only smooth Poet of those times . . ."; French Fogle, ed., *The Complete Prose Works of John Milton*, vol. V, Part I (New Haven and London, 1971), p. 15.

[17]See Merritt Y. Hughes, "Spenser's Acrasia and the Circe of the Renaissance," *Journal of the History of Ideas* 4 (1943), 381-99; A. Bartlett Giamatti, *The Earthly Paradise and the Renaissance Epic* (Princeton, 1969).

[18]Criticism of the allegorical method on the grounds of verisimilitude and probability are frequent in neoclassical artistic as well as literary criticism. Samuel Johnson censured Milton for mixing real and allegorical persons in *Paradise Lost*, but nevertheless granted the poet a restricted use of conventional personifications like Fame and Victory. The Abbé du Bos (1725) similarly attacked the "mingling of real and allegorical figures" in painting because it destroyed verisimilitude; and on these grounds he censured Rubens' introduction of allegorical persons in his painting of the birth of Louis XIII. The poetry of painters "does not consist so much in inventing idle fancies [*chimères*] or 'jeux d'esprits,' as in conceiving what passions and what sentiments one should give to people according to their character and . . . condition of life. . . ." Though du Bos permitted the artist to employ "traditional allegorical figures," he objected to modern allegorical inventions. Sir Joshua Reynolds likewise objected to Rubens' mixture of real and allegorical figures, but nevertheless argued that whatever "the disadvantages of allegorical poetry," allegorical painting was a different affair; if it could produce a "greater variety of ideal beauty" and a "more various and delightful composition," or provide a "greater opportunity" for the artist to exhibit his skill, it was justifiable. Lee also calls attention to Lessing's objection to the "modern fashion of allegorical pictures" (Rensselaer W. Lee, *Ut Pictura Poesis: The Humanistic Theory of Painting* [New York, 1967], pp. 22-23).

In the criticism of painting and poetry alike, the allegorical mode could serve as a topic for defense or condemnation. Apologists cited allegorical content as justification against charges of vanity or falsity or sensuality. The allegorical method could

The Lamb and the Elephant

be extolled as proper not only to both of these arts but as characteristic of Scripture and mystical theology. Conversely, it could be censured as incompatible with the principles of correct imitation and the true laws of literature and art. The belief that classical epic contained hidden moral or metaphysical allegories and that modern heroic poetry or painting should likewise possess an allegorical significance persisted well into the seventeenth century, receiving formal expression in Le Bossu's influential treatise on epic poetry. In Félibien's view that the painter should "represent great events" like the historian, pleasing subjects like the poet, or "mounting still higher, be skilled to conceal under the veil of fables [*savoir couvrir sous le voile de la fable*] the virtues of great men, and the most exalted mysteries," Rensselaer Lee detects the influence of "the Renaissance theory of epic poetry," current in seventeenth-century France—the belief that the epic contains a "hidden meaning beneath the veil of the action" (Lee, p. 19 and 19*n*). In *The Dunciad Variorum* Pope can simultaneously parody the allegorical method while exploiting it to the hilt as a source not only of ridicule and satire, but of genuine beauty and power. The invention of his mock-epic hinges on an allegorical conceit. For the composition or disposition of his fable he depends largely on his chief machining-person, the personification of Dulness. The deliberate mixture of real and allegorical persons is of central importance in this poem, for argument and design, for epic machinery, and for the elaboration of the poet's satiric strategy. As in other allegories, the method of mixing real historical figures with personified abstractions enables him to emphasize both the universal and the particular example, subsuming (so to speak) a large number of concrete and specific individuals under a clearly conceived and sensuously presented universal. As in other allegories of invective or indictment, the incisiveness of the poet's satire results in large part from a dual emphasis on the sensuous image of an abstract vice (on the one hand) and of particular individuals subject to this vice (on the other)—a clear and forceful representation of the essence and extension of a concept. Through this method of combining personification and exemplum, allegorical and historical individuals, other poets had indicted moral vices and the violation of the laws of society. Pope employs essentially the same technique to indict the vices of literary style and trespasses against the rules of art and sense.

Glossing his parody of heroic epic with a parody of literary scholarship, Pope cites the sixteenth- and seventeenth-century commonplace that heroic poetry must contain an allegory, citing Le Bossu's treatise on epic poetry as an authority. According to "Martinus Scriblerus of the Poem," the composer of the *Dunciad* has wrapped "this truth"—i.e. that *Dulness* and *Poverty* are the "Causes creative" of dull authors—"in an *Allegory* (as the constitution of Epic poesy requires) and feigns, that one of these Goddesses had taken up her abode with the other, and that they jointly inspir'd all such writers and such works. He proceedeth to shew the *qualities* they bestow on these authors, and the effects they produce: Then the *materials* or *stock* with which they furnish them. . . . The great power of these Goddesses acting in alliance . . . was to be exemplify'd in some *one, great* and *remarkable action*" (*The Poems of Alexander Pope*, vol. 5. The Dunciad, ed. James Sutherland [New York, 1943], 50).

Recent criticism has emphasized the allegorical element in mannerist painting. Blunt observes that Florentine mannerists "generally turn for their subjects either to the glorification of the Medici or to allegorical mythology, so involved that a volume is needed to explain a fresco cycle such as Vasari's in the Palazzo Vecchio" (Anthony Blunt, *Artistic Theory in Italy, 1450-1600* [London, Oxford, New York, 1962], p. 87). In his opinion the "themes of most Mannerist fresco-cycles are so obscure that they can only have been chosen by a trained theologian . . ." (p. 131). According to Blunt, the Council of Trent had encouraged clarity and accuracy in pictorial representation, but permitted the use of allegory insofar as it was simple

Imitation and Allegory

and intelligible and conformed to ecclesiastical doctrine. Both Molanus and Gilio da Fabriano agreed that the artist could introduce into his paintings "*probable* facts or ideas" based on "the authority of 'wise and learned men.'" In criticizing Michelangelo's *Last Judgment*, however, Gilio argued that even if the painter had tended to "interpret the words of the Gospel mystically and allegorically," he ought to have given the primacy to the literal meaning before all the others, "keeping to the letter as often as possible" (Blunt, pp. 111-13). Similarly, in Vasari's painting the *Immaculate Conception*, Friedlaender emphasizes the "petrification of all emotional content into allegorical abstraction"; in contrast, Lodovico Caracci's *Madonna degli Scalzi* was "one of the main instigators of the seventeenth-century representation of the Immaculata stripped of allegorical and symbolic trimmings . . ." (Walter Friedlaender, *Mannerism and Anti-Mannerism in Italian Painting* [New York, 1965], pp. 56-57).

[19]Cf. Samuel Johnson in *Milton Criticism*, ed. James Thorpe (New York, 1969), pp. 82-83. For Milton's personification-allegory, see A. L. Keith, "*Personification in Milton's Paradise Lost*," *EJ* 17 (1929), 399-409. In an interesting discussion of the allegory of Sin and Death, Anne Davidson Ferry, *Milton's Epic Voice: The Narrator in "Paradise Lost"* (Cambridge, Mass. 1963), pp. 122-46, argues that Milton uses allegory as "an example of fallen modes of language" and that by "the equation of allegory with fallen vision in *Paradise Lost*, the episode of Sin and Death . . . becomes a kind of serious parody of what is presented as a false literary style." On Milton's Sin and Death, see also Robert B. White, Jr., "Milton's Allegory of Sin and Death: A Comment on Background," *Modern Philology* 70 (1973), 337-41. A valuable study by Professor Clay Hunt (unpublished as of this date) explores the interrelationship between literal and allegorical levels in *Paradise Lost*.

Chapter V

IMAGE AND IDEA:
IMITATION AND ALLEGORY

>>>>>>:<<<<<<

Despite the continuity of medieval and Renaissance tradition—in poetics and rhetoric, in attitudes toward the classics, and in conceptions of the nature and functions of allegory—there were also substantial differences. These were not fundamental, however, and usually they involved different degrees or points of emphasis rather than radically divergent approaches or ideals. Medieval poets were, on the whole, less hampered by critical theory and ancient models. Possessing a more restricted knowledge of antiquity and a scantier and less systematic body of poetic theory, they could afford to treat classical theory and practice with greater liberty. Exercising their own invention, they could adapt the materials of classical literature to contemporary fashions without adhering strictly to classical models. They were free to rework motifs from Virgil and Ovid and Lucan into medieval *ballades* and dream-visions, or (like Chaucer) to combine the conventions of the *Somnium Scipionis* and Dante's visionary journey with those of the French erotic vision.

They were also able to treat the literary genres and the principles of structural organization and "realistic" or symbolic representation with greater license. Italian poets of the fourteenth century were, in several respects, more free to experiment with formal organization and to exercise their own originality in structuring their poems than were their compatriots in the late sixteenth and early seventeenth centuries. Despite its range and variety and its frequent inconsistency, Renaissance critical theory narrowed the scope for individual imagination so far as the principles of genre, plot structure, and decorum in style and character and subject matter were concerned. Writing in the early trecento and in a genre that had not been rigidly defined by classical or contemporary theory, Dante, for instance, possessed far greater liberty than his cinquecento and seicento successors. Few of these would have cared to stake their reputation and their life's work on a poem so original, if not irregular, in structure and style as the *Commedia*—tightly organized according to the poet's own principles of structure rather than those of classical poetics, and regular in its irregularity.

1.

Though medieval poets with any pretensions to learning could not be altogether ignorant of allegorical interpretations of Biblical and classical literature, they did not apply allegorical methods consistently in actual composition. Considerations of genre and subject matter and the expectations of their audiences usually influenced their methods of presentation. Though they frequently concluded their beast fables with a concluding *moralitas*, drawing an appropriate and profitable inference from the story, such moral *exempla* were not necessarily allegorical. The audience had little reason to suspect a covert allegorical sense underlying every character, scene, or episode in the fable.

The medieval dream-vision, to be sure, was frequently allegorical; and indeed the popularity of this genre resulted, in large part, from its ability to adapt the allegorical method and the element of the supernatural, the mysterious, and the marvelous to a narrative framework that could meet the requirements of verisimilitude and probability. This conventional fiction, serving as a transitional device for conveying the narrator out of the real world and into a visionary realm, would be especially useful for a poet addressing his audience in person (as Chaucer is believed to have done) and relating fantastic adventures in which he himself was the protagonist. Dante achieved an impressive variation on the vision tradition by depicting his *alta fantasia* or *visione* as an actual journey, and it is significant that a sixteenth-century critic (Jacopo Mazzoni) attempted to justify this apparent breach of verisimilitude by arguing that the *Commedia* was actually a dream-vision. The poet (he suggested) was imitating the dream of a journey, not the journey itself.

Personifications and allegorized characters and events are not uncommon in "philosophical epics,"[1] where they are sometimes asso-

The Lamb and the Elephant

ciated with the visionary journey or the dream-vision. In epics or romances dealing with heroic ages, the marvelous could be taken for granted; one expected wonders and "ferlies," for the histories themselves were crowded with tales of giants and ogres, enchanters and fays. In describing the wonders of Arthur's realm, the narrator did not need the fiction of a dream-vision, though medieval writers did, in fact, utilize this technique to link the narrator with the heroic past and the heroic dead. In the Welsh *Dream of Rhonabwy* the narrator beholds Arthur and his knights through the medium of an incubation dream; and in Irish saga, the ghost of Fergus appears to recount *The Great Cattle-Raid of Cooley*.

In the earlier stages of their development the method of chivalric epic and romance appears to have been predominantly literal rather than allegorical. In contrast to extended dream-visions or allegorical journeys such as the *Roman de la Rose* and the *Commedia*, the chivalric romances belonged to "historical" poetry. The events they described pertained to the remote past rather than to the present. Their setting was generally a real or legendary location—Camelot or Troy or Paris, Broceliande or Ardennes—rather than an allegorical landscape or figurative castle. Their protagonist was a legendary or historical personage (Arthur or Charlemagne or Theseus, Lancelot or Roland, Aeneas or Hector or Troilus) rather than the poet himself (Dante or Guillaume de Lorris). The characters whom the hero usually encounters—other knights and ladies, hermits and sorcerers, ogres and fays and miscellaneous monsters—are rarely personified abstractions. In the alliterative *Morte d'Arthur* King Arthur may dream of Fortune and her wheel, but (unlike certain heroes of Renaissance epic and romance—Orlando and Adonis and Rinaldo) he does not encounter her personally. The poet's subject matter, in short, was (or pretended to be) a *historia* rather than a vision or a parable or a fictional *argumentum*.[2]

In practice, of course, many of these stories and personages and settings were the author's own invention. Nevertheless, however fabulous his subject matter, he frequently maintained the fiction of following an older authority—a stylistic convention that, in view of the frequently ambiguous boundary line between poetry and history, may be relevant to the claims of Geoffrey of Monmouth. The authority himself might be legendary, or begotten by a scribal error like Chaucer's Lollius; and even after citing a real authority the poet often felt free to alter the narrative as he saw fit. The personages of one cycle might be shifted to another, and legendary ancestors could be invented for the poet's patron without his dropping the pretense of historicity. Such fabrications are common in Renaissance romance-epic. Boiardo transfers Morgain-le-Fay from the Arthurian tradition to the Roland cycle; Ariosto not only invents the story of Roland's madness, on the analogy of the madness of Hercules and Lancelot, but introduces the mythological figures of Atlas (already allegorized as an astrologer and hence an appropriate prototype for a magician) and the Harpies. Tasso, in turn, transfers Rinaldo—already celebrated as a Carolingian hero in Ariosto's *Orlando Furioso* and in Tasso's own *Rinaldo*—to the setting of the First Crusade.

2.

On the nature and extent of allegory in medieval romance scholars still disagree. Like the *mirabilia* of the *Odyssey* and Ovid's *Metamorphoses* and the apocalyptic imagery of the Scriptures, the sundry wonders of the romances—monsters and fays and apparitions—lend themselves readily to allegorical interpretation. Nevertheless many of them may be little more than what they appear to be on the surface: the conventional paraphernalia of the supernatural, an inheritance from the pagan and Christian marvelous. It was the marvelous—along with the celebration of love and valor, courtly manners and chivalric ceremony—that constituted the chief appeal of the romance in the Renaissance as in the Middle Ages; and it was this element of *maraviglia* that Tasso consciously sought to preserve in the heroic poem, rationalizing the marvelous by basing it on the Christian supernatural and defending its value in epic poetry by appealing to the authority of Aristotle.[3]

The marvelous in medieval romance could exist in its own right, though it could on occasion, like the wonders and "ferlies" of dream-visions, become the vehicle of allegorical senses. The symbolic dreams of Arthur and Troilus (and, for that matter, the dream of Chaunticleer in Chaucer's mock-epic) are significant primarily

The Lamb and the Elephant

for the plot; they are enigmatic visions, revelations of present conditions or prophecies of future events, whose meaning is subsequently made apparent by the action itself. As symbolic and "significant" dream-visions, they are analogous to the enigmatic prophecies of the Apocalypse and the allegorical dreams of medieval poets. They reveal present or future situations and events through cryptic symbols that are not always apparent to the dreamer and demand explanation, just as the dreams of Pharaoh and Nebuchadnezzar require interpretation by Joseph and Daniel. This method serves not only to arouse suspense, but also to emphasize a crucial incident in the narrative. This type of dream, expressing prophecy through symbol, performs much the same function in the development of the plot as other kinds of omens or signs (such as augury from the flight of birds, lucky or unlucky days or hours, and the like), which are likewise proleptic and symbolic.

The mythological machinery in Chaucer's Knight's Tale is essentially an astrological allegory, as J. M. Manly and Chauncey Wood have recognized. In emphasizing the planetary associations of the major pagan divinities, Chaucer is following the conventions of "natural" allegory,[4] without sacrificing the moral symbolism of the ancient gods. The fusion of these two different modes of allegoresis is made easier by the traditional influence of the planets on psychological as well as physiological character or temperament. Nevertheless, the allegorical element in the Knight's Tale is limited. Saturated as it is with Boethian commonplaces, it may be plausibly interpreted as a moral *exemplum*, but hardly as a sustained allegory.

Though the author of chivalric epic might sometimes profess to instruct as well as entertain, combining *prodesse* with *delectare*, this was a conventional formula—like the poet's concomitant but inconsistent claims that he is recounting a tale never told before and that he is relating historical fact based on the authority of earlier chroniclers or poets—and one cannot always take him at his word. Moreover, in this genre (as contrasted with other literary species, such as the philosophical epic and the dream-vision) his normal means of combining profit with delight is the method of the *exemplum* (with or without passages of moral commentary or a concluding *moralitas*) rather than the method of allegory. Though he may make occasional use of allegorical techniques in various episodes, he often utilizes them primarily as narrative devices—means of introducing and rationalizing the marvelous or foreshadowing the principal events in the plot—and only secondarily as devices for conveying ethical doctrine. In such cases, both profit and delight reside essentially in the narrative example. This in turn may serve as a hortatory or dehortatory argument, illustrating the nature and rewards of virtues and vices and proposing patterns for emulation or avoidance.

3.

In the chivalric epics and romances of the Renaissance, the allegorical element is often more prominent than in those of the Middle Ages. Though this is often merely a difference in degree—and we should not overestimate its importance—it is apparent in the differences between the *Teseida* or *Filostrato* and the Knight's Tale or *Troilus and Criseyde* on the one hand, and the *Orlando Innamorato* or *Orlando Furioso* and the *Faerie Queene* on the other. In the major romance-epics from Boiardo to Spenser there would appear to be increasing emphasis on allegory. Aside from the allegorical gardens and palaces prominent in all of these Renaissance romances, portraying the illusions of sensual pleasure through the fiction of enchantment, allegorical elements become operative in the plot, linking various persons and episodes—and eventually, in Spenser's epic, providing the conceptual framework for the formal organization of his narrative. In Ariosto's poem, the ring of reason, the Hippogriff of imagination, and perhaps (as commentators have suggested) the several horses of irrational appetite occur throughout the poem in association with different scenes and characters and events. Ariosto has adapted them to the conventional romance technique of *entrelacement*, or interweaving the several strands of the narrative. As narrative devices they strengthen the interrelationships between the numerous subplots, and as allegorical symbols they help to create the impression of thematic unity in a diffuse and episodic poem. From time to time, usually in the introductory stanzas to various cantos, the poet himself sometimes draws a moral inference explicitly or advises the reader to look for a hidden meaning.

Though the symbolic content of the *Orlando Furioso* was greatly exaggerated by sixteenth-century commentators, their interpretations helped to shape Spenser's conception of the romance as a vehicle of moral truth under the guise of allegorized wars and amours, and Milton's similar view of the same genre as the medium of profounder truths than the apparently "vain or fabulous" surface meaning.

The allegorical element in the epics of Trissino and Tasso presents a different problem. Both poems were deliberately modeled on classical epics, and opportunities for allegory were accordingly limited. Nevertheless, Homer's fable of Circe provided a precedent for introducing a symbolic palace or garden of sensual pleasure and intemperance like those in the romances of Boiardo and Tasso. Though Trissino's account of the enchantress Acratia is only an episode, Tasso's pagan sorceress Armida plays an active role throughout the plot. She is the literary descendant of the classical Circe and the romantic Alcina. Her pleasure garden belongs to the tradition of Boiardo's fays and Ariosto's enchantress, and her victim Rinaldo is enslaved by inglorious ease and sensual delight in the same manner as Alcina's victim Ruggiero.

Misleading and imprisoning a large detachment of Godfrey's knights and subsequently detaining Rinaldo on her enchanted island in the Atlantic, Armida plays one of the principal roles in the delaying action. The enchanted grove near Jerusalem, infested by devils in order to prevent the construction of siege machinery, is another narrative device for delaying the fulfilment of the epic enterprise. Tasso has modeled this fiction partly on an episode in Lucan's *Pharsalia;* at the siege of Marseilles, Caesar's army destroys a sacred grove consecrated to sinister Celtic divinities near the city. Tasso's forest is also reminiscent, however, of the magic trees and the enchanted woods and parks of medieval and Renaissance romance; moreover, like the latter it is clearly associated with sensual lust. In attempting to cut the first timber, both Tancred and Rinaldo are confronted by apparitions of their respective mistresses. The forest is of central

Image and Idea

importance in the construction of Tasso's plot, for the attack on the Holy City has been frustrated for the greater part of the poem by the need for siege machines, and the enterprise cannot succeed until Rinaldo returns from captivity and exile. The forest motif and the Armida motif are closely related, therefore, both in their symbolic significance and in their importance for the principal delaying action. In both of these instances, Tasso employs symbols of sensual lust as a method of organizing and developing his plot, rationalizing his symbolic fictions by representing them as the effects of sorcery. Indeed, magic performs a multiple office in the poem, prompting the principal delaying actions, associating the opponents of the Crusaders with infernal powers, lending verisimilitude and probability to the marvelous, and functioning as a symbol for the enticements of sensual pleasure. In allegorical interpretations of the Circe myth and Ariosto's Alcina, the sorceress had already become a symbol of *luxuria* and intemperance or even a figure of the *meretrix*. Tasso could exploit these associations all the more effectively since the majority of his readers would already have been familiar with them.

Armida's palace and the enchanted wood are romantic and allegorical elements in an epic that consciously attempted to combine the variety of the romance and its erotic adventures with the unified structure and martial argument of classical epic. In accordance with neo-Aristotelian principles, the narrative must be probable and verisimilar on the literal level, and Tasso explicitly distinguishes the functions of imitation and allegory. Though much of his own "allegory" of the poem appears to have been an afterthought, the fact that he found it advisable to allegorize his epic at all, and that Graziani subsequently allegorized his own heroic poem on the conquest of Granada in very similar terms, is significant. It reflects the continued vitality of the Renaissance allegorical tradition at the crucial stage when neoclassical principles were challenging the methods of the romance—not only demanding a unified plot with a single principal hero instead of a multiplicity of interlacing narratives describing the enterprises of different heroes, but also insisting on verisimilitude and probability in imitation instead of improbable and incredible fictions.

Unlike Mazzoni, who had defended Dante's improbabilities as

credible on an allegorical level, Tasso was not concerned, apparently, with justifying his mimetic method on the grounds of allegorical content; according to his own aesthetic principles, his imitation ought to appear probable and "like the reality" regardless of its hidden significance. The primary function of his *allegoria* was to emphasize the moral significance of his work and thereby undermine the accusations of levity or immorality that his critics were raising and would continue to raise. Such appeals to the allegorical content of a work—justifying improbable fancies as the vehicle of philosophical certainties, fabulous vanities as the medium of grave and sententious doctrines, and apparent vices as hieroglyphs of virtues—were a conventional argument in literary apologetics; and in this respect Tasso's *allegoria* to the *Jerusalem Delivered* performs essentially the same rhetorical function as Boccaccio's allegorization of pagan myth, and Ariosto's insistence on the hidden moral significance of his romance. Whatever other ends they may serve, these appeals to a higher level of meaning are defensive arguments against possible moral objections by adverse critics. Finally, in adding an *allegoria* to his epic, Tasso is not only inviting comparison with rival epics in the vernacular (for both Dante's *Commedia* and Ariosto's romance-epic had been subjected to extensive and intensive allegorical analysis); he is also placing his heroic poem more firmly in the tradition of classical epic. Both Homer and Virgil had been lauded for the profound ethical and physical or metaphysical doctrines concealed in their works.[5] In providing a similar allegory—based on Christian moral theology as well as classical ethics—Tasso is stressing the continuity of the *Gerusalemme Liberata* with the epic tradition, but he is also and simultaneously emphasizing the superiority of the Christian ethics underlying his own allegory to the pre-Christian doctrines underlying the poetic fables of Homer and Virgil.

In perhaps the majority of chivalric epics and romances of the late Middle Ages and the Renaissance, the allegorical element is subordinated to narrative interest. Usually it is confined largely to isolated episodes or to the roles of certain fays and sorceresses. Alternatively, as in the case of Tasso and Graziani, the moral allegory may (in large part) be extrinsic—superimposed more or less arbitrarily on the entire poem—a pattern of meaning external to the plot and characters rather than inherent in the narrative design. In Spenser's romance-epic, however, the allegorical pattern is inherent in the plot structure, the choice of characters, and the subject matter of the majority of episodes. Among chivalric romances this poem is remarkable not only for the large number of personified abstractions and of characters who themselves are thinly disguised images of abstract virtues and vices, but also for the degree to which allegorical significance governs the development and interplay of character and action. The marvelous has been invested with symbolic meaning to a greater extent than had been customary in the chivalric tradition, and the moral allegory is implicit in the formal organization of this epic and the relationship between principal hero and secondary heroes or between the plot of the epic as a whole and the plots of its component books. The direct intervention of Prince Arthur (magnificence and/or divine grace) at crucial moments in the action of the individual books exhibits the characteristic of magnanimity as a universal virtue comprehending all the others, while his quest of Gloriana (glory) reflects the ethical doctrine that the end or final cause of magnanimity and heroic virtue is honor and glory. Within each book, moreover, the relation of the hero to his lady, his associates, and his enemies is conditioned by traditional ethical concepts: the end and object of this particular virtue, its adjuncts and attributes, and its logical contraries, the excess and defect of the Aristotelian mean.

The structure of the complete work, as Spenser conceived it, reflects the influence of both ethical and literary tradition and of both medieval and classical motifs. By devoting a separate book to a particular knight as patron or pattern of a particular virtue, but integrating all twelve books into a single poem, and all twelve heroic virtues into the figure of a single pattern-hero, Spenser was endeavoring in his own way to achieve what Tasso and other Italian poets had attempted by somewhat different means—to reconcile the epic principles of unity of action and the central image of a perfect and complete heroic exemplar, endowed with the cycle of heroic virtues, with the romantic principle of variety of incident, setting, and character. The twelve books devoted to twelve heroes illustrating the moral virtues would correspond not only to Virgil's twelve-book epic, but also to the twelve labors of Hercules and the twelve paladins of France. The addition of twelve more books devoted to the political virtues, in turn, would bring the total number to twenty-four, like the twenty-four book epics of Homer.

Spenser amply merited the epithets Milton bestowed on him: "sage and serious." His poem is unusual among chivalric epics insofar as it generally places primary emphasis on the moral allegory rather than on the fierce wars and faithful loves that are its announced subject and that theoretically serve as vehicles and symbols for the allegorical senses. This is more characteristic, on the whole, of the two first and final books than of the third and fourth books (which critics have usually regarded as containing earlier material). This is one of the principal differences between Spenser's epic and those of Ariosto and Boiardo; and it results, in large part, from the poet's conscious application of the commonplaces of Renaissance allegorical theory to the actual planning and composition of his poem. His poem differs from its romantic predecessors not only in the degree to which chivalric combats and amours are overburdened with the superstructure of moral, religious or political significance but also in its fidelity to Renaissance ideals of the allegorical function of poetry.

Although many poets boasted of allegorical profundities, their claims were often exaggerated, and the weighty moralities that their commentators professed to discover were often little more than exegetical afterthoughts. It is as though Spenser, mindful of the claims that Fornari had made for Ariosto, Tasso for the *Gerusalemme*, and numerous commentators for the *Aeneid* and the *Iliad* and the *Odyssey*—had consciously set out to compose the moral and historical allegory that these poets had supposedly attempted in their own works. His poem differs from the earlier romances, to which it is so frequently indebted, not because he held a different conception of allegory from the majority of Renaissance theorists, but because, unlike the majority of romancers, he apparently took the theory seriously—and acted upon it in composing his own epic romance.

The epics of Spenser and Tasso are interesting not only as diverse solutions to the problem of reconciling epic unity and martial heroism with the narrative variety and erotic themes of the romance, but also as different attempts to achieve a compromise between ideals of credible imitation (verisimilitude and probability) and allegorical content. In *The Faerie Queene*, surface probability and verisimilitude are frequently sacrificed to allegorical content; the latter is genuinely inherent in the narrative structure and the interrelationships among the epic persons; credibility, verisimilitude, and probability are to be found rather in the correspondences between allegorical and literal levels than on the literal plane. The image of a personified abstraction seems convincing because its concrete physical attributes and its particular words and actions are appropriate to the general idea that they help to define. The decorum consists in the accommodation of appropriate concrete particulars to a universal idea. This is an altogether different kind of verisimilitude and probability and decorum from that which neoclassical critics demanded of the poet and which severely limited the imaginative vision of judges as sensible as Samuel Johnson. Spenser's allegorical mode, achieved at the partial expense of verisimilitude, represents one solution to the Renaissance tension between surface lifelikeness and covert allegorical content. Tasso's epic, which tends at times to subordinate allegorical significance to surface verisimilitude, constitutes an alternative solution.

Both in its romantic form and content and in its preference for symbolic or allegorical statement over probable or lifelike imitation, *The Faerie Queene* would appear to be provincial and old-fashioned by contemporary Italian standards, the product of a cultural lag. In contemporary Italy, Spenser's epic would have seemed irregular indeed by neo-Aristotelian standards; and in Florence or Rome or Venice a major poet might well hesitate before violating classical ideals of structural unity and mimetic verisimilitude so openly.

4.

The fashionable ideals of restoring the arts and sciences of antiquity and of imitating or adapting classical models were perhaps more frequently honored in the breach than in the observance. At times they were little more than rhetorical commonplaces. Nevertheless, they often complicated the problems of the Renaissance allegorist. On the one hand, he had been encouraged to look for covert moral or theological truths under the cortex of pagan fable. Imitation of classical poetry and art would, accordingly, involve not merely fidelity to the principles of external form but also a comparable attempt to enrich the doctrinal content of a poem or painting through allegorical senses. On the other hand, the major literary theorists of antiquity had insisted on verisimilitude and probability and decorum in literary or plastic imitation. The poetic fable must appear convincing, plausible, and significant on the literal plane, regardless of any deeper allegorical content. Violations of verisimilitude in the principal Greek and Latin epics and dramas were few. With the notable exception of the pagan marvelous (which could be rationalized in terms of the religious beliefs of antiquity as well as on the allegorical level), these were restricted largely to personifications like Fame and Fortune. The more closely a Renaissance poet imitated the major dramatic or heroic poems of antiquity, and the more scrupulously he adhered to the doctrines of Horace and Aristotle as he understood them, the less scope he had for free allegorical invention. The ideal of imitating the ancients thus tended both to encourage and to discourage the use of allegory.

The Ovidian tradition offered greater scope for fantasy and for exploitation of the marvelous. Besides providing a source book of classical myths and legends for medieval or Renaissance poets, it suggested the manner in which an imaginative writer might invent his own myths or adapt the fables and marvels of Celtic and Germanic tradition to the conventions of his art. In imitating the example of Ovid, he would be less bound by the principles of verisimilitude and probability; and with a freer exploitation of the marvelous he might also possess ampler scope for adapting and altering traditional myths, combining them with fables and legends derived from postclassical sources or with fresh inventions, and investing them with new significance.

Renaissance allegorical romance was, on the whole, an eclectic tradition, combining mythical and allegorical conventions derived from various sources—classical and medieval, pagan and Christian—

and sometimes overlaying these elements with a Celtic and Oriental veneer to enhance the sense of the marvelous and of distance in space or time. The spells of Celtic fays and Saracen sorceresses combined with Ovidian or Virgilian metamorphoses, the charms of Homer's Circe and the songs of Sirens. Atlas and the Harpies and the Perseus-Bellerophon myth entered Carolingian romance, along with Arthurian figures like Morgain-le-Fay. Renaissance magicians and their enchanted gardens and palaces were frequently composite images, retaining the allegorical associations of their classical analogues and prototypes. Boiardo's Fallerina and Alcina (the former, queen of the Orkneys; the latter, a fay and sister to Morgana) are enchantresses partly modeled on Circe. They are emblems of sensual lust, just as his Morgana, partly modeled on Fortuna or Occasio, represents material prosperity. Though these are fays, introduced into the story of the Carolingian hero Orlando, they exhibit the features and moral significance of classical prototypes. Ariosto's Alcina—seductress, witch, and symbolic fisher of men—is another Circe-Siren figure. Like Tasso's Armida, she is a symbol of carnal pleasure and the allurements of the senses. In both instances the vicious spells are broken, and the hero liberated from voluptuous bondage, through the agency of reason.

On occasion the Circe figure became an actual personification, like Trissino's Acratia and Spenser's Acrasia (incontinence). Both Circe and the Sirens had been allegorized, moreover, as types of the *meretrix;* this association also may be implicit in Ariosto's fable of Alcina. The *voluptas*-magician motif and the intemperance-metamorphosis image were equally popular in masques and pageants and allegorical tableaux, like the *Ballet comique de la reine* and Milton's *Comus.* They recur in the Dalila episode of *Samson Agonistes*, though as metaphor rather than as allegory. As harlot and symbolic enchantress, equipped with charmed cup and warbling charms, Dalila is reminiscent of Circe, just as Samson's "effeminate bondage" recalls the amorous captivity and effeminacy of Ariosto's Ruggiero and Tasso's Rinaldo in the palaces of Alcina and Armida. The motifs of sensual blindness and rational insight, of stripping the sorceress to expose the ugliness of vice, and of escape through repentance (Metanoia) belong to the same tradition. Samson, too, has been blinded,

The Lamb and the Elephant

imprisoned, and transformed through Dalila's enchantments, and his repudiation of the metaphorical sorceress links him with the Renaissance allegorical tradition.

The motif of the voluptuous life and inglorious ease and the conversion from vice to virtue through the exercise of reason are favorite themes in the Renaissance. Moreover, writers and artists of the period possessed an exceptionally wide range of symbols and exempla for illustrating them: the Judgment of Paris, the Choice of Hercules, Scipio's Dream, the Pythagorean Y, Hercules and Iole or Omphale, Achilles on Scyros, Virgil in the Basket, Samson and Dalila, Odysseus and Hermes and Circe, Odysseus and Hermes and Calypso, Odysseus and the Sirens, Aeneas and Dido. The personifications of virtue and vice are sometimes represented as estranged sisters or warring princesses, as in Ariosto and Trissino. Sometimes the choice between the active, contemplative, or voluptuous life is depicted through the symbolism of inscribed gates, as in Colonna's *Hypnerotomachia Poliphili*. Frequently vice is represented as an enchantress or fay, while the life of pleasure (the *vita voluptaria*) is figured as a sensual paradise of delights, a parody of the *hortus deliciarum* of Genesis, or as an enchanted palace: the garden of Mirth (Deduit) in the *Romance of the Rose*, the palace of Venus in the *Parliament of Fowls* and the glassy temple of the same divinity in the *House of Fame*, or the dwellings of Fallerina and Alcina, Armida and Acrasia, the palace of Comus, the enchanted groves of *Paradise Regained* and *Jerusalem Delivered*. Sometimes reason is represented as a magic ring of exceptional virtue or a benevolent princess, as in Ariosto; sometimes as a guide who performs the offices of Mercury, like Spenser's Palmer, the Attendant Spirit of *Comus*, and the sage who instructs Rinaldo's fellow-Crusaders how to effect the hero's rescue.

The medieval chivalric epic usually maintained the pretense of narrating *res gestae*—deeds of love and valor and courtesy—and though it might function as a moral *exemplum* its primary method was that of straightforward narration or of interlacing narratives rather than the allegorical mode. The element of the marvelous consisted primarily in the spells of fays and sorcerers, giants and other monsters, enchanted castles, shape shiftings, and occasional symbolic

Image and Idea

dreams and prophecies. The philosophical epic, on the other hand, was more frequently conceived as a unified and coherent allegory; and the dream-vision offered even greater opportunities for apparently free (though in fact close-knit) fantasies—improbable marvels whose actual coherence and probability were intelligible only in terms of their allegorical significance.

In contrast to the enchanted groves and castles of the chivalric romances, those of the dream-vision are sometimes elaborated symbolically in great detail. The heavily symbolic gardens of Alcina and Armida and Acrasia represent a conflation of allegorized classical motifs with the allegorical gardens and palaces of medieval visionary literature and with the enchanted castles and parks of medieval chivalric romance. The figure of Nature in Spenser's romance and Chaucer's dream-vision derives ultimately from the philosophical epic of Alain de Lille. The personification of Reason in the *Romance of the Rose* is a fusion of Boethius' Dame Philosophy and the Biblical Sapientia. Medieval dream-vision and philosophical epic usually made far more extensive use of personification-allegory than contemporary chivalric literature and (as in Chaucer's image of Fame) frequently based their descriptions of these allegorical *personae* on details derived from a fairly wide range of classical or medieval sources. Renaissance romancers often emulated their eclecticism, basing their own symbolic tableaux on elements drawn from classical, medieval, and earlier Renaissance works. In Spenser's romance the allegorical element is further complicated by the addition of apocalyptic imagery and the influence of medieval religious allegories, fusing the motifs of the pilgrimage of human life and the imagery of Christian warfare with the romantic quests of knights-errant, with interpretations of the labors of Hercules and other classical heroes as the triumph of virtue over monstrous vices, with the conception of Aeneas' travails as an allegory of the life of man, and perhaps with the exegesis of medieval and Renaissance epic enterprises as the pursuit of beatitude.

Renaissance epic and romance, like the dramas and lyrics, the satires and encomia, the histories and dialogues of the period, frequently exhibit greater continuity with medieval tradition than their authors recognized. The debate of body and soul and the allegorical

The Lamb and the Elephant

journey of salvation survive into the seventeenth century. In *Paradise Lost* E. M. W. Tillyard perceives an epic elaboration of the morality theme of Everyman, and other scholars have detected similar survivals of medieval motifs in English and Continental drama. Sixteenth-century satire continues the tradition of *Piers Plowman*. Metaphysical lyrics exploit scholastic terminology as a source of wit. Sonneteers elaborate the conventional topics of the *encomium mulieris*, the cult of "refined love," the motifs of constancy and inconstancy in affection, love and friendship, and the *donna angelicata*. The hexaemeral tradition as elaborated by medieval encyclopedists recurs, as Virgil Whitaker points out, in Bacon's image of the Six Days' Works in *The Advancement of Learning* and *New Atlantis*.[6] The medieval anatomy of folly extends through Brant and Erasmus and Burton to reappear, with Ariostan accretions, in Milton's Limbo of Vanity. Milton's *History of Britain* draws heavily on medieval histories and chronicles as well as on classical and Renaissance writers. The philosophical epic survives in the romantic allegories of Spenser and Phineas Fletcher and Henry More, and in Milton's neoclassical epics. In many of these works one encounters rather a transformation of medieval traditions than a radical break. The conventional forms and materials have been "reformed," in varying degrees, after classical models or after Renaissance Italian or Flemish or English examples. The reformation of secular art and learning, like the reformation in theology, was, on the whole, less radical and less thorough than it often claimed to be. It was rather a remodeling, a renovation, of traditional structures than an altogether new edifice erected on different foundations.

On the surface, however, the break with the medieval past is frequently more impressive. Critical emphasis on the principles of the classical genres and humanistic curricula centered on classical authors of the "best" periods tended to discourage close imitation of late classical and medieval works and to depreciate the medieval genres. Though the romance was sufficiently hardy to outlive the Renaissance and, stripped of its allegorical accessories, undergo a transformation into the novel; the dream-vision, which had offered apparently inexhaustible opportunities for allegorical elaboration, became increasingly obsolescent, though never entirely obsolete.

Image and Idea

Again, several of the late Roman works which had exerted so strong an influence on the method or content of medieval dialogue and dream-vision tended to be eclipsed by the writings of earlier (and, in fact, notably superior) authors. The philosophical epics and allegorical visions of the Middle Ages had frequently been heavily indebted to the mythological and astronomical imagery of Martianus Capella's allegory of the Liberal Arts, to the oneirological and metaphysical discussions and stellar imagery of Macrobius' commentary on Cicero's account of Scipio's visionary dream, and to Boethius' ethical dialogue on the inconstancy of Fortune, the distinction between true and false goods, and the nature of true felicity. All three of these works are predominantly prose, though the *De Nuptiis* and the *De Consolatione* combine verse and prose in a fashion *(prosimetrum)* that medieval commentators associated with Petronius' *Satyricon*. Nevertheless they influenced, directly or indirectly, the writings of both Latin and vernacular poets. The work of Alain de Lille and Bernard Silvestris, of Dante and Chaucer and Jean de Meung, would, in some respects, have been significantly different without the combined influence of two or more of these works.

In the Renaissance these late classical treatises did not immediately lose their popularity. All three books remained in print throughout the period, but editions were apparently more numerous in the earlier Renaissance than during the seventeenth century. The Latin text of the *Consolatio* was frequently reprinted during the late fifteenth century and throughout the sixteenth century, as well as translations into English, Dutch, German, French, Italian, and Spanish. There were several incunabular editions of Macrobius' commentary on the *Somnium Scipionis*, numerous printings in the sixteenth century, and notably fewer in the seventeenth. Though the *De Nuptiis* was published in its entirety in fifteenth- and sixteenth-century editions, its popularity thereafter seems to have declined, although selected portions of this pedagogical allegory, such as the discussions of rhetoric or of music, were occasionally reprinted in the seventeenth century.

All three of these books continued to be read throughout the Renaissance; and, if C. S. Lewis is correct, Spenser borrowed a detail from Martianus Capella for his account of the books and papers vomited forth by the monster Errour. Yet they were already obsolescent, and they never regained the importance they had once possessed for medieval authors. Instead of relying on Boethius and Macrobius, as their medieval predecessors had done, Renaissance poets could turn directly to the writings of the Stoics and Platonists themselves in the original tongue or in competent translations. Philological studies and new scientific discoveries diminished the pedagogical value of Capella's allegory of the Liberal Arts. The declining authority of these works, which had exerted so strong an influence on medieval allegorical literature, together with the decline of the dream-vision as a literary genre, the increasing demand for verisimilitude and probability in poetic imitation on the literal level, and the preference for classical authors of an earlier period as models, contributed to the differences between late medieval and Renaissance styles and methods.

5.

Finally, in endeavoring to teach, delight, and persuade, both medieval and Renaissance authors or artists could accomplish these ends on the literal as well as the allegorical plane, through example as well as through symbol. Through "correct" imitation—probable and verisimilar images of actions or characters or passions—they could depict the nature of virtues and vices as well as through metaphorical or transumptive methods. Even though appeals to the allegorical content of poetry and myth persist throughout the Renaissance, toward the end of the period apologists for their art tend to place primary stress on the ethical value of the poetic exemplum, echoing Horace's praise of Homer, or on the ability of the poet's imitation to purge the passions, following Aristotle's lead. The defensive argument that poetry represents the forms or Ideas of virtues and vices rests ultimately on Aristotle's statement that the poet is more philosophical than the historian inasmuch as the poet expresses the universal Idea. The further argument—advanced by Horace, Valvasone, and Milton—that the poet teaches more effectively than the philosopher is based on the superiority of the concrete sensuous example over abstract logic as an instrument of instruction. The additional defense, echoed by Sidney, that the poet persuades to virtue more successfully than the philosopher derives partly from Platonic and Ciceronian rhetorical theory. According to the *Phaedrus* and other dialogues, the realm of universals is invisible and can be contemplated only by the eye of the intellect—by the gods and separated souls in the heaven above the stars—or by philosophers through the process of dialectic. Of all the Ideas, only beauty remains visible to the sensuous eye, arousing love for physical beauty and ultimately leading the soul back to the invisible Idea of absolute beauty. Yet if men could behold the beauty of *phronesis*, they would instinctively be rapt by love of her. In *De Officiis*, Cicero quotes Plato's remarks on the beauty of *sapientia* and applies it specifically to *honestas* (moral goodness); and a host of Renaissance writers, including Bacon, Brinsley, and Milton, subsequently applied this *topos* to the beauty of virtue.[7] Medieval writers may also have encountered it in the *De Officiis*, as well as through the tradition of Augustinian rhetoric (recently explored by Richard McKeon, Marcia Colish, J. A. Mazzeo, and others).

Since both of these Platonic commonplaces concern the persuasive force of beauty and the interrelationship between the invisible archetype and its sensuous embodiment, both held significant implications for rhetoric and poetics. The conception of physical beauty as a visible emblem of divine beauty and the idealization of love as a means of intellectual ascent from earthly to celestial goods and from the illusory world of sense to the archetypal realm of Ideas could serve as a *topos* for praising the beauty of a mistress and the nobility of human love, for lauding the works of nature or those of art, for glorifying earthly love and beauty or for exhorting from these to their celestial counterparts. Frequently associated with medieval conventions of chivalric love and sometimes combined with classical or Christian images—feminine personifications like the Biblical Sapientia or Boethius' Dame Philosophy, or the Liberal Arts, Scriptural types like the bride of the Canticles or Rachel and Leah, and analogies between the Holy Spirit and secular love—these motifs reappeared in the idealized encomia of mistresses, real or allegorical, in late medieval and Renaissance erotic verse. They survived in the fashionable court-Platonism of the sixteenth and seventeenth centuries, silvering passion with the pale cast of philosophical terminology, to recur in the revived Platonism of the German and English romanticists.

Equally significant, however, are the rhetorical associations of Plato's allusion to the beauty of *phronesis* and Cicero's remarks on *honestas*. The *Phaedrus* is a dialogue on rhetoric, and *De Officiis* concerns the ethical instruction essential for a skilled and responsible orator. Both writers are arguing that rhetorical eloquence should be based on philosophical learning, on knowledge of truth. A similar attitude underlies Ramus' insistence that rhetoric presupposes dialectics, and that the orator must turn to logic for the invention and disposition of his arguments. The same point of view recurs frequently in Milton's writings. In *Comus* it differentiates the Lady's chaste eloquence from the specious rhetoric of her tempter, and the *honestas* of her music with its "sober certainty of waking bliss" from the soporific music of Circe and the Sirens and the sensual music of the enchanter himself. In *Paradise Lost* it distinguishes the discourse of divine and angelic persons, and of man himself before the Fall, from the sophistries of Belial and Satan. In *Paradise Regained* it underlies the contrasting rhetoric of Christ and Satan (truth and falsehood) and the condemnation of the eloquence of Greece. Similarly, in *An Apology for Smectymnuus*, Milton defines "true eloquence" as "none but the serious and hearty love of truth...."[8]

Aesthetic categories could, accordingly, serve as the vehicle of ethical categories, *visibilia* as the mirror of *invisibilia*,[9] instructing and persuading through portraying the beauty of virtue and the foulness of vice. Even after his fall from heaven, the Satan of *Paradise Lost* can still be rapt by the sight of beauty—the splendor of the newly created universe, the beauty of Eve, the virtue of Zephon:

>   ... abasht the Devil stood,
> And felt how awful goodness is, and saw
> Vertue in her shape how lovly.

That the Lady of *Comus* can behold "visibly" the forms or Ideas of the theological virtues Faith and Hope and the "unblemish't form of Chastity" is a poetic tribute to her purity of soul.[10] For the

Image and Idea

majority of men, the forms of the virtues are invisible. Nevertheless, the masque itself serves as a means of making these virtues apparent, insofar as the Lady herself exemplifies, manifests, and "illustrates" them. She does not only "see" the Ideas of the virtues visibly; through her own victorious trial she makes them visible to the spectators. In the same way Satanic temptation can manifest or illustrate the high worth of Job or the merit of the Christ of *Paradise Regained*. The action or suffering of the hero or heroine becomes a concrete example and visible emblem of a universal and invisible idea.

The aesthetic and rhetorical force of the concrete image as a means of instruction and persuasion could be applied to art as well as literature, and indeed to the works of nature (the rhetoric and art of God), as well as to the productions of human art. Both painters and poets claimed to be imitating essences and ideas—investing abstractions with sensuous form, expressing universals through particulars, rendering the sundry virtues and vices perceptible to the senses as well as comprehensible to the mind. By thus embodying the idea in an image, they managed simultaneously to delight the senses, instruct the intellect, and move the will. For those who believed that the ideas themselves had originally been abstracted from sensory data, the method of poetry and painting could apparently parallel the normal process of human learning. For those who thought that ideas were innate but obscured by sense-experience and could be recovered systematically only through dialectic, the poem or picture—insofar as it imitated a universal idea and thus presented a refined image to the mind—might constitute a higher level of knowledge than ordinary sense experience. Despite Plato's censure of poets as imitators of imitations, they might lead the spectator upward on the scale of contemplation or ladder of love from sensible to intelligible objects, from the visible to the invisible. For those who extolled the veiled symbols of mystical theology over the logical methods of demonstrative theology, the method of the sister arts might seem to parallel the method of divine revelation. It was by analogy with Scriptural visions and parables that Boccaccio justified the fables of the ancients, arguing that poetry itself is a mode of theology. In at-

The Lamb and the Elephant

tempting to give concrete expression to abstract ideas, both of the sister arts utilized such rhetorical devices as allegory, personification, and exemplum.

6.

Normally serving as inductive proof—an inference from the concrete particular to the abstract universal—the exemplum has frequently assumed a variety of forms and styles in poetry. The author may set forth his "proofs" or examples in a complete story, as in Chaucer's Nun's Priest's Tale or the summary of the *Aeneid* in *The House of Fame*. Alternatively, he may relate a series of brief tales illustrating the same point, like the tragedies in Chaucer's Monk's Tale and *The Legend of Good Women*. He may insert a few short exempla into a longer narrative exemplum, like Chaunticleer's anecdotes of prophetic dreams and Chaucer's references, in Book I of *The House of Fame*, to faithful women whose tragic ends had paralleled Dido's fate. In other cases, where the poet is reluctant to divert attention from his principal tale to other stories, a mere catalog of names may suffice, as in the list of love's victims depicted on the walls of Venus' temple in *The Parliament of Fowls*.

In medieval visionary literature the principal exemplum may take the form of a dream, while a similar story with an analogous situation or significance may serve as the point of departure for the narrative and the occasion for the dream. Ovid's tale of Ceyx and Halcyone performs this compound function—as occasion for the dream journey, as prelude, and as a preliminary and analogous exemplum—in *The Book of the Duchess*, while the eschatological vision of the *Somnium Scipionis* plays a similar role in *The Parliament of Fowls*.[11] The narrator of the exemplum may himself be an examplar of the vice or virtue he is describing (as Chaucer's Pardoner exemplifies avarice or cupidity, the Wife of Bath sensual lust and desire of sovereignty). The examples may be presented through direct narration or description, through the arguments of characters in the story, through the device of reading a book or observing persons and events depicted in sculpture or painting or stained-glass windows.

Exempla of virtues and vices could easily become stereotyped conventions, and it required considerable poetic skill to present them

Image and Idea

with freshness and variety. Few medieval or Renaissance poets have displayed the range and variety of invention that Dante achieves. The various *loci* or places that the traveler visits in his speculative journey, and the rewards and punishments he beholds there, exhibit the general character and essential nature of these virtues and vices. The persons he encounters in this moral cosmos as particular examples of virtue or vice often illustrate these qualities not only in their accounts of their own past actions, and those of their fellows in reward or punishment, but also in their characteristic speech and action. In accordance with decorum, the spirits in Hell and Heaven exhibit the essential qualities of character for which they have been beatified or condemned. Those in Purgatory, on the other hand, are usually characterized through the method of opposition; in speech and action they normally display the virtues diametrically opposite to the particular vices for which they are atoning.

Dante's method leaves him free to concentrate on a few primary examples of a specific vice or virtue, focusing largely on persons and events from recent or contemporary Italian history. As a result, he is able to create the illusion of a dramatic and personal interrelationship between the poet and his examples, endowing them with concrete and individual personality. In placing primary emphasis on the contrast between the living voyager and the dead shades who aid or hinder or consult with him, he expertly exercises art to conceal art, consciously playing down the technical realities of the situation—the fact that rhetorically and poetically these figures are, after all, little more than exempla. It is the poet himself, not Minos or Rhadamanthys or Pluto, who has assigned them their moral significance and their position in Hell or Purgatory or Heaven—and who preserves the polite fiction of surprise in encountering them there.

Except for the distinction (consistently maintained) between the one living man and the multiple spirits of the dead, Dante is consciously underplaying the functional differences between poet and exempla, thereby endowing the latter with the illusion of reality. The poet and his examples of virtues and vices react personally and sometimes violently, with tears or laughter, delight or grief, scorn or pity, love or hate; in this way he endows moral concepts with dramatic and sensuous immediacy. Inductive proofs have been in-

The Lamb and the Elephant

vested with individual personality and a concrete existence over and above their generic and ethical meaning. These phantasms are *eidola* and phantoms in a multiple sense: shades of the dead, images imprinted in the fantasy of the contemplative and visionary protagonist, shadows or emblems of ethical abstractions and moral universals, and fictive images created by the poet.

Exemplary figures like Francesca da Rimini, Filippo d'Argenti, Ciacco, Count Ugolino, and the multitudes of their near-contemporaries who crowd the circles of Hell and Purgatory and Heaven, lend historical immediacy and verisimilitude to the poet's presentation of moral universals, bringing the abstract concepts into sharper definition and clearer focus. At the same time, the eschatological framework into which the poet has fitted these moral or political examples not only clarifies their ethical significance, but also enhances their demonstrative value as the objects of the poet's satiric or eulogistic judgment of current conditions in church and state and of the virtues and vices of contemporary society. These examples and proofs acquire additional rhetorical force through being imaginatively conceived and dramatically realized in terms of concrete personal and historical details. Such examples include not only the poet's near-contemporaries, but the ancients themselves: Ulysses and Capaneus, Virgil and Statius, Cato, and St. Peter.

In addition to these "dramatic" exempla, where the man who represents the particular vice or virtue frequently recites his own story, the poet introduces his particular instances and inductive proofs through other devices as well: catalogs of names, voices heard in the air, pictures on walls and pavements, the comments that the poet's eschatological guides and spectral interlocutors make about other spirits in beatitude or torment.

7.

In defending their respective arts as instruments of instruction and delight, both poets and painters stressed the power of concrete sensuous images to convey abstract ethical ideas or invisible spiritual realities. The apologist for poetry often writes as though his were a visual rather than a verbal medium, capable of rendering virtue visi-

Image and Idea

ble and placing distant scenes or abstract universals literally before the eye. In the drama, the masque, or the dumb show the poet could, indeed, like the painter, rely on direct visual presentation; but in other cases he must depend on the ecphrasis or description, painting through words the forms and attributes of personified concepts or the design and furnishings of symbolic mansions and allegorical gardens.

On occasion the writer may consciously approximate the method of the painter, presenting his allegorical or symbolic figures and scenes as though they were actually verbal descriptions of pictures and statuary. In classical prose the *Tablet of Cebes* and in poetry the descriptions of the shields of Achilles, Hercules, and Aeneas provided literary precedents. Technically, a description was an "imperfect definition," and in poetry and painting alike such symbolic figures provided a convenient method of defining a concept, contrasting it with its logical contrary, depicting its principal causes and effects and attributes, and perhaps introducing historical or legendary exempla as well. In an allegorical triumph of Fortune or Chastity or Fame, a representation of the Choice of Hercules or the Judgment of Paris, or a vision of Heaven or Hell, the methods of the painter and poet may differ little except for the inevitable limitations of medium; and with little adaptation the figures and their attributes could be converted from one medium into that of the sister art. To a limited extent this is often true of setting as well—the allegorical garden or palace or the moral geography of the Otherworld. Dante's cosmological schema functions essentially as a schema of ethical categories (to the dismay of Croce, who denied that its objective "structure" could be true "poetry"). His topography is essentially an organized system of *topoi;* and his places *(loci)* an arrangement of *loci communes.* On a lesser scale, the category of place also serves on occasion as allegorized "commonplace" in the symbolic dwellings and gardens of classical, medieval, and Renaissance literature. Whether the writers themselves—Claudian and Ovid, Chaucer and Guillaume de Lorris, Lydgate and Milton and Spenser—consciously intended to exploit this double sense of *topos* is another matter.

The question of the analogy between visual organization and the formal organization of discursive treatises has been raised, and an-

The Lamb and the Elephant

swered in rather different ways, by several scholars. Erwin Panofsky compared the Gothic cathedral to a scholastic summa, arranged according to "a system of homologous parts and parts of parts." Stressing the "synchronous development" of Gothic architecture and scholasticism, he observed that "early Scholasticism was born at the same moment and in the same environment in which Early Gothic architecture was born in Suger's Saint-Denis."[12]

Herbert Read in turn has argued that "a plastic realization of the underlying metaphysical concepts was essential to the Medieval synthesis." Regarding "the history of mind or intellect as the history of artistic development," he argues that "it is only in so far as the artist establishes symbols for the representation of reality that mind, as a structure of thought, can take shape. The artist establishes these symbols by becoming conscious of new aspects of reality, and by representing his consciousness of these new aspects of reality in plastic or poetic images." Though willing to accept conditionally Panofsky's "notion of synchronicity," he challenges the view that the Gothic style "presents a unified appearance because it is a reflection of the great philosophical synthesis represented by medieval scholasticism."[13]

In *The Art of Memory* Frances A. Yates comments that "if Thomas Aquinas memorised his own *Summa* through 'corporeal similitudes' disposed on places following the order of its parts, the abstract *Summa* might be corporealised in memory into something like a Gothic cathedral full of images on its ordered places." According to St. Thomas Aquinas, "Man cannot understand without images *(phantasmata)*; the image is a similitude of a corporeal thing, but understanding is of universals which are to be abstracted from particulars." Though sensibilia are memorable per se, intelligibilia cannot "be apprehended by man without a phantasm." Hence one remembers "gross and sensible" things more easily than things of "subtle and spiritual import...." To remember "intelligible notions more easily," one should "link them with some kind of phantasms...." Elsewhere St. Thomas explains the Scriptural use of corporeal imagery to describe spiritual things on the ground that "it is natural to man to reach the intelligibilia through the sensibilia because all our knowledge has its beginning in sense." A later Domini-

Image and Idea

can (Bartolomeo da San Concordio) similarly declares that the invention or "finding out of images is useful and necessary for memory" inasmuch as "pure and spiritual intentions slip out of memory unless they are . . . linked to corporeal similitudes."

Miss Yates further suggests that Dante's *Inferno* could conceivably be regarded as a "kind of memory system for memorising Hell and its punishments, with striking images based on orders of places. . . . If one thinks of the poem as based on orders of places in Hell, Purgatory, and Paradise, and as a cosmic order of places in which the spheres of Hell are the spheres of Heaven in reverse, it begins to appear as a summa of similitudes and exempla, ranged in order and set out upon the universe." The "principles of artificial memory, as understood in the Middle Ages, would stimulate the intense visualization of many similitudes in the intense effort to hold in memory the scheme of salvation, and the complex network of virtues and vices and their rewards and punishments. . . ." The *Commedia* would thus "become the supreme example of the conversion of an abstract summa into a summa of similitudes of examples, with Memory as . . . the bridge between the abstraction and the image."[14]

In Dante's *Commedia* the correlation of commonplace and physical locality can be accepted as an observable fact, though the artistic and rhetorical principles underlying this arrangement require further investigation. Precisely how far this topical organization derives from the arts of memory (as Miss Yates suggests) and from rhetorical and logical conceptions of the topics of invention is still uncertain. In addition to such influences Dante's arrangement was undoubtedly conditioned by the kind of organization conventional in medieval visions of the Otherworld. Many of these apocalyptic or eschatological visions involved a close correlation of ethical *topos* and physical topography, disposing the various categories of sinners or saints in different localities. Such arrangements (one might argue) do not necessarily involve a command of rhetorical theory. They are implicit in the Biblical separation of sheep and goats and symbolism of the right and left hands of the divine judge. The principle of local distribution according to rank or profession or office was conventional in medieval, as often in modern, assemblies; and the separate grouping and arrangement of culprits according to the nature and gravity of their misdeeds are not uncommon even in ordinary penal institutions.[15]

Though Dante (and perhaps other medieval and Renaissance poets and artists) may indeed have been influenced by the tradition of the *Rhetorica ad Herennium*, his chief concern is not to facilitate the memory of an orator but to strike the imagination of his readers through sensuous images and exempla disposed in a clearly defined and readily comprehensible schema, thereby informing the intellect and moving the will. This arrangement serves aesthetic as well as rhetorical and doctrinal ends. Imposing a symmetrical and harmonious structure on a multiplicity of details, demonstrating the order of Providence and the decorum (so to speak) of divine justice, it achieves (like Milton's "cosmic epic" three centuries later) a balanced and coherent design through the juxtaposition of opposites, through a pattern of contrary principles that define and complement each other. In Saint Augustine's thought this is an aesthetic as well as a logical ideal, a principle of beauty.[16]

In both epics the formal design is, in a sense, an image of providential design; it embraces the contrary forces and ends of good and evil, virtue and vice, and their opposite rewards, integrating these *contraposti* and antitheses into a harmonious and symmetrical pattern. The "contrary music" of the poem (to borrow Miss Webber's phrase)[17] imitates the order and decorum of Providence, the antithetical beauty of the Augustinian universe. In Dante's comedy the structure of this design is essentially static, for the fable of this allegory is essentially a contemplative pilgrimage. The chief progession is that of the narrator and observer himself in his journey to God (for the poem, as Singleton observes, is essentially an *itinerarium mentis ad Deum*) through a hierarchically and topically ordered cosmos. This static logical structure provides a framework for constant movement—the motion of the celestial spheres, the downward flow of the rivers of Hell—and most of the characters and *personae* in the poem are represented in motion. In this context the opposition between motion and stasis becomes symbolic, as in the contrast between Satan frozen almost immobile at the center of the world and the rapid movement of the spheres at the circumference of the universe. The nature and direction of their movements likewise becomes

Image and Idea

symbolic: right and left associated with righteousness and unrighteousness; up or down with the love of *spiritualia* or *temporalia*; the movement of the human spirit toward its true and its natural *locus* and *patria* or its perversion to false and illusory goods. As Singleton has noted, Dante's change of direction at the center of the earth, his turn to reascend toward the stars, symbolizes the conversion of the will. Speed or slowness of movement, ease or difficulty of ascent are symbolic of the comparative corruption and purity of the spirit, the relative bondage and freedom of the will. "Rational" and "irrational movements" in the astronomical sense—motion conformable or contrary to that of the fixed stars and the primum mobile—are indicative of the harmony or opposition of the human will to the divine will and the love of God.[18] In Milton's tragic epic, on the other hand, the pattern of antitheses—the eschatological counterpoint or moral *contraposto*—is for the most part dynamic; he depicts the divine decree and its execution primarily through the imitation of an action. The justice of God's ways to men, and the operative control of Providence throughout the narrative of the loss of Paradise, from Satan's initial recovery to the expulsion of Adam and Eve, are vindicated and affirmed in and through the narrative action itself. Like the beauty of Augustine's cosmos, the harmony of Milton's poetic "heterocosm" depends on the antithetical "rhetoric" of Providence, the divine exploitation of evil as well as good to accomplish an uncontrollable and irresistible intent, and to produce greater good out of permitted and foreseen evil.[19]

Augustine had argued the moral beauty of the world, emphasizing the antithesis of good and evil. Other late classical and medieval writers had praised its physical beauty, stressing the principles of order—its harmony, proportion, and symmetry. Dante combines both arguments, portraying the moral order of the universe symbolically through its physical order and depicting the various "state[s] of souls after death" and the strictly proportioned distribution of "reward or punishment by justice" according to "merits or demerits in the exercise of . . . free will"[20] through the systematic organization of physical space. The gradations of the cosmos reflect the grades of justice; degrees of height and depth, like some tropological altimeter, demonstrate the grades of honor and dishonor,

The Lamb and the Elephant

merit and demerit. This topographical representation of ethical concepts and the conventional *topoi* of demonstrative and judicial rhetoric does not seem, however, to have been conceived primarily as a mnemonic aid, nor does it necessarily derive from the arts of memory. As a scheme of visualization and representation, it is directed largely to the understanding (and to the imagination and the will) and only secondarily to the memory; it serves less as an instrument of recall than as an aid to comprehension. There is no inherent conflict, however, between these ends; and Dante's topical method might serve all of the faculties of the mind—assisting memory as well as understanding.

This coincidence of topical and topographical patterns not only befitted the subject of the poem and the "branch of philosophy" ("morals or ethics") to which it belonged. It also served the end or "aim" of the poem: "to remove those living in this life from a state of misery, and to bring them to a state of happiness"[21]—assisting the poet to outline the essential structure of Christian ethics through a spatial schema and to depict separated substances through corporeal imagery and abstract concepts through concrete sensuous images and exempla. It facilitated clear visualization of the basic design of his poem and of the moral pattern underlying his symbolic cosmos. It provided a lucid, logical, and clearly articulated framework for organizing a vast number of mythological and historical figures and episodes, for incorporating eulogies and denunciations of dead and living persons, and for introducing moral and political digressions, passionate reflections on contemporary trends and events in church and state. Dante was still writing within a tradition (exemplified also by Averroes' commentary on Aristotle's *Poetics*) that conceived the office of the poet in terms of demonstrative rhetoric. He conferred blessings or curses, eulogy or reprehension, praise or blame. Dante's topical method permitted him not only to portray the nature and rewards of virtues and vices, but to extol or excoriate particular individuals or entire towns and cities and political factions, exalting them to the skies or (literally and figuratively) damning them to Hell. His rigidly schematized maps of Heaven and Hell and Purgatory provided topics for praising or condemning his contemporaries. Easily visualized and comprehended and readily remembered, serving imagination and understanding as well as memory, this was a framework appropriate not only for his theme and the literal and allegorical significance of his poem, but for his polemical intent.[22]

8.

Both medieval and Renaissance writers displayed similar diversity in emphasizing the ethical significance of their exempla. In some instances the poet himself draws the inference, as in the *moralitas* of Chaucer's beast-fable. At other times he may leave this task to the reader. The audience of *The Parliament of Fowls*, for instance, would presumably have been quite capable of inferring an appropriate conclusion about the consequences of love from the particular examples of famous loves depicted in Venus' temple. Helen and Semiramis, Troilus and Tristram have (as Professor Robertson observes) served their own lusts rather than the common good, and their pursuit of sensual pleasure has ended tragically for themselves or for others. The triumphs of Venus have resulted in the fall of princes and ruin of states. Here as elsewhere the poet points his moral with delicacy and tact, representing the voluptuary life by oblique but conventional symbols—figures of Venus or Eros, the walled garden or paradise of love and pleasure, the inscribed gateway—and portraying moral servitude and submission to passion through the decorum of feudal service or religious observance. Essentially these tragic lovers are examples of retributive justice, and they function poetically and rhetorically as admonitory instances of the wages of sin and the rewards of vice. Nevertheless, Chaucer tempers poetic justice with mercy. Softening his sentence of condemnation through the metaphor of religious devotion and feudal homage, he suggests obliquely that the primary blame for their misery rests not with the lovers (who have served passion and pleasure like loyal vassals) but with the feudal suzerains—the god or goddess of love, or a mortal woman; a ruling passion or a reigning mistress—who have repaid their services so ill. The formal conventions of the medieval social order, both secular and spiritual, have been transferred to the formal order of art. The ceremony of feudal homage and religious devotion has become the ceremony of poetry.

The Lamb and the Elephant

There is ironic wit, as well as a regard for decorum, in such adaptations of social to literary convention. The traditional structure of the moral order and the pattern of poetic justice are well apparent under the feudal and religious imagery. In *The Parliament of Fowls*, for instance, the tragic exempla depicted in Venus' temple—stories of lovers who had pursued their own pleasure instead of the public good—point a moral that, expressed with subtlety and courtesy, would not have been irrelevant to the society and court of Richard II.

The same *topoi* and symbols recur frequently in Renaissance poetry. In the *Hypnerotomachia Poliphili* the protagonist encounters three inscribed gateways representing the active, contemplative, and voluptuous lives. Understandably, the youthful dreamer chooses the ways of pleasure. The amorous paradise reappears in the Circean gardens and groves of Boiardo and Ariosto, Trissino and Tasso, Spenser and Milton. The images of "tyrannic" love and of erotic bondage and captivity survive in Renaissance verse, though much of the feudal and religious parody has been discarded.

9.

Renaissance poetic theorists stressed the superiority of concrete example over abstract precept not only in instructing the mind (as Horace had done), but also in stirring the passions and moving the will. As Varchi and other critics maintained, both rhetoric and poetics endeavored to persuade—to move as well as teach or delight—but, whereas the orator relied primarily on the enthymeme, the poet depended chiefly on the example. In the epic criticism of the period, literary and ethical values were closely interlinked; Homer and Virgil, Ariosto and Tasso were judged as moralists as well as stylists, and in the opinion of more than one critic the literary excellence of a heroic poem depended partly on the moral excellence of its hero.

Despite the diversity or inconsistency of heroic norms in Renaissance epic theory and practice, both critics and poets frequently conceived the epic person as a "pattern-hero," exemplifying a wide range of heroic virtues in their perfection—piety and valor, wisdom and temperance, love and constancy—virtues active and contemplative, moral and theological, acquired and infused, natural and supernatural, private and public. This idealization of the epic hero as a complete and perfect ethical exemplar is in large part a response to the interaction between moral, epistemological, and narrative principles in contemporary literary theory. In the first place, by emphasizing unity of action, neo-Aristotelian criticism tended to focus attention on a single enterprise undertaken and executed primarily through the ingenuity, daring, or piety of a principal hero, rather than on a variety of actions performed by several different champions, as in the multiple plots and episodic narratives of many of the romances. For a neoclassical poet, accordingly, it would be preferable to concentrate the heroic virtues in the epic person—and perhaps his principal adversaries and companions—rather than to distribute them among a large number of different warriors. Secondly, composite formulas for the epic hero—such as strength of mind and body, active and contemplative heroism, wisdom plus fortitude, valor and piety—had been inherited from classical epic or ethics, along with the conception of heroic virtue as superhuman excellence and the ideal of magnanimity and righteousness as universal virtues comprehending all the others. Hence the "just man," the "magnanimous man," and the "perfect hero" might well exhibit a cycle of heroic virtues rather than a more modest excellence limited to a single quality. Insofar as the poet sought, in accordance with Aristotelian, neo-Platonic, and Horatian principles of ideal imitation, to delineate the perfect ideas of magnanimity, justice, and heroic virtue in a perfect exemplar, he would tend to invest his "pattern" of a hero—whether pagan or Christian, antique or chivalric or modern, Stoic or Platonic or Aristotelian—with a variety of heroic virtues and merits. Finally, the conventions of Renaissance encomium—praising a patron or sovereign or hero for several virtues rather than for fortitude alone—tended to concentrate the patterns of heroic excellence in a single figure.

Though the method of the allegory and that of the exemplum are not identical, they may overlap; and in some of these pattern-heroes of Renaissance epic and mythography the force of the exemplum depends in part at least on the allegorical intent. In such cases the example and the allegory point to the same abstract and universal

The Lamb and the Elephant

Idea. Mythographers and poets and artists alike had ingeniously moralized Hercules and his disparate labors into a perfect and universal hero who had manifested the complex of heroic virtues. Tasso had apportioned the heroic virtues among several heroic exemplars —Godfrey, Rinaldo, Tancred, and others—partly on the analogy of Agamemnon and Achilles and Odysseus, and partly through the influence of faculty psychology. His heroic norms are primarily concentrated, however, in Godfrey as idealized leader and Rinaldo as idealized warrior, while their pagan opponents provide examples of heroic force or cunning disassociated from Christian piety. His principal method for conveying the norms of heroism is the narrative exemplum, but the superimposed "allegoria" serves essentially the same purpose. Spenser likewise combines the methods of allegory and exemplum, but with greater emphasis on the former than in Tasso's poem. The protagonist of each book of the *Faerie Queene* serves as the pattern-hero for a particular virtue, while Prince Arthur ("magnanimity") provides the pattern of a universal hero, endowed with the complex of private virtues.

NOTES

[1] Ernest Robert Curtius, *European Literature and the Latin Middle Ages*, trans. Willard R. Trask (New York and Evanston, 1953), pp. 38, 120, 198, 360-62.

[2] Charles G. Osgood, *Boccaccio on Poetry* (Indianapolis and New York, 1956). Boccaccio (pp. 48-49) defines fiction *(fabula)* as "a form of discourse, which, under guise of invention, illustrates or proves an idea; and, as its superficial aspect is removed, the meaning of the author is clear." He distinguishes four kinds of fiction, represented respectively by Aesop's fables, Ovid's *Metamorphoses*, the epic poetry of Virgil and Homer (and the comic poetry of Plautus and Terence), and "old wives' tales." The first "superficially lacks all appearance of truth," as when "brutes or inanimate things converse." The second kind sometimes "superficially mingles fiction with truth." The third is "more like history than fiction," while the fourth "contains no truth at all, either superficial or hidden." Osgood (pp. 164-65) suggests that Boccaccio's "distinctions seem to be based" on Macrobius' commentary on the *Somnium Scipionis* (1.2) "with some suggestion of Cicero's *De Inventione*" (I. 27). According to the pseudo-Ciceronian *Rhetorica ad Herennium* (I. 8. 13), a *fabula* is "neither true nor probable, like those of tragedy; a *historia* is remote in time, but a fact; an *argumentum* is fiction, yet possible," like the stories of the comedies. According to Servius' commentary on Terence, *argumentum*, the story of comedy is "fictitious, something which could happen, i.e., something verisimilar"; *fabula* is "matter that is neither true nor verisimilar"; and history is "actual deed *(res gesta)*." See Marvin T. Herrick, *Comic Theory in the Sixteenth Century* (Urbana, 1964),

140

pp. 60-61; cf. T. W. Baldwin, *Shakspere's Five-Act Structure* (Urbana, 1963), pp. 66-67.

Though Boccaccio stresses the analogy between the third kind of poetic fiction and the manner of history (the implicit link being their verisimilitude on the literal level), he emphasizes the allegorical sense that this kind of poetry often possesses over and above its literal meaning. This higher, hidden sense is more characteristic of epic poetry than of comedy: "The third kind is more like history than fiction, and famous poets have employed it in a variety of ways." Though heroic poets like Virgil and Homer "seem to be writing history" in episodes like the "description of Aeneas tossed by the storm" or the "account of Ulysses bound to the mast to escape the lure of the Sirens' song," nevertheless "their hidden meaning is far other than appears on the surface." On the other hand, although Plautus and Terence also "employed this form" of poetic fiction, these comic poets actually "intend naught other than the literal meaning of their lines. Yet by their art they portray varieties of human nature and conversation, incidentally teaching the reader and putting him on his guard. If the events they describe have not actually taken place, yet since they are common, they could have occurred, or might at some time."

According to the *Rhetorica ad Herennium*, trans. Harry Caplan (Loeb Classical Library: Cambridge, Mass. and London, 1954), pp. 22-25, "The kind of narrative based on the exposition of the facts [in negotiorum expositione] presents three forms: legendary, historical, and realistic [fabulam, historiam, argumentum]. The legendary tale comprises events neither true nor probable [Fabula est quae neque veras neque veri similes continet res], like those transmitted by tragedies. The historical narrative is an account of exploits actually performed (Historia est gesta res), but removed in time from the recollection of our age. Realistic narrative recounts imaginary events [Argumentum est ficta res] which yet could have occurred, like the plots of comedies." In his *Commentary on the Dream of Scipio*, trans. William Harris Stahl (New York, 1952), pp. 84-85, Macrobius declares that fables may serve two purposes: "either merely to gratify the ear or to encourage the reader to good works." The latter kind of story, which "draws the reader's attention to certain kinds of virtue," can be subdivided into two types: 1) fables, like those of Aesop, in which both setting and plot are fictitious, and 2) the *narratio fabulosa*, which "rests on a solid foundation of truth,... treated in a fictitious style." The latter includes performances of sacred rites, poets' tales of the deeds and ancestry of the gods, and "the mystic conceptions of the Pythagoreans," presenting the truth in the "form of a fable." Philosophers restrict themselves to the kind of *narratio fabulosa* which presents "a decent and dignified conception of holy truths, with respectable events and characters... beneath a modest veil of allegory."

In *An Apology for Smectymnuus* Milton relates how his "younger feet" had wandered "among those lofty fables and romances which recount in solemn cantos the deeds of knighthood founded by our victorious kings" and how "even those books which to many others have been the fuel of wantonness and loose living" had proved to him "so many incitements ... to the love and steadfast observation" of Chastity (Milton, *Complete Poems*, ed. Hughes, p. 294). In *Il Penseroso* he alludes to the "sage and solemn tunes" of "great Bards" who have sung "Of tourneys and of Trophies hung, / Of Forests, and enchantments drear, / Where more is meant than meets the ear" (Hughes, p. 75). In *Comus* he applies the same argument to the marvels of classical myth (and perhaps, as Hughes suggests, to medieval and Renaissance romance):

> ... 'tis not vain or fabulous.
> (Though so esteem'd by shallow ignorance)
> What the sage Poets taught by th' heav'nly Muse
> Storied of old in high immortal verse

The Lamb and the Elephant

> Of dire *Chimeras* and enchanted Isles,
> And rifted Rocks whose entrance leads to hell,
> For such there be, but unbelief is blind.

Cf. Hughes, p. 102. Hughes suggests that Homer and "all the poets down to Spenser ... were in Milton's mind"; John Milton, *Paradise Regained, The Minor Poems, and Samson Agonistes,* ed. Merritt Y. Hughes (Garden City, New York, 1937), pp. 245n-246n.

[3] Osgood observes that according to Aristotle's *Rhetoric* (III. 2) "poetry can create wonder by strange matter and expression, as rhetoric should not" (p. 160). Cf. Aristotle's *Poetics* on "the improbable" as the "most usual basis for the astonishing" and its suitability for epic more than for tragedy "because the actor is not seen" (Allan H. Gilbert, ed., *Literary Criticism: Plato to Dryden* [Detroit, 1962], p. 106).

[4] Jean Seznec, *The Survival of the Pagan Gods,* trans. Barbara F. Sessions (New York, 1961), pp. 37-83; Chauncey Wood, *Chaucer and the Country of the Stars: Poetic Uses of Astrological Imagery* (Princeton, 1970); Geoffrey Chaucer, *Canterbury Tales,* ed. John Matthews Manly (New York, 1928), pp. 132-44.

[5] As Hallett Smith observes, translators are often superreaders, and Chapman is as inclined to see allegory or symbol in Homer as Harington in Ariosto. Professor Smith has kindly called my attention to a relevant passage in Fontenelle's *Dialogues of the Dead;* in a conversation with Aesop, Homer disavows any allegorical intent. See also Allen, *Mysteriously Meant;* and Domenico Comparetti, *Vergil in the Middle Ages,* trans. E. F. M. Benecke (London, 1895).

[6] Virgil K. Whitaker, *Francis Bacon's Intellectual Milieu* (Los Angeles, 1962).

[7] See John Milton, *Complete Poems and Major Prose,* ed. Merritt Y. Hughes, pp. 95n, 505n, and my "Herbert's Platonic Lapidary," *Seventeenth-Century News.*
Plato's criticism of rhetoric must be read in the light of his contrast between knowledge and opinion and between real and apparent truth. As Ernst Cassirer observes, (*The Individual and the Cosmos in Renaissance Philosophy,* tr. Mario Domandi [New York and Evanston, 1963], pp. 16-18), "Plato's vision of the world is characterized by the sharp division he makes between the sensible and the intelligible world, i.e. between the world of appearances and the world of ideas. The two worlds, that of the 'visible' and that of the 'invisible', ... do not lie on the same plane and, therefore, admit of no immediate comparison. Rather, each is the complete opposite ... of the other." In Cassirer's opinion, "Aristotle's criticism of the Platonic doctrine begins with his objection to this separation of the realm of existence and the realm of ideal 'meaning'. ... The barrier between 'appearance' and 'idea' in the Platonic sense disappears. The 'sensible' and the 'intelligible,' the 'lower' and the 'higher,' the 'divine' and the 'earthly' are joined by a single, steady nexus of activity."
In *The Mirror of Language: A Study in the Medieval Theory of Knowledge* (New Haven and London, 1968), Marcia L. Colish reexamines the "medieval theory of verbal signs" formulated by Saint Augustine and held by the majority of medieval epistemologists. "The medieval conception of symbolism was fundamentally linguistic." Saint Augustine, Saint Anselm, Saint Thomas Aquinas, and Dante "all share the same verbal epistemology," and each expresses it through "one of the modes of the trivium"—in the modes of rhetoric, grammar, dialectics, and poetics respectively (pp. x, 10). Tracing the influences of Cicero, Aristotle, and Plato on Saint Augustine's "sign theory" or "verbal theory of knowledge" (pp. 61-68), Professor Colish analyzes Dante's poetic theory in the light of medieval conceptions of the relationship between rhetoric and poetics (pp. 224-85). In medieval tradition she finds "two basic applications of rhetoric to poetry.... Some writers

carry over antisophistic principles to poetry, thus endowing the poet with the power and the duty to express the true and the good and to move the reader toward them. Others concentrate instead on the technical aspects of poetic decoration, borrowing from rhetoric its figures, allegories, tropes, and colors, and applying them to poetry as canons of adornment." Though these "two approaches rarely occur unmixed with each other between the seventh and the thirteenth centuries," they nevertheless appear to be "drawing further apart" in the twelfth and thirteenth centuries. Observing that "the rhetorical idea of poetry as a medium of education and as a moral stimulus was also retained by medieval commentators who, following the Platonic tradition, thought that the truth of poetry was either covered with fictitious veils or nonexistent," Professor Colish finds that "Carolingian scholars perpetuated the theory of poetic fiction" but that in the twelfth and thirteenth centuries "the idea of poetic fiction underwent some modifications and was supplemented by a strong scholastic stress on the falsity of poetry" (pp. 234-35). For Carolingian views on verisimilitude in the poetic fable, see p. 235; and for the "Ciceronian correlation between eloquence, wisdom, and virtue" in the *ars dictaminis* of Dante's period, see p. 241. For Saint Augustine's views on "redeemed eloquence" see p. 38 and passim. See also Richard McKeon, "Poetry and Philosophy in the Twelfth Century: The Renaissance of Rhetoric," *MP* 43 (1946), 217-34; McKeon, "Rhetoric in the Middle Ages," *Speculum* 17 (1942), 1-32; Morton W. Bloomfield, "Symbolism in Medieval Literature," *MP* 56 (1958), 73-81; Helene Wieruszowki, "*Ars Dictaminis* in the Time of Dante," *Medievalia et Humanistica* 1 (1943), 95-108.

[8]Gilbert, *Literary Criticism: Plato to Dryden*, p. 138*n*.

[9]D. W. Robertson, Jr., *A Preface to Chaucer* (Princeton, 1962), pp. 25-26.

[10]Milton, *Complete Poems*, ed. Hughes, p. 95*n*.

[11]For the exemplary function of "introductory reading from a book in the early love-visions," see Paul G. Ruggiers, "The Unity of Chaucer's *House of Fame*," *SP* 50 (1953), pp. 16-29. For Chaucer's rhetoric and poetic, see Traugott Naunin, *Der Einfluss der mittelalterlichen Rhetorik auf Chaucers Dichtung* (Bonn diss., 1929) and Robert O. Payne, *The Key of Remembrance: A Study of Chaucer's Poetics* (New Haven, 1963).

[12]Erwin Panofsky, *Gothic Architecture and Scholasticism* (Latrobe, 1961), pp. 4, 51.

[13]Herbert Read, *Icon and Idea* (New York, 1965), pp. 53, 63, 72.

[14]Frances A. Yates, *The Art of Memory* (Chicago, 1966), pp. 70-79, 87, 95-96. See also Yates, *Giordano Bruno and the Hermetic Tradition* (New York, 1969), pp. 191-204; A. D. Nuttall in *The Metaphysical Poets*, ed. Frank Kermode (Greenwich, Conn., 1969), pp. 155-56. Louis L. Martz, *The Poetry of Meditation* (New Haven, 1954) emphasizes the importance of composition by place in the sixteenth and seventeenth-century meditative tradition.

Miss Yates's study traces the system of memory *loci* and images from classical antiquity through the Middle Ages and the Renaissance. According to the *Rhetorica ad Herennium* (widely cited in the Middle Ages and once attributed to Cicero), "The artificial memory includes backgrounds and images (Constat . . . ex locis et imaginibus)." By background or places *(loci)* the author means "such scenes as are naturally or artificially set off on a small scale, complete and conspicuous, so that we can grasp and embrace them easily by the natural memory—for example, a house, an intercolumnar space, a recess, an arch, or the like. An image is, as it were a figure, mark, or portrait (Imagines sunt formae quaedam et notae et simulacra) of the object we wish to remember; for example, if we wish to recall [the genus of] a horse, a

The Lamb and the Elephant

lion, or an eagle, we must place its image in a definite background"; *Rhetorica ad Herennium,* pp. 208-09, and Yates, pp. 4-16. As Miss Yates suggests, the sophists may have made a "lavish use" of the system of artificial memory, Aristotle noted the value of *topoi* in remembering "things themselves" (Yates, pp. 30-31). St. Albertus Magnus stressed the importance of the art of memory for ethics and rhetoric; "since human life consists in particulars it is necessary that it should be in the soul through corporeal images; it will not stay in memory save in such images"; Yates, p. 67. Miss Yates notes Fludd's attempt to "present his philosophy visually or in 'hieroglyphics' " (pp. 324-26) and observes that the "prenotions" and "emblems" upon which Bacon's "art of memory" is built correspond to the "places and images" of the older mnemonic systems. In Bacon's opinion, "Emblem reduceth conceits intellectual to images sensible, which strike the memory more." What is sensible "always strikes the memory stronger, and sooner impresses itself than the intellectual"; (Yates, p. 371).

While recognizing the distinction between "an externalized visual representation in art proper" and "the visual pictures of memory," Miss Yates examines certain fourteenth-century Italian paintings on allegorical and eschatological subjects from the point of view of the art of memory—in the light of medieval emphasis on forming "corporeal similitudes for the moral 'teachings of the ancients' " and on recalling the invisible joys and torments of heaven and hell (Yates, pp. 91-94).

[15]Such schematic arrangements, moreover, are frequently conditioned by the exigencies of art. Like the painter, the poet must normally endow his *personae* (whether real or allegorical) with a setting and a background. If his method is allegorical or transumptive (metaphorical), his setting and disposition are likely to be topical. Whether he followed a mnemonic system or not, the allegorical significance of his images and places would be substantially the same, and the design and style of his work would be conditioned by the same principles of poetic or pictorial composition. In many cases the final results would be remarkably similar, and it would be difficult to prove definitively that a particular work had or had not been composed according to a system of memory *loci.* Metaphors of place and personifications are not uncommon in Scripture, and the image of the seven-pillared house of Sapientia in particular may have influenced Dante's *Paradiso* and possibly the pillared hall of the goddess Fame in Chaucer's vision. The celestial spheres, already heavily allegorized through their associations with various Olympian gods as well as the Sirens and the Muses, had frequently provided a localized frame of reference for abstract concepts or separated substances—the liberal arts, various categories of virtue, the angelic hierarchies and intelligences. The possibility of Dante's systematic use of memory *loci* raises the question of whether Martianus Capella and Alain de Lille also utilized such a system.

[16]In Book XI of *The City of God,* after discussing the fall of the angels and demonstrating that "the flaw of wickedness is not nature, but contrary to nature, and has its origin, not in the Creator, but in the will," Saint Augustine argues that God caused him to "be cast down from his high position and to become the mockery of His angels—that is, He caused his temptations to benefit those whom He wishes to injure by them." God created the devil good, but had "already foreseen and arranged how He would make use of him when he became wicked."

Having demonstrated this point, Augustine then argues that "the beauty of the universe . . . becomes, by God's ordinance, more brilliant by the opposition of contraries." God would never have created any angel or man, "whose future wickedness He foreknew, unless He had equally known to what uses in behalf of the good He could turn him, thus embellishing the course of the ages, as it were an exquisite poem set off with antitheses. For what are called antitheses are among the most elegant of the ornaments of speech. . . . As, then, these oppositions of contraries lend beauty to the language, so the beauty of the course of this world is achieved by the opposition of contraries, arranged, as it were, by an eloquence not of words, but of things." Thus in Ecclesiasticus 15, "Good is set against evil, and life against death: so is the sinner against the godly." See *The City of God*, trans. Marcus Dods, Modern Library (New York, 1950), pp. 361-62.

[17]Cf. Joan Webber, *Contrary Music: The Prose Style of John Donne* (Madison, Wis., 1963).

[18]For "rational" and "irrational" motions in microcosm and macrocosm, see Chauncey Wood, *Chaucer and the Country of the Stars*, pp. 231n, 243n.

[19]For reexamination of comparative criticism of the *Commedia* and *Paradise Lost*, see Irene Samuel, *Dante and Milton: The "Commedia" and "Paradise Lost"* (Ithaca, N.Y., 1966).

[20]*Dantis Alagherii Epistolae*, ed. and trans. Paget Toynbee, 2d ed. (Oxford, 1966), p. 201.

[21]Toynbee, p. 202.

[22]The issues that Miss Yates has raised are important not only for the analysis of Dante's artistic method, but also for the topical arrangement of figures—exempla and personifications—in other medieval and Renaissance poems. Symbolic gardens and buildings—gardens of Love and Incontinence, temples of Venus, palaces of Fame or Fortune, Honor or Wisdom, houses of Care or Holiness—frequently serve as topical frameworks, like the general "headings" in commonplace books, for the personified attributes of an abstract idea (often represented as a divinity or a sorceress) and for characteristic exempla. Such arrangements occur in the *Romance of the Rose*, in Chaucer's dream-visions, and in the Renaissance epics or romances of Boiardo and Ariosto, Spenser and Tasso. Whether they were regarded largely as a poetic and rhetorical convention already well established in late classical antiquity and elaborated in medieval and Renaissance literature must await further research.

Chapter VI
INVENTION AND DESIGN:
IDEA AND FORM

LIKE THE study of anatomy, the definition and differentiation of styles and genres are possible only through the dissection of organic or quasi-organic forms. Literary criticism can on occasion become a kind of aesthetic vivisection—a violence against art in the interests of art, just as anatomy is violence against nature for nature's sake. Like the techniques of the machine shop, or the laboratory, the method of the critic is one of systematic disjunction and reconstruction, an eclectic and selective process that is no less creative than destructive. Disintegrating the structures of concrete and particular works into their component elements, combining these with the dismantled accessories of other works, constructing out of the debris the designs of a model comedy or epic or tragedy, the definitions of tropes and schemes, or categorical distinctions of style—it involves synthesis no less than analysis. Its emblems are the bath of Medea, the patchwork quilt and the mosaic, the synthetic automobile of the amateur mechanic, the synthetic man of Dr. Moreau or Dr. Frankenstein.

The ideas of styles and genres are, for the most part, abstractions achieved by analysis and comparison of passages in works of diverse authorship and subject matter and period. Like other arts, rhetoric and poetics create their own paradigms or models—ideal structures that may bear as little resemblance to aesthetic phenomena, and the concrete realities of literature and art, as the paradigms and modules of the twentieth-century scientist. Isolating and combining details drawn from a wide variety of works, abstracting definitions and principles, and fitting these abstractions into a logical and coherent theoretical structure, they achieve a rational and ideal synthesis that may (one hopes) possess a validity and integrity of its own. Nevertheless, this is, and must remain, a different kind of synthesis, and possesses a different structure, from that of the concrete works of

Invention and Design

art with which it began. The artificial synthesis of the poet or orator and that of the theorist of eloquence belong to different orders of reality.

The methods of the historian or critic are not those of the creative artist, but they are nonetheless relevant for him insofar as he allows them to condition his own practice. In the theory-ridden period of the late cinquecento and seicento, the poet's representation of abstract universals and concrete particulars was inevitably conditioned by general ideas of style and genre as well as by specific models. The literary theories of the age are not irrelevant to his work, but they can rarely serve as authoritative or reliable guides. In addition to theory, the critic must consider contemporary models and fashions, the individual (though perhaps indefinable) sensibility of the writer, and, above all, the problems of composition and imagery peculiar to a specific work dealing with a particular subject matter and designed for a specific function, a specific location or occasion, or a particular audience.

The fascination of the Beyond—that metaphysical precipice that attracts speculation like the cliffs of Gadara—is the obsession of most Alexandrian eras. The scholarship of our own age is no exception. Physics has become metaphysics, and history has merged into metahistory. The boundaries between criticism and "meta-criticism" are equally uncertain.

In the study of form and style, the literary historian can analyze or compare the techniques of particular authors and works with relative precision. When he transcends these modest but sensible limitations in attempting to isolate and define period styles, to explain their origin and psychological or social significance, and to relate them to the sensibility of the age or to twentieth-century theories of structure and expression, he is apt to overtax the capacities of his own methodology. Renaissance theory is frequently an unreliable guide for the interpretation of Renaissance works, and twentieth-century concepts are often anachronistic. Though the historian cannot dispense with either Renaissance or modern criteria, he must apply them not only with flexibility and caution, but with no little skepticism. If modern theories are apt to be irrelevant, Renaissance critical opinion is frequently inconsistent or strongly conditioned by polemical intent; and its value for practical criticism is restricted by its abstract character, its normative orientation, or its endeavor to support or censure the practice of the moderns by comparison with the doctrine or example of the ancients. Neither Renaissance nor modern theories of form and style can serve as definitive guides, and in ascertaining the significance of structural or expressional modes in a particular work, the critic must rely on an eclectic methodology, adapting his critical assumptions and techniques to the specific poem. He must be a casuist, though (one hopes) a judicious one.

Analogies between literary and plastic forms and styles can be useful only when the formal and stylistic principles consciously shared by poets and artists have been ascertained and when the compositional or expressional elements peculiar to each art have been analyzed. Before attempting to correlate "classical" (i.e. High Renaissance), mannerist, and baroque styles in art and literature, or to explain them as spontaneous expressions of a contemporary sensibility or world-view, the literary historian should consider the common theoretical principles that may underlie both painting and poetry—the emphasis on unity of design, accommodation of style to subject, marvel and probability, and resemblance to nature; the conception of painting and poetry alike as imitations of action and character, passion and thought; the sensuous manifestation of invisible objects of reason or faith, abstract ideas or spiritual substances or states of soul; the stress on depicting or arousing the emotions, affects of secular or religious love, pity or terror, wonder or delight; the emphasis on the dramatic representation of external and internal events. All of these concepts are commonplaces of Renaissance literary theory, and many of them occur not infrequently in treatises on art. Though some of them have been regarded by recent critics virtually as *differentiae* of mannerist or baroque sensibility and style, they are, for the most part, thoroughly conventional. The task for the cultural historian is to ascertain how and why mannerist and baroque artists, and certain writers of the period, managed to embody these concepts or express these values more forcefully than their predecessors. The answer probably lies in meticulous formal and stylistic analysis, and in a recognition of the specific technical problems that different cinquecento and seicento artists and poets faced in attempting to imitate the motions of body and spirit and to solve the conflicting demands of probability and admiration, tradition and novelty.[1]

I.

In some respects the Renaissance poet or painter moved more easily and more freely between the divided and distinguished worlds of practice and theory, particulars and universals, than his modern descendants. The end of his rhetorical and poetic theory, his arts of logic and manuals of painting, was practice; and he was usually well aware that he could not write or paint well simply by following the book, by relying exclusively on the rules. Exercise was also essential, along with wide reading and experience, observation of nature and study of classical and modern exemplars, and individual taste, judgment, and invention. Quintilian had stressed imitation and exercise as well as precept as methods of learning, and many of the theorists of the period—High Renaissance, mannerist, baroque, neoclassical—recognized the importance of all of these factors, even though their emphasis might vary in different polemical contexts.[2] Both Friedlaender and Posner note a "conservative, academic undercurrent in late Mannerism," and "mannerist" theorists frequently acknowledge the importance of study and exercise, familiarity with the art of antiquity and the High Renaissance, and knowledge of anatomy.[3] Conversely, most of their opponents acknowledged the importance of individual talent and the role of imagination in invention. Few of them would have reduced the principles of formal composition to an exact reproduction of the object. Verisimilitude did not mean literal and meticulous fidelity to the object, just as imitation did not, as Atkins suggests, mean slavish copying of classical models. Though the painter must use judgment and taste in developing and ordering the inventions of his imagination, he must exercise the same qualities in applying the rules of his art and in borrowing from ancient and modern artists or from nature.

Like the theorists, moreover, creative writers and artists had been trained to analyze and dissect the works of nature or of art, to abstract the principles of design, and to consider the process of composition as an intellectual and rational technique, though assisted

The Lamb and the Elephant

by individual imagination or inspiration. In theory the work of art was an ideal construction—a reconstruction rather than an exact rendition of nature—and in giving it structure and design, the painter, like nature herself, not only imitated the idea of whatever species he had occasion to portray, but also observed an ideal canon of proportions, proceeding (like nature) through the "certainty" of mathematical method. In reconstructing nature and the works of nature, he operated according to the same laws and principles whereby nature herself had originally proceeded. Though the mannerists themselves sometimes disregarded natural proportions or depreciated the value of mathematical studies, they nevertheless insisted on the superior beauty of their own uncanonical proportions as reflections of an archetypal idea of absolute Beauty; and in imitating this idea they claimed to be working as nature, or the Creator of nature, had worked—following the method of nature or nature's God rather than merely copying its results, and preferring creative to created nature as a model.

Such arguments were, for the most part, commonplaces in Renaissance eulogies of the arts. They served to demonstrate the nobility of the artist and to justify his resort to fiction. In the late trecento Boccaccio had extolled the poet's free invention and ability to create "unheard of things," and the quattrocento artist Cennino had transferred this argument to the painter. Later theorists similarly followed Boccaccio in associating the method of poetry with that of mystical theology. Poets and painters alike had praised their disciplines as divine arts and had claimed divine inspiration and rapture. Moreover, comparisons between the methods of different arts—painting, architecture, sculpture, poetry, geometry, and the like—and those of the Creator were conventional in Renaissance apologetics. In attempting to prove the *honestas* or nobility of his art, its antiquity or its divine origin, the apologist sometimes endeavored to trace it back to the creation of heaven and earth—or (like Milton) beyond the first creation. The lofty claims that Lomazzo and other late cinquecento or seicento theorists made for the transcendental inspiration and vision of the artist and the similar claims that Sidney and other English apologists made on behalf of the poet were familiar *topoi* in Renaissance polemics and critical theory.

Invention and Design

In Renaissance Italian theories of painting, Rensselaer Lee distinguishes several variant (and, in his opinion, incompatible) conceptions of mimesis. The notion of "literal imitation," already apparent in the fourteenth century, was "the natural accompaniment" during the following century "of a realistic point of view and practice among those artists who were striving strenuously to capture the perfect illusion of visible nature," like the ancient painters who had "created so convincing an illusion of life that animals and men . . . mistook their art for reality." Sixteenth-century writers advanced a theory of ideal imitation based partly on Aristotle and Horace and partly on the example of the painter Zeuxis as related by Cicero and Pliny. This approach entailed the imitation of an ideal nature—an attempt to surpass nature herself by selective imitation of nature or through close study of the art of antiquity.[4]

A third variant was the neo-Platonic theory of ideal imitation fashionable near the end of the sixteenth century, but strongly influenced by the fifteenth-century Platonist Ficino. In Lee's opinion, Lomazzo temporarily diverted "the theory of imitation entirely from Aristotelian channels by declaring that ideal beauty, the image of which one sees reflected in the mirror of his own mind, has its source in God rather than in nature." This theory "differs fundamentally from the earlier theory of Dolce who finds an outward standard of perfection in the antique, not an inward standard in the image of ideal beauty in the mind's eye." Finally, in 1664, Bellori "resumed and brought to fruition what had been until the late sixteenth century the normal Italian mode of thinking about the arts," redefining the idea that "an artist should imitate . . . as an image of selected and embellished nature which the painter forms in his imagination after the empirical method of Zeuxis." Since the ancient sculptors had used the "Idea meravigliosa," modern painters and sculptors ought to study the most perfect of ancient sculptures as guides to the "emended beauties of nature."[5]

In Bellori's discussion of ideal art, Lee finds an incompatible mixture of mystical Platonism and Aristotelian empiricism, an incongruous blend of *a priori* and *a posteriori* approaches to the idea of beauty. Nevertheless, though it is true that both of these concepts occur in Bellori's treatise, his "philosophical inconsistency" may not be so fundamental as recent historians have suggested, nor his breach with earlier neo-Platonic critics so decisive as modern scholarship has inferred. The inconsistency resides essentially in certain facets of Aristotelian and Platonic theory—notably the question of the origin and ontological status of ideas—in the light of twentieth-century interpretations of Plato and Aristotle. Bellori was writing against the background of a series of Renaissance attempts, including the effort of Jacopo Mazzoni, to reconcile Platonic and Aristotelian doctrines. Medieval schoolmen, moreover, had achieved a partial resolution of the problem in the conceptualist distinctions between the *universale post rem, in re,* and *ante rem.* There is no basic contradiction in positing the existence of an archetypal idea of beauty in the divine mind, which the artist approaches gradually through abstraction from particular things. The real contradiction lies in the difference between Aristotle's emphasis on sense perception as the source of our ideas (and deductive reasoning as partially dependent on the results of induction) and the Platonic conception of innate ideas.[6]

The ascent of the mind to the idea of absolute beauty through love of beautiful objects, as described in the *Phaedrus* and the *Symposium*, is an ascent by degrees from particulars to the universal, from sensuous to intelligible objects, through a process of progressive abstraction.[7] Though this ascent from the visible to the invisible is hardly identical with Aristotelian induction, it is not inconsistent with the latter.[8] For Renaissance writers, already accustomed to synthesizing Plato and Aristotle and Horace, or to playing them against one another, the two methods of abstraction might seem complementary; they could be regarded not only as parallel to each other, but also as analogous to the ascent from images to ideas and first principles that Plato had found in various arts and sciences—in arithmetic, geometry, and astronomy and, above all, in dialectic.[9]

The mannerist's emphasis on divine inspiration, in turn, and his insistence on the independence of individual genius from rules and models, are primarily a reaffirmation of commonplaces of the European poetic tradition. These doctrines are by no means peculiar to mannerist theory, nor are their antitheses usually regarded as irreconcilable. The same theorists who emphasize conformity to the rules

Invention and Design

often extol the divine inspiration of the poet or painter, recognizing the necessity of natural talent in addition to the principles of art. The classical Renaissance critics who insist on conformity to nature frequently make allowance for poetic license. Though Plato playfully elaborates the theme of the poet's divine *furor*, he also lays down the strictest of laws, aesthetic as well as moral and political, concerning poetic imitation. Though Horace ridicules the mad bard and the fantastic poet or painter who joins incongruous things together, he allows both "an equal right to indulge their whims" within limitations, and he elsewhere describes himself as the victim of an "amabilis insania."[10] Both natural ability and art are necessary; there is little use in "study without wit," or in "wit without training."[11]

Similarly, though Longinus regards genius as the principal source of excellence in style, he also emphasizes the importance of art and "imitation and emulation of the great prose writers and poets of antiquity." Maintaining that there can be an "art for reaching the heights or plumbing the depths," he argues against the opinion that "a body of precepts" cannot be "applied to such matters. The great man, they hold, is born and not taught, and the genius is what he is only by the gift of nature. The productions of native ability are thought to be ruined when subjected to the dry-as-dust technologist. But I believe this popular notion can be proved false, if only we consider that while in the strongest emotions Nature is a law unto herself, yet even she does not like to work rashly and entirely without method." Great qualities sometimes require the curb, sometimes the spur. One must "learn from art that there are some things in language that depend on nature alone."[12]

Analogous views on the interdependence of art and nature, and of the roles of imitation and inspiration, occur in the critical observations of Renaissance poets. Milton extolled the divine inspiration of poetry and the laws of the several genres, debating whether to follow natural or artificial order in the construction of his plot. Ben Jonson, like Quintilian before him, emphasized the importance of nature as well as exercise, imitation,[13] and study, associating natural wit with poetic rapture and maintaining that "Arts and Precepts availe nothing, except nature be beneficiall and aiding." He took "this labour in teaching others, that they should not be always to be taught, and I would bring my Precepts into practise. For rules are ever of lesse force and valew then experiments...." The poet must perfect natural ability through exercise, study, and the imitation of the "best writers," for "without Art Nature can nere bee perfect, & without Nature Art can clayme no being." Though a poet's liberty should not be confined "within the narrowe limits of laws which either the *Grammarians* or *Philosophers* prescribe," since there were "many excellent Poets that fulfill'd" these laws before their discovery, nevertheless "whatsoever Nature at any time dictated to the most happie, or long exercise to the most laborious, that the wisdom and Learning of *Aristotle* hath brought into an Art, because he understood the Causes of things; and what other men did by chance or custome he doth by reason; and not only found out the way not to erre, but the short way we should take not to erre."[14]

The divine origin of poetry and painting and the *topos* of celestial inspiration were too convenient as arguments in eulogies and apologies for both arts to be recklessly discarded. These commonplaces coexist in Renaissance treatises side by side with discussions and analyses of the rules and principles of imitation; one encounters them in neoclassical writers like Milton and Ben Jonson, as well as in anticlassical apologists. Conversely, few critics were so rash as to dismiss the rules altogether. Usually they achieved a compromise between the claims of individual talent and the authority of ancient or recent example, the forms of external nature and the rules of art.

The importance of neo-Platonic principles in mannerist aesthetics should not be exaggerated. On the whole, they were not so much operative principles as apologetic arguments—defenses against the charge of violating probability, verisimilitude, and decorum. In effect, the mannerist apologist is countering the accusations of his opponents by appealing to the Deity Himself. If he breaks the rules of imitation, it is because he is divinely inspired. If his forms seem unnatural, it is because he is following the Creator of nature and imitating an archetypal Idea superior to natural forms. Such arguments are intended to refute the charge of distorting nature by appealing to a power above and beyond nature and her objects.

Invention and Design

These arguments are frequently couched in neo-Platonic terms. They might just as easily have been developed into an aesthetic based on the opposition between Nature and Grace; but this line of argument could have increased the theorist's vulnerability to hostile criticism, exposing him to condemnation on theological as well as purely artistic grounds.

In some of these paintings or poems, moreover, apparent violations of verisimilitude and probability could be defended paradoxically as both probable and verisimilar, insofar as they represented a heightened state of emotion, the irrationality of the lover or the devotion of the saint. In art, distorted forms and an unrealistic treatment of space or light and shadow could enhance the visionary quality of the work as a deliberate appeal to the imagination, a conscious representation of a fantasy. In literature the same effect could be achieved by hyperbolic and far-fetched imagery and emotionally charged figures.

This facet of the art of the period could parallel or reinforce contemporary techniques of meditation, with their emphasis on imaginative realization of religious scenes or theological doctrines as a means of stirring the emotions and moving the will. It is, however, only *one* facet of contemporary literature and art; and it parallels only *one* aspect of the meditative tradition. A highly realistic art, it might be argued, could serve the same devotional ends as well or better. There were, moreover, numerous variations in meditative techniques, varying in their appeals to the intellect, the imagination, and the senses. Some of these sought to stimulate devotion by stimulating the senses and stirring the imagination, others by exploiting the commonplaces of Ramist logic and rhetoric.

2.

Theoretical differences concerning the source of the artist's ideas of design—the actual works of nature or mathematical principles and quantitative measurements, antique statuary or modern painting, formal rules or supernatural inspiration—are less significant for the formation and development of his style than the kind of design he preferred and his principles of composition. Whatever its epistemological basis, Zuccaro's *disegno interno*,[15] when reduced to its essentials and divested of its neo-Platonic trappings is little more than the design in the artist's mind, the preliminary idea or pattern that he will subsequently realize on canvas or in fresco. It does not differ *essentially* from the mental design that most painters or poets—Aristotelians, Platonists, or naive realists—form before commencing a work. What Zuccaro is asserting is little more than what Aristotle had required of the poet—that he conceive the pattern and form of the work as a whole before actually setting it down. Zuccaro's "Mannerist pun" on *disegno* as "*segno di Dio*"[16] and his metaphorical description of the artist's internal design as "a spark of divinity" are rhetorical embellishments of an aesthetic commonplace, the divine inspiration of the poet or painter. The majority of Renaissance theorists saw little or no contradiction between assertions of divine inspiration and the importance of formal rules and classical models. The supernatural inspiration of the poet and the power of natural *ingenium* (or *vis mentis*) are commonplaces of the classical tradition and of medieval and Renaissance poetics, and the strictest of epic poets frequently retain the convention of invoking pagan or Christian divinities for aid.

Though Zuccaro's assertion that painting does not need to "learn rules or means for its own art" from mathematics[17] conflicts with views expressed by Alberti and Leonardo and Dürer and other "early Humanist artists," the contradiction is perhaps less fundamental than it seems, and Blunt may have exaggerated the antirational elements in mannerist composition and style. Both earlier and later theorists stressed the value of mathematical measurements for a variety of reasons—verisimilitude and accuracy in the reconstruction of nature and especially in linear perspective, foreshortening, and the proportions of figures; the conception of symmetry, harmony, and mathematical proportion as the source of beauty in design, both in nature and in classical sculpture and architecture; the Platonic and neo-Pythagorean emphasis on mathematics as the basis of the natural order as well as the order of art, underlying physics and metaphysics and psychology, astronomy and music; the analogy between "mundane" and "human" and "instrumental" music, and the "hidden powers of harmony" implicit not only in

Invention and Design

the macrocosm but in the microcosm of the human body and the human soul. The emphasis on mathematics in Renaissance art and late Renaissance or post-Renaissance efforts to reconstruct physics and metaphysics, ethics and politics on a mathematical basis for the sake of greater accuracy and certitude cannot be divorced from the context of Renaissance Platonism. In emphasizing one facet of the Platonic tradition—the immanence of the idea of beauty, and the superiority of the abstract idea to natural forms—mannerist theorists like Lomazzo and Zuccaro tended to underemphasize another and equally important aspect of Platonism: the importance of mathematics in the ascent of the mind from the realm of sense and opinion to the realm of abstract ideas and intellectual truth. Finally, the arguments that Alberti, Leonardo, and other artists advanced for the close association between mathematics and the visual arts cannot be divorced from apologetic expediency. Such arguments served to exalt the status of the painter by associating him with the liberal arts.

The arguments of Lomazzo and Zuccaro do not, in fact, define or affect the essence of the mannerist style or explain its principal characteristics. Though they could and did provide plausible defenses to justify its apparent violations of the rules of nature or art, they could have served just as well as apologetic arguments in support of virtually any other style that had been censured for ignoring canonical proportions.

Some of the apparent inconsistencies in late cinquecento and seicento theory, moreover, are already implicit in quattrocento treatises on painting. Cennino begins his *Libro dell' Arte* by emphasizing the painter's freedom of imagination and the parallel with the poet's liberty of invention, but concludes his book with rules for "copying and imitating things from nature," casting life masks or entire human figures, including the artist's "own person" from living models.[18] His stress on the artist's power to portray *invisibilia* and to invent and compose objects that do not exist in nature serves primarily as a rhetorical argument for the nobility or *honestas* of his art. Painting "calls for imagination, and skill of hand, in order to discover things not seen, hiding themselves under the shadow of natural objects, and to fix them with the hand, presenting to plain sight what does not actually exist. And it justly deserves to be enthroned next to theory, and to be crowned with poetry. The justice lies in this: that the poet, with his theory . . . is free to compose and bind together, as he pleases, according to his inclination. In the same way, the painter is given freedom to compose a figure, standing, seated, half-man, half-horse, as he pleases, according to his imagination."[19]

Alberti similarly appeals to the topics of nobility and utility. Painting "contains a divine force which not only makes absent men present, . . . but moreover makes the dead seem almost alive." It "contributes to the most honourable delights of the soul," and the master painter who "sees his works adored will feel himself considered another god." Furthermore, painting is "most useful to that piety which joins us to the gods and keeps our souls full of religion."[20] Alberti's primary emphasis, however, falls on the painter's relationship to nature. In discussing the mathematical basis of painting he considers "the roots in nature which are the source of this delightful and most noble art." A picture is essentially a "cross-section of a visual pyramid, artificially represented with lines and colours on a certain plane according to a given distance, centre and lights." The three principal parts of painting—"circumscription, composition, and reception of light"—are "taken from nature."

Alberti consistently stresses the importance of verisimilitude. Painting "strives to represent things seen," and should achieve "good relief and a good likeness of the subject. . . ." In seeking "grace and beauty of things" in the composition of planes, there is "no more certain and fitting way . . . than to take them from nature, keeping in mind in what way nature, marvellous artificer of things, has composed the planes in beautiful bodies." The painter may learn the movements of the body from nature, "even though it is difficult to imitate the many movements of the soul." The painter's *"istoria* will move the soul of the beholder when each man painted there clearly shows the movement of his own soul," and these "movements of the soul are made known by the movements of the body." The painter should portray the "observed planes of any body" in such a way that "at a certain distance and in a certain position from the centre they appear in relief, seem to have mass and to be lifelike."

Invention and Design

In the interest of greater accuracy and fidelity to nature, Alberti recommends the use of "an intersection"—a "thin veil" marked out in parallels and placed "between the eye and the thing seen, so the visual pyramid penetrates through the thinness of the veil." The artist who "forces himself to represent things as he sees them in our veil" will "paint things taken from nature sweetly and correctly."[21]

Despite his admiration for the lost arts and sciences of "our most vigorous antique past," Alberti does not favor an uncritical imitation of the antique. The Florentine moderns "should not be slighted in favour of anyone famous in antiquity in these arts." The principles of correct mathematical construction were "hidden and unknown" to ancient sculptors and painters, and one "scarcely sees a single antique [i]storia aptly composed." He advises against copying the "figures of other painters"; if one must "copy the works of others," it would be better to "copy a mediocre sculpture than an excellent painting," since "sculpture is more certain than painting" and it is "easier to find relief in sculpting than in painting."[22]

Besides decorum ("take care that all the members are suitable"; "all the members ought to conform to a certain appropriateness"), he stresses other principles conventional in rhetorical theory—"copiousness and variety." Like Cicero, he requires the practitioner of his art to be "a good man and learned in liberal arts." Just as rhetoricians had compared the orator to Hercules Gallicus, captivating the ears of men and drawing them after him through the persuasive force of eloquence, Alberti praises the *istoria* "so agreeably and pleasantly attractive that it will capture the eye of whatever learned or unlearned person is looking at it and will move his soul." Finally, like the rhetoricians who had analyzed the passions and the language of expressive gesture, he stresses the movements of the soul and the motions of animate and inanimate things.[23]

3.

Since poets and painters were often compelled to borrow technical terms and theoretical concepts from rhetoric, there are sometimes significant resemblances in their theories of composition and their ideas of disposition—their principles for constructing a short or long

The Lamb and the Elephant

poem, an oration or an epic, a sentence or a drama, a painting or a building or a statue. Treatises on the visual and verbal arts tended to conceive the art of composition as a process of synthesis and combination—the systematic construction or reconstruction of an object out of clearly definable parts.

In studies of the organic arts—rhetoric or grammar, logic or poetry —as in discussions of the arts of design, the writer frequently employed the method of analysis as a preparation for creative synthesis, dissecting natural or artificial models into their component sections or members or motifs, and teaching the method of imitating and perfecting the parts and recombining them into a new synthesis. Critics of the visual arts likewise subdivided the complete design into sections and subsections; these were, in a sense, comparable to the divisions and subdivisions of a periodic sentence or to the quantitative parts of an oration or dramatic poem. Theoretically the principle of decorum in imitation and expression was as applicable on the lowest level as on the highest; levels of style must be observed in the simplest elements of composition—in the choice and arrangement of words or in the quality and disposition of lines and planes and colors—as in the most complex. Visual and verbal style would vary with the nature and arrangement, quality and quantity, of the elements of composition.

In the composition of a periodic sentence, the component parts —letters and syllables, words and phrases and clauses, "commas" and "cola,"—corresponded roughly to the component elements of the painter's *istoria*—planes and members and bodies. In the visual and verbal arts alike, the master demonstrated his skill in the proper construction, proportion, and coordination of each part and in integrating and combining them into a unified and harmonious whole.[24]

Insofar as their methods of instruction and composition involved both analysis and synthesis, literary and artistic theory both tended to emphasize the elements of design as well as unified and integrated structure, the accuracy and articulation of the part as well as the integrity and symmetry of the whole. According to contemporary doctrine the art of composition consisted in the judicious and harmonious combination of parts; and similar ideals of symmetry and balance, or asymmetry and vehemence, sometimes underlie the

Invention and Design

design of a painting or a poem, a drama or an oration or an edifice, and the construction of brief or extended sentences or paragraphs. Just as the turns or reversals of thought may correspond to the changes and alterations of external events, the turns in the argument of an epigram or sonnet may correspond to the reversals or peripeteias of heroic and dramatic poetry. The formal principles for composing a well-knit plot and a well-turned period may not be altogether different.

The technical assumptions that poets and artists shared in common made it easier for one art to borrow and adapt stylistic principles or modes from the other. Both shared similar (though variable) notions of the relationship between invention, disposition, and expression in the composition of a painting or poem. Both shared a common debt to rhetoric and logic. Frequent parallels between the arts in literary and artistic criticism from Aristotle and Horace into the eighteenth century and beyond emphasized the analogy between the inventions of poet and painter and orator, between the disposition of a plot, the design of a painting, the structure of an oration, or between ornaments or colors of rhetoric and those of the painter. Poets and painters frequently derived their inventions from the sister art—sometimes directly, sometimes through the mediation of emblem-books, mythographies, and iconologies. That there should likewise be cross-influences in notions of disposition and style is not surprising.

Treatises on rhetoric and poetic and the visual arts frequently acknowledged similar principles for acquiring and exercising these arts—study of the masterpieces of antiquity, mastery of the "rules," verisimilitude and probability, grace or marvel, clarity or obscurity, the importance of natural talent or *ingenium*, appeal to the senses and to the imagination and emotions as well as to reason, the force of inspiration, and the value of concealing as well as displaying art. Aristotle's definition of poetry was extended to painting; this too was defined as the imitation of an action, and the unities were likewise regarded as normative for the visual arts as well as for epic and drama. Even architecture was redefined as an art of imitation.

Both poets and painters acknowledged the principle of decorum, and different categories of painting had been correlated, according to their subject matter, with literary genres. In theory, and less frequently in practise, literary style varied with subject and genre. To what extent did similar concepts of decorum influence pictorial modes? To what extent did the Renaissance artist consciously accommodate his manner to the level of his subject, seeking *vaghezza* and grace in one type of subject matter, *asprezza* and grandeur and magnificence in another, employing different modes for satiric themes, for heroic and tragic arguments, and for scenes of erotic dalliance and sensual delight? To what extent did regard for the unities condition the composition of his figures and their organization in space? or concern for the imitation of action influence his treatment of movement? To what extent do the distortions of mannerist (and, in some instances, of baroque) art parallel the disturbed syntax and contrived difficulties of the magnificent style? Does the compressed and "unreal" space in mannerist painting—the tendency toward composition through massed human figures—partly reflect a conscious emphasis on the imitation of human action? Are the qualities of Michelangelo's late paintings partly explicable in terms of the *genus grande*? Are they conditioned not only by his essentially sculpturesque approach to problems of modeling and composition, but also by a deliberate endeavor to achieve the heroic or tragic style appropriate to his subject matter, to arouse pity and terror and marvel? Is it in the interests of the "grand style" that he invests his figures with superhuman and heroic proportions, sacrificing grace to severity and strength, and the ornament of color to vigor and vehemence of design?

One should not press these questions or arguments—for neither painters nor poets are consistently logical or subservient to theory —but one should not ignore the possibility that some at least of the characteristics of mannerist and baroque art spring from the influence of Renaissance poetic theory and from a conscious effort to imitate human actions by emphasizing movement, to achieve in design the structural integrity and unity of the poetic fable, and to observe in different genres appropriate distinctions in levels of style.

The conscious striving for emotional effect—or *affect*—in seicento art is paralleled in the drama of the period. Its roots, however, lie partly in contemporary poetic theory, with its emphasis on the deliberate excitement of the passions as an essential function of art.[25]

Invention and Design

By arousing and purging the emotions, the poet or artist enhanced the tranquillity of the state as well as the internal peace of the individual. An art of deliberate perturbation might theoretically result in greater tranquillity of mind than the "harmonious visions" of "classic" art. Contemporary theories of meditation had emphasized the role of the sensuous imagination in stirring the emotions and directing them to devotional ends. Rhetorical theory had analyzed and classified the passions in elaborating the conception of affective proof. In attempting to persuade or move his public, the artist, like the poet, found his most effective method to be the direct appeal to the emotions through the imagination and the senses.

Like the poet and the rhetorician, the painter sought both *enargeia* (vividness) and *energeia* (vehemence) in style. Besides vividness and distinctness, his images must possess vehemence and force—energy and strength like that of the great orators and poets. The qualities that modern critics have most frequently emphasized in baroque art are qualities that rhetorical theory had conventionally associated with the *genus grande* or sublime.

The heightened subjectivity in seicento art and literature is consistent with critical emphasis on verisimilitude or naturalness in the imitation of thought and character. In the visual arts one encounters the evolution of a style in painting capable of expressing emotion and ecstasy, imitating the objects of secular or religious passion in a passionate manner, and suggesting the experience or act of vision in portraying the objects of vision. In prose style and poetry one encounters the development of a style capable of portraying the dynamic process of thought. In comparing these developments critics have sometimes treated them as spontaneous expressions of the "baroque impulse" and the inner conflicts of "baroque man." In the context of the literary and artistic theory of the period, however, they represent the technical fulfillment of conventional mimetic ideals—the imitation of action and the representation of character and thought (*Ethos* and *Dianoia*) as dynamic processes.

4.

How does one depict abstract universals or (more difficult still) invisible and inconceivable spiritual essences through particular and

The Lamb and the Elephant

sensuous forms—and yet endow these forms with verisimilitude and decorum? This had been a recurrent problem in Renaissance poetics and art. Boccaccio had compared the methods of poetry and mystical theology and maintained that the poet conceals the abstract idea in an allegorical fiction or invention. Tasso argued that the poet necessarily imitates human actions and, like the painter, must accommodate spiritual substances to human perception by endowing them with human characteristics.[26] Though supporting the allegorical conception of poetry, he maintained that the imitation (i.e., the representation of action on the literal level) must possess verisimilitude and probability. Aristotle's argument that the poet, unlike the historian, depicts the universal through the particular had been reinforced by the conception of the poem as exemplum. Though Plato had regarded poetry as an imitation thrice removed from reality and had distinguished sharply between icastic and fantastic mimesis (imitation of existing and nonexisting things), he had nevertheless conceded that the poet does, indirectly, imitate ideas in copying the forms of nature, which are copies of ideal forms. As the works of nature are shadows of reality, works of art are shadows of shadows. According to Hermetic doctrine, natural objects bore the signatures imprinted upon them through the influence of the heavens. According to Scripture, the heavens themselves were, in a sense, the rhetoric and art of God, declaring his glory and showing his handiwork; and the "invisible things" of God "from the creation of the world are clearly seen, being understood by the things that are made...."[27] If the world was an enigmatic mirror, dimly reflecting the divine face, so was the *speculum* of poetic allegory and painting. If faith was the "evidence of things not seen," a poetry or art consecrated to the faith could likewise mirror the ideal, giving visible expression to the invisible and shadowing the intelligible in sensuous form.

Like their medieval predecessors, poets and painters of the Renaissance possessed a theory of art which could be applied alternatively or simultaneously to philosophy or theology, to the objects of reason or of faith. It could serve as a basis for allegory or for naturalistic representation or for both. Though the emphasis on verisimilitude and probability, like the stress on unity of action, became more pronounced after the publication and diffusion of

Invention and Design

Aristotle's *Poetics*, these principles had been commonplaces of medieval poetics, and theorists on painting had emphasized truth to nature long before Aristotle's treatise had begun to remold Italian critical thought. Medieval poets had frequently rationalized their allegories through the device of a dream-vision or (like their Renaissance successors) through the agency of witchcraft. The tension between the marvelous and the probable, already apparent in medieval literature, became a central issue in cinquecento and seicento artistic and literary controversy. Persisting well into the eighteenth century, it helped to shape the controversy between the apparently conflicting (though not inevitably contradictory) claims of allegorical method and naturalistic imitation. Despite large areas of disagreement, however, both parties generally accepted the principle of ideal imitation. Both, as a rule, agreed that art and literature should portray the universal, even though they differed as to how, precisely, this should be done.[28]

Notes

[1]For a re-examination of the "variable meanings of *style* in the eighteenth century," see David A. Hansen, "Redefinitions of *Style*, 1600-1800," in *New Aspects of Lexicography: Literary Criticism, Intellectual History, and Social Change*, ed. Howard D. Weinbrot (Carbondale and Edwardsville, Ill.; London and Amsterdam, 1972), pp. 95-116, 186-89. Among recent studies of sixteenth- and seventeenth-century style in poetry and prose, see Annabel M. Patterson, *Hermogenes and the Renaissance: Seven Ideas of Style* (Princeton, 1970), pp. 44-68; Stanley E. Fish, *Self-Consuming Artifacts: The Experience of Seventeenth-Century Literature* (Berkeley, Los Angeles, London, 1972); Earl Miner, ed., *Seventeenth Century Imagery, Essays on the Uses of Figurative Language from Donne to Farquhar* (Berkeley, 1971); Ronald David Emma and John T. Shawcross, eds., *Language and Style in Milton* (New York, 1967); Stanley Stewart, *The Expanded Voice: The Art of Thomas Traherne* (San Marino, Calif., 1970); Josephine Miles, *Renaissance, Eighteenth-Century, and Modern Language in English Poetry: A Tabular View* (Berkeley, 1960); Morris W. Croll, *Style, Rhetoric, and Rhythm*, ed. J. Max Patrick et al. (Princeton, 1966); Richard Foster Jones et al., *The Seventeenth Century* (Stanford and London, 1965); idem, *Ancients and Moderns*, 2d ed. (Berkeley and Los Angeles, 1965); Stanley E. Fish, ed., *Seventeenth-Century Prose: Modern Essays in Criticism* (New York, 1971); George Williamson, *The Senecan Amble, Prose Form from Bacon to Collier* (Chicago, 1966); Karl R. Wallace, *Francis Bacon on Communication and Rhetoric* (Chapel Hill, 1943). Rosalie L. Colie, *Paradoxia Epidemica, The Renaissance Tradition of Paradox* (Princeton, 1966); K. G. Hamilton, *The Two Harmonies: Poetry and Prose in the Seventeenth Century* (Oxford, 1963); George Philip Krapp, *The*

The Lamb and the Elephant

Rise of English Literary Prose (New York, 1915); Thomas K. Whipple, *Martial and the English Epigram from Sir Thomas Wyatt to Ben Jonson* (Berkeley, 1925); D. L. Clark, *Rhetoric and Poetry in the Renaissance* (New York, 1922); R. J. Crane, *Wit and Rhetoric in the Renaissance* (New York, 1937); Wilbur S. Howell, *Logic and Rhetoric in England, 1500-1700* (Princeton, 1956); Sister Miriam Joseph, *Rhetoric in Shakespeare's Time* (New York, 1962); Wesley Trimpi, *Ben Jonson's Poems: A Study of the Plain Style* (Stanford, 1962); W. Fraser Mitchell, *English Pulpit Oratory from Andrewes to Tillotson* (New York and Toronto, 1932); Jerrold E. Seigel, *Rhetoric and Philosophy in Renaissance Humanism: The Union of Eloquence and Wisdom, Petrarch to Valla* (Princeton, 1968); Robert Adolph, *The Rise of Modern Prose Style* (Cambridge, Mass., and London, 1968); James Sutherland, *On English Prose* (Toronto and London, 1957); F. P. Wilson, *Seventeenth-Century Prose* (Berkeley and Los Angeles, 1960); Joan Webber, *The Eloquent "I": Style and Self in Seventeenth-Century Prose* (Madison, Milwaukee, London, 1968); idem, *Contrary Music: The Prose Style of John Donne* (Madison, 1963); Brian Vickers, *Classical Rhetoric in English Poetry* (London and New York, 1970); idem, *Francis Bacon and Renaissance Prose* (London, 1968); idem, ed., *Essential Articles for the Study of Francis Bacon* (Hamden, Conn., 1968); Leonard Nathanson, *The Strategy of Truth: A Study of Sir Thomas Browne* (Chicago, 1967); Paolo Rossi, *Francis Bacon: From Magic to Science*, trans. Sacha Rabinovitch (Chicago, 1968).

For discussion of mannerist and/or baroque styles in literature and art, see Wylie Sypher, *Four Stages of Renaissance Style* (Garden City, N.Y., 1955); Arnold Hauser, *Mannerism, The Crisis of the Renaissance and the Origin of Modern Art*, trans. Eric Mosbacher (New York, 1965); Austin Warren, *Richard Crashaw, A Study in Baroque Sensibility* (University of Louisiana, 1939); René Wellek, "The Concept of Baroque in Literary Scholarship," *JAAC* 5 (1946), 77-109; Wolfgang Stechow, "Definitions of the Baroque in the Visual Arts," *JAAC* 5 (1946), 109-15; Roy Daniells, "English Baroque and Deliberate Obscurity," *JAAC* 5 (1946), 115-21; idem, "Baroque Form in English Literature," *UTQ* 14 (1945), 393-408; idem, *Milton, Mannerism and Baroque* (Toronto, 1963); R. A. Sayce, "The Use of the Term Baroque in French Literary History," *Comparative Literature* 10 (1958), 246-53; Heinrich Wölfflin, *Principles of Art History*, trans. M. D. Hottinger (New York, 1950); Walter Friedlaender, *Mannerism and Anti-Mannerism in Italian Painting* (New York, 1965); Erwin Panofsky, *Idea, A Concept in Art Theory*, trans. Joseph J. S. Peake (Columbia, S.C., 1968); Riccardo Scribano, *Manierismo, barocco, rococo: concetti e termini* (Rome, 1962); M. Treves, "Maniera, the History of a Word," *Marsyas* 1 (1941), 69-88; John Shearman, *Mannerism: Style and Civilization* (Harmondsworth and Baltimore, 1967); Jean Rousset, *La littérature de l'âge baroque en France. Circe et le paon* (Paris, 1953); Franklin W. Robinson and Stephen C. Nichols, Jr., eds., *The Meaning of Mannerism* (Hanover, New Hampshire, 1972); Joseph Mazzeo, *Renaissance and Seventeenth-Century Studies* (New York, 1964); Karl Borinski, *Die Antike in Poetik und Kunsttheorie, von Augsgang der klassischen Altertums bis auf Goethe und Wilhelm von Humboldt* (Leipzig, 1914); Julius Schlosser-Magnino, *La letteratura artistica*, trans. Filippo Rossi (Florence, 1935); Paola Barocchi, *Trattati d'arte del cinquecento fra manierismo e controriforma*, vols. 1 and 2 (Bari, 1960-1962); Enrico Castello ed., *Rettorica e Barocco* (Rome, 1955); Ruth C. Wallerstein, *Studies in Seventeenth-Century Poetic* (Madison, 1950); Carl J. Friedrich, *The Age of the Baroque, 1610-1660* (New York, 1952); Rudolph Wittkower, *Art and Architecture in Italy, 1600-1700* (London, 1958); Mario Praz, *Studies in Seventeenth-Century Imagery*, 2 vols. (London, 1939); James V. Mirollo, *The Poet of the Marvellous: Giambattista Marino* (New York and London, 1963); Paul Meissner, *Die geistesgeschichtlichen Grundlagen des englischen Literaturbarocks* (Munich, 1934).

Invention and Design

On problems of periodization, see Roger Murray, "A Case for the Study of Period Styles," *College English* 33 (1971), 139-48. Meyer Schapiro's essay "Style," in *Anthropology Today*, ed. A. L. Kroeber (Chicago, 1953), pp. 387-412, provides a valuable critique of the concept of style held by Wölfflin, Riegl, and other art historians. I am indebted to Dr. Robert R. Wark, Curator of the Huntington Art Collection, for this reference; Professor David A. Hansen of the University of California at Riverside has kindly called my attention to the reprint of Schapiro's essay in J. V. Cunningham, ed., *The Problem of Style* (Greenwich, Conn., 1966), pp. 19-56.

According to Alastair Smart, *The Renaissance and Mannerism Outside Italy* (London, 1972), the term Renaissance has frequently been applied, loosely and inaccurately, to the "flowering of the northern artistic genius around 1400" as exemplified by the sculpture of Claus Slater and "the new style of painting perfected by Jan Van Eyck." Nevertheless the "ideal that inspired the Italian Renaissance—the revival and emulation of the culture of antiquity—was not to exert any profound influence upon painting and sculpture outside Italy until the sixteenth century." Although northern artists had responded to "realistic" tendencies in the Gothic world of Giotto and the Lorenzetti, their vision had been "moulded essentially by medieval traditions, and the development of the new style in northern Europe must properly be seen as the consummation of the Late Gothic spirit." Like Johan Huizinga, who regarded this art as the creation of the waning Middle Ages, Smart argues that those art historians who have detected Renaissance elements in this new northern style have wrongly confused the Renaissance with realism. In Germany and the Netherlands alike, the northern Renaissance actually begins with Dürer. Noting the influence of Raphael and Michelangelo on Jan van Scorel and of Leonardo on Quinten Massys and Gossaert, Smart stresses the role of sixteenth-century Netherlandish painters in disseminating Italian Renaissance influences in other countries. Their attempts to "graft Italian High Renaissance forms onto the still flourishing Netherlandish tradition" are "the natural accompaniment of the spread of humanism to northern Europe..." (Smart, pp. 8-10, 126; cf. pp. 129, 137-40, 177-78; for France, England, and Spain, see pp. 180-84, 190-91, 201, 206).

[2]According to the *Rhetorica ad Herennium* orators can acquire the faculties of invention, arrangement *(dispositio)*, style *(elocutio)*, memory, and delivery by three means: theory, imitation, and practice ("arte, imitatione, exercitatione"). "Ars est praeceptio, quae dat certam viam rationemque dicendi. Imitatio est qua impellimur, cum diligendi ratione, ut aliquorum similes in dicendo valeamus esse. Exercitatio est adsiduus usus consuetudoque dicendi." ("By theory is meant a set of rules that provide a definite method and system of speaking. Imitation stimulates us to attain, in accordance with a studied method, the effectiveness of certain models in speaking. Practice is assiduous exercise and experience in speaking"), trans. Harry Caplan (Cambridge, Mass., and London, 1954), pp. 6-9.

As J. W. H. Atkins observes, Quintilian "endorses the familiar doctrine of the need for natural capacity, which should be fertilised by art and improved by practice"; *Literary Criticism in Antiquity* (Cambridge, 1934), II, 263-64. Quintilian is in general agreement with the opinion of earlier authorities who had added to the demand for *natura, ars*, and *exercitatio* "a further demand for imitation of the best writers." He insists "that only the best writers were to be imitated, and that they were to be imitated with discernment and judgement"; he protests against the tendency in his own time to take decadent writers as models and to copy the defects rather than the merits of the best authors. He regards "the development of a writer's native powers" as one object of imitation, and affirms that "imitation should not be limited to any one style, since various circumstances called for different styles." Imitation should not be regarded as "a matter of mere words"; what "was really to be imitated were the methods of this or that writer; his judgment, his arrangement, his appeal to the emotions, as well as his vocabulary, his use of Figures and the rest." Imitation alone is not enough, and "its real function lies not in the reproduction of earlier methods of expression but in conducing to the discovery of new effects and to the development of style in general." Here, Atkins suggests, Quintilian apparently is in agreement with Horace, who held similar views of imitation (ibid., pp. 278-80). As Atkins correctly observes, imitation was "to become the watchword of the Renascence," though he overstates the amount of "slavish copying" in the Renaissance conception of imitation (pp. 278-79). Atkins suggests that "a restatement of classicism . . . forms the main elements of Quintilian's creed. . . ." To counter the stylistic abuses of his day he advances "a new orthodoxy of his own. . . , taking reason or nature as his guide, and discarding as his basis the authority of the Greeks —that principle which since Cicero's day had been accepted by theorists as axiomatic" —and emphasizing nature, art, exercise, as well as decorum, correctness and the "imitation of sound models. . . ." Noting his influence on Elyot, Jonson, and other English writers, Atkins points out the similarity of Quintilian's views to those of the eighteenth-century critics who found "Nature and Homer" the same (ibid., pp. 295-98). See H. E. Butler, trans., *The Institutio Oratoria of Quintilian* (London and New York, 1922), IV, 15-23, 75-91, on study and imitation of the best authors, the utility of poetry and history and philosophy for the orator, on drawing from other authors "our stock of words, the variety of our figures and our methods of composition," and on the relation between invention and imitation and judgment. Cf. ibid., vol. I (1921), pp. 383, 385 on judgment and invention, p. 395 on *res* and *verba* (matter and words), and p. 397 on art, nature, practice, and imitation. See Elizabeth J. Sweeting, *Early Tudor Criticism* (Oxford, 1940), and Ruth Wallerstein, *Studies in Seventeenth Century Poetic* (Madison, 1950) on the influence of Quintilian's concept of imitation in the Renaissance.

Donald Lemen Clark, *John Milton at St. Paul's School* (New York, 1948), p. 7, distinguishes three divergent views on rhetoric in antiquity: 1) Plato's "moral philosophical" condemnation of rhetoric as concerned with "appearances, opinion, and pleasure" instead of "reality, truth, and the good life"; 2) Aristotle's "philosophical scientific" theory of rhetoric as closely allied with dialectic; and 3) the "practical educational view of the rhetoricians from Isocrates" (who referred to himself as a philosopher rather than rhetorician and to his school as a school of philosophy) "to Cicero to Quintilian, who praised rhetoric, practiced it, and taught it as an essential attribute of the free citizen." For John Colet's essentially Erasmian emphasis on the study of such authors "that hathe with wisdome joyned the pure chaste eloquence," and for the views of Valla and Erasmus concerning "the classical authors of the best period for the study of vocabulary, ornament, and style," see pp. 100-06. The division into nature, art, and exercise as essential elements for the mastery of eloquence had become a commonplace by the fourth century B.C., though Protagoras is credited with the "earliest statement of the analysis" and though Diogenes Laertius reports Aristotle as regarding "natural endowment, study, and constant practice" as essential for education; pp. 126-29. In his discussion of the curriculum at St. Paul's School in London, Clark follows this division: "Textbooks for Precepts," "Authors for Imitation," "Exercises for Praxis." See also the related studies of Renaissance education by Virgil K. Whitaker, *Shakespeare's Use of Learning* (San Marino, Calif., 1953); Thomas W. Baldwin, *William Shakspere's Petty School* (Urbana, 1927); idem, *William Shakspere's Small Latine and Lesse Greeke* (Urbana, 1944); Frances A. Yates, *The French Academies of the Sixteenth Century* (London, 1947); W. H. Woodward, *Desiderius Erasmus Concerning the Aim and Method of Education* (Cambridge, 1904); idem, *Studies in Education During the Age of the Renaissance,*

Invention and Design

1400-1600 (Cambridge, 1906); idem, *Vittorino da Feltre and Other Humanist Educators* (Cambridge, 1897).

In "Rhetoric in the Middle Ages," Richard McKeon stresses the influence of rhetoric on "three distinct lines of intellectual development during the Middle Ages": 1) "the tradition of rhetoricians themselves, who found their problems assembled ... in the works of Cicero and Quintilian"; 2) "the tradition of philosophers and theologians who found in Augustine a Platonism ... formulated in terms ... simplified from Cicero's rhetorical distinctions"; and 3) the logical tradition which passed as Aristotelian yet "followed Aristotle only in the treatment of terms and propositions and resorted to Cicero in the treatment of definitions and principles." In regard to the first, medieval rhetoricians followed Cicero in discussing "civil philosophy as the subject matter of rhetoric." As for the second, rhetoric had influenced Augustine "both in his reactions against it and in his assimilation and use of devices borrowed from it. ..." In McKeon's opinion, Augustine "differentiated two eloquences and two arts, much as Plato had proved rhetoric a pseudo-art in the *Gorgias* and yet had illustrated the method of the true rhetoric based on dialectic in the *Phaedrus*." Augustine's dialectic transforms the judgment that Cicero had expressed in *De inventione* —"that wisdom without eloquence is of little benefit to the state and eloquence without wisdom a great danger"—and these terms acquire two meanings. "The wisdom and eloquence of the world are to be contrasted to eternal wisdom and eloquence. ..."

In discussing the logical tradition of the Middle Ages, McKeon notes the extension of "the devices of rhetoric to logic" and the common use of "places" for purposes of discovery by rhetoricians and dialecticians alike. The subordination of rhetoric to logic was usually based on its "concern with hypotheses rather than with theses." He notes the three-cornered dispute between three traditions of rhetoric—that assimilated to dialectic and proof; that assimilated to theology and edification; and a third tradition indifferent to both of the others. The three main lines of medieval rhetorical development recur during the Renaissance. For Zabarella, Varchi, and Robertelli, rhetoric was a part of rational philosophy subordinate to logic. The tradition in which rhetoric "dominated the arts" continued into the Renaissance in both theological and secular tradition, assimilating "all philosophy and all subjects" to rhetoric (as in the doctrines of Nizolius and Majoragius) or transferring the method of discovery from rhetoric to dialectic (as in the thought of Rudolph Agricola and Ramus). The tradition in which rhetoric had "become a discipline of words, independent alike of philosophy and dialectic, finally established verbal distinctions" which influenced the theories of mathematics, physics, and symbolic logic: McKeon's essay appears in R. S. Crane, ed., *Critics and Criticism, Ancient and Modern* (Chicago, 1952), pp. 260-96. Cf. pp. 290n, 291n for references to scholarship on medieval *artes dictaminis* and *artes praedicandi*, and p. 292 for references to thirteenth-century translations of Aristotle's *Rhetoric* and Demetrius' *De elocutione*. See also Marsh H. McCall, Jr., *Ancient Rhetorical Theories of Simile and Comparison* (Cambridge, Mass., 1969); William Nelson, "The Boundaries of Fiction in the Renaissance: A Treaty Between Truth and Falsehood," *ELH* 36 (1969), 30-58; J. A. G. Tans, ed., *Invention et Imitation: Etudes sur la littérature du seizième siècle* (The Hague, 1968); Cesare Vasoli, *La dialettica e la retorica dell' Umanesimo: Invenzione e "methodo" nella cultura del XV e XVI secolo* (Milan, 1968); John D. Boyd, *The Function of Mimesis and Its Decline* (Cambridge, Mass., 1968).

[3] Walter Friedlaender, *Mannerism and Anti-Mannerism in Italian Painting* (New York, 1965), p. xvii.

[4] Rensselaer W. Lee, *Ut Pictura Poesis: The Humanistic Theory of Painting* (New

York, 1967), pp. 9-12. According to Varchi, the end of poetry and painting was "to imitate nature as far as possible," but both poet and painter might "use some discretion" in concealing imperfections in their subject. In Ludovico Dolce's opinion, the painter should strive "not only to imitate, but to surpass nature," portraying "in a single body all the perfection of beauty that nature scarcely displays in a thousand." In seeking this idealized nature or "perfettione di bellezza," the artist might emulate Zeuxis by going "direct to nature, and selecting the fairest parts from a number of individuals," thus producing "a composite figure more perfect than commonly exists." Alternatively, like Apelles and Praxiteles, he might "use as perfect a single model" as he could find, correcting her imperfections by a study of the marble and bronze statuary of antiquity, which "contain all the perfection of art."

In this doctrine, Lee finds the influence of Aristotle's statement that poetry expresses the universal, and Horace's advice to the poet to follow Greek exemplars. Literary theorists of the sixteenth century frequently claim "that poetry is like painting in its power to idealize nature." Fracastoro declares that, whereas others consider the particular *(singulare)*, the poet considers the universal idea, and Scaliger praises Virgil for providing ideas and examples of natural things more perfect than the works of nature—a *topos* that Pope would echo in his *Essay on Criticism* apropos of Virgil's imitation of Homer (Lee, pp. 9-12); cf. p. 13 on Alberti and Raphael.

In classical antiquity and in the Renaissance Erwin Panofsky (*Idea, A Concept in Art Theory*, trans. Joseph J. S. Peake [Columbia, S.C., 1968], p. 14) perceives two opposing conceptions of art "set naively side by side"—as inferior to nature "insofar as it merely imitates nature, at best to the point of deception" and as superior to nature inasmuch as it improves upon "the deficiencies of nature's individual products" and "independently confronts nature with a newly created image of beauty." Plato himself distinguished (*Idea*, p. 3) between painters who merely imitated sensory appearances and those who attempted to portray the Ideas, fixing their sight alternately on the true forms of the beautiful, just, and rational and on "that which merely passes for all this among men...." In the *Orator* Cicero (*Idea*, pp. 12-13) provides an essentially "rhetorical description of artistic creation," praising Plato as a master and teacher "not only of thought but also of speech" and basing his conception of ideal sculpture and oratory on the Platonic theory of ideas. Phidias did not model his statues of Zeus and Athena on actual human beings, but on "a sublime notion of beauty" which he beheld in his own mind, directing his hand and art according to this ideal likeness. Similarly, we "see the image of perfect eloquence in the mind and only seek to comprehend its copy with the ears." For Plotinus (*Idea*, pp. 26-27) the artist does not "simply reproduce the visible," but goes back to the "principles in which nature itself had found its origin." The artist's mind shares the nature of "the creative *Nous*," and the Idea he beholds in his mind is a living "vision." St. Augustine (*Idea*, p. 35) sees visible beauty as "only a feeble likeness of the invisible." Medieval philosophy (*Idea*, pp. 40-41) compared the artist with "the *deus artifex* or *deus pictor*," holding that "the artist worked, even if not from an Idea in the real, metaphysical sense, at least from an inner notion of form, or 'quasi-idea,' that preceded the work." In the Renaissance (*Idea*, pp. 48-51, 64-66) the ideas of *imitatio* and *electio*—"truth to nature and beauty," the "requirement of formal and objective 'correctness' " and the idea of "rising above nature," imitating reality and "improving upon it"—coexist side by side, as in antiquity. In the High Renaissance, "the art-theoretical doctrine of Ideas, insofar as it is concerned with the principle of beauty..., seems almost like a more spiritualized form of the old selection theory —spiritualized in the sense that beauty is achieved not by an external combination of separate parts but by an inner vision that combines individual experiences into a new whole."

Contrasting medieval and Renaissance attitudes toward art, Panofsky argues that

Invention and Design

the latter removed "the object from the inner world of the artist's imagination," placing it "firmly in the 'outer world'"; moreover, in its concern with the problem of beauty Renaissance thought differed "essentially" from "the medieval doctrine of Ideas" (*Idea*, pp. 50, 64).

On the conception of beauty as symmetry, see *Idea*, pp. 29, 53-55, 72, 221, 236. On icastic and fantastic imitation, see pp. 5, 215, 242. On the distinction between internal and external design, see pp. 61-62, 75-93, 220-34. On the relationship of rules to individual genius, see p. 219. On idea and allegory, see p. 237. On Ficino's influence on mannerist or baroque theory see pp. 97-99. On different senses of *idea*, see p. 66, and on different meanings of *maniera* see pp. 238-41. On the analogy between the *modus operandi* of art and nature, see p. 42. On the conception of art as "restoring" nature to its pristine and unfallen perfection, see p. 95.

In *Studies in Seicento Art and Theory* (London, 1947), Denis Mahon re-examines what he terms "the Agucchi-Bellori phase of the classic-idealist theory" of art and reinstates "the good Monsignore" (Giovanni Battista Agucchi) "into his proper position, as the precursor of Bellori, within the general scheme elaborated by Dr. Panofsky." Noting a "fundamental discrepancy between art and theory" during the seicento, when "the prevailing artistic language was the baroque" but "the predominant trend in art theory was strongly accentuated in the opposite direction, towards the classic," Mahon attempts to explore "the precise character of the interrelation of art with theory in certain specific cases"—notably the admiration expressed by Agucchi, Mancini, and other early seventeenth-century theorists for the paintings of the Carracci and Domenichino, and the influence of such classicizing criticism on Guercino's change of styles after his brief visit to Rome (pp. 3-5).

In his *Trattato* on painting Agucchi contrasted the popular or "vulgar" painters who merely seek exact imitation of nature and visible likeness with the nobler and more enlightened artists who "embody in their conception that excellence of beauty and perfection which nature herself (though in practice invariably prevented by a multiplicity of material circumstances) would nevertheless wish to attain" and who "represent the world [*le cose*] not as it actually is, but as it ideally ought to be, bringing together . . . those elements of beauty which . . . nature has contrived to scatter here and there, perfect parts of necessarily imperfect wholes." Whereas the public approves "a close imitation of nature," the *huomo intendente* "lifts up his thoughts to that *Idea del bello* which nature shows that she wishes to achieve. . ." (pp. 62-63). On the one hand, Agucchi condemns the neglect of beauty for the sake of resemblance ("similitudine") alone; but, on the other hand, he also censures "what we should now describe as the Mannerist style," for its lack of verisimilitude —"maniera lontane dal vero e dal verisimile." The best style or *maniera*, in his opinion, is "connected with the *Idea* in theory and with the Caracci, Raphael and the *statue antiche* in practice. . ." (pp. 64-65).

In Agucchi's theory of the Idea of the beautiful in painting, Mahon recognizes the influence of Aristotle's *Poetics*—especially the distinction between serious-minded and trivial-minded poets, who are concerned respectively with "noble themes" and "the affairs of the vulgar," and the doctrine that "the highest form of art involves idealized imitation, the ennoblement of the actual" (pp. 125-30). Cf. Aristotle, *On the Art of Poetry*, trans. Ingram Bywater (Oxford, 1951): "As Tragedy is an imitation of personages better than the ordinary man, we in our way should follow the example of good portrait-painters, who reproduce the distinctive features of a man, and at the same time, without losing the likeness, make him handsomer than he is" (p. 57); "The poet being an imitator just like the painter or other maker of likenesses, he must necessarily in all instances represent things in one or other of three aspects, either as they were or are, or as they are said or thought to be or to have been, or as they ought to be. . . . For the purposes of poetry a convincing impossibility is preferable to an unconvincing possibility; and if men such as Zeuxis depicted be impossible, the answer is that it is better they should be like that, as the artist ought to improve on his model [tò gàr parádeigma deî huperéchein]" (pp. 85-86, 91); "The distinction between historian and poet . . . consists really in this, that the one describes the thing that has been, and the other a kind of thing that might be. Hence poetry is something more philosophic and of graver import than history, since its statements are of the nature rather of universals, whereas those of history are singulars. By a universal statement I mean one as to what such or such a kind of man will probably say or do—which is the aim of poetry, though it affixes proper names to the characters. . ." (p. 43). Cf. S. H. Butcher, ed., *Aristotle's Theory of Poetry and Fine Art* (New York, 1951), p. 35; see also Butcher's chapters on "Poetic Truth" and "Poetic Universality in Greek Literature," ibid., pp. 163-97, 389-407.

Mahon challenges the view that Agucchi's *Idea* is "nothing more or less than the neo-Platonic *Idea* of the Mannerist period." In his opinion, Agucchi expresses the "typically Renaissance conception of the collection and synthesis of already existing natural beauties," and his praise of the Carracci "brings out his anti-Mannerist point of view." Agucchi represents the Carracci as "having rescued art from the *maniere lontane dal vero* [*e dal verisimile*] by a return to nature, and it is on this foundation that the new *Idea* is possible," through "a thorough study of nature, then its ennoblement by elimination of faults, selection of the best, and synthesis 'con finezza di giuditio . . .'" Like Raphael, the Carracci had studied the works of antiquity in order to form the *Idea* of a beauty that does not exist in nature except through the collection and judicious synthesis of beauties scattered and dispersed in many objects (Mahon, pp. 139-40). Cf. pp. 141-54, on parallels between Agucchi's "idea of beauty" and the views of later seventeenth-century critics such as Bellori and Dufresnoy; see also pp. 157-91, for the critical doctrines of Zuccaro and Roncalli, for Roman and Tuscan conceptions of the early cinquecento Venetians as "somewhat unsophisticated imitators of nature," and for Salvator Rosa as an example of "discrepancy between theory and practice in the Seicento."

Mahon identifies Cicero's *De inventione* as the source of the story, so frequently repeated during the fifteenth and sixteenth centuries, of the painting of Helen that Zeuxis executed for the Crotonians; variant versions refer to the subject of this work as Venus or even as Juno (Mahon, p. 134n.).

[5] Lee, pp. 13-16.

[6] In considering Renaissance discussions of visual or verbal imitation, the student must bear in mind not only the variety of theories concerning the origin and the ontological status of ideas, but also the different senses of *idea*. This term may be applied to the image or *eidolon* of an object impressed on the senses from without, to an innate idea pre-existing in the mind of God or angel or man, to an image existing in the imagination or memory, to a universal concept abstracted from particulars, to a composite image combining selected details from particulars, or to the design that the artist conceives in his own mind and transfers to paper or canvas. Rhetorical and poetic theorists refer to the *idea* of a species of style or poetic genre, the idea of a vocation or office (such as the perfect orator or poet or painter, the perfect prince or warrior or priest) or to moral universals, such as the idea of virtue or vice, felicity or misery. For certain rhetoricians, the word is an image of an idea or thought, and the idea itself an image of a thing. For a strict Platonist, on the other hand, things themselves are images of ideas. For the nominalist, universals are words or "names"; for the realist, they are metaphysical realities, prior to and more "real" than concrete particulars.

In Renaissance accounts of ideal imitation one should not confuse speculations on

Invention and Design

the Idea of Beauty with a general theory of universals. Much of the material collected by Panofsky in *Idea* and summarized by Lee centers specifically on the idea of the beautiful rather than on moral universals in general, or on the ideal forms of particular species or genres of created beings. Moreover, since Plato himself had distinguished beauty from other universals as the only archetypal idea still visible to the senses in the world below, there is probably less inconsistency in the mixture of Platonic and Aristotelian conceptions in Renaissance art theory than recent historians have assumed. Most Renaissance theorists associated the idea of beauty with symmetry and proportion (often under the influence of Vitruvius). In many of their disputes the real point at issue was precisely how far the individual artist was free to embody his own notions of beauty in his composition, even at the risk of violating verisimilitude and classical canons of proportion. Both sides in the controversy tended to regard art as the image of an idealized and refined nature, and to view the act of creation or composition as a realization of nature's principles—operating as nature worked. The "independents" or "anticlassicists" (as they have sometimes been called) often held theoretical views similar to those of their opponents. Nevertheless, they frequently found it convenient to base their polemical strategy on the rights of natural genius, on freedom of invention and composition, and on the superiority of an intuitive sense of beauty rather than on mathematical, anatomical, and other "academic" studies.

Though the idea of the beautiful should not be confused with other universals (nor Renaissance discussion of the ideal pattern or formal design of a work of art or literature confused with discussion of the ideal patterns or paradigms of the moral or intellectual or political virtues), they are nevertheless interrelated, and (like Plato in the *Phaedrus*, Aristotle in the *Poetics*, and Cicero in the *Orator*) Renaissance writers could apply arguments associated with the ideal imitation of beauty to the ideal imitation of other qualities. The notion of ideal imitation was, in fact, ambivalent, and could embrace both aesthetic models or archetypes. Just as Aristotle had cited the example of Zeuxis in regard to delineation of the ideal type or paradigm (*Poetics*, Chap. 25) and Cicero had compared his idea of the orator to Phidias' ideal conceptions of Zeus and Athena, the Florentine poet Antonio Francini could compare Milton's selective quest for the ideal of moral virtue to Zeuxis' choice of the rarest beauties as a model for his portrait of Helen ("E per poterla effigiare al paro/ Dalle più belle Idee trasse il più raro"). An artist almost divine, Milton has beheld the noblest men in all the lands in order to fashion the idea of every virtue: "L'ottimo dal miglior dopo scegliea / Per fabbricar d' ogni virtù l'Idea." See H. C. Beeching, ed., *The Poetical Works of John Milton* (New York, 1935), p. 119.

In Panofsky's opinion (*Idea*, pp. 64-65) a preoccupation with the problem of beauty differentiates the art-theoretical doctrine of Ideas in the High Renaissance from the medieval doctrine of Ideas. Moreover, though the Renaissance view seems "almost like a more spiritualized form of the old selection theory," it also differs from the classical view. Even though the selection theory was a commonplace in antiquity, classical thinkers had not identified the Idea with the paradigms "obtained by choosing from among the most beautiful things." Renaissance thinkers, however, "understood the Idea concept in the light of a fundamentally novel attitude toward art which identified the world of ideas with a world of heightened realities."

Finally, insofar as a work of art realized the universal—an Idea achieved through either Aristotelian induction or Platonic dialectic (or, in the case of beauty, an Idea already inherent in the fallen soul), it could serve the ends of contemplation and action. Yet it could also become an instrument of self-perfection, a means of reascent to the realm of ideas. Through presenting an idealized image, the sensuous vehicle of a universal abstracted from particulars, it facilitated the movement from multiplicity to unity, from the Many to the One. In addition to its ability to teach, per-

The Lamb and the Elephant

suade and delight, and to purge the passions, it also possessed (in neo-Platonic terms) the ability to hasten the purification of the soul, its dissociation from flesh and matter, its progressive spiritualization and regeneration, and its reunion with the divine.

In an essay "On Metaphysical Poetry," *Scrutiny* 2 (1933), 222-39, James Smith defines "metaphysical" poetry as "that to which the impulse is given by an overwhelming concern with metaphysical problems; with problems either deriving from, or closely resembling in the nature of their difficulty, the problem of the Many and the One." Such problems are, however, usually involved in theories of "ideal art" and of the knowledge and representation of universals. Insofar as the poet or painter endeavored to portray paradigms of species and archetypes of virtues or vices in and through idealized and exemplary figures—or to depict an "Idea della bellezza" that nature could only realize imperfectly and had scattered through myriad particulars —he was inevitably concerned with the problem of the One and the Many.

Smith's essay emphasizes the distinction between the metaphysical conceit and other kinds of conceits and metaphors, as well as the differences between true metaphysical poetry, and "baroque poetry" and the poetry that Samuel Johnson called "metaphysical." In contrast to dead and inert metaphors which have lost the quality of tensions, "within the metaphysical conceit, . . . even when it is being dwelt on by the mind, tension between the elements continues." In Smith's opinion, metaphysical poetry springs from a "concern with problems with which the universe must always present mankind." Though it is not "confined to either one age or country," nevertheless the conditions under which it is produced are "somewhat rare in occurrence." He perceives "traces of it . . . in Virgil; in Tasso of the *Aminta*, not of the *Gerusalemme*; but most of all, outside England, in the Spain of the Philips." In some of Calderón's dramas, "not the language merely, but the action is a metaphysical conceit: it is at once fleshly and spiritual, and the one, it seems, because of the other."

Nevertheless the emphasis on the image as a vehicle of the idea, and on *sensibilia* and *visibilia* as aids to the knowledge of *intelligibilia* and *invisibilia*, is a recurrent theme in epistemology and mnemonics, in demonstrative and mystical theology, in rhetoric and poetics and art theory, in the art of meditation, and in Renaissance pedagogy. Humanist educators and apologists had stressed the superiority of poetic images and examples, to scholastic precepts and syllogistic demonstrations. John Milton bases his pedagogical method on epistemological method, the natural order of *sensibilia* and *intelligibilia* in the normal process of learning. Echoing St. Paul's Epistle to the Romans, he declares that "because our understanding cannot in this body found itself but on sensible things, nor arrive so clearly to the knowledge of God and things invisible as by orderly conning over the visible and inferior creature, the same method is necessarily to be followed in all discreet teaching." See Hughes, *Complete Poems and Selected Prose*, p. 631.

For Milton, as for Plato, true eloquence is the offspring of virtue. *The Reason of Church-Government* (Hughes, p. 640) commends Plato's advice that, "seeing that persuasion certainly is a more winning and more manlike way to keep men in obedience than fear," laws of "principal moment" should be prefaced by a discourse showing "how good, how gainful, how happy it must needs be to live according to honesty and justice; which being uttered with those native colors and graces of speech, as true eloquence, the daughter of virtue, can best bestow on her mother's praises, would so incite and in a manner charm the multitude into the love of that which is really good, as to embrace it ever after...."

[7] "But of beauty," according to the *Phaedrus*, "I repeat again that we saw her there shining in company with the celestial forms; and coming to earth we find her here too, shining in clearness through the clearest aperture of sense." For "beauty only

174

Invention and Design

has this portion, that she is at once the loveliest and also the most apparent." He "whose initiation is recent, and who has been the spectator of many glories in the other world, is amazed when he sees any one having a godlike face or form, which is the expression or imitation of divine beauty; and . . . some 'misgiving' of a former world steals over him. . ." (B. Jowett, trans., *The Works of Plato* [Tudor Publishing Co., New York, n.d.], III, 409-10). "For he who would proceed rightly in this matter," Diotima advises Socrates in the *Symposium*, "should begin in youth to turn to beautiful forms; and first, if his instructor guide him rightly, he should learn to love one such form only. . . ; and soon he would himself perceive that the beauty of one form is truly related to the beauty of another. . . , and will become a lover of all beautiful forms; this will lead him on to consider that the beauty of the mind is more honorable than the beauty of the outward form. . . , and at last the vision is revealed to him of a single science, which is the science of beauty everywhere. . . . And the true order of going or being led by another to the things of love, is to use the beauties of earth as steps along which he mounts upwards for the sake of that other beauty, going from one to two, and from two to all fair forms, and from fair forms to fair actions, and from fair actions to fair notions, until from fair notions he arrives at the notion of absolute beauty, and at last knows what the essence of beauty is" (Jowett, II, 340-42).

For the neo-Platonic commonplace that earthly love may be a means of ascent to divine love, and devotion to female beauty a stage to the adoration of divine beauty, see A. J. Krailsheimer, *The Continental Renaissance, 1500-1600* (Harmondsworth, 1971), pp. 143, 147.

For Abelard and conceptualism, see W. Windelband, *A History of Philosophy*, trans. James H. Tufts (New York, 1901), pp. 272, 298. According to Windelband, it was essentially Abelard's theory "that became the ruling doctrine in the formula accepted by the Arabian philosophers (Avicenna), '*universalia ante multiplicitatem, in multiplicitate et post multiplicitatem*'; to universals belongs equally a significance *ante rem* as regards the divine mind, *in re* as regards Nature, and *post rem* as regards human knowledge."

[8]In the *Topics* Aristotle distinguishes induction and reasoning as two different species of dialectical arguments. Induction is "a passage from individuals to universals. . . ." It is "more convincing and clear" than reasoning, "more readily learnt by the use of the senses," and is generally applicable "to the mass of men. . ." (McKeon, p. 198). According to the *Posterior Analytics*, induction "proves not what the essential nature of a thing is but that it has or has not some attribute." It serves to "establish a universal on the evidence of groups of particulars which offer no exception. . ." (p. 165). Even though "the act of sense-perception is of the particular, its content is universal," and we must "get to know the primary premisses by induction; for the method by which even sense-perception implants the universal is inductive" (pp. 185-86).

[9]B. Jowett, trans., *The Works of Plato*, II, 262-94.

[10]Ernst Robert Curtius, *European Literature and the Latin Middle Ages*, trans. Willard R. Trask (New York and Evanston, 1953), p. 474.

[11]Allan H. Gilbert, ed., *Literary Criticism: Plato to Dryden* (Detroit, 1962), p. 141.

[12]Gilbert, pp. 147-48, 154, 163.

[13]The principle of imitating selected models (in addition to theory and practice) as a method of learning an art is common to Renaissance artistic, poetic, and rhetorical theory. Painters and poets could find this principle clearly expressed in the *Rhetorica ad Herennium*. This treatise, which medieval authors had erroneously regarded as

an original work by Cicero, recommended imitation as a means of developing the five faculties essential for good oratory: invention, disposition, style, memory, and delivery. See *Rhetorica ad Herennium*, ed. and trans. Harry Caplan, pp. 6-9, "All these faculties we can acquire by three means: Theory, Imitation, and Practice [arte, imitatione, exercitatione]. By theory is meant a set of rules that provide a definite model and system of speaking. Imitation stimulates us to attain, in accordance with a studied method, the effectiveness of certain models in speaking. Practice is assiduous exercise and experience in speaking."

In *The Scholemaster*, Ascham defines imitation as a "facultie to express livelie and perfitlie that example which ye go about to folow" and distinguishes three kinds of imitation "in matters of learning." Comedy and tragedy provide "a perfite *imitation*, or faire livelie painted picture of the life of everie degree of man." In regard to the second kind of imitation—"to folow for learning of tonges and sciences the best authors"—Ascham notes the "great controversie" as to "whether one or many are to be folowed: and if one, who is that one; *Seneca* or *Cicero*; *Salust* or *Caesar*; and so forth in Greeke and Latin." The third kind of imitation pertains to the second: "as, when you be determined whether ye will folow one or mo, to know perfitlie, and which way to folow, that one; in what place; by what meane and order; by what tooles and instrumentes ye shall do it; by what skill and iudgement ye shall trewelie discerne whether ye folow rightlie or no." See O. B. Hardison, Jr., ed., *English Literary Criticism* (New York, 1963), pp. 59-61. In Ascham's opinion, Sturmius surpassed all other writers on this subject, declaring "who is to be followed, what is to be followed, and, the best point of all, by what way and order trew Imitation is rightlie to be exercised" (p. 64).

The alleged "classicism" of the Renaissance cannot be dissociated either from its theories of ideal representation or from its interpretations of the principle of verisimilitude. For many writers and artists of the sixteenth century (as for many of the eighteenth century) the works of the ancients might well seem the most reliable "rule" or "guide" for imitating either the realm of nature or the realm of ideas—or both.

Nevertheless the imitation of classical models might complicate as well as resolve the problem of achieving a "convincing" or "probable" likeness. The principle of verisimilitude—shared by classical, medieval, and Renaissance writers alike—was, in practice, relative rather than absolute. It varied not only with subject and genre, but also with the knowledge and expectations of the audience. In certain contexts, an image might appear the more convincing the closer it conformed to the manners of the writer's own contemporaries; in other contexts he must emphasize historical or geographical distance to make his image seem probable (even though his historical or geographical details might in fact be far from accurate). In certain genres, variants of epic and romance, an image might seem the more probable in proportion to its defiance of the ordinary conventions of behavior; the image of a hero, an enchantress, or a pagan princess might paradoxically seem most persuasive when most marvelous and (from a normal point of view) most incredible.

Increased familiarity with the manners and conventions of antiquity on the part of Renaissance audiences (in comparison with medieval audiences) might heighten the demand for historical distance in order to achieve verisimilitude and "probable" likeness. Nevertheless in actuality the historical knowledge of Renaissance readers or spectators, their expectations from the poem or painting, and the mixture of classical and modern conventions by the poet or painter himself were variable. An audience of tradesmen and an audience of antiquarians would not possess the same notions of "convincing" or probable behavior. To the former, a historically accurate portrait of classical worthies might well seem unrealistic or pedantic, while to the latter a flagrant disregard of historical milieu might produce ludicrous anachronisms.

Even the most erudite of writers and audiences, however, generally tended to reinterpret classical civilization in the light of their own values. By considerable ingenuity and hermeneutic or rhetorical skill, literary critics frequently converted the warriors of classical epic into model Renaissance gentlemen. Similarly even in works addressed to highly literate and sophisticated audiences, poets often invested the ancients themselves with the *ethos* of an idealized Renaissance prince. Conversely, in treating their own contemporaries, or in portraying Biblical personages, Renaissance writers and artists sometimes tended to "classicize" their subjects, imposing upon modern England or Italy and upon ancient Palestine the manners and mores of Greece and Rome. The basic question (to which Renaissance poets did not, either in practice or in theory, give a consistent answer) was whether the distance between antiquity and modernity should be accentuated or minimized in the interests of historical decorum. In practice, the imitation of classical models (whether in formal literary structure, in style, or in norms of character and thought) often tended to blur rather than accentuate the difference between the ancient and modern worlds. Accepting classical standards (or his own conception thereof) as definitive and normative, the poet or painter sometimes applied the same neoclassical schemas to his images of ancient Greeks and Romans, personages of the Old and New Testament, and his own contemporaries. Along with the contrary tendency (to accommodate the mores of antiquity to contemporary manners in the interest of verisimilitude) this frequently resulted in a "mixed" schema for the representation of ancient and modern alike, a variable blend of both classical and contemporary elements. It seems unwise, therefore, to press the difference between medieval and Renaissance representations of historical distance too far; both involved a mixture of antique and modern conventions.

[14] Hardison, pp. 275-86.

[15] Anthony Blunt, *Artistic Theory in Italy, 1450-1600* (London, Oxford, New York, 1962), pp. 88-98.

[16] Ibid., p. 142n. Blunt observes that Zuccaro is "only rarely" inclined toward neo-Platonism: "He gives Plato himself as the source for his theory of Ideas, though it is more exactly Neoplatonic...." Cf. pp. 140-47.

[17] Ibid., p. 145.

[18] Cennino d'Andrea Cennini, *The Craftsman's Handbook*, trans. Daniel V. Thompson, Jr. (New York, 1954), pp. 123-30.

[19] Ibid., pp. 1-2.

[20] Leon Battista Alberti, *On Painting*, trans. John R. Spencer, rev. ed. (New Haven and London, 1966), pp. 63-64. "In all this discussion, I beg you to consider me not as a mathematician but as a painter writing of these things. Mathematicians measure with their minds alone the forms of things separated from all matter. Since we wish the object to be seen, we will use a more sensate wisdom" (p. 43).

[21] Ibid., pp. 40, 52, 67-69, 72, 77, 89, 94.

[22] Ibid., pp. 39, 58, 94-95.

[23] Ibid., pp. 72-81, 89, 95.

[24] In classical and Renaissance theories of style, the principles for sentence structure are sometimes analogous to those for the disposition of orations and poems or for artistic designs. For Longinus, "fitting and dignified arrangement" is the fifth source of the sublime and "serves to hold all the others in union...." Like other critics, he stresses the emotional effects of harmony and order. Harmony is "not merely an

The Lamb and the Elephant

instrument of persuasion and pleasure to men but also has wonderful power for expressing great and strong feeling." Literary composition, "as a harmony of words natural to man and laying hold not of his ears alone but of his very spirit, sets in motion manifold ideas of words, thoughts, actions, beauty, and melody. . . ." The speaker's audience share his emotions and feelings "as he brings together great conceptions in the verbal structure he erects." Composition "is of the greatest importance in giving weight to noble passages, in the same way as the synthesis of the parts gives beauty to the body, for any one member cut from the others and taken by itself is of no great account, but when they are all together they make up a perfect harmony. . . . In such well-rounded sentences greatness depends almost entirely on the union of a multitude." In a sentence of Demosthenes, one cannot add or subtract a syllable without reducing its grandeur or its energy (Gilbert, pp. 191-93). Aristotle had similarly defined beauty in terms of order (Bywater, p. 40) and demanded a plot so tightly constructed that "the transposal or withdrawal" of any incident would "disjoin and dislocate the whole" (Bywater, p. 42).

Longinus' emphasis on variety and unity in the orator's arrangement of words is paralleled in Renaissance discussions of unity and variety in the visual arts and in epic or dramatic plot or style. His insistence on the power of harmony to persuade and move has numerous analogues in classical and Renaissance statements of the persuasive force of beauty. In his dialogue on rhetoric *(Phaedrus)* Plato had stressed the power of beauty to move the beholder, arguing that moral wisdom *(phronesis)* would ravish the sight if it were visible. In the *Republic* and other dialogues he had discussed the power of music over the passions, and Aristotle had emphasized the same point in his *Politics*.

In the myth of Hercules Gallicus, Renaissance exegesis found an emblem of the power of oratory to draw men by the ears; this image was subsequently extended to the poet and to the painter's appeal to the eye. In verbal discourse, in music, and in the visual arts, harmony and symmetry of composition possessed the power to move and persuade. In this respect the visual arts could share a common end with rhetoric as well as poetic, and it is possible that in the character of their linear rhythms, their disposition of light and heavy masses, their use of loose and disjointed or closely-knit structures, their exploitation of balance or antithesis or asymmetry they may have consciously aimed at particular emotional effects, as did the poet and the rhetorician. Moreover, just as the elongation of rhetorical periods and their component members (words, phrases, clauses) was a traditional means of achieving stylistic elevation through conscious departure from ordinary usage in discourse, the deliberate elongation of painted or carved figures and their component members might serve a comparable end in art.

When the mannerist apologists defended their distortions in the name of a higher ideal of beauty existing as a *disegno interno* in the mind—an idea superior to natural forms and derived directly from the divine archetype of the Beautiful—they were speaking essentially of an idea of composition. The doctrinal foundation of their argument was Plato's statement that, alone of the transcendental ideas, beauty is still visible on earth and to the eye of sense. Their remarks concerning the intuitive perception of beauty should not be misapplied to the universal ideas of wisdom or virtue or to other archetypal norms which the poet and painter alike were theoretically supposed to imitate. These could, as a rule, be known only through abstraction from sensuous particulars and the systematic use of dialectic—or, alternatively and indirectly, on the authority of the philosopher or the theologian. Just as Horace had counseled the poet—and Cicero the orator—to consult the Greek philosophers, Renaissance painters sometimes sought detailed instructions for their themes and inventions from scholars and ecclesiastics, in addition to the writings of the poets themselves and mythological or iconographical manuals.

Invention and Design

Alberti, in turn, followed Vitruvius in defining beauty as "a kind of harmony and concord of all the parts to form a whole which is constructed according to a fixed number, and a certain relation and order, as symmetry, the highest and most perfect law of nature, demands." In beautiful architecture the "business of the mind is the choice, division, ordering and things of that kind, which give dignity to the work" (Blunt, pp. 15-16).

[25] See "'Passions Well Imitated'; Rhetoric and Poetic in the Preface to *Samson Agonistes*," in Joseph Anthony Wittreich, Jr., ed., *Calm of Mind, Tercentenary Essays on Paradise Regained and Samson Agonistes in Honor of John S. Diekhoff* (Cleveland and London, 1971), pp. 175-207.

[26] Cf. Torquato Tasso, *Prose*, ed. Francesco Flora (Milan and Rome, 1935), pp. 324-25). Drawing an analogy between poet and painter, Tasso doubts whether poetry imitates "alcuna azione in quanto divina; perché in quanto tale peraventura non si può imitare con alcuno di quegli instrumenti che sono propri de la poesia. . . . Laonde se il pittore, quantunque dipinga Giove e Marte, Iside ed Osiri, non è pittore d'altra forma che de l'umana o di quella di fiera, perché la divinità non può da lui essere imitata; cosí il poeta di queste forme e di queste azione non è imitatore, ma de le umane principalmente o propriamente. Tanta è dunque la diversitá fra l'imitatore de le cose divine e de le cose umane, quanta fra quelle che sono propriamente idee, e queste che chiamiamo imagini e simolacri." Cf. Castelvetro and Milton on the representation of divine and invisible persons or events through sensuous media and human terms. Tasso cites Aristotle's observation that many feigned *(fingono)* the lives of the gods—like their figures and images—in the likeness of those of men. Cicero declared that Homer had attributed *(trasportate)* human things to the divine, and divine to us, "volendoci dare a divedere ch'egli aveva descritti gl'Iddii come uomini, e le passioni umane come divine: perché il parlare e l'consigliarsi sono umane azioni; e l'adirarsi e 'l muoversi a compassione, passioni de gli uomini" (Tasso, ed. Flora, p. 324).

[27] D. W. Robertson, Jr., *A Preface to Chaucer* (Princeton, 1962), p. 152.

In elucidating "the basic difference between the function of art in medieval contexts and in later times," E. H. Gombrich resorts to "the philosophic distinction between 'universals' and 'particulars.'" In his opinion "the return to the classical ideal of 'convincing' image in the Renaissance did not necessarily change the nature of the problem, it only created more exacting standards for the rendering of universals . . . . But in one respect the importance of these fresh standards can hardly be overrated. As in classical times, the narrative was again to be presented to the beholder as if he were an eyewitness to imaginary events" (*Art and Illusion: A Study in the Psychology of Pictorial Representation*, 2d. ed., rev. [Princeton, 1961], p. 152).

Chapter VII
INVENTION AND DISPOSITION: THEME AND STRUCTURE

>>>>>>:<<<<<<

FEW POETS or painters could altogether ignore contemporary theories of composition and imitation, or such rhetorical terms and concepts as invention and disposition, *ingenium* and judgment. These terms were polysemous, however, and sometimes possessed different senses in different arts. Invention (literally "finding") originally referred to the choice of argument; the orator selected his proofs from among the commonplaces (topics) of invention. This term was later extended to other arts and sciences. The poet's theme or subject was his "argument" or invention;[1] and the rhetorical background of medieval poetics is apparent in terms like *troubadour* and *trouvère*. Musical compositions are "inventions"; so are scientific discoveries and technological innovations, thanks to Bacon's rhetorical education.[2] The same term was also applied to the "conceit," an image or argument based on the correspondence between two different things or ideas, and it thus became closely associated with wit and ingenuity. The same designation could also be applied to an entire poem or story, and to an emblem or device. In painting, "invention" could refer to the subject, to a symbol or iconographical motif, or on occasion to composition and design as well.[3] Thus Vasari observes that Pontormo and many other painters had "imitated Dürer in his motifs *(invenzioni)*"; this, he continues, was "not in itself reprehensible," but it is "extremely regrettable that he took over the German manner lock, stock, and barrel, down to the facial expression and even in movement."[4] The term occurs frequently in cinquecento and seicento art theory and survives well into the eighteenth century. Bevilacqua has noted the rhetorical implications of Reynolds' discussion of "inventions" in the *Discourses*.[5]

Invention and Disposition

I.

At an early date, invention became associated with *ingenium* (natural talent or genius, cleverness or wit) and with the faculty of imagination or fantasy. For theorists of the late sixteenth and seventeenth centuries, *ingenium* or wit was virtually identical with facility and originality of invention; it was the primary source of clever *concetti* and witty *acutezze* (points). Judgment in turn was associated with disposition and design. Horace had stressed the importance of judgment for the poet, and this principle occurs frequently in the artistic and literary criticism of the period.

The invention and judgment of arguments also belonged to logic,[6] thus paralleling two of the five conventional parts of rhetoric (invention, disposition, memory, elocution, delivery).[7] Ramus subsequently eliminated this duplication by assigning invention and disposition to logic and leaving elocution (style) and delivery to rhetoric. Though his influence on subsequent treatises on logic and rhetoric and on manuals of Reformed divinity is apparent, his impact on poetry is more difficult to trace, in spite of the valuable researches of Rosemond Tuve. Ramus' system is essentially a simplification of the Aristotelian system rather than a radical revision, and poets could have achieved substantially the same results through following the traditional logicians and rhetoricians. Ramus' subordination of rhetoric to logic, moreover, is in part an implementation of Plato's insistence that the rhetorician is apt to mislead unless he is already in possession of certain knowledge; eloquence must be based on truth (a *topos* that would receive poetic elaboration in the last book of *Paradise Regained*), and truth can best be achieved through dialectic. Nevertheless, there were many features of the Ramist system in addition to its comparative simplicity that should have made it attractive to poets. In teaching, Ramus himself illustrated various forms of argument through quotations from classical poetry and oratory; and his successors, including Downham and Milton, continued this practice. His *Dialectica* and the complementary *Rhetorica* of Talon were frequently employed as textbooks in English schools. Finally, his discussion of the invention of arguments could readily be used in conjunction with treatises on *ingenium*, facilitating the invention of conceits and their development as instruments of logical proof.

Though invention was normally associated with choice of argument, and judgment with disposition, theorists did not consistently maintain this distinction. Just as artists sometimes extended invention to include design or disposition, Tasso argued that the poet must exercise judgment as well as invention, selecting a subject matter capable of receiving the "form" of the poetic fable. There are three things that the heroic poet must consider: "to select a matter fit to receive the most excellent form that the poet's artifice attempts to introduce; to bestow such a form; and lastly to invest it with the rarest ornaments that are appropriate to its nature." According to Philoponus' commentary on the third book of Aristotle's *Prior Analytics,* Tasso continues, one must not only consider the species of the "cose subiette" but also the matter and "la disposizione a ricever le forme. . . ." The poet must not only exercise art in forming the matter, but also display judgment in recognizing it, selecting a subject naturally capable of every ornament and perfection. The poet's choice of argument belongs therefore (in Tasso's opinion) to judgment rather than to invention.

In invention, moreover, the poet possesses greater freedom than the orator. In judicial cases the matter is often ordered by chance and necessity, but in poetry it is frequently subject to choice. The poet is permitted to feign, "e la finzione è riputata invenzione. . . ."[8] Steering a middle course between critics who associate poetry with the false and those who associate it with history, Tasso advises the heroic poet to eschew "gli argomenti finti," but concedes him the license to feign and invent and to mix truth and fiction in constructing his fable, since his object is the universal idea rather than the concrete particulars of history.[9] Horace had similarly praised Homer for skilfully blending false with true, and so employing fiction that "beginning, middle, and end all strike the same note. . . ."

Like Tasso, Milton's nephew Edward Phillips believed that the heroic poet ought to choose as his subject "a brief, obscure, or remote tradition, but of some remarkable piece of story," that could provide scope for amplification through "feigning of probable circumstances." In this and "in proper allegory," invention "principally

Invention and Disposition

consisteth"; and the "well management" of invention is "no other than decorum...."[10] Mazzoni similarly allowed the poet to mingle his own inventions with the facts of history, while Castelvetro argued that the poet's subject ought to be entirely his own invention.

The ambiguities of the terms "invention" and "disposition" in Renaissance criticism and the tendency to blur the distinction between them reflect the difficulty that critics experienced in correlating and reconciling the terminology of logic and rhetoric and in imposing this terminology on literature and the visual arts. One critic might reserve the term invention for a fictional subject devised by the poet. Another might apply it indiscriminately to a feigned or to a historical argument. A third might deny this title to a historical subject but apply it to the fictional details, incidents, and characters invented by the poet in amplifying an argument derived from history and structuring his plot; in this case, invention might overlap with disposition. In some instances such variations in terminology may reflect older traditions concerning the nature of poetry—the medieval conception of the poet as a maker of fictions and fables, the classification of epic and romance as "historical" poetry.

In the late Renaissance the meaning of these terms is further conditioned by Aristotle's comparison of the tragic plot—"the first essential, the life and soul . . . of Tragedy"—to the "simple black-and-white sketch of a portrait."[11] If invention includes the idea or design in the painter's mind (as it did for Alberti and Dolce and other theorists), then it might conceivably embrace the ideal form of the poem in the poet's mind. Tasso's emphasis on adaptability to epic or tragic form as a criterion in selecting a subject for heroic or tragic poetry is based primarily on Aristotle's discussion of the tragic plot and of the "kinds of incident" that arouse terror or pity. The "finest tragedies," Aristotle had insisted, "are always on the story of some few houses . . . that may have been involved, as either agents or sufferers, in some deed of horror," and for a well-constructed plot poets are "still obliged to have recourse to the families in which such horrors have occurred." Though the "traditional stories . . . must be kept as they are," there is nevertheless "something left to the poet himself; it is for him to devise the right way of treating them."[12] Tasso and Phillips similarly allow the poet to feign or invent details and episodes for the sake of amplification, probability and verisimilitude, or for emphasizing the universal.

Conceits are "inventions" in a different sense, and they normally bear a rather different relationship to disposition or design. As figures of thought they are usually ornaments of style—the external ornament that the poet applies after inventing his subject and arranging it. A conceit is not, as a rule, the argument of a longer poem, nor does it usually provide a basis for the structure of the fable.[13] In epic, tragedy, and comedy, its function is essentially ornamental, and it belongs usually to elocution rather than to invention or disposition. Nevertheless, in shorter poems such as the epigram, the sonnet, or the madrigal, a conceited invention or device may constitute the actual argument, and the structure may hinge on the elaboration and development of this conceit. Allegories, as Gascoigne and Phillips recognized, are also "inventions"; in an allegorical drama (such as the masque) or the "dark conceit" of an epic or romance, the poet's device (or "extended metaphor") may constitute the principal argument and the foundation of a "metaphoric structure." In the majority of epics and dramas, however, the conceit is extrinsic to both argument and structure. It is subsequent—not prior—to the processes of invention and disposition of theme or subject matter.

Renaissance theorists sometimes differ in the degree of emphasis they accord to invention and disposition. Where Boccaccio defines the poet's function chiefly in terms of allegorical invention, Aristotle and his Renaissance commentators not only define poetry in terms of imitation, but especially stress the disposition of the plot. In their discussions of poetic fictions, Renaissance critics alternatively emphasized the fictive subject or the introduction of fictive details in elaborating a subject based not on fiction but on historical truth. For some commentators, the poet's office consisted primarily in inventing a fable; for others, it consisted principally in the disposition or construction of his fable. The former stressed the fictional or nonfictional character of the argument; the latter the poet's artistry in plot-construction.

2.

By stressing the importance of probability in the representation

Invention and Disposition

of an action, Renaissance critical theory tended to link the theory of art and poetry with that of rhetoric. For Plato, rhetoric and probability had belonged primarily to the realm of opinion. For Aristotle, rhetoric had been the counterpart of dialectic; it discerned "the real and the apparent means of persuasion" just as dialectic discerns "the real and the apparent syllogism."[14] Its propositions were "Complete Proofs, Probabilities, and Signs."[15] In contrast to logical demonstration, which reasons from "true and primary" premises, dialectic "reasons from opinions that are generally accepted."[16]

Aristotle's emphasis on probability or necessity in the poetic fable and on "convincing" or persuading the audience had brought the art of poetry—and especially the art of plot-construction—close to the frontiers of other organic arts: logic, dialectic, and rhetoric. The poet's function was not to describe the "thing that has happened," but to describe "a kind of thing that might happen, i.e. what is possible as being probable or necessary." This emphasis on the probable or necessary underlies Aristotle's doctrines concerning the universal element in poetry, on the use of historic names in tragedy, and on plot structure and unity of action. By a universal statement Aristotle means "one as to what such or such a kind of man will probably or necessarily say or do—which is the aim of poetry...." A "likely impossibility" is preferable to an "unconvincing possibility."[17] Tragedy adheres to the historic names because "what convinces is the possible...." The tragic hero passes "by a series of probable or necessary stages from misfortune to happiness," or vice versa. Aristotle censures the episodic plot, which observes "neither probability nor necessity in the sequence of its episodes," and he praises Homer for observing unity of action in the *Odyssey* instead of depicting the hero's entire life and including incidents that "had no probable or necessary connexion with one another...." In a tragic *peripeteia* the "change from one state of things within the play to its opposite" occurs "in the probable or necessary sequence of events...." In the characters, as in the incidents of the play, the poet must "endeavour always after the necessary or the probable; so that whenever such-and-such a personage says or does such-and-such a thing, it shall be the probable or necessary outcome of his character; and whenever this incident follows on that, it shall be either the necessary or probable consequence of it." There "should be nothing improbable among the actual incidents."[18]

Like the rhetorician and the dialectician, the poet was concerned with the probable.[19] In depicting the "element of Thought" *(Dianoia)* the poet must make a more direct use of rhetoric. In "the speeches of Tragedy" *Dianoia* "falls under the arts of Politics and Rhetoric; for the older poets make their personages discourse like statesmen, and the moderns like rhetoricians."[20]

Since Aristotle compares the plot of tragedy to design in painting (the "simple black-and-white sketch of a portrait"), his remarks on probability and unity in the construction of the poetic fable could be (and sometimes were) transferred to pictorial art. In attacking their opponents or predecessors for faulty design, seicento critics frequently based their arguments on Horatian or Aristotelian doctrines.

Poet and painter alike, moreover, faced the additional problem of reconciling the probable with the marvelous. Aristotle had emphasized both of these apparently conflicting qualities. In his opinion, incidents arousing pity and fear produce "the very greatest effect on the mind when they occur unexpectedly and at the same time in consequence of one another; there is more of the marvelous in them then than if they happened of themselves or by mere chance." Moreover, even "matters of chance seem most marvelous if there is an appearance of design . . . in them." A plot "of this sort is necessarily finer than others." The "chief factor in the marvelous," however, is the improbable. Though the marvelous is "certainly required in Tragedy," the epic "affords more opening for the improbable . . . because in it the agents are not visibly before one." The marvelous is a "cause of pleasure," and impossibilities are justifiable if "they make the effect of some portion of the work more astounding."[21]

Aristotle's views on the well-constructed plot, the nature of beauty, and the relationship of parts to the whole could be adapted to the criticism of pictorial composition. If plot is "the first essential, the life and soul" of tragedy, then design—the closest "parallel in painting"—would be the life and soul of a picture. If the plot consisted in a "combination of incidents,"[22] the painter's *disegno* was composed of a combination of planes and members and bodies. A

Invention and Disposition

well-constructed painting, like a "well-constructed Plot," must be "a beautiful whole made up of parts," exhibiting "a certain order in its arrangement of parts" and possessing "a certain definite magnitude." If the poet's "story, as an imitation of action, must represent one action, a complete whole, with its several incidents so closely connected that the transposal or withdrawal of any one of them will disjoin and dislocate the whole,"[23] the same principle of economy and complete integration of parts in a unified whole could apply to the painter's design and *istoria*.

3.

Seicento art and literature were not created in a cultural vacuum —in complete detachment from each other or from the social and intellectual tensions of the century. Nor, on the other hand, do they form a cultural continuum. They belong to different compartments, separate and discrete disciplines; but these compartments are not hermetically sealed. Though the art theorists of the period were usually conscious of the principles of invention, composition, and style that they held in common with poets and rhetoricians, in addition to a common stock of topics and universals, they were also aware of the different techniques imposed upon them by different media and the principles and methods peculiar to each art.

Since seventeenth-century poetry and painting were not composed in strict isolation, they cannot be effectively studied in isolation; like the critics of the period, the modern literary historian can learn much from the parallels between the sister arts. At the same time he must avoid overstressing the analogies between them, the tendency to interpret literary techniques in terms of technical solutions to purely pictorial problems, and vice versa, or to look for the same historical pattern in the development of visual and verbal arts or in the contemporary evolution of science and society. Positing a parallel and virtually synchronous development in the art and thought of an age is a mode of "aesthetic occasionalism" common to students of *Geistesgeschichte* and period styles. The literary historian cannot arbitrarily assume that the literature and art of a period are correlative modes for expressing the same sensibility or spirit of the age, and he must guard against allowing his stereotypes of

The Lamb and the Elephant

seventeenth-century art or society to prejudice his interpretation of literature. To overstress the interrelationship between the visual and verbal arts can be as misleading as to ignore it altogether.

In interpreting the literature of the seventeenth century, the literary critic is frequently prejudiced by his conception of its art; and his views of the latter, in turn, have often been shaped by his opinions of the intellectual and spiritual crises of the period. Having interpreted baroque art as a visible statement of the century's political and psychological conflicts, he finds a comparable expression of the same tensions in contemporary literature.

The technical problems that the late Renaissance painter faced in organizing a composition in space are not identical with those that confronted the poet in achieving formal organization in time. Some of the principal features of mannerist and baroque styles are a conscious response to problems peculiar to the visual arts. In such instances the search for parallels in contemporary literary style is apt to distort both of the sister arts. The crowded foregrounds of certain mannerist pictures and the baroque preference for a freer and looser organization of massed bodies in space are, in large part, alternative solutions to compositional problems inherited from the artists of the High Renaissance.

In attempting to achieve the illusion of three-dimensional space on a two-dimensional surface, earlier artists had frequently relied on optical perspective as the basis for spatial organization and on modeling in *relievo* to suggest the plastic volumes of the human form. In arranging their planes and grouping their figures, however, they did not always succeed in linking foreground and background. As Wölfflin observes, "the sixteenth century is more planimetric than the fifteenth." We see "art, as soon as it has mastered perspective and spatial depth, consciously and consistently acknowledging the plane as the true form of beholding." "Yet the classic plane style had its limited period. . . . There comes a moment when the plane relation slackens and the receding sequence of the picture begins to speak, where the contents of the picture can no longer be grasped in plane sections, but the nerve lies in the relation of the foreground to the background parts." "If primitive style is unconsciously a plane style and classic consciously so, we can call the art of baroque consciously a-planimetric. It repudiates the obligation to the compelling frontality of the work, because only in this freedom did the semblance of living movement seem to it accessible." Baroque painters frequently "intensify the recessional movement by an 'exaggerated' foreground"—a technique that Leonardo had deliberately avoided because it impaired clarity, regarding it "inadmissible to alienate things in the perspective representation which are in reality closely related."[24]

Though Wölfflin's description of the evolution of cinquecento and seicento style tends to bypass the mannerist phases analyzed by Friedlaender, both historians emphasize the technical problems in the representation of bodies in space and their influence on stylistic development. Though this was by no means the only contributing or determinative factor, it was a consideration of crucial importance, and it provides a more reliable method of approach (as Wölfflin sensibly observed) than vague appeals to expressional content or to the doctrine of the "imitation of nature."

The earlier Renaissance quest for naturalness in the representation of bodies in space (and, on the part of certain artists, for mathematical accuracy and certitude in representation), had succeeded in rendering three-dimensional space plausibly and (in Blunt's opinion) "rationally," but in solving these problems it had raised others. Having learned how to represent three-dimensional space, the artist now faced the problem of organizing it in a unified and "natural" composition. The carefully contrived perspectives of High Renaissance art had achieved unity of viewpoint, but the result in many cases was not merely to dissociate foreground from background and to break up recessive depths into a series of horizontal planes, but also to produce the effect of a deliberately contrived composition, the impression of a carefully arranged stage setting or the ordered perspective of a peep show. Certain so-called mannerist painters apparently met these difficulties by deemphasizing the background and stressing the foreground instead, elaborating Michelangelo's precedent and utilizing the plastic volumes of the human figures themselves and their interrelationships as the principal elements in the composition or deliberately bypassing the spatial achievements of the High Renaissance and returning to northern or primitive methods of composition. If their treatment of space seems "unreal" or "irrational" to us, it is partly because these artists intentionally disregarded the mathematical composition of space as inessential to their design and preferred instead to organize their design like sculptors in terms of the "volumetric stances" of the figures themselves. They solved the problem of organization largely by compressing space into the foreground plane and by sacrificing "naturalness" (as their critics objected) to their principles of formal arrangement.

On the other hand, the baroque artists (who, in Friedlaender's opinion, were consciously reacting against the distortions, the slapdash techniques, the dense and overcrowded compositions, and the apparent unnaturalness of the later mannerists) met the problem of unified spatial organization in a different way, linking foreground and background by emphasizing recessional movement and disposing the masses of figures in an apparently looser and freer arrangement in space (i.e. through "open form").

Though we should not exaggerate the influence of theory on actual practice, it seems unlikely that seicento painters could have been entirely indifferent to the principle of unity of action and of plot or design. This principle had significantly reformed the Renaissance dramatic and epic tradition; and, though painters may have felt greater freedom than poets to disregard it, it had significantly influenced Renaissance artistic as well as literary criticism. The concern of many baroque painters for unified composition[25] is consistent with one of the principal doctrines of contemporary poetics and art theory.[26]

4.

Since composers in any art form must consider problems of arrangement, proportion, and emphasis in organizing the parts of a work into a unified whole and a coherent design, the tension between "multiplicity and unity" (or "multiple unity and unitive unity") that Wölfflin finds in sixteenth- and seventeenth-century art is sometimes apparent also in the verbal arts. In most instances, however, the parallels are not close, and here again the fashionable analogies with classic, mannerist, and baroque styles may be forced and misleading. In the composition of sentences it is actually the periodic model (so closely associated with Ciceronian influence), rather than the loose sentence or the "exploded period" of "anti-Ciceronian" prose, that achieves unity most successfully.[27] Like the dramatic plot, Cicero's "reflex" or periodic style possesses "independently in itself a beginning and ending, and a length easily taken in at a glance." It "easily conveys information" and it is "*pleasing* from its being the opposite of that which is indefinite. . . ." In contrast, the older "continuous" style "has no termination" and "is unpleasant, from its being indefinite; for all like to descry the end."[28] In this case, Croll's attempt to force art-historical categories upon literary history leads to contradiction; though the contrast between the definiteness and indefiniteness of loose and periodic structure may correspond in part to Wölfflin's antitheses between closed and open form (and perhaps clearness and unclearness as well), it actually contradicts his schema of multiplicity and unity.

In dramatic and epic theory, the problem of multiplicity and unity centered largely on the question of multiple actions versus unity of action. Critics defended the multiple plots of contemporary drama and romance on the grounds that variety is a source of beauty and delight, or attacked them for violating a fundamental law of poetics, the example of the ancients, and the rules of Aristotle. A number of poets—Tasso, Spenser, Guarini, and others—endeavored to preserve variety either by closely linking subplots with the central action or by introducing a variety of minor episodes within a single plot structure.

In the sonnet form, various poets—Della Casa, Tasso, Milton—attempted to achieve a more integrated composition by deliberately deemphasizing the divisions between octave and sestet, and between the two quatrains of the octave, through enjambment. Similarly, by emphasizing run-on lines and extending patterns of sense and syntax beyond the formal limits of the line, writers of blank verse avoided the regular stanzaic divisions of rhymed verse; this technique gave them greater freedom and flexibility in constructing periods and verse-paragraphs, facilitating variety in unity. By thus blurring or disguising formal and quantitative divisions the poet could impart

The Lamb and the Elephant

greater energy and continuity to the movement and development of his thought as well as a higher degree of unity. In the miniature drama of a sonnet, as in the more extended plot of epic or tragedy or the designs of frescoes and domes, "the detail of the pattern is movement."[29]

5.

"For the Renaissance," Wölfflin declared, "beauty and absolute visibility coincide. . . . Everything is completely revealed, and is meant to be assimilated at the first glance." The baroque, on the other hand, took into account "the mysterious obscuring of the form, veiled distinctness."[30] In the development from High Renaissance to baroque painting and architecture he finds a progression from absolute to relative clearness parallel to other changes in the "schema" of representation.

Literature possesses its own forms of chiaroscuro. As qualities of style, clarity and obscurity are traditional concerns of the orator, and few poets or artists of the Renaissance could have been altogether ignorant of the long history of these concepts in rhetorical and poetic theory. "The perfection of Diction [*lexis*]," according to Aristotle's *Poetics*, "is for it to be at once clear and not mean." Since the clearest diction (which employs "the ordinary words for things") is mean, the poet must lend distinction to his speech through "unfamiliar terms," such as "strange words, metaphors, lengthened forms, and everything that deviates from the ordinary modes of speech." These "will save the language from seeming mean and prosaic, while the ordinary words in it will secure the requisite clearness." The most effective means of rendering the diction both clear and non-prosaic is "the use of the lengthened, curtailed, and altered forms of words. Their deviation from the ordinary words will, by making the language unlike that in general use, give it a non-prosaic appearance; and their having much in common with the words in general use will give it the quality of clearness."[31]

Aristotle develops these points in greater detail in his *Rhetoric*. Excellence of style consists "in its being clear . . . and neither low, nor above the dignity of the subject, but in good taste; for the style

Invention and Disposition

of poetry ... is not low, yet it is not becoming in prose." Since a departure from ordinary usage imparts dignity to style, the orator should give his "phrase a foreign air; for men are admirers of things out of the way, and what is an object of admiration is pleasant." In accordance with the "rule of good taste" he should raise or lower his style according to the subject, yet manage to "escape observation in doing this, and not appear to speak in a studied manner, but naturally...." Whereas an apparently natural manner tends to persuade, the appearance of artifice tends to dissuade, for "people put themselves on their guard as though against one who has a design upon them, just as they would against adulterated wine." Combining clarity with a "foreign character," the orator's art should "elude observation."[32] Since this conjunction of clarity and strangeness can be found in a good metaphor, the use of appropriate metaphors, preferably based on analogy, is one of the principal sources of elegance in style.

While acknowledging the merit of clarity, later writers on rhetoric and poetics also recognized the advantages of obscurity. Metaphors might lend obscurity as well as clarity to style; and, as extended metaphor, allegory might serve as an instrument for either veiling or visualizing universal ideas. An easy mystery, slightly hidden in an easily penetrable darkness, made possible the pleasure of discovery and offered a dual and paradoxical delight—the attractions of the indeterminate and the determinate, the vague and the distinct, the far and the near, the veiled and the revealed. The spectators who enjoyed the combination of obscurity and clarity and of hidden and revealed form in baroque art—and the readers who applauded the obscurities of Góngora—had already learned the pleasures of obscurity from Renaissance allegories, hieroglyphics, and *imprese* (devices). The tension in metaphysical poetry between metaphor and meaning, between the image and the concept it signified, was roughly analogous to the tension between literal and allegorical senses in medieval and Renaissance poetry, but it could also be (and has been) compared to the mingling of light and dark, clarity and obscurity, in painting. Though one should not push this analogy very far, it is not improbable that a taste for verbal ambiguities and for the intellectual interplay of literal and symbolic senses in mythical and scriptural interpretation should also find delight in the visible interplay of light and shadow in pictorial art.[33]

As both poets and artists made diverse uses of obscurity, it cannot be reduced to a simple symbolic formula, nor can it be regarded as an expression of any single aspect of the sensibility of the age. In satire, obscurity was traditional—partly for the poet's well-being and his safety from libel suits or personal assaults, partly in order to enhance the element of asperity and roughness, and partly in order to extend the range and efficacy of the writer's attack by leaving its objects indefinite. In heroic poetry and tragedy, obscurity was regarded as a means of lending additional force and gravity to style and increasing its ability to arouse terror or admiration. In differing contexts, it could suggest earthly ignorance or the depths of divine knowledge, the limits of human reason or the mysteries of divine truth. Though certain artists could invest chiaroscuro with symbolic sense, as an emblem of spiritual light and darkness, many were concerned less with the figurative senses of clarity and obscurity, than with the opportunities they afforded for subtle gradations or violent contrasts in shading. Like other contraries, light and shadow appeared more clearly through their opposition; they served to accent certain elements in a painting and subordinate others, combining the pleasures of distinct cognition and dim surmise. Establishing an agreeable tension between the partially revealed and the hidden, they provided a means for heightening emphasis, dramatic suspense, and rhythm.

6.

In Croll's opinion, the "whole theory of *concettismo* is derived from Aristotle's *Rhetoric*," especially the section on enthymenes and metaphors.[34] This is an oversimplification, certainly—and most students of the seventeenth century would probably regard it as such—but it nevertheless contains a substantial measure of truth. Tesauro openly acknowledges his debt to Aristotle, quoting extensively from the *Rhetoric* and the *Poetics;* and other seicento writers on *concetti* must have been thoroughly familiar with both works. Recent scholarship has stressed the importance of the *Rhetoric* in

Invention and Disposition

Jesuit courses of instruction. Most of Aristotle's doctrines had become commonplaces of rhetorical theory, however, and it is sometimes difficult to distinguish between the direct and indirect impact of his influential treatise. Moreover, there are dissimilarities as well as similarities between his views on style and those of the *concettisti*.[35]

Like Gracián and other seventeenth-century writers, Aristotle emphasizes the role of natural genius in the invention of metaphors; but Longinus and Horace had also acknowledged the importance of natural talent as well as art in rhetorical or poetic compositions. Both Gracián and Aristotle stress the perception of similarity or correspondence between dissimilar things as the basis of the conceit (Gracián) or the metaphor (Aristotle). Like many of *concettisti*, Aristotle regards metaphor (and its variants: the enigma, the paradox, the pun, the proverb, and the hyperbole) as a source of *energeia* in style. He, too, recognizes the delight that results from deception, from the sudden reversal of expectation, and from admiration and surprise.[36]

On the other hand, the chief virtue of style, in his opinion, is clarity. He condemns far-fetched metaphors and warns that the abuse of metaphor may lead to frigidity in style. He emphasizes the "clearness and sweetness" of metaphor as well as its strange or "foreign" air. In prose he prefers the periodic or "reflex" sentence to the loose or "continuous" model.

Some of the *concettisti* or metaphysicals combine familiar diction with an extensive resort to metaphorical analogies, and it is possible that this use of ordinary words (except for scholastic idioms and other terms of art) in conjunction with metaphorical conceits may have been conditioned by Aristotle's dual emphasis on clear diction and strange or "foreign" metaphors. On the whole, however, *concettismo* would appear to be an extension of (or indeed an aberration from) Aristotle's principles of style rather than a close application or adaptation.

7.

Later critics have sometimes exaggerated the tensions between naturalistic and ideal imitation in the Renaissance. For critics of the period, there was usually no essential conflict, and when they did emphasize this distinction it was often in a polemical context. In the poetic or pictorial treatises of the Renaissance these concepts are often closely associated. Far from being mutually exclusive, they were complementary. The question was not as a rule disjunctive—whether universal ideas *or* natural objects were to be imitated. Poets and artists were fully aware that abstract ideas were invisible and could only be apprehended by abstraction from the senses, and that spiritual substances could be conceived or visualized only through similitudes and enigmas ("through a glass darkly"). Things above nature must be represented through the forms of nature, invisible substances through visible accidents, and intellectual abstractions through the medium of the senses. The ideal forms of natural species, the essential form of Beauty, the ideas of moral and theological virtues could be fully and most clearly known only in and through the intellect. The difference between "ideal" and "realistic" imitation was largely a difference between an intellectual and a sensuous art.

The poet or painter might, of course, ignore ideal content altogether—as many did—or impose a moral or religious *significatio* arbitrarily, to lend weight and gravity to his work or to defend it against accusations of bawdry or manslaughter or triviality. If he did, however, take the principle of ideal imitation seriously and attempt to mingle *utile* with *dulce*, there was no real conflict between the imperatives to imitate universals and to portray the particular forms of nature. As exemplum or as allegory, the natural form served as image or as symbol of the abstract universal. There was no dissociation between natural and ideal representation, for he was in fact representing both. Insofar as the end of his imitation was persuasion and instruction as well as delight, he must make his icon not only pleasing or forceful, but also plausible, portraying the forms of nature and human actions with probability and verisimilitude. In short, he must construct a convincing image of nature, and to do so he must know how nature (or the creator of nature) operates.

It is not surprising that the author of the *Historia Animalium* should compare a well-constructed plot to a living organism, "as a beautiful whole made up of parts, or a beautiful living creature...."[37] Nor is it remarkable that an architect (whose constructions must,

Invention and Disposition

after all, obey mathematical principles if they are to stand) should regard architecture as an imitation of nature and advise the builder to follow the laws and methods of nature. Ancient architects (Alberti declared) accepted nature as their model, "collected the laws, according to which she works in her productions as far as was humanly possible, and introduced them into their method of building." Treatises on painting similarly emphasized the certitude of mathematics. Through the study of perspective, quattrocento painters managed, as Blunt observes, to go "beyond the naïve and tentative imitation of the natural world and . . .to reconstruct it with the sureness which comes from reliance on absolute rules."[38] In much the same way, the study of anatomy could assist the artist in imitating and reconstructing the world in miniature, the human microcosm. For greater accuracy in portraying an actual scene or individual, he could take measurements, or employ such technical aids as Alberti's veil or the plaster casts described by Cennini, or for a more normal or idealized reconstruction he could study the disposition and proportions of antique sculpture or a scheme of mathematical ratios, like Dürer's formulas for proportion. Treatises on ethics or on rhetoric and poetics provided systematic discussion of varieties of character and passion, and later treatises on art contained detailed instructions for depicting them by means of facial expressions, gestures, and stance. For the attributes of mythological figures he could consult iconographical manuals and mythographies.

Like the learned poet or orator, the *pictor doctus* could, if he chose to do so, rely on a formidable battery of scientific and artistic aids in reconstructing natural forms to render his *istoria* probable and therefore persuasive. In seeking verisimilitude, or likeness to nature, he attempted to apply the principles of nature, to reconstruct natural forms in the light of the laws whereby nature herself had constructed them. Nature delighted in harmony, proportion, and symmetry,[39] and he emphasized these qualities in that second nature —art. Space was mathematically organized and natural bodies possessed weight and measure; in his own works he tended to stress primary rather than secondary qualities, and hence rendered the mass and forms of bodies more convincingly than their appearance. In theory he conceived harmony primarily as a ratio of parts, and composition as an arrangement of figures and members; in practice he sometimes sacrificed the impression of unity to clear articulation of parts. Many of the characteristic features of Wölfflin's "classic" art—an art of "being" rather than "appearance"—are consistent with this conception of art as a composition of parts, and with the endeavor to achieve verisimilitude less through superficial appearance than through fidelity to the natural laws, mathematical or scientific, underlying the construction of natural forms. Insofar as it was mathematically constructed, this was essentially an "abstract" art, and it would probably have won Plato's qualified approval. The art that replaced it, seeking verisimilitude through greater emphasis on surface appearance, shifting tones of light and shadow, patches of color, and other secondary qualities, would doubtless have reminded him of that illusionist art which he associated with sophistic.

A Renaissance poem or painting is not an intuitive projection of either the individual or collective unconscious, the spontaneous expression of the sensibility of an age or a sense of reality—the manifestation of a *Weltanschauung* or a *Zeitgeist* or the instinctive reflection of a mode of perception or conception.[40] It is, on the contrary, a premeditated construction, a consciously composed artifact. Once achieved, however, it may condition all of these.[41] *Raumgefühl*, the feeling for space, is apparently the product, not the cause, of the painter's mastery of perspective. The qualities of repose or restlessness, harmony or violence, proportion or distortion that we perceive in quattrocento or seicento pictures are not so much reflections of the artist's temperament or the sensibility of his age as they are projections of our own emotional responses—"affects" which the painter may (or may not) have consciously intended to arouse. We should not mistake the artist's schemas in representing reality for automatic reflections of his sense of reality. At the same time, we should recognize the possibility that his modes of representation could and sometimes did provide a suggestive schema for apprehending and interpreting both *visibilia* and *invisibilia*, natural and supernatural realities.

For the majority of Renaissance poets, the most important preliminary considerations in their art of representation and expression were invention and disposition: the choice of subject matter and its formal arrangement. The poem was less a copy of nature than a

Invention and Disposition

reconstruction of nature, less a reflection of reality than a reorganization of reality—a conscious imposition of form on matter, the achievement of an artificial (rather than a strictly organic) unity through the systematic integration of parts (and parts of parts) into a harmonious whole.

The principal schema of representation (and conception)—to borrow Wölfflin's phrase—was in fact the design itself. This was not an unpremeditated response—an instinctive reflection of the poet's personal vision and his natural or habitual way of perceiving and conceiving reality. It was, on the contrary, an artificial construction designed to condition the percepts and concepts of his spectators. Renaissance art might indeed be a "vision of reality," to borrow Yeats's phrase, but it was normally a constructed rather than a spontaneous vision. However much the poet might attempt to disguise his art in the interest of illusion, it remained nonetheless an artificial vision of forms and ideas abstracted from nature, achieved through study and laborious exercise and perpetuated in and through an artifact. It was a painstakingly fabricated image rather than an intuited Gestalt, a rational construction rather than a spontaneous psychological projection. Moreover, like the image in a mosaic, it was designed for contemplation at a distance, from the viewpoint of the audience rather than from the artists' scaffolding. The Renaissance icon, in poetry and perhaps in painting also, was the product not so much of a mode of perception as of a method of composition. It was less an expression of subjective sensibility than an imitation of objective reality—a representation of universal essences in and through sensuous forms.

The Lamb and the Elephant

Notes

[1] In stressing the painter's creativity and freedom of invention as an argument for the nobility of his art, Cennini was employing arguments that Boccaccio had marshaled in support of the poet. After defining poetry itself as an art of invention and expression—"a sort of fervid and exquisite invention, with fervid expression, in speech or writing, of that which the mind has invented" *(fervor quidam exquisite inveniendi, atque dicendi, seu scribendi quod inveneris)*—Boccaccio argues its *honestas* or nobility by describing its divine origin and its sublime effects. In this passage he follows the conventional rhetorical division—*inventio, dispositio, elocutio*—but significantly stresses its significance for the allegorical character of poetry: "This fervor of poesy . . . impels the soul to a longing for utterance; it brings forth strange and unheard-of creations of the mind; it arranges these meditations in a fixed order, adorns the whole composition with unusual interweaving of words and thoughts; and thus it veils truth in a fair and fitting garment of fiction" (Charles G. Osgood, *Boccaccio on Poetry* [Indianapolis and New York, 1956], xxv, 39). Poets "compose their inventions" under divine help and guidance (p. 41). Instead of making "their inventions void and empty, trusting in the superficial appearance of their tales to show their eloquence," they have concealed their philosophical or theological "meaning or intention . . . beneath the superficial veil of myth. . ." (pp. 52-53). It is not "one of the poet's various functions to rip up and lay bare the meaning which lies hidden in his inventions," but to conceal it from "the gaze of the irreverent. . ." (p. 59). Since they possess the license to "sacrifice the literal truth in invention. . . ," poets should not be regarded as liars "who lean with their whole weight upon mere inventions" (pp. 64-65). Poets "never veil with their inventions anything which is not wholly consonant with philosophy as judged by the opinions of the Ancients. . . . The poet conceives his thought by contemplation, and, wholly without the help of syllogism, veils it as subtly and skilfully as he can under the outward semblance of his fiction" (p. 79). Dionysius the Areopagite (i.e. pseudo-Dionysius) proves that "divine theology employs, with its other instruments, poetic inventions" (p. 86). Natural theology is "found in great poets since they clothe many a physical and moral truth in their inventions. . ." (p. 122).

For Boccaccio, poetic invention is virtually identical with the poet's fiction or *fabula* and with the allegorical method. He defines fiction itself as "a form of discourse, which, under the guise of invention, illustrates or proves an idea; and, as its superficial aspect is removed, the meaning of the author is clear" (p. 48), and he draws a sharp distinction between the inventions of rhetoric and those of poetry. Though "rhetoric has also its own inventions," nevertheless "among the disguises of fiction rhetoric has no part, for whatever is composed as under a veil, and thus exquisitely wrought, is poetry and poetry alone" (p. 42). Moreover, "oratory is quite different, in arrangement of words, from fiction"; the latter has "been consigned to the discretion of the inventor as being the legitimate work of another art than oratory" (p. 61). Though the obscurity of poetry may seem to violate the "old rule of the orators, that a speech must be simple and clear," such obscurity belongs to the method of poetry, which employs the veil of fiction in order to "make truths which would otherwise cheapen by exposure the object of strong intellectual effort and various interpretation, that in ultimate discovery they shall be more precious." Saint Augustine had commended the "obscurity of the divine word" since it stimulated diverse "opinions about the truth, each reader seeing some fresh meaning in it." Men may "go away the richer, because they have found that closed which might be opened in many ways, than if they could open and discover it by one interpretation." The

Invention and Disposition

obscurity of Scripture serves to "exercise him that shall afterward receive it." For Boccaccio, who specifically applies Augustine's "attitude toward the obscurities of Holy Writ" to "the obscurities of poetry," the poet's invention is essentially the veil of allegorical fiction, exquisitely wrought and designed to conceal and adorn a philosophical or theological truth (pp. 60-61).

In Gascoigne's opinion the "first and most necessarie poynt" in making a "delectable poeme" is "to grounde it upon some fine invention," containing *aliquid salis*, "some good and fine devise, shewing the quicke capacitie of a writer." He advises the poet to "studie for some depth of devise in the Invention, and some figures also in the handlyng thereof," avoiding the trite and obvious. In praising a lady, he would eschew hackneyed figures such as "hir christal eye" and "cherrie lippe" and "finde some supernaturall cause" for extolling her "in the superlative degree" or else "undertake to aunswere for any imperfection that she hath. . . ." Similarly, in disclosing his "pretence in love," he would either "make a strange discourse" of an intolerable passion, or "pleade by the example of some historie," or resort to allegory or the "covertest meane that I could. . ." (O. B. Hardison, Jr., ed., *English Literary Criticism: The Renaissance* [New York, 1963], pp. 75-76).

Puttenham associates the "inventive parte of the mynde" with the imagination or fantasy, and Sidney praises the vigor of the poet's invention, which lifts him above the restrictions of nature and enables him to create "things either better then Nature bringeth forth, or, quite a newe, formes such as never were in Nature. . . ." For the same author, the fictive narrative of poetry serves as "an imaginative groundplot of a profitable invention" (Hardison, pp. 156-57, 104, 128).

Emphasizing the poet's freedom of invention, Sidney draws a sharp distinction between true or "right Poets" and didactic poets who deliver "sweetly uttered knowledge" of moral or natural philosophy, history or astronomy. Since the latter do not follow their own invention, it is debatable "whether they properly be Poets or no," and they resemble "the meaner sort of Painters" who "counterfet onely such faces as are sette before them. . . ." True poets, on the other hand, are like the more excellent painters, "who, having no law but wit, bestow that in collours upon you which is fittest for the eye to see," like the artist who depicts "the constant though lamenting looke of *Lucrecia*. . . ; wherein he painteth not *Lucrecia* whom he never sawe, but painteth the outwarde beauty of such a vertue." For Sidney, the "skil of the Artificer standeth in that *Idea* or fore-conceite of the work, and not in the work it selfe. And that the Poet hath that *Idea* is manifest, by delivering them [i.e. Xenophon's Cyrus and Virgil's Aeneas, et al.] forth in such excellencie as he hath imagined them" (Hardison, pp. 106, 105).

Castelvetro, on the other hand, had argued that "poetry is the similitude and likeness of history," that "the matter of poetry should be like the matter of history and resemble it, but . . . ought not to be the same," and that the poet should relate a story "imagined by himself about things that have not happened," making it "not less delightful nor less like the truth" than actual history. The world jeers at "such thefts as these of the inventions of others," for the "essence of a poet consists in his invention. . . ." Though many poets "have borrowed from histories or other poets part or all of their poems," they should be blamed and despised rather than acclaimed (Allan H. Gilbert, ed., *Literary Criticism: Plato to Dryden* [Detroit, 1962], pp. 305-06, 324). In discussing the "incredible possible," Mazzoni argues that the poet may borrow from history but "add many things from his own invention." When "the history is not known in detail," he is free to "enlarge and particularize the history by introducing his own inventions without fear of transgressing the credible," and this kind of story is "better and more perfect than all the others." Alternatively, he may transmute and falsify "history that is true or at least recorded in some writer. . ." (p. 390).

For Dryden (preface to *Annus Mirabilis*), invention is closely associated with

The Lamb and the Elephant

wit and the "faculty of imagination." Adapting the conventional rhetorical classification (invention, disposition, elocution) and the distinction between invention and judgment to "the proper wit of an heroic or historical poem" (which consists in "the delightful imaging of persons, actions, passions, or things" rather than in "the jerk of sting of an epigram," the "seeming contradiction of a poor antithesis," or the "jingle of a more poor paronomasia"), he distinguishes the "first happiness of the poet's imagination" as "invention, or the finding of the thought"; the second as "fancy, or the variation, driving, or moulding of that thought, as the judgment represents it proper to the subject"; and the third as "elocution, or the art of clothing and adorning that thought so found and varied, in apt, significant, and sounding words. . . ." The "quickness of the imagination is seen in the invention, the fertility in the fancy, and the accuracy in the expression." See John Dryden, *Of Dramatic Poesy and Other Essays*, ed. George Watson, 2 vols., Everyman's Library (London and New York, 1962), I, 98.

In *A Parallel between Painting and Poetry*, Dryden argues that "Invention is the first part, and absolutely necessary" to both arts, even though "no rule ever was or ever can be given how to compass it. A happy genius is the gift of nature," and "without invention, a painter is but a copier, and a poet but the plagiary of others." Under the "head of invention" Dryden (like other theorists) places "the disposition of the work; to put all things in a beautiful order and harmony, that the whole may be of a piece." In their compositions poet and painter alike must conform to "the texts of ancient authors, to the customs and the times," observing the principle of decorum and excluding all that is "not proper or convenient to the subject. . . ." Though Du Fresnoy makes "*design*, or *drawing*, the second part of painting," Dryden finds no parallel here with poetry, since "the rules which he gives concerning the posture of the figures are almost wholly proper to that art, and admit not any comparison, that I know, with poetry" (Watson, II, 194-96). In the "third part of painting, which is called the chromatic, or colouring," he finds a parallel in diction and verbal ornament: "Expression, and all that belongs to words, is that in a poem which colouring is in a picture" (Watson, II, 203). Cf. Murray W. Bundy, "'Invention' and 'Imagination' in the Renaissance," *JEGP*, 29 (1930), 535-45.

Though Horace offers to show where the poet's "materials will be found," and advises the writer to make his "inventions . . . consistent," his primary emphasis falls on disposition, the "force and charm of arrangement." He himself would aim at a poem so "deftly fashioned out of familiar matter" that others would attempt to emulate it in vain; such is "the power of order and arrangement." The "secret of all good writing is sound judgement." Though he recognizes that natural ability and *ingenium* are necessary for the poet as well as art and training, Horace stresses the importance of close examination of classical models ("study the Greek masterpieces") and critical revision and correction ("censure the poem that has not been pruned by time and many a cancellation—corrected ten times over and finished to the fingernail"). He ridicules the notion that the poet can rely on inspiration alone and neglect art, challenging Democritus' belief that "genius is happier than miserable art." He praises verisimilitude as essential for credibility and pleasure ("I shall bid the clever imitator look to life and morals for his real model, and draw thence language true to life"; "fictions made to please should keep close to the truth of things; your play should not demand an unlimited credence") (Gilbert, pp. 129-41).

[2]See Paolo Rossi, *Francis Bacon, From Magic to Science*, trans. Sacha Rabinovitch (Chicago, 1968); Karl R. Wallace, *Francis Bacon on Communication and Rhetoric* (Chapel Hill, N.C., 1943). Bacon's nomenclature for the four "Arts Intellectual" in *The Advancement of Learning* derives from the conventional terminology of the five parts of rhetoric. Since "man's labour is to *invent* that which is *sought* or *pro-*

Invention and Disposition

pounded; or to judge that which is *invented*; or to *retain* that which is *judged*; or to *deliver over* that which is *retained*," the intellectual arts must be four: "Art of Inquiry or Invention; Art of Examination or Judgment; Art of Custody or Memory; and Art of Elocution or Tradition." Distinguishing sharply between invention of arts and sciences and invention of speech and arguments, Bacon maintains that the latter is not truly an invention, but "a *Remembrance* or *Suggestion*, with an application; which is the cause why the schools do place it after judgment, as subsequent and not precedent." Properly "to invent is to discover that we know not, and not to recover or resummon that which we already know. . ."; see Hugh A. Dick, ed., *Selected Writings of Francis Bacon*, Modern Library (New York, 1955), pp. 285-90. Under invention of speech and arguments Bacon includes general and special topics. These "*marks* or *places*" not only "furnish argument to dispute probably with others," but also "minister unto our judgment to conclude aright within ourselves" (p. 292). Judgment concerns "the natures of Proofs and Demonstrations"; the art of Memory is built on prenotion and emblem; and the fourth art deals with the organ, method, and illustration of tradition (pp. 293-300). Williamson observes that in Bacon's inductive method "invention and disposition coincide." Ramus had "treated method under Judgment," and though Bacon transferred it to Elocution, "he continued to think of it as judgement rather than disposition" (George Williamson, *The Senecan Amble: A Study in Prose Form from Bacon to Collier* [Chicago, 1951], pp. 155-56).

³Cf. Leon Battista Alberti, *On Painting*, trans. John R. Spencer, rev. ed. (New Haven and London, 1966), pp. 31, 91. In "beautifully composing the *istoria*," Alberti declares, the "greatest praise consists in the invention. A beautiful invention has such force . . . that even without painting it is pleasing in itself alone. Invention is praised when one reads the description of Calumny which Lucian recounts was painted by Apelles. . . . Therefore I advise that each painter should make himself familiar with poets, rhetoricians and others equally well learned in letters. They will give new inventions or at least aid in beautifully composing the *istoria* through which the painter will surely acquire much praise and renown in his painting." In Alberti's view, ancient architects had "rightly maintained that nature, the greatest of all artists in the invention of forms, was always their model" (Anthony Blunt, *Artistic Theory in Italy, 1450-1600* [London, Oxford, and New York, 1962] p. 19). Leonardo compares the "inventive faculty" of the painter to the creative power of God. The painter surpasses nature "by the invention *(fintione)* of endless forms of animals and herbs, plants and landscapes." By "means of drawing" he must "show to the eye in visible form the idea and invention which exists first in his imagination. . ." (Blunt, pp. 36-37). Lee observes that the term *inventio* "regularly included the choice of subject as well as the general planning of the composition. . ." (Rensselaer W. Lee, *Ut Pictura Poesis: The Humanistic Theory of Painting* [New York, 1967], p. 17).

Alberti defines composition as "that rule in painting by which the parts fit together in the painted work." Subdividing the complete composition or *istoria* into successively smaller units—bodies, members, and planes—he defines circumscription as "a certain rule for designing the outlines of the planes. . ." (Alberti, p. 70). As "bodies are part of the *istoria*, members . . . parts of the bodies," and "planes part of the members," the "primary parts of painting" are the planes; and "that grace in bodies which we call beauty is born from the composition of the planes" (p. 72). The painter's fame consists primarily in the "composition of bodies" (p. 75), and in attempting "to express life in things" he must portray "every part in motion," while preserving grace and "appropriateness" (p. 74).

In Alberti's threefold division of painting *(circonscriptione, compositione, receptione di lumi)* Panofsky recognizes an "indirect adaptation . . . of the rhetoricians' *inventio, dispositio, and elocutio: inventio* being partly included by Alberti under

The Lamb and the Elephant

compositione. . ." (Lee, pp. 70-71). In Lee's opinion, Dolce's classification *(inventione, disegno, colorito)* is a "direct adaption" *(sic)* of the same rhetorical classification. According to Dolce, "L'inventione è la favola, o historia, che'l Pittore si elegge da lui stesso, o gli è posta innanzi da altri per materia di quello che ha operare," while "il disegno è la forma, con che egli la rappresenta." Dolce also observes that invention derives from two sources, history and the painter's own *ingegno*. From history the artist simply derives the matter, but from *ingegno* proceed (in addition to "orderly arrangement and disposition of figures and decorum") the attitudes, variety, and energy of the figures. This is "parte commune col disegno." Thus, in Lee's opinion, Dolce conceives invention as "the choice of the history that he would represent, and the general plan of the picture, according to principles of good disposition and decorum, that he would work out in his mind" (pp. 70-71). Creighton Gilbert, "Antique Frameworks for Renaissance Art Theory: Alberti and Pino," *Marsyas*, 3 (1946) demonstrated that Paolo Pino, not Ludovico Dolce, "first clearly divided the labor of the painter into the three categories of *disegno, inventione*, and *colorire*, which correspond to the three major divisions of the art of rhetoric among the ancients" (Lee, p. viii).

In his instructions to Taddeo Zuccaro for the cycle of paintings at Caprarola, Annibale Caro declares that "besides the invention, we must look to the disposition of the figures, the attitudes, the colour, and a number of other considerations, all in accordance with the descriptions that I find of the subjects which seem to me suitable" (Blunt, p. 131*n*).

The threefold division (invention, disposition, and elocution) is common in poetic theory as well as in treatises on rhetoric (Lee, p. 71). This classification is apparent in Tasso's *Discourses on the Heroic Poem*. After defining the heroic poem in the first book, he proceeds to the selection of subject matter in Book II, to the problem of poetic form and disposition in Book III, and to elocution in Books IV, V, and VI.

[4] Walter Friedlaender, *Mannerism and Anti-Mannerism in Italian Painting* (New York, 1965), p. 3.

[5] See Vincent M. Bevilacqua, "*Ut Rhetorica Pictura*: Sir Joshua Reynolds' Rhetorical Conception of Art," *HLQ* 34 (1970), 59-78. For the views of Sperone Speroni concerning the analogy between rhetoric and painting, see Ruth Wallerstein, *Studies in Seventeenth Century Poetic* (Madison, Wis., 1950), pp. 8-15, 28-29, 50-56, and Bernard Weinberg, *A History of Literary Criticism in the Italian Renaissance*, 2 vols. (Chicago, 1961), pp. 169-71. Just as the painter depicts the faces and bodies of men, the orator paints "con lo stile delle parole" the truth (which is the proper object of speculative doctrines). In Weinberg's opinion, Speroni "places the whole essence of poetry in ornament." From the "process of applying a method of invention, disposition, and elocution there results a fairly consistent poetic. The plot, from invention, must be single and simple . . . so that a proper amount of ornamentation may be added. . . . If the poet strikes a proper balance between invention and elocution, . . . he is . . . worthy of the highest praise. . . ." Miss Wallerstein examines St Augustine's "special Christian application" of the "conception that style takes its form immediately from thought," and emphasizes his view of language as primarily "the immediate embodiment of thought." Tracing the Augustinian tradition in style through the Middle Ages and the Renaissance, she observes that in the course of this development the conception of style as the immediate exprssion of thought (which had first found clear expression in Socratic and Platonic criticism of the Sophists) was "worked out in terms of an allegorical and schematic view of the Bible, a symbolistic view of nature and of human reason." But she also notes that Augustine "helped to kindle in the sixteenth and seventeenth centuries a view of the integral relation of expression to the movement of the thinking mind which was quite independent of sym-

Invention and Disposition

bolism and allgory and quite critical of it." John Hoskins' *Directions for Speech and Style*, ed. Hoyt H. Hudson (Princeton, 1935), treats the order of nature itself as a kind of divine rhetoric. In his opinion (p. 2), "the conceits of the mind are pictures of things and the tongue is interpreter of those pictures. The order of God's creatures in themselves is not only admirable and glorious, but eloquent; then he that could apprehend the consequences of things, in their truth, and utter his apprehensions as truly were a right orator." Cicero had "said much when he said, *dicere recte nemo potest nisi qui prudenter intelligit*." In the *Orator* Cicero had stressed the relationship between philosophy and eloquence, maintaining that "whatever ability I possess as an orator comes, not from the workshops of the rhetoricians, but from the spacious grounds of the Academy" and declaring that philosophy is "essential for the education of our ideal orator . . . for no one can discuss great and varied subjects in a copious and eloquent style without philosophy. . ." ; (trans. H. M. Hubbell, Loeb Classical Library [Cambridge, Mass., and London, 1939], pp. 313-15).

Hanna H. Gray, "Renaissance Humanism: The Pursuit of Eloquence," in *Renaissance Essays*, ed. Paul O. Kristeller and Philip P. Wiener (New York and Evanston, 1968) notes "the pervasive influence of rhetoric" on the ideas and vocabulary of art theory, of historiography, and of moral philosophy. She observes (pp. 208-09) that "their presuppositions about eloquence identified the humanists with no one school of philosophy" and that "even in the disputes carried on among humanists over the relation between rhetoric and philosophy . . . the ultimate issue lay in the definition of eloquence rather than in totally opposed views as to its value." Umberto Pirotti (Eric Cochrane, ed., *The Late Italian Renaissance, 1525-1630* [New York and Evanston, 1970], pp. 187-90) discusses the contrasting attitude of "Aristotelians" toward the use of eloquence. Boccadiferro "carried on an anti-literary tradition," disdaining "rhetorical finery" and maintaining that stylistic ornament "is not required in the sciences." Benedetto Varchi, on the other hand, "criticized both the stylistic awkwardness of all the philosophers who had written in Latin after Boethius and the vain chatter of those who renounced matter for words alone. In his opinion words and things had to be solidly united, for " 'no one can be truly eloquent without doctrine, nor truly learned without eloquence.' " Pirotti further suggests (pp. 204-05) that, though "integral Aristotelianism has usually been seen as completely separate from humanism," nevertheless "in at least one sense philosophy was a close cousin of humanism in its attempt to restore and to take possession of a great monument of pagan antiquity. . . . Though it was born in the Middle Ages, Aristotelianism is to some extent a typical expression of the Renaissance."

In his essay "Historiography: The Art of History in the Italian Counter Reformation," Giorgio Spini stresses Patrizi's unwillingness to submit to "the authority of Cicero, Lucian, or Pontano" and his demand for a "dispassionate, personal inquiry toward a defintion of history . . . upon which a completely new historical methodology can be built." Though Lucian had perceived a "possible distinction between historiography and rhetoric," he had failed to develop it, and it remained for Patrizi to bring forth "for the first time . . . a concept of history not as oratory, but as science" (Cochrane, pp. 97, 101).

[6]For the division of logic (or dialectic) into *inventio* and *judicium* by John of Salisbury and other medieval or Renaissance logicians, see Wilbur Samuel Howell, *Logic and Rhetoric in England, 1500-1700* (Princeton, 1956) and Catherine M. Dunn, ed., *The Logike of Peter Ramus* (Northridge, Calif., 1969). This classification recurs in Rudolph Agricola's *De Inventione Dialectica*, in Peter Ramus' *Dialectica*, and in later treatises. Professor Howell observes that, like Aristotle and Cicero, Agricola accords the most "detailed and systematic treatment" to invention rather than judgment. Professor Dunn notes that Ramus "inverted the traditional order of studying

the two parts of logic," considering it "more natural first to find the topics of discourse and then to order and arrange them"; he assigns to invention "all the topics or places of investigation" and to disposition "anything concerned with the arrangement of material—proposition, syllogism, and method" (Dunn, pp. xiv-xviii).

According to Ramus' definition, "Invention . . . teachethe to invente argumentes," while "Judgement and disposition . . . teachethe to dispone and place orderly the argumentes invented, to the ende we maye judge well and rightly: for we judge of every thing according to the disposition thereof." The "first place of invention" and the "fountayne of all sciences" is cause, inasmuch as "that matter is known perfectly, whose cause is understanded. . ." (Dunn, pp. 10, 41).

Milton's *Art of Logic* observes that "Ramus follows the ancients, Aristotle, Cicero, and Fabius, in dividing dialectic into invention and judgment." Invention is "too broad a term," however, and judgment is not really "the second part of logic, but an effect common to both parts and springing from both. . . ." Milton himself prefers to classify the two parts of logic as "the invention of reasons or arguments and the disposition of them," for "to what except arguments can invention and disposition pertain?" This division possesses the authority of several classical writers: Plato "adds disposition to invention," Aristotle "adds *táxin*, which is the same," while Cicero declares that invention and disposition "pertain not to oratory but to reason" (Columbia edition, Vol. XI, pp. 21-25). Drawing an analogy between the parts of grammar and logic, Milton describes *dispositio* as "the syntax as it were of the arguments, not merely for judging well, as Ramus holds, for that is too narrow, but for thinking well, which is the general end of logic. . . ." He disagrees with those who regard *judicium* as the second part of logic, "since according to their opinion judgment is the end and product of this second part, to wit, of disposition" (CE, XI, 295-97).

[7] See Ernst Robert Curtius, *European Literature and the Latin Middle Ages*, trans. Willard R. Trask (New York and Evanston, 1953), p. 68. "Rhetoric as an art . . . has five divisions: *inventio* (*euresis*, invention), *dispositio* (*taxis*, disposition), *elocutio* (*lexis*, diction), *memoria* (*mneme*, memory), *actio* (*hypocrisis*, delivery)." Cf. Thomas Wilson (Hardison, p. 33), "Invention of matter," "Disposition of the same," "Elocution," "Memorie," "Utterance." For Wilson, Invention is the "finding out of things true, or things likely, the which may reasonablie set forth a matter, and make it appear probable. The places of *Logique*, give good occasion to find out plentiful matter." Disposition is "the setling or ordering of things invented for this purpose, . . . an apt bestowing, and orderly placing of things, declaring where every argument shall be set, and in what maner every reason shalbe applied for conformation of the purpose" (Hardison, pp. 33-34). Invention was closely associated with verisimi'itude and probability. According to Cicero's *De Inventione* I, 7 and the pseudo-Ciceronian *Rhetorica ad Herennium*, I, 2, invention is "excogitatio rerum verarum aut veri similium, quae causam probabilem reddant" (Osgood, p. 156).

[8] Torquato Tasso, *Prose*, ed. Francesco Flora (Milan and Rome, 1935), pp. 341-42.

[9] Ibid., pp. 375, 380-87.

[10] Gilbert, pp. 133, 672.

[11] Aristotle, *On the Art of Poetry*, trans. Ingram Bywater (Oxford, 1951), p. 38.

[12] Ibid., pp. 51-55.

[13] In translations or discussions of Aristotle's *Poetics*, the term *Dianoia* (referring to the thought or reasoning of the characters) was sometimes rendered as *concetto* and *concetti* or as *sententia*. Because of the ambiguity of the latter term, theorists sometimes interpreted Aristotle's *Dianoia* in terms of sententious and gnomic sayings,

Invention and Disposition

such as aphorisms and apothegms and proverbs; cf. Tasso's discussion of *Dianoia* in *Discorsi del poema eroico*.

[14] Richard McKeon, ed., *The Basic Works of Aristotle* (New York, 1941), pp. 1325-29.

[15] Ibid., p. 1336.

[16] Ibid., p. 188; cf. p. 209.

[17] Bywater, p. 84.

[18] Ibid., pp. 41-46, 56-57.

[19] In the *Topics* Aristotle defines a dialectical problem as "a subject of inquiry that contributes either to choice and avoidance, or to truth and knowledge.... For some problems it is useful to know with a view to choice or avoidance, e.g. whether pleasure is to be chosen or not, while some it is useful to know merely with a view to knowledge, e.g. whether the universe is eternal or not..." (McKeon, pp. 196-97). A thesis, in turn, is "a supposition of some eminent philosophy that conflicts with the general opinion.... Or it may be a view about which we have a reasoned theory contrary to men's usual opinions..." (p. 197). Aristotle's "thesis" thus corresponds in part to Renaissance conceptions of paradox; but he includes paradox along with fallacy among the five aims of sophistic reasoning (p. 210).

The matter of dialectical problems may, accordingly, overlap the concerns of *Ethos* and *Dianoia* in tragedy, though the latter are separate and should not be confused. "Character in a play ... reveals the moral purpose of the agents, i.e. the sort of thing they seek or avoid," while Thought "is shown in all they say when proving or disproving some particular point, or enunciating some universal proposition" (Bywater, pp. 38-39).

Though the poet as imitator is distinguished from the rhetorician and dialectician through his mimetic function, his imitation of an action tends to become a mode of rational demonstration insofar as it is probable or necessary. In Renaissance drama there is, in fact, frequent interaction between dialectical or rhetorical reasoning and the events of the plot. In Milton's sketch for a drama on Phinehas, the protagonist's act of homicide precipitates a controversy over the justice of his deed, which is finally resolved by the divine testimony, the direct intervention of the Deity. The dramatic situation in *Samson Agonistes* gives rise to similar controversies, which are finally settled by the dénouement of the drama. The dramatic action itself thus serves as an instrument of proof. The poet is in effect employing two interacting modes of the rhetorician's logical proof—the enthymeme (in the debates of the characters) and the exemplum (in the dramatic action). The action or dramatic situation gives rise to the problem—the proposition or thesis; the speeches of the characters bring the controversial issues into focus; the dénouement of the plot resolves them.

[20] Bywater, p. 38; cf. p. 66.

[21] Ibid., pp. 45-46, 83-84, 87.

[22] Ibid., p. 38; cf. p. 36.

[23] Ibid., pp. 40-43.

[24] Heinrich Wölfflin, *Principles of Art History*, trans. M. D. Hottinger (New York, 1950), pp. 73-74, 109, 206-07.

[25] Ibid., pp. 155-95.

[26] The problem of linking part to part in order to achieve a more unified composition is common to both visual and verbal arts. The lines of bodies or drapery,

The Lamb and the Elephant

pointing fingers, side glances, half-turned figures are common devices of the painter —a pictorial syndeton, linking the elements in a pictorial composition. Just as the prose stylist links words or members in the sentence through conjunctions, the dramatist links scenes through *parasceve* or preparation. The absence of such links within a sentence (asyndeton) was a conventional rhetorical device for acheiving elevation in style.

[27]In contrasting the hypotactic structure of the complex sentence with the paratactic structure of the co-ordinate sentence, Williamson lists several variants in terminology. For Aristotle, they are periodic and continuous; for Demetrius, compacted and disjointed; for Quintilian, compacted and resolved; for Williamson, well-knit and loose; for the majority of modern grammarians, periodic and loose (Williamson, pp. 37-38).

For the influence of the "experimental philosophy" on English prose style, see Richard Foster Jones, "Science and English Prose Style in the Third Quarter of the Seventeenth Century" and "The Attack on Pulpit Eloquence in the Restoration," in Richard Foster Jones, *The Seventeenth Century* (Stanford, Calif. and London, 1965), pp. 75-142. Distinguishing the scientific "revolution in style" from the Anti-Ciceronian movement, he argues that, though both were motivated by "the desire to discover knowledge which would more fully satisfy the demand for reality," the "stylistic movements that accompanied them pursued different and divergent courses. The Anti-Ciceronian style found its theories in Aristotle and its models in such Latin writers as Lucan, Juvenal, Persius, Tacitus, Pliny, and especially Seneca; science renounced Aristotle and all his works, and sought for no models in the ancients" (Jones, p. 165). Morris W. Croll, on the other hand, argues that the "scientific cult of unrhetorical speech from 1650 onward is a second, later stage in the history of the same naturalistic tendency that shows itself in the Anti-Ciceronian victory at the end of the preceding century. It did not create a new, a rival style to the Anti-Ciceronian; it only introduced certain changes within the *cadres* of that style." See *Seventeenth-Century Prose: Modern Essays in Criticism*, ed. Stanley E. Fish (New York, 1971), p. 91.

[28]*Aristotle's Treatise on Rhetoric*, trans. Theodore Buckley (London, 1850), pp. 229-30.

[29]Merritt Y. Hughes observes that in the translation that Milton made of Psalms I to VIII in August, 1653, the poet was already stressing "the sense variously drawn out from one verse into another. . . ." He cites Lawrence Binyon's objection that several of these versions "failed to give the effect of their models by 'moving in a continuous motion' with 'pauses without reference to the stanzas' "; John Milton, *Complete Poems and Major Prose* (New York, 1957), p. 161*n*.

[30]Wölfflin, *Principles*, pp. 223-24.

[31]Bywater, pp. 75-76.

[32]Aristotle, *Rhetoric*, trans. Buckley, pp. 207-10; Book III, Chapters 2-11.

[33]In Tasso's opinion, obscurity frequently lends gravity to style, inasmuch as all that is plain and open is customarily disprized. Brevity is required in the grave style more than in all the others, "percioché il molto nel poco si mostra molto piú grave. . . ." Symbols and allegories enhance gravity. An unpleasant sound may impart gravity, whereas sweetness or tenderness of sound, and equality (of parts or members) tend to destroy it. *Contraposti* and contrary sentences composed with affected diligence and vicious art are inimical to gravity. Nevertheless, *contraposti* tend to swell the verse; and, when mixed with "la figura de la gravitá," they render speech more notable, magnificent and beautiful. As we seek beauty and magnificence above

Invention and Disposition

all else, we praise those poems and orations which are simultaneously most exact and most magnificent (Tasso, ed. Flora, pp. 516-17). Of all the figures of thought which enhance gravity, prosopopoeia is foremost (p. 517). The low style (the tenuous or subtle style), however, avoids oblique modes of speech because they are obscure, and employs the natural order of speech. Above all else it requires that probability which the Latins call *evidenza*, the Greeks *energia*, and the Italians *clarity* or *expression*; this is the virtue that makes us almost see the things that are narrated (p. 521).

Like Aristotle, Tasso regards clarity without baseness as the virtue of elocution. Though the orator should seek clarity with appropriate height, the poet employs a more sublime speech than befits the orator. Like Aristotle, he observes that unusual words make discourse more venerable and produce marvel, for the marvelous is always accompanied with delight. Metaphors are more suited to the orator. Tasso agrees with Aegidius, the interpreter of Aristotle, as to the three *proprietà* of the metaphor: that it be taken "da cose convenevoli, da vicini, e da manifeste. . . ." Others (cf. Aristotle) add that the metaphor should be taken from "cose belle e grate a la vista. . ." (Flora, pp. 460-61). Since the invention of fitting metaphors requires knowledge of "la similitudine de le cose ne la dissimilitudine," their invention seems to belong properly to philosophical talents *(ingegni)*. Plato above all others invented metaphors and used them unsparingly (p. 462). Allegory contributes to grandeur of style. It was rightly said that allegory is similar to night and darkness. Hence it should be used in mysteries and therefore in "mysterious poems" like the heroic poem. Enigma and allegory are possibly the same in species or at least in genus (ed. Flora, pp. 486-89).

Wölfflin notes the baroque distaste for "unnatural" clarity in the representation of objects. "While classic art aimed at revealing the motive in absolute clarity, the purpose of the baroque is not to be unclear, but to make clarity look like an accidental by-product" (*Principles*, p. 206). "In absolute clearness there lies a motive of that fixation of the figure which the baroque eschewed on principle as something unnatural" (p. 222). In so-called "picturesque lighting" the "play of light . . . has become independent of the object. . ." (p. 200). Poets and painters of the period could also make use of the imagery of light and darkness traditional in Christian and neo-Platonic mysticism.

[34]*Style, Rhetoric, and Rhythm; Essays by Morris W. Croll*, ed. J. Max Patrick et al. (Princeton, 1966), p. 77n; see Aristotle, *Rhetoric*, Book II, Chapters 22-24 and Book III, Chapters 8-15.

[35]Several of the most significant theoretical treatises on the conceit appeared long after the principal "mannerist" painters and poets. The first edition of Baltasar Gracián's *Arte de Ingenio* was published at Madrid in 1642; the second edition was published in 1649 as *Agudeza y arte de Ingenio*. Matteo Peregrini's *Delle acutezze* was published at Genoa in 1639. Emanuele Tesauro's treatise *Il cannocchiale aristotelico, o sia Idea delle argutezze heroiche, volgarmente chiamate imprese, e di tutta l'arte simbolica et lapidaria . . . esaminata in fonte co' rettorici precetti del divino Aristotele, che comprendono tutta la Rettorica, et Poetica elocutione* was published at Torino in 1654. See Morris W. Croll, *Style, Rhetoric, and Rhythm*, p. 77n; Guido Morpugo Tagliabue, "La retorica aristotelica e il barocco," in *Retorica e barocco*, pp. 119-96; Cochrane, p. 379n., 389n., Curtius, p. 294.

The second edition of Tesauro's book, published at Venice in 1663, added two new treatises—one on "preachable conceits" and the other on emblems ("due nuovi trattati, cioè de' concetti predicabili et degli emblemi"). The altered title emphasized the rhetorical character and function of the book: *Il Cannochiale aristotelico, o sia Idea dell' arguta et ingeniosa elocutione, che serve a tutta l'arte oratoria, lapidaria et simbolica. . . .*

The Lamb and the Elephant

For a study of the seventeenth-century conceited or pointed style as a mode of "literary mannerism," see Klaus-Peter Lange, *Theoretiker des Literarischen Manierismus: Tesauros und Pellegrinis Lehre von der "Acutezza" oder von der Macht der Sprache* (Munich, 1968).

[36]For Aristotle, metaphor ranks (along with antithesis and *energeia*) among the elegancies and "approved beauties" of style. The "power of inventing" these belongs "either to the man of high natural genius, or to one of talent chastened by discipline. . . ." To receive "information with ease, is naturally pleasant to all"; but, whereas "foreign expressions are unintelligible" and "words of common use" are already understood, metaphor produces the effect of pleasure in the highest degree. When "the poet calls old age 'stubble,' he produces in us a knowledge and information by means of a common genus." The "similes of the poets also produce the same effect. . ." (Buckley, pp. 234-35). Of the four types of metaphor "from genus to species, or from species to genus, or from species to species, or on grounds of analogy" (Bywater, p. 72), the analogical metaphor "which is constructed on similar ratios" is the best (Buckley, p. 236). Metaphor is also a source of *energeia*, and to produce this effect, its terms should be "appropriate and not obvious"; just as in philosophy, "it is the privilege of one who conjectures happily, to discern the point of similitude. . . ." The "greatest number of elegances arise from metaphor, and from additionally deceiving the hearer; for the point becomes more clear that he has learnt something, from the meaning being the opposite (of what it was supposed), and the mind seems to say, 'How true is this! I however was wrong.'" The "elegancies of proverbial expressions arise from one's meaning not what he says. . . ." For the same reason, enigmas, paradoxes, and puns are pleasing. Proverbs are "metaphors from species to species," and hyperboles recognized as such are also metaphors (Buckley, pp. 240-46).

Since exotic or compound words and new coinages offend against good taste, being too far removed from common usage, they must be used "sparingly, and in very few places. . . ." In prose only metaphors and words "of *ordinary* use, and in their *original acceptations*" are available, since "these are the only words which *all* persons employ. . ." (Buckley, p. 209). Metaphors possess "in an especial manner" the qualities of "clearness and sweetness, with an air of being foreign"; and in employing them the speaker must rely on his own talent, since "it is not possible to derive [them] from any other person" (Buckley, p. 210). To be appropriate they must be "constructed on principles of analogy. . . ." To embellish his subject, the orator draws his metaphors from "such things coming under the same class as are better"; to debase his subject, he derives them from "such as are worse." Metaphors should not be far-fetched, but should be based on "kindred objects" of the same species. They can be extracted from "neatly constructed *enigmas*," since "it is on the principles of metaphor that men construct enigmas. . . ," and the transfer should be made "from objects which are *beautiful*. . ." (Buckley, pp. 210-13). The simile is essentially a metaphor, but it is seldom useful in prose "since it carries with it the air of poetry" (Bywater, pp. 75, 78). Cf. Aristotle, *The Art of Rhetoric*, trans. John Henry Freese (Cambridge, Mass., and London, 1959), pp. 398-99; "We ought therefore to aim at three things—metaphor, antithesis, actuality" *(metaphoras antitheseōs energeias)*; and pp. 404-07; "We have said that smart sayings are derived from proportional metaphor and expressions which set things before the eyes. We must now explain the meaning of 'before the eyes' and what must be done to produce this. I mean that things are set before the eyes by words that signify actuality *(hosa energounta sēmainei)*." Thus through the use of metaphor Homer frequently "speaks of inanimate things as if they were animate; and it is to creating actuality [*energeian*] that his popularity is due. . . . For in all these examples there is appearance of actuality [*energounta*] since the objects are represented as animate. . . ."

Invention and Disposition

Since the technical terms *energeia* (energy, vigor) and *enargeia* (vividness, distinctness, clearness) are normally distinguished by rhetoricians—and since Aristotle's *energeia* has sometimes been virtually equated with *enargeia*—the comments of Edward Meredith Cope on this passage should be consulted: *The Rhetoric of Aristotle with a Commentary by . . . Cope*, rev. and ed. John Edwin Sandys (London and Cambridge, 1877), III, 110n-111n, 125n-127n. Energeia (here translated as "vivid representation") is "principally shewn in *animation*, literally and metaphorically, in a vivid, vivacious, style, and in animating, vivifying, inanimate objects; investing them with life, motion, and personality. . . . This sense is borrowed from the metaphysical use of the term, to express 'realization,' as opposed to . . . the mere capacity or potentiality of life and action." Quintilian distinguishes *energeia* from *enargeia* (Sandys, p. 111n.): *energeia* confinis his (est enim ab agendo dicta) et cuius propria virtus, non esse quae dicuntur, otiosa. . . . Praecipueque ex his oritur sublimitas quae audaci et proxime periculum translatione tolluntur, quum rebus sensu carentibus actum quendam et animos damus. . . ." On the other hand, "*enargeia*, quae a Cicerone *illustratio* et *evidentia* nominatur, quae non tam dicere videtur quam ostendere: et affectus non aliter, quam si rebus ipsis intersimus, sequentur." Cf. Sister Miriam Joseph, C.S.C., *Rhetoric in Shakespeare's Time* (New York and Burlingame, 1947 and 1962), pp. 320-21, on *enargeia* and *hypotyposis* as "generic names for a group of figures aiming at lively description and counterfeit representation"; Richard A. Lanham, *A Handlist of Rhetorical Terms* (Berkeley and Los Angeles, 1969), p. 40 on the distinction between *enargeia* (vividness) and *energeia* (vigor); Madeleine Doran, "The Language of *Hamlet*," HLQ 27 (1964), 259-78.

Aristotle's *Rhetoric* also associates *energeia* (one of the three principal elegancies of style) with the ability to "place the object before your eyes; for it needs must be, that one sees more clearly what is actually in the course of being done, than what is *about* to be." Buckley (p. 236) somewhat misleadingly translates this term as *personification*, since "the effect is produced by representing inanimate objects as the agents in any thing. . . ." In Aristotle's opinion, "those expressions which represent the object as in action, do all of them produce the setting before the eyes. . . ." *Energeia* is "an imitation"; and, though it differs from metaphor, it is often associated with the latter. Homer frequently employs it, "putting inanimate things as animate, by means of a metaphor. . ." (Buckley, pp. 239-40).

Like energy, rhythm has become a cliché in criticism of baroque style; and, like *energeia*, it is a conventional rhetorical concept. In the *Rhetoric* (Book III, Chapter 8), Aristotle argues that the diction in prose "ought to be measured, yet without metre; for what is destitute of measure is displeasing and indistinct" (Buckley, p. 226). Since rhythm involves ratio or proportion (p. 227), it is potentially relevant to the visual as well as the verbal arts and the arts of music and dancing. Since diverse rhythms are associated with different levels of style and with different emotional effects, the distinction between different kinds of rhythm is almost as important in art criticisms as in rhetoric and poetic. To speak in general terms about the rhythm of a particular painting or sculpture without analyzing its qualities and comparing or contrastng it with the rhythm of other works is almost as meaningless as passing allusions to the rhythm of a Ciceronian oration or a Jacobean sermon. Broken and interrupted rhythms can be a source of surprise, moreover, in the visual as in the verbal arts, a turn counter to expectation and a means for heightening admiration or passion.

[37] Bywater, pp. 40-51.

[38] Blunt, pp. 19, 50.

[39] Cf. Blunt, p. 19. Erwin Panofsky observes (*Meaning in the Visual Arts* [Garden City, N.Y., 1955] p. 65) that the Greek artist-theoretician started "with the human

figure, organically differentiated into torso, limbs, and parts of limbs, and subsequently tried to ascertain how these parts related to each other and to the whole. The "basis of the Polyclitan canon," he observes "is not a principle of mechanical identity, but a principle of organic differentiation." Graeco-Roman rhetorical and poetic theory similarly emphasized the relationship of the members (and parts of members) to one another and to the whole in the composition of sentences, and the interrelationships of the parts of a well-constructed poem or oration. Panofsky (pp. 68-69) analyzes Vitruvius' conceptions of proportion, symmetry, and *eurhythmia;* and Blunt (p. 15) notes the influence of Vitruvius on Alberti's definitions of beauty in *De Re Aedificatoria:* "a certain regular harmony of all the parts of a thing of such a kind that nothing could be added or taken away or altered without making it less pleasing," and "a kind of harmony and concord of all the parts to form a whole which is constructed according to a fixed number, and a certain relation and order, as symmetry, the highest and most perfect law of nature, demands." Vasari, in turn (Blunt, p. 91), regarded "the judgement of the eye" as a better guide for achieving the proportions of figures than mathematical measurement.

[40] Attempts to correlate High Renaissance and baroque styles with static or dynamic world-views are not uncommon in recent criticism, but they are usually based on a distortion of intellectual history. In the symmetry and formal order of Renaissance "classic" art, many critics perceive a reflection of the cosmos itself as order and hierarchy. In the restless forms of baroque art, on the other hand, they find an expression of worldly mutability and illusion, the conception of nature as process, the world as flux, and life as a dream. To prove the point they can, of course, cite documentary parallels, but all too often they have (voluntarily or involuntarily) weighted the evidence. Both of these conceptions were, of course, commonplaces that coexist in both periods; and there is little justification for arbitrarily associating one conception with "classic" and the other with "baroque."

In seventeenth-century poetry and prose, antithesis—especially when associated with *acutezza* as in the pointed antithesis and *contraposti* of the epigram—could serve the ends of logical demonstration as well as rhetorical persuasion, adding sharpness and clearer definition to the ideas and concepts the author desired to emphasize as well as adorning style. In *The City of God,* trans. Marcus Dods, Modern Library (New York, 1950), pp. 361-62, Saint Augustine praised the use of antithesis ("the opposition of contraries" or "contrapositions"—i.e. *contraposto* or counterpoint) as one of the most elegant ornaments of speech. According to logical theory, "contraries laid together more evidently appear"; see my *Milton's Epic Characters* (Chapel Hill, N.C., 1968), pp. 39-41. Antithesis could function both as an ornament of style and a "dissentany argument," defining a concept or proving a proposition by opposing it to its contrary. The use of the terms *contraposto* in art theory and *counterpoint* in music represents an adaptation of rhetorical and poetic terminology to the sister arts.

[41] See Stanley E. Fish, *Self-Consuming Artifacts: The Experience of Seventeenth-Century Literature* (Berkeley, Los Angeles, London, 1972), on Renaissance literature as artificial construct.

Chapter VIII

THE END OF THE RENAISSANCE: THE PROBLEM OF PERIODIZATION

>>>>>>:<<<<<<

MOST HISTORIANS of the Renaissance have experienced the embarrassments of periodization. In compiling a bibliography or planning a seminar, one must decide whether to include Milton and Dante, and whether to classify mannerists and the baroque artists as "late Renaissance" or "post-Renaissance." This is an operative expediency, forced upon us not by the nature of the subject but by our own *modus tractandi;* and in such instances we are usually aware that in clarifying history we are falsifying it.

Curtius experienced a similar embarrassment in delimiting the Middle Ages: "When I tried to grasp the beginnings of the medieval world, I was led back to imperial Rome and to late antiquity in general. Some features of the medieval mind would emerge in the first century of our era, some would point back to the Hellenistic epoch. On the other hand, most of them survived the so-called Renaissance and were well alive until the end of the seventeenth century.... I seemed to discover that there was no such thing as the Middle Ages which I had been looking for."[1] Developing Trevelyan's suggestion that the "real break" in modern history occurs not in the sixteenth but in the eighteenth century, Curtius argued that "medieval forms of life subsist until about 1750" and that the "Industrial Revolution has meant a much more radical change than the Renaissance or the Reformation."[2] Perhaps this is true if one is thinking primarily in terms of social and economic history. Many students of English literature, however, would be inclined to locate the major, and decisive, transitions in the preceding century; and, indeed, the origins of the Industrial Revolution are to be found in seventeenth-century science. "In 1600," as Douglas Bush has observed, "the educated Englishman's mind and world were more than half medieval; by 1660 they were more than half modern."

Moreover, "what distinguished the seventeenth century from the sixteenth was not so much the arrival of new ideas and forces as the accumulated and irresistible pressure of old and new ones in potent combination and interaction."[3]

The course of the Renaissance cannot be plotted like the trajectory of a bullet or the structure of a play. It was a drama with multiple plots and counterplots. Its movements in different arts and sciences were not synchronous; they did not consistently follow the same direction or progress at the same rate in different countries. Attempts at periodization—arbitrary though they often are—must take into account local traditions, cross-influences, cultural lag, and (on occasion) deliberate archaism. To seek initial and terminal dates for the Renaissance as a whole can only result in falsification. The most one can do is to focus one's inquiry on particular arts and sciences in particular countries. These did not develop or decline simultaneously, burgeoning and withering with changing climates of opinion, even though Renaissance conceptions of the cycles and seasons of history—the parallel development of eloquence and empire, and the influence of the stars or the Creator of the stars on the fate of arms and arts and society alike—may once have encouraged such a view. The notion of the decline of Renaissance civilization was conditioned, in part at least, by neoclassical ridicule of late Renaissance styles as corruptions of taste, by academic elevation of certain High Renaissance paintings into "classics" in their own right and models for close study and imitation, and by the shift in intellectual leadership from Italy to western Europe. Moreover, the concept of artistic decadence was implicit in neo-Aristotelian conceptions of the ideal paradigms of the genres and in Aristotle's own account of the origins and evolution of literary species. In his opinion, the various genres of poetry had developed naturally, "through their original aptitude, and by a series of improvements for the most part gradual" until they had achieved their natural form, and ceased evolving. Like comedy, tragedy "began in improvisations," advancing "little by little, through their [the authors'] improving on whatever they had before them at each stage. It was in fact only after a long series of changes that the movement of Tragedy stopped on its attaining to its natural form."[4]

End of the Renaissance

For critics who accepted this frame of reference, further changes or developments beyond the "natural form" of a genre might seem decadent; insofar as these departed from the natural form or "idea" of tragedy or comedy or epic, they would appear to be corruptions of form and style. Nevertheless, such principles did not necessarily imply the stagnation of the arts. There was still ample scope for improving and refining them. Neoclassical writers were aware of defects in their Renaissance predecessors. Although they might question their own ability to equal the latter in originality and power, they were frequently more confident of surpassing these rivals in correctness and polish. The minor genres in particular—satire and verse epistle, burlesque, epic and the verse essay—offered opportunities for exercising invention and judgment. Stricter critics had exposed the frailties of the classical masters themselves. For all their originality and creative excellence, these had sometimes fallen short of realizing the "perfect idea" of a heroic poem or tragedy. Unable to profit by recent critical refinements on Aristotelian and Horatian doctrine, they had also been ignorant of Christian truth and the new cosmology.

1.

Neither neoclassical strictures against seventeenth-century metaphysical poetry nor seicento complaints against the degeneration of pictorial art since the great masters of the early cinquecento can be regarded as unbiased testimony, clear evidence of the decadence of Renaissance culture and the end of the age. There is, in fact, no single point where the observer of the Renaissance can exclaim, like a spectator at a play, "*This* is the climax or turn," "*this* is the commencement of the falling action," or "here at last is the catastrophe." Confronted with the imperative of filling out the death certificate for an era, Italians and Englishmen, art historians and scientists are as likely to differ as the watchers at the deathbeds of John Donne's "virtuous men": "some...say, 'Now his breath goes,' and some say, 'no.'"

Most of them would probably agree that the Renaissance had expired well before the end of the seventeenth century, but they would still have to search for a plausible diagnosis. Some would accuse the Reformation or the Counter-Reformation, the repressive force of the Inquisition or the disintegrative dynamic of Protestantism, the extremes of too much or too little toleration and the "wars worse than civil" of religion—the Pharsalias and Philippis of the Church Militant. Some would blame the sack of Rome, the policies of the Hapsburgs, and Spanish influence over the papacy and the states of Italy and the Netherlands. Others would detect symptoms of schizophrenia or manic-depressive tendencies. In the distortions of mannerist and baroque art, the eccentricities of metaphysical poetry, and the ambiguities of tragicomedy they would recognize signs of cultural neurosis and hysteria. The "exploded periods" of Senecan prose and the "broken knowledge" of the aphoristic style reflected the disintegration of the established world-view and the dogmas of the established church, the collapse of the old systematic philosophies and the old certitudes, the dissolution of what had still survived of the medieval synthesis of arts and sciences and of political and spiritual authority. In art and poetry they perceived further evidences of disintegration. The traditional forms of art and nature alike appeared to dissolve into ecstasies and hallucinatory visions, and ecstatic visions in turn to dissolve in tears. El Greco's figures appeared to dissolve into waves of light, undulations of ectoplasm. Rubens' corpulent saints soared into the empyrean like colored balloons at a village fête, miraculously defying the laws of gravity. The instruments of the Passion floated weightless in space. Paintings and statues of apotheoses, apparitions, and mystical raptures became in effect feats of levitation. Baroque poets, in turn, tended to dissolve the object into metaphor and conceit, to obscure the theme in the play of wit and the concatenation of images, to blur the distinction between objects by shifting their attributes (as in Crashaw's "wounded heart" and "bleeding eyes," "flaming fountain" and "weeping fire") or (as in Góngora's "feathered citharas") to fashion a new and hybrid creature by combining the attributes of object and image. In the tension between imperial ambitions and contempt of the world in baroque society, these observers would find proof of maladjustment and alienation; and in the devotional literature of the period an inconclusive dialogue between Eros and Thanatos, libido and death-wish—an unstable mixture of erotic and religious melancholy.

End of the Renaissance

Others, finally, would emphasize the disguised or overt challenge to authority, not only in church and state but in most branches of organized, traditional learning. They would stress the epistemological crisis of the seventeenth century; growing awareness of the unreliability of the traditional learning and the conventional scientific and philosophical methods; recognition of the limitations of human reason and the need to assist it by means of a reliable art of invention and judgment, discovery and proof; above all, the quest for certitude, the search for new and valid methodologies in natural philosophy and metaphysics as in ethics and politics. They would point to the influence of Bacon and Descartes, the stimulus of new scientific discoveries, the rise of "experimental" and "mechanical" philosophy. The Renaissance, they might suggest, had died either by suicide or by parricide, perishing by its own agency or by the very forces it had generated. The revival of learning (including the atomic materialism of antiquity, several varieties of classical skepticism, and the mechanical and mathematical treatises of Alexandrian scientists) had rendered the major philosophical systems of the ancients increasingly suspect, and their scientific learning obsolescent. In the light kindled partly by the ancients—and by the light of nature, which the ancients themselves had revered—their deficiencies in observation and logic, their errors in induction and deduction, had become clearly and embarrassingly evident.

One would not expect a unanimous verdict, and perhaps each of these diagnoses contains an element of truth. All have been—and still are—advanced as causes for the end of the Renaissance. Many of them have been regarded as post-Renaissance phenomena, though this is not (one feels) an altogether satisfactory classification. Only the last of these factors—the influence of "new philosophy," which itelf developed out of the fruitful conjunction of Greek scientific thought and Renaissance science, the interaction of active and contemplative ends—effectively undercut the authoritative classical tradition in one major branch of learning, natural philosophy, and led directly to the Newtonian cosmos of the Enlightenment and ultimately to modern experimental methods and technology.

The Renaissance classical tradition survived, albeit somewhat changed, well into the period of the Enlightenment and beyond.

The Lamb and the Elephant

The controversies over the relative merits of ancients and moderns during the seventeenth and early eighteenth centuries were, in large part, a duel between the *litterae humaniores* and the new science. Despite their external form (which frequently involved a systematic comparison between ancient and modern representatives of the several branches of learning, juxtaposing classical and modern dramatic poets, ancient and recent mathematicians or geographers or medical authors), the real point at issue was, as a rule, less the ostensible rivalry with antiquity—Greek science versus English science, Latin poetry versus French or Italian poetry—than the rivalry between contemporary science and the classical literary tradition still influential in contemporary criticism and education. In certain respects this was more than the conventional *querelle des anciens et des modernes* ("a constant phenomenon of literary history and literary sociology"). It belonged to a different, though related, war—which was likewise a "quarrel of clerks." It was, in fact, another battle in the *querelle des arts*, another episode in the longstanding rivalry between science (or philosophy) and poetry.[5] In many instances, the conflict between ages was less significant than the tension between rival arts. On the whole, the strongest defenders of the "modern" camp were the partisans of the new science; and the most powerful supporters of the ancients were the advocates of neoclassical principles and humanistic values in literature. Both, in fact, would win in the end—the victory falling to antiquity in poetry and criticism, and to modernity in philosophy and science. The civilization of the Enlightenment would, in large part, represent an alliance of the new philosophy with neoclassical literary principles —the best of both ages.

Underlying the question of the relative superiority of ancients and moderns, moreover, was the practical issue of precisely how far, if at all, the methods and examples of the ancients should condition those of the moderns—not only in literature and art but (more significantly) in philosophy and science. The chief issues in the Ancients-and-Moderns controversy were not only questions of superiority (the ostensible point of the controversy) but also questions of authority—the relative or absolute value of classical precepts and precedents and the dependent or independent status of modern

End of the Renaissance

writers vis-à-vis the *auctoritas* of antiquity. At stake was the comparative force of tradition and innovation—in the sciences as well as in humane letters. The central issue, in many cases, was methodology. In asking "which age is better?" the disputants were, in effect, debating questions of method: "what authors should one follow (if any) and how?" and "what principles and techniques, what methodologies, could best achieve the ends of the several arts and sciences?" For the poet or artist, these questions involved the rival claims of original genius and the authority of rules and traditional models—his freedom (or lack of freedom) to exercise his own originality in invention, disposition, and style. They were even more significant, however, for the philosopher and the scientist, since they involved the crucial issue of certitude and the search for a valid and reliable methodology in the investigation of nature and human society and substances above and beyond nature—the study of physics and metaphysics and politics.

In mannerist or baroque literature and art the tension between ancient and modern, between classical precedent and new invention, is sometimes apparent in claims to freedom and originality in theme, design, or expression *(inventio, dispositio, or elocutio).* Frequently this assertion of partial independence from classical models and principles is a reaction less against the classics themselves than against neoclassical or pseudo-classical trends in contemporary criticism; and not infrequently the partisans of "new" styles of expression and new forms of design turned to classical authors for models and principles. Thus the *novum genus dicendi* drew heavily from Aristotle's discussion of metaphor and from the example of Martial in poetry, and Seneca and Tacitus and Pliny in prose. In the same way, defenders of the moderns in philosophy and science might appeal to the skeptical thought of Sextus Empiricus or the atomic Epicureanism of Lucretius. Arguments and styles that on the surface appeared to be "anticlassical" might, in fact, be little more than "anti-Ciceronian," "antischolastic," or "anti-Galenist."

2.

In considering the several "symptoms" of the old age of the Renaissance, the civilization of the eighteenth century offers a useful point of comparison, since (if the term has any meaning at all) it belongs to a "post-Renaissance" age. Several of the forces and movements commonly associated with the end of the Renaissance had lost much of their energy and momentum. In western Europe, Reformation and Counter-Reformation fervor, once white-hot and irresistible as a lava flow, had lost its incendiary zeal and sought the milder shades and grottoes of pastoral care. In England and France alike, rational churchmen faced more insidious adversaries than schismatics and heretics—reasoned disbelief and witty infidelity, distrust of dogma, the authority of revelation, the natural theology of deism, the enthusiastic religion of nature and the cult of the sublime. Mannerist extravagance and baroque excess had been moderated to the refinements of rococo or neoclassical forms, and the High Renaissance masters and antique statuary restored to positions of eminence in academies of design. Metaphysical wit had been clipped and pruned; its inventions curbed by judgment and the limitations of classical decorum, its points and *argutiae* sprinkled discreetly over heroic couplets. Even Attic salt could be unpalatable in excess. Herbert's subtle devotional poetry now inspired Anglican and Nonconformist hymns. The metaphysical and Marinist traditions, fashionable in the late Renaissance, had been bypassed or altered virtually beyond recognition; and both neoclassical and romantic (or "preromantic") poets tended to resume the Renaissance tradition, the latter reviving the Spenserian stanza and blank verse, the former continuing the Renaissance imitation and assimilation of classical models. Though contemporary tastes in landscape were strongly affected by seicento painters like Salvator Rosa, this influence merged with that of Longinus' rhetorical treatise and the poetry of Milton; all three were subsumed under the same category, the sublime.

In the age of the Enlightenment two of the forces allegedly responsible for the end of the Renaissance were still operative—the shift of cultural leadership from Italy to western Europe and the growth of the new science. English dramatists and critics turned more readily to French poets and theorists than to Italians. The alliance of physics, mathematics, and mechanics had produced a

End of the Renaissance

new and satisfactory model of the universe (*fiat Newton, fiat lux*); the new technology, pregnant with the "mechanical muse" and with prophecies of Satanic mills, carried the seeds of social as well as industrial revolution. Nevertheless, the patterns established in the Renaissance were still operative. Frenchmen and Englishmen still traveled to Italy to inspect classical ruins and Renaissance paintings, bringing back drawings of Roman capitals and facades, prospects of Rome and Venice, and miscellaneous marbles. They learned, once again, to enjoy Dante (in spite of Voltaire's ridicule of the *Commedia* as a "salmagundi" of a poem), to appreciate the irregular beauties of Ariosto, and to sketch the encounters of Tasso's Armida and Rinaldo. Poets might eulogize the new science, but they sometimes regarded it as a dangerous rival, a potential threat not only to religion and society but to humane literature.

The Enlightenment erected its own observatories and fortresses, its offensive and defensive weapons, on the foundations of Renaissance humanism. Peter Gay has effectively summarized the affinities between the two periods. Both movements were "dominated by men of letters" and "moral realists"; both "admired classical antiquity, especially ancient Rome." In addition to their admiration for Cicero, the eighteenth-century *philosophes* read and extolled many of the classical authors influential in the late cinquecento and the seicento—Lucretius and Lucan, Seneca and Tacitus, Martial and Juvenal and Horace—and they inherited the humanists' contempt for the darkness of the Middle Ages. Nevertheless, there were significant contrasts. Antiquity "appeared to them in rather different guises: the antiquity of the Enlightenment, classical, differentiated, and influential especially through its critical world-view, did not confront the Humanists as a ready-made finished product; it had to be discovered."[6]

The political and cultural influence of Spain and of France undoubtedly altered the character of late Renaissance civilization,[7] but one is reluctant to identify this transmigration of arms and arts with the end of the Renaissance, even in Italy. During the sixteenth century, Englishmen had borrowed Italian Renaissance fashions not only directly from Italian sources but indirectly through French and Spanish media. British authors translated or adapted the sonnets

The Lamb and the Elephant

of Desportes and DuBellay, French translations of Italian *novelle* and classical works, and the plays of Spanish dramatists. The essays of Montaigne, the writings of French historians, and the treatises of Spanish authors—Guevara, Vives, Huarte—were widely read. Though Spanish literature—the works of Cervantes, devotional treatises, plays and lyrics—continued to influence English writers throughout the seventeenth century, Italian literature remained a major influence on English poetry until the Restoration. Milton wrote Italian poetry and corresponded with his Italian friends, praised the Italian commentaries on poetic theory and the poetry of Dante and Petrarch and Tasso, echoed Ariosto, consulted the Italian historiographers, adapted Italian fashions in the sonnet, the canzone, the madrigal, and blank verse. Donne read Italian as well as Spanish poets, and Marino and other seicentisti were translated or imitated by Crashaw and the circle of poets associated with Thomas Stanley. Though critics may be partially correct in stressing the medieval element in Spanish Renaissance and baroque literature, as well as in English metaphysical and Italian seicento poetry, the Italian impact on seventeenth-century English literature includes neoclassical as well as romantic and baroque influences. The neoclassical currents of the Italian Renaissance, which had already reached England directly, would be reinforced—or indeed remodeled—by the influence of French neoclassical criticism and poetry. These, in turn, had been influenced not only by the ancients themselves but by Italian theory and practice, either directly through Italian poets and critics or indirectly through Dutch theorists like Daniel Heinsius and Vossius. The result of the French impact on English literature was to undercut the English and Continental metaphysical tradition (including the formerly influential work of Théophile de Viau) and to reemphasize the authority and example of the ancients. Essentially it represented a victory of the stricter classical orientation of the Renaissance over certain irregular or (loosely-labeled) anticlassical trends in late Renaissance styles. Moreover, it is roughly paralleled by a neoclassical reaction against baroque (sometimes labeled "Gothic") irregularities in the arts of design.[8]

One hesitates to identify the end of the Renaissance with these shifts in power—as though Clement were Belshazzar, Charles V a

End of the Renaissance

Cyrus redivivus, and Louis XIV a new Alexander—or (in England) to link it with a change of dynasties, the transition from the Elizabethan to the Jacobean age. One is also reluctant to identify the changes in English and Continental literary taste near the end of the sixteenth century—such as the Jonsonian adaptations of the plain style or the vogue of metaphysical poetry and Senecan prose—as "post-Renaissance" phenomena. Jonson's critical thought, strongly influenced by Heinsius and by Horace, belongs essentially to the Italian Renaissance tradition. His comedies and tragedies build on the Renaissance Terentian and Senecan tradition. His shorter poems—verse epistles and satires, epigrams, erotic lyrics, epithalamia—belong to minor classical genres. His "plain style" in poetry is strongly influenced by the example of Anacreon and Horace, the Latin elegiac poets, and Martial. His masques draw their motifs from Renaissance mythography and from Cesare Ripa's *Iconologia*.

Metaphysical poetry and Senecan prose, in turn, may have involved a conscious reaction against certain aspects of fashionable but overworked Renaissance styles—a richly ornamented but threadbare Petrarchism and a polished and vacuous and pedantic Ciceronianism. Nevertheless, both of these may be regarded rather as late Renaissance than as post-Renaissance styles. The Senecan tradition was strongly indebted to classical models; the metaphysical mode reflected the influence of classical poets and rhetoricians in addition to medieval and Renaissance themes. Many of the rhetorical devices characteristic of seventeenth-century German baroque poetry had long been conventional in the poetry of the English and Italian Renaissance. Similarly, the mannerist developments out of (and sometimes away from) High Renaissance styles, and the baroque reformation of mannerism in its turn, might perhaps be better described as late Renaissance than as post-Renaissance.

In art and literature especially, attempts at periodization tend to break down or to introduce meaningless barriers. Strictly speaking, seventeenth-century neoclassical movements, in art and literature alike, are partly a conscious return to the Renaissance tradition, partly an extension of the Renaissance movement and a deliberate effort to polish and refine its styles. As recent criticism has observed, there is a clearly defined line of influence from Italian neo-

The Lamb and the Elephant

Aristotelian dramatic theory to that of Daniel Heinsius, from Heinsius to the neoclassical French tragedians, and thence to the English stage.[9] Does the distinction between Renaissance and post-Renaissance clarify or obscure this pattern of development? Again, one normally assigns the neoclassical poetry of Milton to the late Renaissance and the dramas of the far less classical Dryden to a later (and post-Renaissance) age. Though these authors looked to different sources for their poetic theories—the one to Italy, the other to France—and thus represent different aspects (or indeed phases) of the neoclassical movement, are the categories "late Renaissance" and "post-Renaissance" really significant in this case? When one turns to their prose style, however, the chronological classifications may seem more justifiable, indicative of the gulf that separates the early Augustan from the late Renaissance humanist.

3.

In the poetry and prose of the late Renaissance, and frequently in its art, one encounters—along with simultaneous attempts to achieve unity and variety, verisimilitude and marvel—movements toward a stricter and a more liberal observance of the rules, toward a tighter and a looser structure, toward greater informality in organization and a severer emphasis on the rules of construction. Critics have frequently associated the search for a looser and less formal arrangement with the individualism and subjectivism of the period, the search for the self, the emphasis on private study or reflection, the attempt to suggest the meditative process—the movement of the mind and the action of thinking—rather than the finished thought. They have noted the analogy between this partial dissolution and "re-formation" of conventional literary and artistic forms and the revaluation of established methodologies and the search for new methods and procedures in philosophy and the sciences. And they have also called attention to the ways in which the recognition of relativity and uncertainty, the search for truth and certitude—the tensions between doubt and assurance or reason and faith—are reflected in correlative styles, whether classical or nonclassical. The epistle, the essay (which developed out of the Senecan epistle), and

End of the Renaissance

the dialogue were often open-ended forms; permitting a relatively free development of thought within a comparatively loose and flexible structure, they could follow the direction of the argument instead of predetermining it, reflect the pattern of thought instead of imposing it.

Nevertheless, whatever the advantage of informality in style and looseness in structure, the writer could not dispense entirely with formal organization. Though looser forms might afford greater scope for the free development of the argument, they did not altogether solve the problem of organization. The philosophical writers of the late sixteenth and early seventeenth centuries commandeered the most varied, and apparently unpromising, genres, forcing them into the service of ethics or physics, Stoic or Hermetic doctrines. Bacon and Pascal utilized the broken knowledge of the aphorism in the cause respectively of experimental method and religion. Descartes adapted the meditation to the method of systematic doubt and the ends of epistemology and metaphysics. Bruno's *Heroic Frenzies* is essentially a commentary (in dialogue form) on a collection of emblems and sonnets, with a mythical frame-narrative that concludes with a eulogy of Queen Elizabeth. Burton employs the genre of the medical treatise for a Menippean satire on the vices and follies —the real and symbolic madness—of all sorts and conditions of men, mixing physical and spiritual remedies, and medical and stoical and Christian consolatories. Browne converts the antiquarian treatise into a vehicle for a meditation on death and the brevity and vanity of earthly glories.

Although the Reformation and Counter-Reformation may have transformed Renaissance society, one would be reluctant to regard them as the Pillars of Hercules that mark its utmost limits—the spiritual termini of a secularized and "gentilizing" age. For every *dévot* who despised Ethnic learning and art as worldly vanities, there were others (no less pious) who cultivated them as ends in themselves or as means to ethical or professional, political or ecclesiastical ends. Though certain partisans of the Reformation might denounce stageplays, others would compose Latin or vernacular dramas as instruments of political or religious propaganda or for academic exercise and instruction. If some reformers condemned

The Lamb and the Elephant

the arts and sciences as vain wisdom, and the pursuit of natural philosophy as idle curiosity, others encouraged scientific experiment for its utilitarian bent. Though the Counter-Reformation censured Patrizi and silenced Galileo, it did not succeed in checking the development of the new science and the substitution of mathematical, mechanical, and quantitative approaches to physics in place of the older qualitative concepts. Though it might endeavor to subject the arts of design to the principles and ends of the faith, it could apply the spur as well as the bit. The extension of an earlier Renaissance tradition—divine poetry, adapting the forms of classical genres to Biblical subject matter—owed much to the stimulus of both movements. Even though these movements tended to divide Europe, and with it the international community of men of humane letters, to split nations and universities, and in certain instances to enhance (paradoxically) the skepticism of learned men, they continued to support the traditional ends of humanist pedagogy, to educate classicists, to train Ciceronian (and anti-Ciceronian) writers and speakers. English writers still managed to imitate or adapt Italian models. Both armed camps of the Church Militant held similar views on the relationship of humane letters to theology, and literary developments (sacred or secular) often followed similar patterns.

The Reformation and Counter-Reformation may have heightened the tension between classical and Christian traditions, which Renaissance humanists had sometimes found embarrassing or had politely ignored; but this represented the renewal of an old conflict rather than a new development. Ever since the patristic age, "Hellenism" and "Christianism" (to employ Budé's phrase) had coexisted, like incompatible but indispensable marital partners, in an indissoluble but often quarrelsome wedlock. There was little doubt as to where the sovereignty resided; it belonged to Sophia, the revealed wisdom of the Scriptures. Nevertheless, the learning of the Ethnics was necessary for understanding, explaining, and for following the Scriptures; in order to teach and persuade and in order to govern, Sophia must employ the arts and sciences of Apollo Musagetes. Though medieval and Renaissance writers and artists might attempt to reconcile and synthesize the two traditions, they were conscious of the differences between them and the difficulty of combining the sacred and the profane. This did not deter Protestant poets like Spenser and Milton or post-Tridentine Catholic writers and artists from using pagan mythological imagery even in treating sacred themes. Seventeenth-century preachers in England and on the Continent continued to employ the devices of classical rhetoric and to imitate the styles of Cicero or Seneca. In the late Renaissance, as in the early Renaissance, the tension between poetry and theology, like the earlier quarrel between rhetoric and logic or poetry and philosophy and the later quarrel between poetry and science, was essentially an argument between rival disciplines, another phase of the *querelle des arts*.

If the hierarchy of arts and sciences could have remained compartmentalized and static—each content with its own subject matter, its own authorities, its own rules and principles, its own instruments and ends, and its just position in the scale of learning according to its degree of certitude, the nobility of its subject, and its relation to the ends of the architectonic and ruling science of theology—the chances of a successful revolt, a *trahison des clercs* against the established order or the development of a radical skepticism, would have seemed slight. Nevertheless, though the ideal of such a hierarchy existed—from the age of Plato and Aristotle throughout the Middle Ages and the Renaissance—it never achieved absolute stability. As in the chain of command at some military headquarters or a Byzantine court, there was frequent reorganization, continual jockeying for positions of greater honor and authority. The interrelationships of logic and rhetoric and poetics, the connections between poetry and theology, the relation of the arts of design to the trivium and quadrivium were subject to frequent redefinition; and the arts and sciences themselves developed and changed through new and sometimes unconventional interactions. Renaissance artists borrowed from optics and anatomy and geometry; physicians studied Hermetic philosophy and alchemy; late-Renaissance scientists applied the principles of mathematics and mechanics to physics; seventeenth-century philosophers endeavored to follow the methods of the geometrist; theologians interpreted the Scriptures through the meth-

The Lamb and the Elephant

ods of humanist philology and historiography and Ramist logic; empiricists invoked the aid of the lowly mechanical arts to reorganize the principles and ends of natural philosophy. In the late Renaissance the traditional boundaries between the learned disciplines (never definitively established) were breaking down, their conventional authorities challenged, and their principles and methods questioned and subjected to radical revision.

Rival authorities tend to undermine the principle of authority. Rival claims to certitude encourage doubt. Conflicting rhetorical appeals may arouse distrust of rhetoric. By the end of the sixteenth century, the variety of opinions among the classical philosophical schools (most of them, with the notable exception of the skeptics, professing to be more than mere opinions, and to teach certainties rather than probabilities) had left several influential thinkers (Bacon and Montaigne and Telesio among them)[10] acutely dissatisfied with the contemporary state of knowledge, especially in natural philosophy and metaphysics, the sciences of the visible and invisible worlds. The conflicting claims of rival churches, in turn, forced the crisis of choice upon the individual conscience; where one could not rely on external authority, he must "doubt wisely," judiciously circumambulating the "cragged, and steep" hill of Truth:[11]

> ... hee that will
> Reach her, about must, and about must goe;
> And what the hills suddennes resists, winne so. . . .

These contradictions, based on the authority of revealed theology, encouraged reliance on natural theology or the less arduous alternatives of skepticism and disbelief.

In this uncertain and unpredictable climate—a climate of opinions, not of certitudes—the traditional role of rhetoric was, to a certain extent, compromised. It could adorn and embellish Truth, but it could not discover her. Unlike logic, which aimed at certainties through infallible syllogistic demonstrations, it derived its arguments from probabilities or apparent probabilities. It could be useful in persuading the multitude to follow Truth—once she had been discovered and uncaverned—but it could not assist the philosopher to

End of the Renaissance

find her out and to exantlate her. This task—the first and primary labor of the intellectual speleologist—devolved upon the logician; and he must first find a reliable spade—an appropriate instrument or *organon*.[12]

NOTES

[1]Ernst Robert Curtius, *European Literature and the Latin Middle Ages*, trans. Willard R. Trask (New York and Evanston, 1953), pp. 586-87.

[2]Curtius, p. 587.

[3]Douglas Bush, *English Literature in the Earlier Seventeenth Century, 1600-1660* (Oxford, 1945), pp. 1-3.

[4]Aristotle, *On the Art of Poetry*, trans. Ingram Bywater (Oxford, 1951), pp. 19, 29-31.

[5]Cf. Curtius, pp. 251-55, 588-93. Attempts to differentiate Renaissance from post-Renaissance society in terms of personal or psychological qualities—subjectivism, individualism, and the like—have sometimes yielded contradictory results. Where students of mannerst or baroque art and literature have emphasized subjectivity of presentation and individuality of style, the meditative tradition in Counter-Reformation devotion and the soul-searching and self-examination of Protestant piety, the development of biography and autobiography and the personal essay, Cochrane argues that in late sixteenth-century Florence, "the art of introspection," which "Petrarch had learned from Augustine and had passed on to all his successors down to the time of Benvenuto Cellini, had disappeared," along with "the very concept of the individual human being as something of value in itself alone, which Burckhardt a century ago and Federico Chabod more recently have defined as one of the chief characteristics of Quattrocento culture" (Eric Cochrane, ed., *The Late Italian Renaissance, 1525-1630* [New York and Evanston, 1970], p. 56). As an example he cites Salviati's eulogy of Benedetto Varchi, which reduces "the real man, living in a particular time and place" to "a collection of cellophane-wrapped 'virtues'. . . ." In actuality, Salviati's method, lauding his master in terms of five abstract qualities, follows the conventional schema of Renaissance eulogy, drawing (perhaps too obviously and too mechanically) on conventional topics of invention. It is a characteristic example of Renaissance humanistic rhetoric rather than a symptom of the end of the Renaissance. See also John Hoyles, *The Waning of the Renaissance, 1640-1740: Studies in the Thought and Poetry of Henry More, John Norris and Isaac Watts* (The Hague, 1971).

In an essay on Paolo Sarpi, William Bouwsma notes two different aspects of "the Renaissance mentality"—a tendency to "liberation and bold adventures of the mind" and a "profound skepticism concerning the limits of the human understanding and a resignation to man's imprisonment in the chaotic immediacy of direct experience" (Cochrane, p. 368). In his opinion, Sarpi's position was a "natural development of the Renaissance emphasis on particular, concrete experience and of its rejection of all-embracing intellectual systems created by men."

Herbert Read, *Icon and Idea* (New York, 1965), pp. 114-15, observes that "there are a few insignificant self-portraits in medieval art, but it is not until we reach Van Eyck and Fouquet that self-portraits with any psychological penetration begin to appear, and then they come thick and fast throughout the Renaissance period." Most of these self-portraits "present only an outer facet of the inner reality," but "with Rembrandt begins an attempt to get below the mask, to render an inner subjective state irrespective of fidelity to outward appearances."

[6]Peter Gay, *The Enlightenment: An Interpretation* (New York, 1966), pp. 98-118, 125, 162-63, 209, 256-69, 321. Gay suggests that "the Renaissance could not take antiquity as casually as the Enlightenment would take it: precisely because it had to be wrested from medieval hands, it remained problematic; many of the Humanists therefore found their true eighteenth-century heirs not in the philosophes but in their opponents, the *érudits*." Moreover, "with few exceptions the Humanists remained within the Christian fold," whereas the philosophes tended to use antiquity as "a well-stocked arsenal to be rifled at will" in their criticism of the contemporary church and state (Gay, pp. 125, 258-69). For Gay, the "four centuries between 1300 and 1700 are the prehistory of the Enlightenment"—centuries that "supplied the Enlightenment with its image of the past, both pagan and Christian, its vocabulary, its philosophical method, and much of its program" (p. 256). Though Gay employs the term "pagan" in a special sense, referring "not to sensuality but to the affinity of the Enlightenment to classical thought" (p. 9), he tends at times to overemphasize this facet of the age, just as an earlier generation of historians frequently exaggerated the "paganism" of the Renaissance. His picture of the age is truer for French than for British writers, and more applicable to Hume and Gibbon than to Swift or Samuel Johnson. This emphasis on the "pagan" aspects of the Enlightenment, though valid for many authors of the period, is less appropriate for others; to fit these into his frame of reference he must resort to oxymoron or paradox: "pagan Christianity," "the Christian component."

Walter Jackson Bate, *From Classic to Romantic: Premises of Taste in Eighteenth-Century England* (New York, 1961), regards the Enlightenment ("a period which extends roughly from the middle of the seventeenth century through the close of the eighteenth") as a "transitional meeting-ground between two dominant epochs of modern thinking." Bate also emphasizes the continuity between Renaissance humanistic values—both ethical and literary—and neoclassical canons of taste (p. 102): "The earlier portion of the Enlightenment marks the final subsiding of the European Renaissance: it comprises the consolidation and in some respects the extreme development of the values it inherited." Like Vico at the turn of the century, neoclassical critics in England and France frequently deplored the neglect of moral knowledge for the scientific examination of external nature (pp. 3-4, 58). Like Renaissance theorists, they argued that the poet and artist should imitate an idealized nature rather than particular models (pp. 10, 21, 80) stressing order and symmetry, decorum and probability, and the importance of judgment as well as invention, reason and the rules of art as well as imagination (pp. 11-92). Dugald Stewart's assertion that, since "there are defects and redundancies" in every natural scene, Milton "would not copy his Eden from any one scene, but would select from each" (p. 117), exercising his taste and his "power of Abstraction," recalls cinquecento and seicento theories of ideal and selective imitation and their accounts of the method followed by Zeuxis. See also Douglas Bush, *The Renaissance and English Humanism* (Toronto, 1939).

[7]In Curtius' opinion (p. 594), "Italy enjoyed the indisputed literary leadership of Europe until about 1530," when it was "supplanted by Spain until about 1650." French culture, dominant for another century, produced the English "Augustan Age." In 1762 Richard Hurd could complain that "French criticism has carried it before the Italian, with the rest of Europe," and "our obsequious and overmodest critics were run down by their authority" and "taste of Letters. . . ." Gay observes (p. 10) that

in the age of the Enlightenment "Paris was the headquarters and French the lingua franca of European intellectuals, and philosophes of all nations were the declared disciples of French writers."

[8] E. H. Gombrich, *Norm and Form: Studies in the Art of the Renaissance* (London, 1966), p. 84.

[9] Cf. J. E. Spingarn, *A History of Literary Criticism in the Renaissance*, 2d ed. (New York, 1954), p. 245, on the transmission of the "tradition of Scaliger" through the Dutch scholars Heinsius and Vossius and its influence on French tragedy and criticism. Spingarn observes (p. 246) that "while French literature had already during the sixteenth century taken from the Italian Renaissance its respect for antiquity and its admiration for classical mythology, the seventeenth century owed to Italy its definitive conception of the theory of poetry, and especially certain rigid structural laws for tragedy and epic." See also Daniel Heinsius, *On Plot in Tragedy*, trans. Paul R. Sellin and John J. McManmon (Northridge, Calif., 1971), pp. xiii-xix.

[10] Cf. Virgil K. Whitaker, "Bacon's Doctrine of Forms: A Study of Seventeenth-Century Eclecticism," *HLQ* 33 (1970), 209-16. For Renaissance skepticism, see Don Cameron Allen, *Doubts Boundless Sea: Skepticism and Faith in the Renaissance* (Baltimore, 1964); Margaret L. Wiley, *The Subtle Knot: Creative Skepticism in Seventeenth-Century England* (London, 1952); Louis I. Bredvold, *The Intellectual Milieu of John Dryden* (Ann Arbor, Mich., 1934).

For the epistemological crisis of the late sixteenth and seventeenth centuries, and the search for more effective methods in philosophy and the natural sciences, see Basil Willey, *The Seventeenth-Century Background* (Garden City, N.Y., 1953); idem, *The Eighteenth-Century Background* (Boston, 1961); C. M. Coffin, *John Donne and the New Philosophy* (New York, 1958); Jason A. Saunders, *Justus Lipsius: The Philosophy of Renaissance Stoicism* (New York, 1955); William A. Sessions, ed., *The Legacy of Francis Bacon, Studies in the Literary Imagination*, vol. 4, no. 1 (1971); Marie Boas, *The Scientific Renaissance, 1450-1630* (New York, 1962); A. Rupert Hall, *The Scientific Revolution, 1500-1800*, 2d ed. (Boston, 1966); Herbert Butterfield, *The Origins of Modern Science*, rev. ed. (New York, 1965); Hugh F. Kearney, *Origins of the Scientific Revolution* (New York, 1964); Andrew G. Van Melsen, *From Atomos to Atom* (New York, 1960); Alexander Koyré, *From the Closed World to the Infinite Universe* (New York, Evanston, and London, 1958); Marjorie Hope Nicolson, *Science and Imagination* (Ithaca, 1962); idem, *The Breaking of the Circle* (New York, 1962); Victor Harris, *All Coherence Gone* (Chicago, 1949); W. J. Ong, *Ramus, Method, and the Decay of the Dialogue* (Cambridge, Mass., 1958); F. H. Anderson, *The Philosophy of Francis Bacon* (Chicago, 1948); C. D. Broad, *The Philosophy of Francis Bacon* (Cambridge, 1926).

[11] Charles M. Coffin, ed., *The Complete Poetry and Selected Prose of John Donne*, Modern Library (New York, 1952), pp. 97-98.

[12] The interrelationships between literary style and epistemological methods in the seventeenth century will receive more detailed examination in a later study.

EPILOGUE

Renaissance moral allegory and exemplum[1] cannot be reduced to a single formula, either in theory or in practice. There are too many variables: different schemes of classification for symbolic levels or senses, the equivocal and polysemous character of the symbols themselves, the complexity of the iconographical and literary traditions from which the poet derived his images and themes, and the diverse contexts—varying not only with subject and genre but also with his own tastes and those of his audience—in which he introduced and adapted traditional motifs. Not only were the symbols themselves ambiguous, frequently capable of both pejorative and favorable interpretations; but the abstract concepts they signified—Nature, Fortune, Virtue, and the like—might involve terms just as equivocal, variously defined, and subject to logical distinctions in meaning and in application. Like their iconographical attributes, the meanings of Fortune, Time, and Occasion overlap. In different contexts their significance may be almost identical or diverse. Time may appear as the moving image of eternity and Fortune as the agent of divine providence, but they may also be conceived as blind and capricious forces, ruled by chance or by indifferent fate. They may be represented as aids to valorous enterprises or as foes to virtuous actions. Occasion may serve as an exhortation to sensual pleasures or to wealth and power, to heroic activity or to patient dependence on divine dispensation. Nature may be conceived in physical or moral terms, lauded or condemned in accordance with either classical or Pauline tradition, represented as the vicar of deity or contrasted with divine revelation and grace—depicted as deformed by sin or as the image of the Creator and the shadow of heaven. The visible forms of nature and the shapes of art may be extolled as copies of intelligible and celestial essences and a means of reascent to the transcendental world, but they may also be depreciated as terrestrial and temporal goods, antithetical to celestial and eternal values, and perverting the appetite from true to false felicity.

Usually such differences of emphasis result from different rhetorical purposes or diverse poetic contexts, rather than from diverse philosophical systems or contrasting world-views. Despite the diver-

Epilogue

sity of Renaissance philosophy and theology, most writers of the period accepted the same ethical system (predominantly Peripatetic, with Platonic and Stoic accretions) and the same moral theology. On the whole, both their symbolic vocabulary and the meanings with which they invested it were conventional. Their variations usually resulted rather from the variety inherent within the tradition itself—or from their own endeavors to adapt a conventional symbol to specific contexts in their own poetic fables or to reconcile the demands of tradition and novelty, probability and surprise, by combining conventional images into a new and composite image capable of evoking the tradition in its complexity—than from different philosophical systems. Though technical disparities in philosophical classification—divergences between Platonic and Aristotelian psychology, between alternative definitions of virtue as a mean between two extremes and as the contrary of a single vice, or divergences between Stoic and Peripatetic conceptions of the passions—might condition a writer's treatment of traditional symbols, they rarely resulted in a radical transformation of the latter.

The most notable exceptions occur in Renaissance hieroglyphic and Hermetic literature, both of which significantly enlarged the writer's thesaurus of symbols but frequently tended to absorb conventional symbols and doctrines as well. Though Valeriano's treatise on hieroglyphics is based on Horapollo's *Hieroglyphica*, he draws extensively on mythography and on symbolic interpretations of natural history. Like Berchorius, he moralizes the iconographical attributes of pagan divinities and the phenomena of nature. His work belongs no less to the tradition of allegorized natural history and mythography than to the tradition of Renaissance hieroglyphics. In an age when the conventional symbols were rapidly becoming trite and hackneyed, the Hermetic writers managed to retain the aura of mystery traditionally associated with allegory through drawing on the vocabulary of the occult arts and sciences—alchemy and astrology, natural magic and the Kabbalah—or through reinterpreting classical myths as allegorical expressions of their own doctrines. In Bruno's treatment of the Diana myth one may recognize a conscious adaptation of a classical symbol as the vehicle of his own philosophical doctrine, expressed through a fable of his own inven-

The Lamb and the Elephant

tion (the questing blind men rendered sightless by the magic of Circe) and combined with a conventional tribute to Queen Elizabeth. In philosophical or scientific works the allegorical mode might serve as defensive tactics in a war of ideas, a rhetorical smoke screen or camouflage to conceal the author's real opinions from the scrutiny of heresy hunters. It could also serve, however, merely as ornament. In the Preface to *The Great Instauration*, Bacon declares that he has not endeavored "either by triumphs of confutation . . . or even by the veil of obscurity, to invest these inventions of mine with any majesty. . . ." Not infrequently, however, the basic doctrines hidden under the veil of Hermetic or Kabbalistic symbols may be more conventional than they appear to be on the surface; under the exotic veneer one may detect commonplaces of mystical theology or of Christian regeneration and salvation.

In "following tradition," as Horace had advised them, Renaissance authors were frequently able to invest the same conventional symbols with diverse significances in different literary contexts without sacrificing the appearance of continuity with classical or contemporary mythographical tradition. That the same symbol might be employed for persuasion or dissuasion in a favorable or a pejorative context is not surprising in view of the prominence of rhetorical studies in contemporary grammar schools. Writers had been trained to argue both sides of a question, drawing their arguments pro and con from the same topics of invention or their contraries. Insofar as classical myth and legend had been allegorized to illustrate moral commonplaces, they could be useful to the rhetorician, though they would possess little or no value in logical demonstration. Thus in *Comus* the Elder Brother argues the invulnerability of chastity by moralizing the myths of Diana and Minerva. The Attendant Spirit, in turn, lends credibility to his account of Comus' sorceries by citing the "heav'nly" authority of ancient myths of Chimaeras and enchanted Isles. In *Areopagitica* Milton utilizes the myth of Isis and Osiris as an argument for liberty of the press. In his *Essays* Bacon cites the myth of Plutus to illustrate the nature of riches, the story of Hercules to describe Christian resolution, and the example of Ulysses as evidence that grave natures are "commonly loving hus-

Epilogue

bands." The Judgment of Paris exemplifies the sacrifice of riches and wisdom to amorous affection; Virgil's pedigree of Fame refers to "false news" as signs of troubles and seditions; and Jupiter's marriage to Metis designates the union of Sovereignty and Counsel.

Opponents might rebut such mythical arguments by citing other myths or exempla, drawn from the same *topos* or its contrary, or by interpreting the same myth in a different way (as theological disputants so frequently did in interpreting Scriptural metaphors and allegories). The poet might confirm or counter the myth or exemplum by comparing it with a Biblical parallel, as in the debate in the *Ecloga Theoduli*—where Alithia (Truth) juxtaposes examples drawn from sacred history to the mythical fables of Pseustis (Falsehood)—or as in Milton's references to the myths of Mulciber and Ophion and the Hesperides in *Paradise Lost*.

Professions of mystery and hidden moral or spiritual significance in Renaissance poetry are sometimes genuine, but they are often little more than a poetic convention and a rhetorical stance, like the poet's claim to divine furor and prophetic vision, his alternative promises to relate events never before narrated in verse or prose and to repeat faithfully the story of his legendary or imaginary authority, his expressions of personal grief or fear for the fate of his characters, and his hyperbolic similes or comparisons. Protestations of moral intent and ex post facto allegories are a response to contemporary theories of what poetry ought to be. Though they are sometimes sincere, they are frequently little more than conventional apologetic devices, forms of ethical proof or techniques for enhancing the gravity and authority of a work. Like contemporary artists who introduced erotic motifs into religious paintings and into exempla of temperance and chastity, or depicted the invisible beauty of virtue through seductive ladies, poets might express the hero's scrimmages with virtues and vices through images of sensual dalliance or martial combat. Whether, like the author of the Song of Solomon, they were consciously portraying the ecstasies of the soul through the pleasures of the senses or whether they were merely rationalizing delight under the pretense of moral utility and profit was a question their critics frequently raised but rarely answered successfully.

The Lamb and the Elephant

The critic should be on his guard against stereotypes or schematic frames of reference, whether these are based on twentieth-century psychology or on Renaissance and medieval poetic theory. While the former often tends to subordinate the principles of conscious composition to unconscious or unpremeditated processes of expression and projection, the latter is frequently too rigid, too abstract, or too ambiguous to serve as a completely reliable guide for interpreting a concrete work. Renaissance poets or critics sometimes differed in their interpretation of the same theoretical treatise or their application of its principles. Poetic fashions and conventions sometimes tended to acquire a momentum of their own and to become virtually autonomous; and attempts to reorient or reform them in accordance with classical example and precept often resulted in compromises that were neither consistent nor entirely successful. In medieval and Renaissance art or literature alike, there is frequently a marked discontinuity between practice and theory.

In theory, the moral office of the poet was well established in both medieval and Renaissance criticism. Horace had declared that "the man who mingles the useful with the sweet carries the day by charming his reader and at the same time instructing him."[2] Aristotle had stressed the ethical function of poetry, subordinating it to the "architectonic" discipline of politics; as Milton and many of his contemporaries interpreted the *Poetics*, tragedy could serve the ends of morality by reducing the passions "to just measure with a kind of delight, stirr'd up by reading or seeing those passions well imitated." The weight of classical authority supported the ethical orientation of poetry; and, despite a few dissenting voices,[3] this was the prevailing doctrine in the Renaissance as in the Middle Ages. In theory, the poet should "mix" the *utile* and the *dulce*. The precise formula for this concoction, however, and the proportions of delight and morality, remained vague. In practice poets usually possessed even greater freedom than the apothecary in the quantities and ingredients of their prescription. They did not possess an exact formula, and the twentieth-century scholar should be cautious in supplying one. In some instances the pill may be entirely confectioner's sugar; in other cases, medicinal wormwood thinly powdered with rhyme.

Epilogue

I.

In interpreting specific works of literature, neither the medievalist nor the Renaissance specialist can trust implicitly in the methodological assumptions and techniques that have proved valuable in other cases. The working hypotheses—the theories of genres and styles, the poet's relationship to classical and contemporary fashions, the categories of allegorical significance and the vocabulary of symbols—that have succeeded with one poem of the period may not be applicable to another poem even of the same genre and on the same theme. The rules of the genres, the imitation of the ancients, allegorical methods of interpretation and composition, and the significance of the same mythical or Biblical or natural symbols varied widely both in theory and practice, not only among different writers but sometimes in different works by the same poet. Renaissance critics frequently disagreed on the relevance of the classical authorities on poetics, on the interpretation of their texts, on the "laws" and principles of the literary kinds, on the comparative excellence of Greek and Latin poets or of ancients and moderns, and on their relative value as models for imitation.

Though the literary theories of the age possessed a common vocabulary—drawn from different and sometimes conflicting traditions—they did not possess a unified and universally accepted poetic doctrine. Moreover, Renaissance poets themselves differed significantly in the rigidity or freedom with which they attempted to follow classical or contemporary models or to observe the "rules" of Aristotle and Horace as they understood them. In practice, the principles of the genres were flexible. The majority of poets were not seeking the critical approbation of the learned, but the favor of courtly, bourgeois, or even popular audiences. Though certain poets might seek to convey moral instruction or religious and political propaganda, others attempted to add pleasure to profit, or endeavored merely to entertain. Some disregarded the allegorical method altogether or introduced occasional allegorical episodes; others composed entire poems as allegories or merely superimposed an allegorical interpretation retrospectively on a narrative originally conceived and executed as a literal fable.

The Lamb and the Elephant

In the light of such diversity both in theory and in practice, attempts to formulate a general idea of the period and its cultural ideals, its aesthetic principles and literary methods, may easily result in misleading stereotypes—oversimplifications like *"the* medieval mentality" or *"the* Renaissance mind," *"the* theory of the genres" or *"the* allegorical method." The diversity of Renaissance art and literature (like the subtlety of Bacon's "Nature") resists such facile generalizations. In spite of a tendency to overemphasize universal concepts—the *idea* of tragedy or epic or comedy, the genera of style, the classes of society, the categories of mankind, the forms of virtues and vices—or to treat the classics themselves less as unique individual works than as exemplary models of these abstract norms, Renaissance critics rarely reached agreement on the definition of these concepts; and in practice this emphasis on universal categories often prejudiced their interpretation and evaluation of particular works. When judged by such idealized paradigms, the poetry of the moderns appeared irregular and that of the ancients defective. With their multiple plots and heroes, their levity and their violations of probability and verisimilitude, the fashionable romance-epics of Boiardo and Ariosto failed to realize the "idea" of the heroic poem. Despite its greater regularity, Tasso's *Jerusalem Delivered* also missed the ideal form of the genre, and its admixture of romantic elements violated epic decorum. Homer's heroes fell short of heroic perfection. The manners of his characters were sometimes "low," and many of his minor *personae* were too base for epic dignity. Even Virgil was defective; inasmuch as Aeneas' piety was pagan rather than Christian, he could not be a *perfect* heroic exemplar. *Paradise Lost,* in turn, was censured for its tragic argument, its unfortunate ending, its neglect of the conventional martial subject matter, and the disproportion between human agents and "machining" persons.

The idealizing tendencies apparent in so much of the thought of the age might stimulate theoretical speculation, but they sometimes proved distinctly embarrassing in practice. Machiavelli recognized their irrelevance for practical politics, just as Bacon perceived their adverse effect on natural philosophy. Similarly, in literary criticism this emphasis on the universal could be a stumbling block, diverting attention from the unique characteristics of a particular work to its

Epilogue

generic attributes and overstressing its conformity or lack of conformity with the rules of its genre. Both in theory and in practice, the qualities of the individual work were often overshadowed by the properties of the ideal epic or comedy or tragedy.

For the twentieth-century scholar, these paradigms of literary genres are significant insofar as they may have conditioned a particular work by a particular poet. Nevertheless, he must realize their limitations. Though they were regarded as universals, they were by no means universal even in Renaissance theory; and in practice (as contemporary critics realized with misgivings) they were often ignored or else altered almost beyond recognition. However valuable they may be for the history of criticism, their utility for the interpretation of particular works is severely limited.

Attempts to impose our own generalizations concerning medieval or Renaissance literature—our own universals of Renaissance epic or tragedy, or baroque or mannerist style, or allegorical method—on specific poems are equally dangerous. Some of the more dubious interpretations of medieval and Renaissance poetry have resulted largely from the misapplication of universals (general conceptions about the period or its literature as a whole) to particular works. Such stereotypes are often useful, for they enable us to ascertain general patterns and trends. Yet essentially they are abstractions from concrete realities—convenient formulas for averages. They do not cover all particulars, nor, on the whole, do they entirely fit the particulars from which they have been abstracted. The green splotches on a map may permit the surveyor to suggest the general outlines of a wooded area, but they provide little assistance to a botanist in identifying the age and height and species of its trees.

Like generalizations about the medieval or Renaissance worldview, general statements about medieval or Renaissance aesthetics may prejudice or distort the interpretation of specific poems—partly because the art and the thought of both periods are too complex and diverse to be reduced to a single formula, partly because the majority of writers had never formulated a systematic *Weltanschauung* or coherent aesthetics. The immediate problems that they faced in composing a particular poem or a specific passage in a specific poem were of a different order and on a different scale. Most of these poets were concerned, not with the larger issues of the nature of the world or of art, but with considerations of theme and structure and style —invention, disposition, and elocution—problems of choosing and organizing the subject matter of a particular poem and communicating it, as effectively as possible, to a particular audience.

2.

The terminology that scholars are compelled to use in analyzing the Renaissance tradition and its relationship to medieval and classical thought and style is almost as vague as the words "classical," "medieval," and "Renaissance" themselves. Though we cannot dispense with terms like "Aristotelianism" and "Pyrrhonism," "scholasticism" and "humanism," "Platonism" and "Stoicism," "Hermeticism" and "Orphism," "Ciceronianism" and "anti-Ciceronianism," "neoclassicism" and "veneration for antiquity," their meaning often varies so widely in different contexts that they are apt to become nonsense-words. They are equivoques, and their very ambiguity is a reflection of the inconsistency and variety of Renaissance thought.

The Renaissance writer—metaphysician or moralist, theologian or natural historian, rhetorician or poet—was usually more eclectic than he realized or cared to acknowledge. Even though he might regard himself as a Platonist or an Aristotelian, a Pyrrhonist or a Stoic in thought, a follower of Cicero or Seneca in prose style, or an imitator of a particular classical author, he rarely relied on a single authority. His interpretation of one classical work was inevitably influenced by his understanding of others; his reading of early classical authors by late classical modern commentaries; and his interpretation of the classical tradition itself by the Judaeo-Christian tradition. As T. W. Baldwin[4] has observed, Renaissance conceptions of Greek and Latin tragedy and of Horatian and Aristotelian poetics were strongly conditioned by Donatus' remarks on Latin comedy. Similarly, as Marvin Herrick and Bernard Weinberg[5] have pointed out, cinquecento commentators read Aristotle's *Poetics* in the light of Horace's *Ars Poetica*. Renaissance Platonists or Aristotelians usually approached their master through commentaries that themselves reflected an eclectic tradition, and their interpretations were

Epilogue

often further biased by the attempt to harmonize the classical authors with one another or with Christian doctrine. Renaissance "schools" of thought were not only interdependent, but within the same "school" or tradition scholars disagreed in their interpretation of the same author and in their application of his doctrines and his logical or rhetorical or poetic methods to contemporary thought and letters.

The notions of "reverence for antiquity," the concept of "imitation," the definition of the literary genres and categories of style, and the theory and practice of allegory were likewise variable and ambiguous. In an age when the citation of authorities—Scriptural or classical, sacred or profane—was scarcely less important in philosophical and scientific controversies than in rhetorical arguments, it was convenient for writers to appeal to classical or Biblical precedent to justify the form, content, or style of their own compositions. According to their source of inspiration, the writings of the ancients constituted divine or human testimony, and might therefore serve as inartificial proofs in controversial arguments. In some instances, accordingly, a writer might find it expedient to underplay his own originality, emphasizing his conformity with classical or Biblical authority and presenting his own inventions rather as an innovation on established tradition, or a restoration of an older and more authoritative tradition, than as something altogether new and unprecedented. Fidelity to tradition and to ancient example was (as we have seen) a commonly recognized means of observing verisimilitude and decorum in narration, characterization, and description. In the Renaissance the force of tradition would be further enhanced by the quasi-legal authority ascribed to certain texts as rules or as models for poetics and rhetoric or for ethics and theology—potential guides and exemplars for both secular and religious compositions.

Discussions of Renaissance reverence for antiquity and imitation of classical models are apt to degenerate into meaningless verbal exercises once the critic passes from the analysis of particular works to large-scale generalizations. The historian must not only define precisely what he means by these terms in a specific context; he must also take into account the differences between medieval and post-Renaissance approaches to the classics and the wide divergences among Renaissance writers or artists themselves in their attitudes toward classical civilization.

The reconquest of antiquity was not, of course, uniquely a Renaissance ideal. At the end of the eighteenth century, as Joseph Wittreich points out, Blake could still aspire to "renew" the lost art of Greece.[6] A sincere though superficial Hellenism underlay the drawings of Flaxman, the statues of Hiram Powers, Goethe's dreams of Helen and classical Walpurga's nights, the plantation architecture of the Mississippi Valley, the classic gowns of revolutionary Paris, the replica of the Tower of the Winds in north Oxford, the provincial Parthenons and Hellenic municipalities scattered across the United States. Politically, the example of antiquity could serve as a symbol for democrats and despots alike, just as Jerusalem—the type of the Church Triumphant—had served the crusaders, expeditionary forces of the Church Militant. Marble togas adorned the statesmen in Westminster Abbey and the statues of Washington. Revolutionary Frenchmen and Americans masqueraded as Roman senators or Athenian democrats. Napoleon, consul and emperor, erected monuments of merit after the high Roman fashion—triumphal column and obelisk and arch. For more than one generation of Europeans the emancipation of Hellas was the visible symbol of the triumph of democracy, the goal of a classical crusade.

This cultivation of the *maniera antica*, in politics as in art, was partly a survival of Renaissance attitudes, partly an extension of reverence for Latin antiquity to that of Greece. From the seventeenth century onwards one encounters, in fact, a series of attempts to "reform" art or literature by a conscious revival or renewal of classical and/or Renaissance traditions. Baroque critics of mannerist art, and subsequently neoclassical critics of baroque, frequently demand a return to the principles of the High Renaissance. The richness and variety—and the ambiguity—of the Renaissance tradition is apparent in the use that both neoclassical and anticlassicist, academic and antiacademic artists and writers could make of it. Early cinquecento mannerists and nineteenth-century Pre-Raphaelites consciously sought inspiration from early Renaissance or "northern" painters. Michelangelo not only stimulated the development of mannerism but influenced painters as diverse as Reynolds and Blake.

Epilogue

Both neoclassical and romantic poets were often indebted to Renaissance epic and drama, and twentieth-century poetry has been strongly influenced by the "metaphysical' revival.

The problem of "periodization"—defining and delimiting the Renaissance, establishing *termini a quo* and *ad quem*, or differentiating and labeling its phases—is no less difficult for the end of the period than for its beginning. In both cases the problem is sometimes enhanced by a tendency to blur the distinctions between the Renaissance as a period, a society, a movement, and a style (or styles). The Italian Renaissance, according to different authorities, was over by 1530, by 1580, by 1600, or as late as 1633. In the opinion of other scholars, it never ended at all; instead, there was a "transfer of creative energies from one field of activity to another."[7]

As these estimates are based on different criteria and different aspects of Renaissance culture—economics and politics, religion and philosophy, poetry and historiography, music and painting—they are not necessarily inconsistent, and it is quite possible that all of them are partially, relatively, and perhaps equally true. Though one is skeptical of attempts to impose an exact chronology on cultural developments, dating intellectual movements and artistic styles by years or decades like pottery fragments, such estimates may be useful as long as one is aware of their relative and conditional character. What is true of one aspect of Renaissance civilization at a particular place and time may not be true of the period as a whole, and to ignore the inevitable qualifying conditions and circumstances is to commit the easiest of logical errors—the fallacy of *secundum quid*. Here again we should recall Sarton's warning against facile generalizations about the Renaissance as a whole and his insistence on the need for precise discussion of specific aspects of the period.

It may also be true—but again in a highly restricted sense—that the Renaissance never ended, that historians have mistaken change and development for decadence, and that efforts to locate the "end" of the period are merely a quest for the tail of the chimera. The "progress" of the arts and sciences, so gloriously acclaimed by Renaissance writers as the principal merit of their age, has not lost its momentum; the influence of Renaissance ideas and styles is with us still; the achievements of the Enlightenment and those of the

The Lamb and the Elephant

Romantics were, in large part, developments based on the achievements of the Italian Renaissance. This view does not really solve the problem of periodization, however; it merely compels us to revise our terminology and invent another name for the period of the quattrocento and cinquecento. It tends, moreover, to define the Renaissance "period" in terms of the influence and diffusion of the Renaissance "tradition." These terms do not have the same meaning, and to equate them is rather like equating classical civilization with the classical tradition. To broaden one's terminology to this extent is to render it virtually meaningless.

Notes

[1] For rhetorical theories concerning the use of exempla at the beginning or in the midst of a composition, see *(inter alia)* John of Garland, *Poetria Nova;* Faral, *Les arts poétiques;* Aristotle's *Rhetoric;* Cicero, *De Inventione; Rhetorica ad Herennium.*

[2] Allan H. Gilbert, ed., *Literary Criticism: Plato to Dryden* (Detroit, 1962), p. 139.

[3] Cf. Castelvetro, "poetry has been discovered solely to delight and to recreate...."; Gilbert, p. 307. Mazzoni, in turn, distinguishes between three modes of poetry, according to the end of imitation, delight, and delighting "profitably"; Gilbert, pp. 384-85. In the first two modes, poetry "is not ruled or governed by the civil faculty."

[4] T. W. Baldwin, *Shakspere's Five-Act Structure* (Urbana, Ill., 1947).

[5] Marvin T. Herrick, *The Fusion of Horatian and Aristotelian Criticism in the Italian Renaissance* (New York, 1961); Bernard Weinberg, "From Aristotle to Pseudo-Aristotle," in Elder Olson, ed., *Aristotle's "Poetics" and English Literature* (Chicago and London, 1965), pp. 192-200.

[6] Joseph Anthony Wittreich, Jr., "Domes of Mental Pleasure: Blake's Epics and Hayley's Epic Theory," *SP* 69 (1972), p. 108.

[7] Eric Cochrane, ed., *The Late Italian Renaissance, 1525-1630* (New York and Evanston, 1970), p. 17; cf. pp. 11-18, 43-44, 56, 73, 93-105, 152, 271-74, 358-85.

INDEX

Abelard, Peter, 175
Accademia della Crusca, 59
Accommodation, principle of, xxxiv, 92-93, 179
Achilles: in Renaissance epic, 63
Action, as object of imitation, xxi, xxv, xxxix, xl, 60, 115, 162-63, 191, 202, 207. *See also* Mimesis
Adonis: in Renaissance epic, 63
Aeneas: in Renaissance epic, 63
Aeschylus, xxvi, 86
Affective efficacy of poetry, xl. *See also* Passions; Catharsis; Rhetoric
Agricola, Rudolph, 21, 51, 169, 205
Agucchi, Giovanni Battista, 171-72
Alain de Lille, xxxviii, 121-23, 144
Alamanni, Luigi, 57, 61-65
Alberti, Leon Battista, 43, 52, 156-59, 177-79, 183, 197, 203-04, 212
Albertus Magnus, St., 144
Alchemy, xxxvi, 75
Allegory, medieval and Renaissance: scholarship on, 98-99
Amadis of Gaul, 62, 80
Anagogy, xxv, xxix, xxxv, 75
Analogy, xvii, xxv, xxxv, xxxvii, 156-57, 193, 209-10. *See also* Correspondences; Metaphor
Anatomy, 35-36, 49, 149, 173, 196
Ancients and moderns controversy, 88, 159, 218-19, 237
Andrew of St. Victor, 76
Anthropology, xxiii
Anti-Ciceronianism, 191, 208, 219, 226. *See also* Cicero and Ciceronianism; Style; Seneca
Anticlassicism, 173. *See also* Mannerism
Antiquity of poetry and allied arts, as rhetorical *topos*, xix-xx. *See also* Apologetics
Antiquity, Renaissance attitudes toward, 25-51
Anti-Renaissance and Counter-Renaissance, 8
Antithesis, 134-35, 144-45, 178, 208-12. *See also* Contraries
Apelles, 35
Aphorism, 216, 225
Apocalypse, 110
Apologetics, xviii-xx, 10, 51, 59, 83, 96, 103, 127, 130, 150, 154, 157, 174, 234-35

Aquinas, Thomas, St., xl, 14, 132, 142
Archaism, 38-41, 55, 80-81
Archetype, xvi, 152, 170-72, 178, 196-97. *See also* Universals; Intelligibilia; Invisibilia
Archias, xviii
Architecture, 23, 50, 53, 59, 132, 161, 179, 203
Areopagus, 69
Argonauts, 62-63
Argument, xxii, xxiii, xxxi, xxxvii, 28, 32-34, 40, 58-65, 72-73, 82-83, 92-94, 111, 113, 126, 150, 154-57, 162, 180-81, 184, 203, 212, 228, 234-35, 238; *argumentum* as distinct literary genre, 108, 140-41.
Ariosto, Ludovico, xv, xxi, xxx, 40, 44, 57, 59, 61-62, 65, 74, 85, 100-02, 109-16, 119-21, 138, 142, 145
Aristotle and Aristotelianism, xviii, xxii, xxv, xxx, xxxiv, xlvi, 12-13, 16, 23, 29, 40-41, 59-61, 66, 71, 84-85, 92-93, 98, 109, 113-15, 117, 124, 136, 139, 142, 151-56, 161, 164-65, 169-73, 175, 178-79, 181-86, 191-95, 205-11, 214-15, 219, 224, 236-37, 240, 244
Arthur, king of Britain, xxx, 40, 62-63, 80, 85, 108-09, 140
Arts, rivalry of (*querelle des arts*), 218
Ascham, Roger, 176
Astronomy and astrology, xxxvi, xliv-xlv, 78, 110, 134-35
Astyanax: in Renaissance epic, 63, 78. *See also* Trojan myth in the Renaissance
Asyndeton, 208. *See also* Style
Atkins, J.W.H., 149, 167-68
Audience, xvii, xxv, xxviii, xxxii, xli, 31, 37, 46, 50, 53, 96, 107, 141, 147, 163, 176-79, 199, 232, 237, 240. *See also* Rhetoric
Augustine, St., Bishop of Hippo, xvi, xli, xliv-xlv, 77, 125, 134-35, 142-45, 169-70, 200-01, 204, 212, 229
Authority, xxi, xxiii, 10, 13, 30-31, 36, 48-49, 60, 87, 105, 108-09, 205, 217-20, 227, 240-41
Averroes, 29, 136

Bacon, Francis, xv, xix, xlv, 10, 49, 68, 73, 78, 122, 125, 144, 202-03, 225, 228, 234

245

Index

Baïf, Jean Antoine de, 56
Baitello, Francesco, 64
Baldwin, T.W., 240
Barga, Pietro Angelio da, 64
Baroque, xli, 9, 148-49, 162-63, 166, 171, 174, 188-94, 209, 211-12, 216, 219-23, 229, 242
Bartolomeo da San Concordio, 133
Basini, Basinio, 63, 65
Bate, Walter Jackson, 230
Beast-fable, 137
Beauty, ideal, 170-71, 174-75, 178, 196
Being, chain of (scale of nature), xxxvi-xxxvii
Bellenden, John, 78
Belloni, Antonio, 64
Bellori, Giovanni Pietro, 151-52, 171-72
Bembo, Pietro, 52, 69
Benamati, Guido Ubaldo, 64
Berchorius, Petrus, 233
Bernard of Chartres, 20
Berni, Francesco, 57
Berti, Bernardino, 64
Bevilacqua, Vincent M., 51, 180, 204
Bible, xvi, xx-xxi, xxiv-xxv, xxxii, xxxvi, 23, 29, 40-41, 62-63, 71-72, 75-77, 81-82, 90-93, 104, 110, 120-21, 125, 133, 145, 174, 177, 194, 204, 207, 226-27, 235, 237, 241
Binyon, Laurence, 208
Blake, William, 242
Blank verse, 55-56
Blunt, Anthony, xlv, 104-05, 156, 177, 189, 197, 203, 212
Boccadiferro, Lodovico, 205
Boccaccio, Giovanni, xv-xviii, 20-21, 27-28, 44, 48, 58, 72, 77, 80, 83, 88, 93, 96, 127, 140-41, 150, 164, 184, 200-01
Boece, Hector, 78
Boehme, Jakob, xxxvi
Boethius, 82, 121-25
Boiardo, M.M., xxi, 57, 59, 62, 65, 74, 95, 109, 111, 116, 119, 138, 145, 238
Bolgar, R.R., 28, 31
Bolognetti, Francesco, 63
Bononome, Gioseffo, 100-01
Borromeo, Charles, St., xlv
Bos, Abbé du, 103
Bouwsma, William, 229
Bracciolini, Francesco, 64
Brinsley, John, 125
Browne, Sir Thomas, xxiv, 9-10, 68, 225
Bruni, Leonardo, 20, 23-24

Bruno, Giordano, 21, 73, 78, 233-34
Budé, Guillaume, 226
Bulgars, conversion of, 64
Bunyan, John, xxxv
Burckhardt, Jacob, 229
Burton, Robert, 225
Bush, Douglas, 213-14

Camoens, Luis de, 61-62, 78, 96
Campion, Thomas, 56
Carracci: family, 171-72; Lodovico Carracci, 105
Caraffa (Carrafa), Ferrante, 64
Caro, Annibale, 57
Cassirer, Ernst, xxiv
Castelvetro, Lodovico, 59, 179, 183, 201, 244
Castle, figurative, 108, 121, 131, 145
Cataneo, Pietro, xlv
Catharsis, xviii, 84, 96, 162-63, 173, 183, 236. See also Passions
Cellini, Benvenuto, 229
Cennini, Cennino, 150, 157-58, 177, 197, 200
Certitude, xxiv, xli, 114, 126, 150, 156-59, 189, 216-17, 224, 227-28
Chabod, Federico, 229
Chapman, George, 73, 142
Character: as object of imitation, xxi, xxxv, xxxix, 37, 53, 60, 81, 106, 115, 129, 163, 171-72, 176, 185-86, 202, 207, 238. See also Mimesis
Charlemagne: in Renaissance epic, 64, 80
Chaucer, Geoffrey, xxvi, xxxviii, 28, 40, 44-45, 55, 57-58, 80-82, 102, 106-10, 120-21, 128, 137-38, 144-45
Cheke, Sir John, 10
Chiabrera, Gabriello, 64
Chrétien de Troyes, 52
Chrysippus, xviii, xli, 14, 84
Cicero and Ciceronianism, xvii-xviii, xxii, xxxviii-xli, 9, 22, 29, 33, 66, 97, 123, 125-28, 140-43, 151, 159, 168-92, 172-73, 178-79, 191, 205-06, 211, 221, 226-27, 244
Cid, the (Ruy Díaz de Bivar), 80
Circe, 112-13, 119, 138, 233-34
Clarity: as attribute of style, xxx, 104-15, 192-95, 210. See also Obscurity
Clark, D.L., 168
Classicism, 25-51, 53-70, 176-77
Cleopatra: in Renaissance epic, 63
Clovis: in Renaissance epic, 64

246

Index

Cochrane, Eric, 229
Cognitive functions of poetry, xl
Colet, John, 168
Colish, Marcia L., 125, 142-43
Colonna, Francesco, 120, 138
Columbus, Christopher, 65
Commonplaces *(topoi)*, xix, xxii-xxiii, xxxvi, xliv, 9-10, 21, 23, 32-33, 52, 72, 100, 118, 125, 129, 131-36, 145. *See also* Argument; Invention; Rhetoric; Dialetic; Logic
Composition, techniques of, xxxiv, 16, 180-212
Conceit and concettismo, xviii, xxiv, xxxvii, 174, 180-84, 194-95, 206, 209-10, 216
Conceptualism, 152, 175
Constantine: in Renaissance epic, 64
Continuity of tradition, xv. *See also* Tradition; Innovation
Contraries, logical, xxxv, 15, 115, 129, 131, 134-35, 144-45, 194, 208, 212, 234-35. *See also* Antithesis; Logic; Rhetoric
Copernicus, Nicolaus, 21
Correspondences, xxxiv-xxxv, xliv-xlv, 71, 100, 156-57, 180, 193, 209-10. *See also* Analogy
Cornazzano, Antonio, 65
Corruption of arts, 17
Cosmology: and cosmic symbolism, xxxv, xliv-xlv, 144, 215-17, 220-21; cosmic epic, 129-35
Counter-Reformation, 8, 48, 205, 215, 220, 225-29
Crantor, xviii, 14, 84
Crashaw, Richard, 216, 222
Credibility: in verbal and visual arts, xl, 83, 89, 113-14, 117, 176, 201
Croce, Benedetto, 131
Croll, Morris W., 191-95, 208-09
Crusades, 64, 109, 112-13
Curtius, E.R., 206, 213, 230

Daniello, Bernardino, 98
Dante Alighieri, xv, xviii, xxvi-xxvii, xxxiv-xxxvi, 26, 55, 58, 60, 73-76, 80, 83, 85, 106-08, 113-14, 123, 129-36, 142-45, 221-22
Davenant, Sir William, xviii
David, son of Jesse: as epic hero, 63
Decorum, xx, xxii, 29, 36-37, 53, 59-61, 79-84, 97, 106, 117-18, 129, 134, 137-38, 154, 159-64, 176-77, 182-83, 192-93, 202, 208-09, 238, 241
Deductive logic, xxv, xxxviii, 152, 175
Delaying action, 113. *See also* Plot
Della Casa, Giovanni, 191
Demetrius Phalereus (pseudo-Demetrius), 208
Denores, Giason, 59
Design, 146-212. *See also* Disposition; Plot; Structure
Dialectic, xxv, 126-27, 152, 169, 173, 178, 185, 205-07. *See also* Logic
Dialogue, 224-25
Dionysius the Areopagite, 200
Disposition, xx, xxii, xxxiv, 42, 126, 146-212, 219, 240-41. *See also* Design; Organization; Plot; Structure
Divine poetry, xx, 62-63, 226
Dolce, Ludovico, 151, 170, 183, 204
Domenichino (Domenico Zampieri), 171
Donatus, xxxviii, 240
Donne, John, xxxi
Downham, George, 181
Drake, Sir Francis, 65
Drama, xxv, xxxiii, xxxvi, 44-45, 57-61, 82, 94, 207, 223-25, 240
Drant, Thomas, 56
Dream and dream-vision, xxv-xxvi, xxxviii, 29, 71-76, 106-10, 121-24, 128-29, 138, 144, 165
Drury, Elizabeth, xxxi
Dryden, John, 86-87, 201-02, 224
Du Bartas, Guillaume de Saluste, Sieur, 62
Du Bellay, Joachim, 55, 58, 69, 222
Dürer, Albrecht, 156, 180, 197
Dufresnoy, Charles, 172
Dunn, Catherine M., 51, 205-06
Durandus, Guglielmus, 102

Ecloga Theoduli, 235
Ecphrasis (description), 131
Education, xviii-xix, xli, 10, 16-17, 23, 31-34, 51-53, 72, 79, 110, 122-25, 143, 167-69, 174, 180-81, 194-95
Elizabeth, Queen of England, xix, xxxi, 40, 47, 66, 78, 225, 234
Elocution, xx. *See also* Style
Emblem, xxii, xxviii, xxxiii, xliii, 33, 46, 71, 144, 161, 180, 203
Empiricism, xix, 151, 154, 163, 208, 217, 225, 228

Index

Enargeia, xli, 163, 211
Enchantment: as literary motif, 112-15, 119, 165
Energeia, 163, 192, 195, 209-11
Enigma, xxi, xxiv, xxvi-xxviii, xxxviii, 71, 73, 110, 164, 195-96, 209-10. *See also* Hieroglyph
Enlightenment, 71, 217-18, 220-21, 230
Enthymeme, xl, 138, 194, 207
Entrelacement, xxx, 111, 113, 120. *See also* Plot; Romance
Epic, xxi, xxviii-xxix, 39-40, 53-70, 79-80, 84-96, 104, 107-17, 120-23, 135, 138-42, 145, 176-78, 182-83, 186, 191-94, 204, 231, 238-39
Epigraphy, 36
Epistemology, xxv, xli, 87, 142-43, 155-56, 174, 225, 231
Erasmus, Desiderius, 21, 33, 76, 168
Ercilla y Zúñiga, Alonso de, 64
Eschatology, 128-35
Este family, 62, 65
Esther: as epic heroine, 63
Ethics, xvi-xix, xxix-xxx, xxxvi-xxxvii, 27, 35, 39, 72, 84-85, 94, 112-15, 126-33, 136-40, 197, 205, 232-33
Etymology, xxxiii, 75
Euripides, xxvi, 86
Example (exemplum and exemplar), xvii, xxvii, xxix-xxxi, xxxiv, xxxix-xl, 17, 32, 41, 51, 53, 62, 66, 84, 89, 93-96, 99, 110-11, 115, 120-24, 128-31, 136-40, 145, 149, 170, 174, 232, 234-35, 238, 241, 244

Fabias, 206
Fairfax, Edward, 44
Fantastic vs. icastic imitation, xxxiii, 164, 171. *See also* Imitation; Mimesis
Félibien, André, 104
Felicity, xxi, 121, 123, 130, 136, 185, 232
Ficino, Marsilio, xlv, 48, 78, 151, 171
Fiction, xxx, xxxiii, xxxix, 14, 41, 71-74, 88, 92-93, 96, 107-08, 113, 130, 140-43, 150, 164, 179, 182-83, 184, 200-02, 233
Filelfo, Francesco, 65
Filelfo, Giovan Mario, 65
Final cause, xxi, xl
Fletcher, Giles, 89
Fletcher, Phineas, 85
Florilegia, xxii, 33
Fludd, Robert, 144

Forest, enchanted: as epic motif, 112-13, 138
Fornari, Simone, 74, 101, 116
Fowler, Alastair, xxxiv
Fracastoro, Girolamo, 78, 103, 170
Francini, Antonio, 173
Francis, of Assisi, St.: in Renaissance epic, 63
Friedländer, Walter, 105, 149, 189, 204

Gama, Vasco da, 62
Gambara, Lorenzo, 65
Garcilaso de la Vega, 69, 78
Garden, symbolic, 131, 138, 145
Gascoigne, George, 184, 201
Gathelus, 78
Gay, Peter, xxxvii, 221, 230-31
Geistesgeschichte, 187. *See also* History and historiography
Genesis, 120. *See also* Bible
Genres, literary: 23, 25, 29-30, 33, 35, 42, 44, 55, 58-61, 74-75, 79, 106-07, 153, 161-62, 176, 214-15, 226, 232, 237, 241; definition of, 146-179; theory of, xxxviii, xli
Geoffrey of Monmouth, 78, 108
Geography, 49
George, St., of Cappadocia, xxxiii, 62
Gestalt, 199
Ghiberti, Lorenzo, 23
Gilbert, Creighton, 204
Gilio da Fabriano, 105
Giorgi, Francesco, xliv
Giorgini, Giovanni, 65
Giraldi Cinzio, G.B., 60, 63
Godfrey of Boulogne, 64-65
Goethe, Johann Wolfgang von, 242
Gombrich, E.H., xxxviii, 179
Gongora y Argote, Luis de, 193, 216
Gonzaga, Francesco, 65
Gonzalo, Fernandez, 63, 65
Gosson, Stephen, xviii
Gower, John, 45
Gracián, Baltasar, 195, 209
Graziani, Girolamo, xv, 63-64, 73, 113-14
Gray, Hanna H., 205
Greek Anthology, 35
Gregory, the Great, St., xv-xvi
Guarini, Giovanni Battista, 59-60
Guercino (Giovanni Francesco Barbieri), 171

Index

Guillaume de Lorris, xxvi, 108, 120, 145

Hardison, O.B., Jr., 176
Harington, Sir John, 44, 11-12, 142. *See also* Ariosto
Harmony, xxxiv, xxxviii, xliv-xlv, 135, 156-57, 160-61, 171, 178-79, 197-99, 212
Harvey, Gabriel, xxxi, 33, 61, 69
Heckscher, William, 21
Heinsius, Daniel, 222-24, 231
Henry IV, King of France, 63
Heraclius: in Renaissance epic, 64
Herbert of Bosham, 76
Hercules, xxxi, 21, 63, 65, 101, 109, 116, 120-22, 140, 234
Hercules Gallicus, 159
Hermeticism, xxi, xxv, xxviii, 16, 46, 71, 87, 164, 233-34
Hero, xvii, xxix, xxx-xxxi, 39, 61-65, 80, 91-92, 102, 108-09, 113-17, 127, 138-40, 185, 238
Herrick, Marvin T., 240
Hesiod, 40, 131
Hexaemeral tradition, 56
Hierarchy, principle of, xix, xxxv, 212, 227
Hieroglyph, xx, xxiv, xxviii, 35, 71, 144, 193, 233. *See also* Emblem
History and historiography, xv, xix, xxiii, xxvii-xxix, xxxvii, 6-7, 18-24, 32-41, 45-46, 51, 61, 72-73, 76, 79-81, 92-96, 108-09, 124, 129-31, 140-41, 147, 164, 172, 176-77, 182-87, 201, 205, 213, 222, 228, 241
Holinshed, Raphael, 78
Homer, xv-xviii, xxx, xxxii, xli, 14, 41, 60-63, 72, 80, 84, 91, 112, 116, 124, 131, 140-42, 168, 170, 179, 182, 185, 211
Horace, xviii, xx, xxii, xxx, xxxviii, xli, 14, 23, 29-30, 37, 52, 57, 59, 66, 69-72, 84, 124, 138-39, 151-53, 170, 178, 181-82, 186, 195, 202, 221, 223, 236-37, 240
Horapollo, 233. *See also* Hieroglyph; Emblem
Hoskins, John, 205
Howard, Henry, Earl of Surrey, 57
Howell, W.S., 51, 205-06
Hughes, Merritt Y., 208
Huizinga, Jan, 7
Humanism, xix, 13-24, 31, 36-37, 43, 48-52, 67, 79-80, 83, 103, 122, 156, 174, 203, 205, 218-21, 226, 228-30

Icastic imitation. *See* Fantastic imitation
Iconology, xv-xvi, xxii, xxvii, xxxiii, xliii, 10, 22-23, 26, 33, 36-37, 46, 71-72, 76-78, 83, 102, 178, 180, 197, 223, 232
Ignatius, St.: in Renaissance epic, 63
Illusionism, xl, 151, 188, 198-99
Imagery, xxxix, xlii, xlv, 91, 93. *See also* Metaphor; Personification; Rhetoric
Imagination, xvi-xvii, xxvi, xxxiv, xxxviii, xlv, 71, 88, 98, 111, 114, 118, 121, 130, 132, 136-37, 149-50, 153-55, 157-58, 163, 171, 181, 201-02
Imitation (*mimesis*), 35, 60-61, 86, 89, 104. *See also* Mimesis
Imprese (devices), xxvi, xliii, 193, 209. *See also* Emblems
Individualism, 229
Inductive logic, xxv, xxix, xxxviii, 93, 128-29, 152, 175
Ingenium, xxii, 42, 149, 152-53, 156-57, 161, 167-68, 171, 173, 180-81, 195, 202, 209-10, 219, 241. *See also* Wit; Conceit; Invention
Innovation, xxi, xxviii, 3-23, 39, 42, 48, 50, 58, 60, 66, 78, 149, 219, 233
Inspiration, xxii, 150, 152-53, 156, 202, 235
Intelligibilia (distinguished from sensibilia), xvi-xvii, xxxiv, xxxix-xli, xlv-xlvi, 51-52, 126-37, 142-45, 152, 157, 164-65, 174-75, 196. *See also* Invisibilia; Universals; Archetypes
Introspection, 229
Invention, xx-xxiii, xxvii, 29, 32-33, 42-43, 72, 78, 88, 92, 97-98, 100, 106, 108, 118, 126, 133, 146-212, 217, 219, 229, 233-34, 240-41
Invisibilia (distinguished from visibilia), xvi-xvii, xxxiv, xxxviii, 51-52, 126-27, 130-31, 136, 142, 144, 152, 163-65, 174-75, 196, 199, 232, 235

Jean de Meung, xxvi, 108, 121, 145
Job, Book of, xvi, 62, 127
Joele, Luigi, 64
John, Don, of Austria, 64
John of Garland, 97, 244
John of Peckham, 23
John of Salisbury, 80
Johnson, Samuel, 86-95, 105, 117
Jones, R.F., 208
Jonson, Ben, 61, 153-54, 223

Index

Joseph, as epic hero, 63
Joseph Bekhor Shor, 76
Joseph of Exeter, 80, 103
Journey motif, 134-35
Judgment (distinguished from invention and from imagination), 149, 180-81, 202-06, 217
Judith: as epic heroine, 62-63

Kabbalah, 233-34

Lancelot, 63, 109
Landscape, symbolic, xliv, 58, 108
Langland, William, xxxv, 45
Learned poet (*poeta doctus*): ideal of, 197
Le Bossu, René, 104
Lee, Rensselaer, W., 103-04, 151, 169-70, 173, 203-04
Leonardo da Vinci, xliv, 49, 156-57, 189, 203
Lepanto, Battle of, 64
LeRoy, Loys, 21
Lewis, C.S., 123
Liberal arts, 124-25
Liburnio, Nicolò, 57
License, poetic, 154, 157-58
Life, images of: as pilgrimage, 121-22; as warfare, 121
Liturgy, xxxiv, 38, 77, 102
Logic, xvii, xxxviii, xlv, 15, 25, 29, 115, 124, 126-27, 134, 149, 160-61, 169, 181-82, 186, 205-06, 212, 227-29
Lomazzo, Giovanni Paolo, 150, 151, 157
Longinus, 153, 177-78, 195, 220
Louis, St., King of France: in Renaissance epic, 63
Lucan, 112
Lucian, 205
Lull, Ramon, 51

Machiavelli, Niccolò, 11, 44, 238
Macrobius, 123, 128, 140-41
Macrocosm-microcosm ratio, xxxv, 101, 156-57
Magic, xxxvi, xxxvii, xlv
Magnanimity, 115, 139
Mahomet II (the Great), Sultan of Turkey, 65
Mahon, Denis, 171-72
Malatesta, Sigismundo, 43, 65
Malherbe, François de, 55
Malmignati, Giulio, 65

Mancini, Giulio, 171
Manly, J. M., 110
Mannerism, xli, 9, 41, 148-67, 171-72, 178, 188-91, 210, 219, 220, 223, 229, 242
Mantuan (Baptista Spagnolo), 65
Marino, Giambattista, xv, 63, 220
Martianus Capella, 123-24, 144
Martz, Louis, xxxiv
Marvel (*meraviglia*) and the epic marvellous, xxi, xxviii, xxxviii, xl, 55, 84, 89, 95, 107-09, 113, 115, 120-21, 141-42, 148-51, 162, 165, 176, 186, 193, 195, 209, 211, 224, 233
Masque, 86, 119, 184
Mathematics, xxxv, xxxvi, 35-36, 49, 150-52, 155-59, 173, 177, 189-90, 197-98, 212, 217
Matthieu de Vendôme, 97
Maurice, Prince of Nassau, 63
Mazzeo, J.A., 125
Mazzoni, Jacopo, xviii, 59, 83, 96, 113, 152, 183, 201, 244
McKeon, Richard, 125, 169
McLaughlin, Mary Martin, 20
Medici, Cosimo de', 65
Medici, Hippolito de', 57
Medici, Lorenzo de', 65
Meditation, 155, 163, 174, 224-25
Meleager: in Renaissance epic, 63
Memory and mnemonics, xvi, 31, 132-33, 143-45, 167, 174, 176, 203, 206
Meretrix, 113
Metaphor, xxv, 73-76, 137, 144, 184, 192-95, 209-16, 219, 235
Metaphysical poets, 9, 42, 174, 193, 195, 215-16, 220-23, 243
Method and methodology, xvii, xix, 6, 13, 33, 72, 129, 144, 147-50, 153, 160-64, 187, 196, 199, 203, 217, 219, 225-28, 236-37
Michelangelo Buonarroti, 52, 105, 189
Middle Ages: Renaissance attitudes toward 25-51
Milton, John, xv-xxvi, xxix, xxxiii-xli, 9-10, 14-15, 21-23, 27, 30, 47-66, 74-96, 103, 112, 116, 119-27, 135, 138, 141-42, 150-54, 173-74, 179, 181-82, 191, 206-08, 220, 224, 227, 230, 234-38
Mimesis (imitation), xvi-xlvi, 31, 36-37, 42-43, 49-50, 58, 69-145, 148-59, 164-212, 226, 230, 236-37, 241, 244
Molanus, Joannes, 105
Montaigne, Michel Eyquem de, 228

Index

Montefeltro, Federico da, 65
More, Henry, 85
Movement: representation of, 158-59, 190-92, 224; symbolism of, 134-35
Music, xxxiv-xxxvi, xliv-xlv
Mussato, Albertino, 23
Myth and mythography, xv-xviii, xxii-xxvii, xxxi-xxxiii, xlii, xliv, 10, 23, 26-27, 33, 36, 41, 71-86, 93, 110, 118-19, 139-40, 178, 193, 197, 200, 223-27, 231-37

Natural philosophy, xxi, xxxvii, 27, 72, 217, 226-27, 233, 238
Nature: as object of imitation, xxi, xxvii, 60, 88, 150-55, 156-59, 164-65, 170-73, 176, 179, 188-89, 196-97, 198-205. *See also* Mimesis
Nelson, William, 102
Neoclassicism, 71, 79, 87, 139, 149, 154, 177, 215, 218-19, 222, 224, 242-43
Neo-Latin literature, 53-54, 62, 69
Neo-Platonism. *See* Plato and Platonism
Nicholas of Lyra, 76
Nobility (*honestas*): as *topos*, xix-xx, 14, 52, 126, 150, 227
Novum genus dicendi, 219. *See also* Anti-Ciceronianism; Seneca; Style
Number symbolism, xxxv, xliv-xlv, 99

Obscurity, as aesthetic principle, xxx, xxxii, 192-93, 200-09, 234. *See also* Clarity
Occultism, xxxvi, xlv, 71
Oliviero, Anton Francesco, 64
Optics, 43
Organization, 131
Ornament, 31
Origen, xvi
Origin of poetry and related arts, xix-xx
Ovid, xv, 72, 82-83, 118-19, 128

Paladins of France, 116
Palladio, Andrea, xlv
Panofsky, Erwin, xliv-xlv, 25-28, 37, 132, 170-73, 203-04, 211-12
Parable, 108, 127
Pascal, Blaise, 225
Passions: as object of imitation, xxi, 177-78, 183, 186, 202, 211, 233, 236. *See also* Mimesis; Catharsis

Pastoral, xxix, 44, 59
Patrizi, Francesco, 205
Patron: eulogy of, 65-66, 78, 139
Paul, St., xxv, 174
Periodization: problem of, 167, 213-31
Period styles, 187
Peripeteia, 185
Perregrini (Pelegrini), Matteo, 59, 209
Personification, xxv-xxviii, 75, 87-90, 95-96, 103, 105, 107, 117-19, 128, 131, 145, 209
Perspective, xxxiv, 23, 156, 188-89, 197-98
Petrarca, Francesco, xviii, 21, 23, 44, 64, 69, 80, 97, 222, 229
Phillips, Edward, 182-84
Philology, 16-17, 23, 31-33, 228
Philoponus, 182
Pico della Mirandola, Giovanni, 23, 78
Pigna, Giovanni Battista, 60, 102
Pino, Paolo, 204
Pirotti, Umberto, 205
Place: category of, 131; composition by, 143. *See also* Commonplaces; *Topoi*; Setting
Plato and Platonism, xvii, xxi, xxiv-xxviii, xxxiv, xli, xlvi, 16, 23, 41, 46, 85-86, 125-27, 139, 142, 151-57, 164, 169-78, 181, 185, 198, 206-09
Plautus, 60
Pleasure: as effect of verbal and visual arts, xxx, xl, 158, 178, 196, 235-37, 244; temptation of, 111-13, 119-20, 137-38, 235-37
Pliny, 151
Plot, xxx, 60, 84-85, 93, 95, 106, 110-15, 139, 153, 178, 182-87, 191-97, 204, 207, 238
Plotinus, 170
Plutarch, 83, 100
Poet: office of, xv-xlvi, 136, 236-37, 244
Pointed style, 181, 210, 212. *See also* Seneca; Style
Politics, xviii-xix, 27, 35, 39, 94, 186, 236
Pontormo, Jacopo da, 180
Pope, Alexander, 87-88, 104, 170
Porcellio (Pandoni, Giovanni Antonio de'), 65
Posner, Donald, 149
Precepts (rules of art): distinguished from example, 17, 50, 53, 59-61, 66, 138, 149, 153-54, 167-68, 174, 176, 197, 202, 218, 227, 237

251

Index

Probability, xxi, xxiv, xxx, xxxviii, 36-37, 71, 79-89, 93, 97, 103-07, 103-21, 124, 148-49, 151-55, 164-65, 171-86, 196-97, 206, 209, 228, 233
Proportion, xxxiv, xxxv, 10, 135, 150, 156-57, 171, 173, 190, 197, 212
Proverb, xxiii, xxxiii, 32-33, 195, 206-07, 210
Psalms, 208. *See also* Bible
Psychology, xxiii-xxxiv, xxxviii, 140
Puttenham, Richard, 201
Pythagoras and Pythagoreanism, xlv, 46, 156

Quadrivium, 227
Quarrel of arts, 218, 227
Quintilian, xxxix, 23, 149, 153, 167-69, 208, 211

Raleigh, Sir Walter, xviii, xxix, 66
Ramus, Petrus, 29, 126, 169, 181, 205-06
Raphael Sanzio, 171-72
Rashbaum, 76
Rashi, 76
Read, Herbert, 23, 132, 229-30
Reformation, 10-16, 40, 48, 215, 220, 225-29
Renaissance: definition of, 3-23, 167, 213-31
Res-verba, 22, 34, 51-52
Reuchlin, Johann, 48
Reynolds, Sir Joshua, 103, 181
Rhetoric: xvi-xix, xxxi, xxxiii, xxxvii-xlvi, 10-12, 14-31, 53, 71-77, 82-83, 89, 123-36, 140-212, 214, 223, 227-29, 234-35, 240-44; ends of, xvii, xl
Rhetorica ad Herennium, xxxviii-xxxix, 29, 97, 134, 140-44, 167, 175-76, 206, 244
Richard de Bury, 80
Rinaldo, 62
Ripa, Cesare, 71, 223
Robertson, D.W., Jr., 137
Rogers, Daniel, 69
Roland (Orlando), 62-63, 80, 100-02
Romance, xxi, xxviii-xxx, xliii, 37, 42, 45, 57-58, 60-64, 71-75, 80, 85, 102, 106-17, 120-22, 138-41, 145, 176, 182-83, 222, 238
Roncalli, Cristoforo, 172
Ronsard, Pierre de, 62, 78, 69, 96-97
Rosa, Salvatore, 172, 220
Ross, James Bruce, 20

Rubens, Peter Paul, 103
Rucellai, Giovanni, 57
Salviati, Lionardo, 229
Sannazaro, Jacopo, 62
Sansovino, Francesco, 97-98
Sarpi, Paolo, 229
Sarrochi, Margharita, 64
Sarton, George, 12, 16, 49, 243
Scaliger, J. C., 69, 170, 231
Scanderbeg, 64
Scholasticism, xviii, 12-17, 23, 42, 132, 174
Scipio Africanus, 64, 123
Scott, Geoffrey, 23, 50
Scotus, Duns, xli, 14
Self-portraiture, 229-30
Semproni, Giovanni Leone, 64
Seneca, 9, 23, 66, 219-24
Sentence structure, 160-61, 177-78, 191, 195, 208, 212, 216. *See also* Style
Sententiae, xxxiii
Setting, 108-09, 115, 129, 131, 133, 144-45
Seznec, Jean, 22-23
Sforza, Francesco, 65
Shakespeare, William, xliii, 45
Sidney, Sir Philip, xviii, xl, 40, 60, 69, 96, 150, 201
Signatures, xx, xxvi, xxxiv, 164. *See also* Correspondences; Hieroglyph
Singleton, Charles S., 134-35
Skepticism, 228-31
Smart, Alastair, 167
Smith, Hallett, 21, 142
Smith, James, 174
Smith, John, 87
Song of Songs, 73, 235. *See also* Bible
Sonnet, 221-22
Sophistic, 198
Spenser, Edmund, xv, xviii-xxi, xxvi, xxix-xxxiv, xli, 14, 40-45, 55-57, 61-65, 69, 78, 81, 85, 92, 111-17, 120-25, 138, 140, 145, 191, 227
Speroni, Sperone, 60, 69
Spingarn, J. E., 231
Spini, Giorgio, 205
Stanley, Thomas, 223
Stewart, Dugald, 230
Stigliani, Tommaso, 65
Structure, 53, 66, 106-07, 113, 115, 117, 130-36, 146-212, 224-25, 240. *See also* Disposition; Design; Plot; Organization

Index

Sturmius, Johannes, 176
Style: xxxiv, xxxviii, xl, 8-9, 16, 29-35, 40-47, 55, 60, 66-67, 106, 176-77, 203-09, 214-19, 222-23, 237, 240-41; definition of, 8-9, 146-79; studies of, 165-66
Subject-matter: in poetry and painting, xix, xxx, xxxiii, 23, 48, 53, 61-65, 69, 94, 106-07, 116-17, 147, 162, 176, 180-83, 204, 226-28, 238, 240
Sublime, the, 163, 177, 220. *See also* Longinus
Syllogism, 174, 185, 228

Tablet of Cebes, 131
Tacitus, 9, 219-20
Taille, Jacques de la, 56
Talon, Omer, 181
Tasso, Bernardo, 57, 62
Tasso, Torquato, xv, xviii, xxi, xxx, xl, 44, 55-65, 71, 73, 85, 96, 109, 112-19, 120-21, 138-40, 145, 164, 179-83, 191, 204-09, 221-22, 238
Tesauro, Emanuele, xliii, 194, 209-10
Testimony, xxiii, xli, 207, 241
Theme, xxii, 33, 180-212, 216
Theology, xvi, xviii-xxiii, xxviii, xxxiv, xli, 10, 14, 21, 27-29, 72, 75-76, 87-88, 104, 114-15, 118, 127, 164, 174, 196, 200-01, 227, 233-35
Thesis, 207
Thompson, Craig R., 21
Thought *(Dianoia)*: representation of, 163, 177, 186, 204-07, 224
Tillyard, E. M. W., 122
Toland, John, 87
Tolomei, Claudio, 56
Topoi, 138-39, 143-45, 154-56, 175-87, 203, 229, 234-35. *See also* Commonplaces; Invention; Rhetoric; Logic; Dialectic
Toscanella, Orazio, 102
Tottel, Richard, 44
Tradition: continuity of, xx, 3-23, 25-51, 53-70, 78-79, 106-45, 149, 217, 219, 233, 240-41. *See also* Innovation
Tragedy, 171-72, 186, 192, 214, 231, 236. *See also* Drama
Transumptive mode, xxvii, 74, 144. *See also* Metaphor
Trent, Council of, 104, 227. *See also* Counter-Reformation
Trissino, Giangiorgio, 61-64, 96, 112, 120, 138

Trivium, 227
Trojan myth in the Renaissance, 103
Tronsarelli, Ottavio, 64
Tuve, Rosemond, 73, 181
Typology, xxi, xxvi-xxix, xxxi, 71, 76

Unities (time, place, action) in dramatic and narrative poetry, 60, 85, 115, 117, 139, 164-65, 178, 185-87, 190-92, 198-99, 207-08, 224
Universals, representation of, xvi, xxxiv, xxxix, xli, xlvi, 41, 51-52, 89, 92-93, 106-79, 184-85, 196, 238-39. *See also* Invisibilia; Intelligibilia
Utility: as rhetorical *topos* and as end of poetry, xix, xxxi, xl, 14, 85, 158, 196, 235, 244

Valerian: Emperor of Rome, 64
Valeriano, Giovanni Pierio, 233
Valla, Lorenzo, 20, 168
Valvasone, Erasmo da, xviii, xli, 124
Varchi, Benedetto, xl, 138, 170, 205
Variety, as aesthetic principle, xxx, 62, 66, 113-17, 129, 139, 159, 178, 191, 224
Vasari, Giorgio, 15, 21, 105, 180, 212
Vaughan, Thomas, xxxvi
Vega, Lope de, 60, 65
Vegio, Maffeo, 63
Verisimilitude, xxii, xxxviii, xl, xli, 36-37, 71, 79-82, 85-89, 93-97, 103, 107, 113, 117-19, 124, 130, 140-43, 148-49, 154-58, 163-65, 171-76, 184-85, 196-98, 202, 206, 224, 241
Versification, 45, 53-55, 58, 69, 191-92, 208
Viau, Théophile de, 222
Vico, Giovan Battista, 230
Vida, Marco Girolamo, 62
Virgil, xv, xxvi, xxx, xxxii, 40, 57, 62-63, 66, 72, 80-83, 116, 128-131, 140-41, 170, 201, 238
Vision, 127, 131, 133, 143. *See also* Dream and dream-vision
Visual arts, xvi-xvii, xx-xxiv, xxvii, xxxii-xxxiii, xxxvi-xxxviii, xlii, 8-9, 18-24, 35-39, 51, 53, 87, 103-05, 127, 130-32, 144, 146-212, 229-30. *See also* Iconology
Vitruvius, 16, 36, 50, 173, 179, 212
Vives, Juan Luis, 17
Vossius, Gerard Jan, 222, 231

253

Index

Wallerstein, Ruth, 204-05
Walter of Châtillon, 28
Warburg, Aby, xxxvii
Watt, Joachim von, 21
Webbe, William, 56
Webber, Joan, 134
Weinberg, Bernard, 98, 204, 240
Whitaker, Virgil, 122
Williamson, George, 208
Wilson, Thomas, 206
Wind, Edgar, 52
Wit, 153, 180-81, 201-02, 209-10, 206. *See also* Ingenium
Wittreich, Joseph, 242
Wölfflin, Heinrich, 50, 188-92, 199, 209
Wood, Chauncey, 110

World, images of: as forest, xxxv; as labyrinth, xxxv; as sea; xxxv, as theater, xvii, xxxv. *See also* Cosmology and cosmic symbolism
World-view (*Weltanschauung*), 212, 239

Xenophon, 201

Yates, Frances A., xlv, 21, 132-33, 144-45

Zeitgeist, 198. *See also* History and historiography
Zeuxis, 151, 170-73, 230
Zinani, Gabriele, 64
Zuccaro (Zuccari), Federico, 156-57, 172, 177